THE GOSPEL OF MATTHEW

The Gospel of Matthew

RUDOLF SCHNACKENBURG

Translated by
Robert R. Barr

WILLIAM B. EERDMANS PUBLISHING COMPANY
GRAND RAPIDS, MICHIGAN / CAMBRIDGE, U.K.

Translated from the German edition, *Matthäusevangelium 1,1–16,20* and
Matthäusevangelium 16,21–28,20, Die Neue Echten Bibel:
Kommentar zum Neuen Testament mit der Einheitsübersetzung,
© 1985 and © 1987 Echter Verlag, Würzburg

Wm. B. Eerdmans Publishing Co.
255 Jefferson Ave. S.E., Grand Rapids, Michigan 49503 /
P.O. Box 163, Cambridge CB3 9PU U.K.

Printed in the United States of America

07 06 05 04 03 02   7 6 5 4 3 2 1

Library of Congress Cataloging-in-Publication Data

Schnackenburg, Rudolf, 1914-
The Gospel of Matthew / Rudolf Schnackenburg;
translated by Robert R. Barr.
p.   cm.
ISBN 0-8028-4438-3 (pbk.: alk. paper)
1. Bible. N.T. Matthew — Criticism, interpretation, etc.
I. Title.

BS2575.52.S3613   2002
226.2'077 — dc21
                                    2002074324

Contents

Contents

Contents

Introduction

1. FORM AND CONSTRUCTION

The Gospel of Matthew stands at the beginning of the New Testament canon and occupies a primary place in it. It is not, however, the first work of the Gospel genre to appear. The first was the Gospel of Mark, which the author of Matthew knew and used. Why and to what end, then, has "Matthew" (the name will stand for the author, without prejudice to his actual identity) written this great Gospel? That will obviously have connections with the community to which he belongs and for which he writes (cf. below, p. 5). He will seek not only to offer this community new material, but also to address it in its situation and to indicate to it what he sees to be the proper direction for a life in accordance with Jesus' message. Although he adopts the geographical framework of the Gospel of Mark and follows much of the arrangement of material used by his predecessor, Matthew has nevertheless created a new work, one that stands on its own.

When we compare Matthew's Gospel with that of Mark, the first elements that strike us are the expansions at the beginning and at the end. Matthew begins with a "prehistory," an account of certain events before the appearance of John the Baptist and before Jesus' baptism. This account, in contrast to the Lukan "infancy narrative," can be called a "Pre-Gospel." First comes a genealogy that focuses on Jesus' descent from David, and before David from Abraham (1:1-17). Next, in an extended appendix to 1:16, the virgin conception of Jesus by the Holy Spirit is announced to Joseph in a revelation (1:18-25). Chapter 2 is intended to establish not only Jesus' birth in Bethlehem, the city of David, and his domicile in Nazareth, but also the destiny of the messianic child as

1

typologically prefigured in the history of Moses. The first two chapters, then, are intended to direct the reader's attention to the person of Jesus Christ from a viewpoint of faith (christologically), and to lay the groundwork for the presentation of Jesus' emergence and activity.

At the end of his Gospel, Matthew offers burial and Easter recitals not to be found in Mark, and intended to strengthen faith in Jesus' resurrection (the guarding of the tomb, 27:62-66; 28:11-15; the appearance to the women, 28:9-10), climaxing in Jesus' appearance to the disciples with the commission to go forth to all peoples (28:16-20). These key sections at the beginning and end flank the rest of the Gospel, which develops Jesus' earthly activity of proclamation and teaching, his salvific deeds and struggles against opposition, and finally presents his destiny of passion and death.

But how has the evangelist ordered his material? His structure is the object of widely varying assessments. We can solve the problem, however, by recognizing the turning point at 16:21, after the scene at Caesarea Philippi. In 4:17 we read, "From that time Jesus began to proclaim . . . ," and in 16:21 we read the formally similar "From that time on, Jesus began to show his disciples that he must go to Jerusalem and undergo much suffering." After the introduction (the emergence of John the Baptist, Jesus' baptism and temptation, and the beginning of his work in Galilee, 3:1–4:16), the first part covers Jesus' public proclamation and activity in Galilee, but with great effect in a wider area (cf. 4:24-25). The second part recounts Jesus' journey to Jerusalem under the weight of his passion, as well as his activity there (16:21–25:46). The confession by Peter at Caesarea Philippi, along with Jesus' promise for his church, is the midpoint and high point of the Gospel, shaped by Matthew in a different way from Mark's form, and has tremendous significance for the evangelist's purposes (cf. below, no. 5). A second climax is then attained in the grand concluding scene (28:16-20).

In the body itself we are struck by Jesus' great discourses, which the evangelist has composed using his own technique. Five of them have a stereotypical conclusion ("Now when Jesus had finished saying these things . . ."; 7:28; 11:1; 13:53; 19:1; 26:1) to set them off. They are the Sermon on the Mount (chaps. 5–7), the discourse to the disciples (dispatch and destiny of the disciples, chap. 10), the parabolic discourse (chap. 13), the instruction to the community (chap. 18), and the eschatological discourse (chaps. 24–25). Whether the evangelist sought to create a New Testament "Pentateuch" is disputed; in any case, he gathered and systematically handled the themes that were important for the Matthean community. But between these great addresses stand reports of Jesus' activity, consciously ordered following the various discourses, as is clear from chapters 8 and 9. Finally, there are other passages containing varied material and perhaps identifiable by their most striking characteristic as "disputes."

Grossly oversimplifying, we arrive at the following overview of the first part: D = important discourse, A = account of activity, C = contention.

> Beginning: the appearance of John the Baptist, Jesus' baptism and temptation, the message and its echo (chaps. 3–4)
>
> D: The gospel as challenging proclamation: the Sermon on the Mount (chaps. 5–7)
>
> A: Jesus' healing activity (chaps. 8–9)
>
> D: The discourse of the dispatch of the disciples (chap. 10)
>
> C: John the Baptist and Jesus: disputes and discussions with opponents (chaps. 11–12)
>
> D: The parabolic discourse concerning the "kingdom of heaven" (13:1-53)
>
> A: Rejection in Nazareth, Herod's enmity, the feeding of the multitudes, walking on the water, healing of the sick (13:54–14:36)
>
> C: Pure and impure, the Canaanite woman, etc., demands for a sign, and conversation concerning leaven (15:1–16:12)
>
> Conclusion and climax: confession of Peter and Jesus' promise (16:13-20)

The second part sticks more closely to the Markan outline. The points of division coincide with the three announcements of the passion (16:21; 17:22; 20:18), followed by passages in a Markan order but complemented with further material. The first proclamation of the passion is followed by Jesus' words about discipleship, the transfiguration, and the healing of the epileptic boy (16:24–17:20). The second proclamation of the passion is followed by the exclusively Matthean pericope on the temple tax, then by the radically recomposed discourse to the community (18:1-20; cf. Mark 9:33-50), with the appended parable of the merciless slave (18:23-35; exclusively Matthean), followed by community themes taken from Mark 10 (Matt. 19:3-30) and concluding with the parable of the vinedressers (20:1-16; exclusively Matthean). The third proclamation of the passion is followed by the pericope on the sons of Zebedee and the healing of two blind men of Jericho (20:17-34). The last stay in Jerusalem (chaps. 21–25) likewise contains a wide variety of complementary material. Instead of the single parable of the wicked vinedressers (Mark 12:1-12) Matthew offers three parables: the two sons, the wicked vinedressers, and the great banquet (21:28–22:14). The "four questions" in Mark 12:13-37 are characterized by Matthew from beginning to end as disputes. The appended brief accusation of the scribes in Mark 12:38-40 becomes a lengthy discourse of woe against the scribes and Pharisees (Matt. 23:1-36). Similarly, the eschatological discourse (chaps. 24–25) is expanded, mostly with material from the Sayings Source, but also with Matthew's own contributions (the parable of the wise and foolish bridesmaids, 25:1-13; the portrait of the judgment, 25:31-46)

With this overview, which offers different divisions from those in the standard translations, the Matthean peculiarities and purposes are as yet little in view: the intent of his shaping of his Gospel will become clearer as we inquire into his sources and his redactional reworking.

2. SOURCES AND REDACTIONAL FORMATION

Identifiable sources for the Gospel of Matthew are the Markan Gospel (cf. above, pp. 1-3) and the "Sayings Source," a collection of sayings of Jesus into whose content we have some insight from parallels between Matthew and Luke. The Source may date from the A.D. 50s. Alongside these two sources, Matthew offers a great deal of material of his own, which stems from oral tradition but also includes his own redactional formations. Matthew has taken over a great deal from the tradition of his community (cf. the expanded series of Beatitudes, 5:3-20; also 6:1-18 and 18:15-20; the "fulfillment quotations"; the guarding of the tomb; and the command to baptize, 28:19). The community tradition has the earmark of Jewish Christianity; but in the development of this tradition a wider horizon of the church is also discernible.

Matthew the "systematician" has a preference for certain numbers in the composition of his material; indeed, he employs an underlying *number symbolism.* He prefers the numbers of perfection and fullness, *three* (thrice fourteen generations in 1:2-17, exercises of piety in 6:1-18, parables in 21:28–22:14; cf. also 12:40; 17:4; 23:8-10) and *seven* (parables, chap. 13; woes, chap. 23; cf. also 12:45; 15:34; 18:22; 22:25). But he also assigns symbolical value to *ten* (miracles of healing, chaps. 8–9; bridesmaids, 25:1; talents, 25:28) and *twelve* (the number of the tribes of Israel; the number of apostles, 10:1; 11:1; 19:28; also 14:20; 26:53). While this is based to a certain extent on tradition, it is nevertheless a Matthean peculiarity to double the number of the acts of healing to heighten the quality of their wonder (two possessed persons, 8:28; two blind persons, 9:27; 20:30).

Behind such literary devices stands not only Semitic sensitivity but also a certain intention in presentation. The *Sitz im Leben* may have been catechesis, developed by primitive Christian scribes (cf. 13:52), teachers, and "catechists" (23:8, 10) for community life. Whether this was a "school" is questionable. However, the evangelist himself is to be found among such teachers. His teaching and instruction, tailored to the situation of the community — its inner difficulties (romantics and gossips, 7:21-23; wicked and unworthy members, 13:41-42; 22:11-14), and external pressures (from Pharisaic Judaism, cf. 5:10-12; 10:18-23; 21:33-46; but also from the world of the Gentiles, cf. 24:9) — is seen especially in the great discourses (cf. above, pp. 2-3) and in the shaping of the parables (the wedding banquet, talents, ten bridesmaids, and universal judgment). The concrete community (the place of Matthew's writing) becomes the place of revelation, and the testing ground, of the universal church, the world of disciples of Christ (28:19): it must maintain itself as a community of "brothers and sisters" (18:5, 20; 23:9). Thus the Gospel of Matthew becomes the eminently "church" gospel.

3. THE "PLACE" OF THE GOSPEL OF MATTHEW: SPIRITUAL MILIEU AND ORIGIN

The Matthean community was probably established in a rather large city made up of Jews, Greeks, and other groups of people ("Gentiles"). It must have been quite a large Christian community, comprising Christians of varying origin, a community with a rather long history, considering the traditions at work in it (cf. 10:5b-6, 23; 15:24 with 8:11; 25:32; 28:19). The language spoken was quality Greek, the commercial language of the time (not translation Greek). The images and parables betray the Jewish biblical background of the tradition but also the general relationships of the (Hellenistic) time (cf. 18:23-34; 25:14-30; 13:45-46). Matthew's sole aim is the Christian proclamation of salvation. Unlike John, he is free of other spiritual currents in the world around, and he is open to the proclamation of the gospel throughout the cultural world (*oikoumenē*) of the time (24:14).

All indications as to the place of Matthew's Gospel point to Antioch in Syria, at that time the third largest city in the Roman Empire (after Rome and Constantinople), a thriving trade center and a place of exchange between West and East. The Christian community arose through the immigration of Christian Hellenistic refugees after the persecution of Stephen in Jerusalem. It maintained good contacts with the mother community, but quickly accepted non-Jews (Greeks) into its ranks and became a great missionary center (Acts 11:19-26). This explains its various groupings: Jewish Christians with an orientation to Jerusalem (cf. Gal. 2:12), Hellenists bent on mission, and a Christianity that, like Peter, adopted a moderate attitude while actively cultivating a profession of Jesus Christ (cf. Acts 11:26). The structure of the community as well, under the leadership of "prophets and teachers" (Acts 13:1-3), corresponds to the essential nature of the Gospel of Matthew. No influence of Paul and his theology is visible. This is consonant with the fact that, after a brief sojourn in Antioch (Acts 11:25-26) and his confrontation with Peter there (Gal. 2:11-14), Paul had little contact with the community.

4. TIME AND CIRCUMSTANCES OF THE COMPOSITION: THE AUTHOR

Matthew wrote after the Jewish War and the destruction of Jerusalem (22:7). The break with Judaism, which had become strong under the leadership of the Pharisaic scribes, had occurred (cf. 27:25; 10:17; 23:34). The tension with these circles who now lived according to strict interpretation of the law is discernible (cf. chap. 23), and the self-awareness of the church as the true "people of God" has been reinforced (21:43). Accordingly, the composition of this work is to be dated around A.D. 85-90. It may have been occasioned in part by the conflict with Judaism, to which the Jewish Christians living in the Christian community were still conscious of many ties; but a "crisis" is not evident. The danger of believers in Christ backsliding into the Jewish religion of the law, of Jewish Christianity divorcing itself from the church (as is testified for the second century A.D.), is not acute. Instead, Matthew seeks to proclaim the fulfillment of Israel's messianic expectations in Jesus Christ ("fulfillment quotations"), the superiority of the gospel to the religion of the Torah (5:17-48), and the constitution of a new community of salvation of both Jews and non-Jews, so as to establish all believers in Christ in the church of Jesus Christ (16:18). This church, which Matthew vividly portrays in their situation in the local community, is his primary concern. That church must produce the expected fruits (7:16-20; 12:33; 21:43). A strong pastoral and missionary aim outweighs polemics and apologetics.

But since the community could gain self-understanding and live out its life only from an assimilation of the proclamation and activity of Jesus the Messiah, Matthew sought to gather all the traditions of the person and work, passion and resurrection, of Jesus Christ into a single document and offer them to his community in an easy-to-grasp form corresponding to its life. To what extent the Christians sought to promote the influence of this Gospel beyond the local area, on other communities of the larger church, is uncertain. Indeed, the Gospel's effect was great, and it became the preferred Gospel of the entire church (cf. below, pp. 11-12).

According to early church tradition based on Papias (around A.D. 130), the author is the apostle Matthew, who is seen in the Gospel itself as the "tax collector" of 10:3. This tax collector, however, who held a banquet for Jesus and his disciples, is called "Levi" in Mark 2:14 (and Luke 5:27), and only the author of Matthew has identified the otherwise unknown Levi with the apostle. This explains the ancient Christian tradition, but without adequate grounds. Nor is the supposition of a "pre-Matthean" Gospel, inferred from the testimony of the Papias text, tenable. The Gospel of Matthew is an original Greek work, and the evangelist may have been a second-generation (Hellenistic) Jew. The frequent view, often represented in more recent scholarship, that Matthew was not a Jew by birth but a Gentile Christian, is scarcely justifiable. He writes for a community that embraces both groups; but he is best regarded as a person with Jewish views and Jewish ways of speaking.

5. ISRAEL, JUDAISM, AND THE CHURCH IN THE GOSPEL OF MATTHEW

The relationship between Israel, Judaism, and the church, as reflected in the Gospel of Matthew, is a matter of dispute. That the community continued to participate in the life of the synagogue is beyond question, based on the content itself (cf. above, p. 6). But despite the divorce from the Jewish religious community, Matthew continues to show a great deal of respect for the ancient people of God, Israel, from whom Jesus the Messiah has descended (2:6, 20, 21; 15:31) and to whom Jesus was conscious of being sent during his life on earth (10:6; 15:24). As Jesus seeks to gather the "lost sheep of the house of Israel," so too his messengers are to proclaim the gospel of the Reign of God, despite opposition and persecution, in "all the towns of Israel" (10:23; 23:34). The "King of Israel" (27:42) lays claim to all of Israel, through the election of twelve apostles (10:1-2). They shall one day sit, at the "restoration" (the eschatological fulfillment), on twelve thrones and "judge the twelve tribes of Israel" (19:28). From the standpoint of salvation history, the ancient people of God has forfeited its place of priority through the rejection of its Messiah. But the church, as the new people of God, cannot disavow its origin in Israel — its rooting in Israel in God's salvific plan and its abiding obligation to the promises and instructions given to Israel (through the prophets). John the Baptist stands at the end of the old order and is the bridge to the new (11:11-14).

"King of the Jews" no longer has any positive resonance (2:2; 27:11, 29, 37); "the Jews" are currently the people who reject Jesus Christ (28:15). Frequently (29 times) their representatives appear as "the Pharisees," often in league with the "scribes"; their negative portrayal is to be explained by the confrontation of the Christian community with the contemporary Judaism led by them, and does not entirely correspond to the depiction of the Pharisees of Jesus' time, with whom Jesus himself had friendly relations, although not without criticism (cf. Luke 7:36; 11:37; 14:1).

The "church," which is so designated in the Gospels only in Matthew 16:18 and 18:17 *(ekklēsia)*, is the community of salvation that Jesus sought to form (16:18) but that was actually constituted only after Jesus' resurrection. It is presented concretely in the local community, in the assembly of those belonging to it (18:17). The concept of church is essential to Matthew's concept of salvation history: the new people of God is most intimately bound up with the

Messiah. He is in their midst (18:20), and he remains with them to the end of the age (28:20). To the person of Peter (16:18-19) as well as to all its members (18:18) he has committed his full authority and has entrusted his work (28:16-20). Questions of constitution are of secondary importance in this community of siblings.

6. PETER AND HIS MEANING FOR THE GOSPEL OF MATTHEW

More than in the Markan Gospel, Peter steps forward as the spokesperson of the circle of the disciples (15:15; 18:21); in addition, he acquires a unique importance for Matthew and the future church. This is evident in the central scene at Caesarea Philippi itself (16:13-19; see above, p. 2). Furthermore, Peter is designated as "first" in the list of the apostles (10:2). In his walking on the water he becomes, in a special scene, the paradigm of faith and doubt (14:28-31), and in a tradition handed down by Matthew alone he stands prominent in the passage concerning the temple tax (17:24-27). By no means are his weaknesses passed over in silence (cf. the denial, 26:69-75); but despite his obtuseness (26:33-35) and his all-too-human denial, he is the rock chosen by God for Jesus' church and the keeper of the full power of the keys. At most we might wonder that he is not, as he is in Mark 16:7, singled out as the addressee of the Easter proclamation (the first appearance!). He is the reliable transmitter of the tradition of Jesus, and at the same time presents the "apostolic norm of the church."

In more recent scholarship, it is even conjectured that the "Gospel of Matthew" may have originally circulated as a "Gospel of Peter" (W. Schenk, "Das 'Matthäusevangelium' als Petrusevangelium," *Biblische Zeitschrift* 27 [1983]: 58-80); at any rate, Peter is the normative apostolic authority for Matthew's church. Accordingly, the Gospel of Matthew has introduced a plurality of specific testimonials concerning this chief of the disciples in the nascent church (cf. John 21:15-19; 1 and 2 Peter), just as, conversely, these passages have occasioned a special appreciation for him in Christianity. The Roman Catholic Church bases its claim of primacy on the primacy of Peter as expressed in Matthew 16:17-19, although in this passage nothing is yet said about a discipleship of the chief apostle.

7. CHRISTOLOGY

Fundamental and determinative for Matthean theology is the proclamation of Christ (Christology) that finds its pregnant expression in the confession of Peter, "You are the Messiah, the Son of the living God" (16:16). It is the confession of the believing community, the confession that Matthew seeks to reinforce and that is found in his presentation. That presentation is one of faith in Jesus the Messiah ("the Anointed One"), the awaited vessel of salvation, and is bound to the Christian conviction that Jesus is the "Son of God." The truth that Jesus is a divine being, indicated even in Mark with the expression "Son of God" (Mark 1:1, 11; 9:7; 15:39), is underscored by Matthew through its adoption in the confession of Peter, through the reverence of the disciples after the walking on the water (14:33), and through the mocking of the Crucified One on the part of unbelievers (27:40, 43). Over against contemporary Judaism, which rejected this Messiah, Matthew is especially concerned to establish the unique, special messianic character of Jesus as attested in the Scriptures, the messianic character that leads logically to the confession of Jesus as the Son of God. The son born of the Virgin Mary is from the Holy Spirit, and is the promised redeemer and "God with us" of Isaiah 7:14 (Matt. 1:20-23) The flight into Egypt, which recalls Moses the liberator of Israel, climaxes in the realization by Christians that "Out of Egypt I have called my son" (2:15) is a reference to Jesus the Messiah. The fulfillment quotations (1:22; 2:15, 17, 23; etc.) enrich the picture of the Messiah. He is also the Servant of God promised in the book of Isaiah (Matt. 12:17-21), and in his destiny he fulfills many other elements of Old Testament prophecy. This explains the abundance of christological designations in the Gospel of Matthew, and the concentration on particular elements that come to light in the Christian image of the Messiah in contrast to that of Judaism.

Jesus, therefore, the shoot of David, is presented as Israel's promised "king of salvation" in Matthew as nowhere else. On him are focused the genealogy (1:1-17), Joseph's adoptive paternity (1:20), the outcry of the blind men (9:27; 20:30-31), the questioning on the part of the people (12:23), the supplication of the Gentile woman (15:22), and the acclamations at the entry into Jerusalem (21:9) and in the temple (21:15). Precisely this son of David is also the Son of God, as Matthew suggests to his readers in the conversation he has about the Son of David (22:42).

But in his Christology Matthew also directs our gaze to the Lord who remains with his community and bound to it. The Old Testament designation for God, "Lord," which even before Matthew was a title of Jesus Christ in the primitive church, receives considerably more mention in Matthew than in Mark (Matt. 7:21-22; 14:28, 30; 17:4, 15; 25:11, and passim). In particular Matthew has many more references to the "Son of Man," who for him is the same as the "Lord," and who has a special relationship to the believing community. In addition to the citations of "Son of Man" taken over from tradition, Matthew names the "Son of Man" ten more times. The Son of Man is the earthly Jesus (13:37;

16:13), the one crucified and raised by God but, most of all, the one to come with power as redeemer and judge (13:41; 16:28; 19:28; 24:39; 25:31), who will demand an accounting of the community. The community draws its life from the fullness of power of the Son of Man (cf. 28:18) and lives in the expectation of his return.

8. OLD LAW AND NEW "RIGHTEOUSNESS"

God's guarantee of forgiveness and salvation, which Jesus proclaims, also generates a strong moral call to the disciples of Christ. The evangelist, who sees the defects and weaknesses in his community, inserts the new ethos of those who await the Reign of God as an inalienable, integral part of his theology. This ethos is condensed in the programmatic address of chapters 5–7 (the "Sermon on the Mount"). In contrast to Judaism with its legal piety, Jesus calls for a "righteousness that exceeds" that of the scribes and Pharisees (5:20). Jesus proclaims a morality, made possible through God's boundless mercy, grounded in trust in his Father, and transcending legal prescriptions, that is directed to the love of God and reaches from love of siblings and love of neighbors all the way to love of enemies (5:43-48). The righteousness given and required by God, which is on a higher level than that of human beings, stamps Matthew's attitude of piety (6:1-18). The quest for it makes all earthly concerns secondary, and overrules them (6:33). The execution of the will of God, or love in action, which is to be practiced in the community (reconciliation and forgiveness, 5:23-24; 6:14-15; 18:31-35) and toward all people (works of mercy, 25:31-46), ties the revelation of God and Christ to the practice of Christian living.

9. SALVATION HISTORY AND ESCHATOLOGICAL FULFILLMENT

From its own history and the present situation, Matthew's community is enjoined to an acute sensitivity to God's work and activity in history. The history of salvation and reprobation reaches its zenith in the destiny of Jesus the Messiah, the beloved Son of God (21:33-43), but also continues in the history of the people of God (cf. 22:1-14). The salvation history introduced by Jesus, and directed toward final redemption within this world and among the powers of the Evil One at work in it (13:24-30, 36-43), leads to one last climax: the coming of the Son of Man for division and judgment (13:47-50; 16:27; 25:31-33, 46). This is why Matthew's view of the future is presented so extensively (chaps. 24–25). The apocalyptic eschatological age is portrayed by Matthew out of concern for the community: love grown cold (24:12), the responsibility of the leaders (24:45-51), and the lethargy of the good (25:1-13). Out of pastoral concern as well, Matthew emphasizes the judgment being passed on the community (7:23; 13:41-42, 50; 18:35; 22:13; 24:51). However, he also holds out the prospect of the entry of the righteous into the Realm of the Father (13:43), a share in eternal life with God (7:14; 18:8-9; 19:29; 25:46). The community that keeps Jesus' word and teaching can be sure (28:20) of abiding to the "end of the age," the great harvest day of God (13:30).

The proximity of the Realm of God, proclaimed by Jesus, does not create a "crisis of imminent expectation" in the community, but it does demand constant readiness and watchfulness (24:42, 44; 25:10-13) since the Son of Man will come at an hour when he is not expected (24:50). He will reward each person according to that one's works (16:27), and will sit in judgment over all people (25:32). The arc spans from creation (13:35; 24:21; 25:34) to the consummation itself. In spite of the apocalyptic portrayal of the eschatological events (24:19-31), the emphasis rests on God's might and inscrutable dealings (20:23; 24:36) — a theology of history that is valid for all of church history and that has survived to this very day.

10. HISTORY OF THE INFLUENCE OF MATTHEW'S GOSPEL AND ITS MEANING TODAY

In the ancient church the Gospel of Matthew had the greatest and most profound influence of all the New Testament writings. Papias, Justin, and the second-century apologetes seized on the words of the Lord in the Gospel of Matthew and cited them almost verbatim since they have a normative character for Christian life. True, the extreme, radical demands of the Sermon on the Mount create impossible challenges, but they also operate as a dynamic, moving force for the realization of Christian existence. Its influence on the Syrian church was powerful (cf. the *Didache,* or "Teaching of the Twelve Apostles"), as it was on the church of Rome, whose claim of the primacy of the Roman bishop developed in terms of Matthew 16:18-19. The first commentary on the Sermon on the Mount was written by Augustine (A.D. 393/94). We have John Chrysostom to thank for ninety homilies on the entire Gospel (ca. 390). Unfortunately, Matthew's anti-Jewish tendency, owing to the circumstances of his time, had a negative effect on the church. In the time of the Reformation, Pauline theology repressed Matthew's "work-happy" spirituality, and in biblical criticism after the Enlightenment the Gospel of Mark came in for more and more attention because of its status as the oldest Gospel writing.

The Gospel of Matthew retains its abiding value as the "church" work that gives Christians direction and guidance in this world. Indeed, its ethos is more current today than ever before, in the requirements of the Sermon on the Mount, the image of the community of siblings as the model of excellence, the confrontation with the seed of the Evil One, and its outlook on the consummation of world history. Driven forward by its self-understanding as salt of the earth and light of the world (5:13-16) and on the commission of the Risen One (28:16-20), the community of disciples of Jesus Christ knows that it has been sent into the world, and into the world it goes, in struggle and need, solace and hope, throughout all time, toward the goal appointed by its Lord.

11. THE SECOND PART OF THE GOSPEL OF MATTHEW (16:21–28:20)

In 16:21 the evangelist emphasizes the subsequent presentation of the broad scope of Jesus' preaching, expressed in Matt. 4:17, of God's dominion with an observation crucial to his total structure — "From that time on, Jesus began to show his disciples that he must go to Jerusalem. . . ." Here he is calling attention to a decisive turning point in Jesus' life, one grounded in God's mysterious counsel (the divine "must"). It is the road to Jerusalem, which brings him suffering and death, and yet, at the end, in virtue of God's decree, leads to his resurrection. Only to the disciples, and thereby to the later church, is this divine salvific route revealed. Following Mark, Matthew marks this path with three announcements of the passion and resurrection (16:21; 17:22-23; 20:17-19), which likewise subdivide the present passage (16:21–20:34). With chapter 21, we have his days in Jerusalem, at the end of which stands the great discourse on the last days, once more as a revelation for the disciples and the later church, given in the form of prophecy and warning (chaps. 24–25). The report of the passion (chaps. 26–27) is followed by the stories of Easter, culminating in the appearance of the Risen One to the disciples in Galilee and his command regarding their mission in the world (chap. 28). In constructing this latter part of his Gospel, Matthew follows the Gospel of Mark more closely than he does in the first part, although supplementing and broadening it in many respects (see Intro., pp. 1-3).

12. SOME SPECIAL MATTHEAN CONCERNS

1. Matthew 16:21–28:20 clarifies that Matthew's Gospel is for the community. The discourse to the disciples, composed in outline in Mark 9:33-50, is expanded by Matthew, after the exclusively Matthean pericope of the temple tax

(Matt. 17:24-27), into a discourse on life in the community (chap. 18). In material peculiar to Matthew (the parables of the workers in the vineyard, 20:1-16; the royal wedding feast, 22:1-14; the ten virgins, 25:1-13; the money entrusted to stewards, 25:14-30; and portrayal of the universal judgment, 25:31-46), the same tendency is evident.

2. The assault on the Jewish leaders becomes more vehement. Jesus' brief words against the scribes in Mark 12:38-40 become a long discourse against the scribes and Pharisees in Matthew (following the Q tradition; cf. Luke 11:39-52), with seven "cries of woe" (Matthew 23). The same polemics, occasioned by apologetic needs in the concrete circumstances of the time, form the background of the story citing the sentinels at the tomb (27:62-66; 28:11-15). However, the Jewish people also come in for a share of the guilt imputed (21:43; 22:7; 27:25; 28:15).

3. Jesus' majesty is more strongly evident in Matthew than in Mark. While Mark only occasionally affords, in the abasement and suffering of the Son of Man, a glimpse of his coming sovereignty and glory, postponing the actual turning point until his death (Mark 15:37-39), Matthew shows signs of his divine power even in the passion (Matt. 26:53-54; 27:19; "Son of God," 27:40, 43).

4. The resurrection event gets more attention. Matthew tells the story of the descent of an angel to roll away the stone (28:2-4) and of Jesus' appearances to the women (28:9-10) and to the eleven disciples (28:16-20). The meaning of Jesus' resurrection rings out in his very death, in the opening of the tombs and the awakening of the corpses of many godly persons (27:52-53). The "Pre-Gospel" of chapters 1and 2 corresponds in some ways to the Easter posthistory.

5. Matthew fashions the concluding scene with the Resurrected One (28:16-20) into a Magna Charta for the church. In this scene, which corresponds to one at Caesarea Philippi (16:16-20), Jesus promises that his church will not be overcome by the powers of death since he himself, the Resurrected One, has founded and maintains it. Matthew opens up a horizon for the mission to all peoples, but it also binds the community to the earthly Jesus' words and works. It shows the new people of God, Israel's legacy, in union with the Lord of its community — the wave of the future. All in all, Matthew seeks to transmit to his community a self-awareness shot through with great theological depth as well as with relevance for its life in this world. This image of the church is gaining the same currency today.

Commentary

THE PRE-GOSPEL (CHAPS. 1–2)

The Genealogy of Jesus the Messiah (1:1-17)

1:1 *An account of the genealogy of Jesus the Messiah, the son of David, the son of Abraham.*

2 *Abraham was the father of Isaac, and Isaac the father of Jacob, and Jacob the father of Judah and his brothers,* 3 *and Judah the father of Perez and Zerah by Tamar, and Perez the father of Hezron, and Hezron the father of Aram,* 4 *and Aram the father of Aminadab, and Aminadab the father of Nahshon, and Nahshon the father of Salmon,* 5 *and Salmon the father of Boaz by Rahab, and Boaz the father of Obed by Ruth, and Obed the father of Jesse,* 6 *and Jesse the father of King David.*

And David was the father of Solomon by the wife of Uriah, 7 *and Solomon the father of Rehoboam, and Rehoboam the father of Abijah, and Abijah the father of Asaph,* 8 *and Asaph the father of Jehoshaphat, and Jehoshaphat the father of Joram, and Joram the father of Uzziah,* 9 *and Uzziah the father of Jotham, and Jotham the father of Ahaz, and Ahaz the father of Hezekiah,* 10 *and Hezekiah the father of Manasseh, and Manasseh the father of Amos, and Amos the father of Josiah,* 11 *and Josiah the father of Jechoniah and his brothers, at the time of the deportation to Babylon.*

12 *And after the deportation to Babylon: Jechoniah was the father of Salathiel, and Salathiel the father of Zerubbabel,* 13 *and Zerubbabel the father of Abiud, and Abiud the father of Eliakim, and Eliakim the father of Azor,* 14 *and Azor the father of Zadok, and Zadok the father of Achim, and*

Achim the father of Eliud, 15 and Eliud the father of Eleazar, and Eleazar the father of Matthan, and Matthan the father of Jacob, 16 and Jacob the father of Joseph the husband of Mary, of whom Jesus was born, who is called the Messiah.

17 So all the generations from Abraham to David are fourteen generations; and from David to the deportation to Babylon, fourteen generations; and from the deportation to Babylon to the Messiah, fourteen generations.

1-17 Matthew 1:1-16 is a genealogy, a literary genre highly regarded in Judaism (Flavius Josephus, *Life of Moses* 1) and necessary for anyone's claim of descent from the priestly line of Levi. The genealogy of Jesus Christ here, however, serves not a historical but a theological purpose. The point is to establish Jesus' authentic descent from "King David" (v. 6), from whose line Nathan promised David that the Messiah would come (2 Sam. 7:13-14). This descent is by way of Jesus' putative father Joseph, of the same line. The family tree here is traced back to Abraham, the forebear of the people of Israel, since ancient Israel has its meaning for Matthew as the source of the new people of God (cf. 8:11; 22:32; Intro., pp. 7-8). With David as the pivotal ancestor, the genealogy is arranged in three periods (Abraham to David, vv. 2-6a; David to the Babylonian Captivity, 6b-11; and from there to Jesus, vv. 12-16) and understood in the framework of number symbolism (thrice fourteen generations) pointing to the Messiah (v. 17). These very unequal, artistically composed periods of time (the first, about 500 to 800 years; the second, about 400 years; and the third, about 600 years) are arranged in this literary genre — verses 2-3a according to the history of the patriarchs in Genesis, verses 3b-6 according to Ruth, and the remainder according to unknown sources. The number fourteen represents twice the sacred number seven, or perhaps the numerical value of the Hebrew letters for David (d = 4, w = 6, d = 4). In the second period the number of forebears is reduced to fourteen through the elimination of three members of the list of kings (between Joram and Uzziah). In the first and third periods respectively, one generation is omitted, perhaps because the pivotal descendants (David and Jesus Christ) are included. The arithmetic, however, remains unclear.

From a historical viewpoint, the list presents other problems as well. The spelling mistakes in the names may partially be owing to errors on the part of copyists. The correct names in the list of kings would be Asa (vv. 7 and 8) and Amon (v. 10). Josiah was the father of Jehoiakim, who is not named, and the grandfather of Jehoiachin (= Jechoniah) (v. 11); the "brothers" should have referred to Jehoiakim. But Matthew is not concerned with historical precision but with the turning point brought about by the Babylonian Captivity. The time before the Babylonian Captivity is characterized in the main by the people's abandonment of God (cf. 2 Chron. 33; 36:1-21). Thereupon a new list begins

— without kings — which leads to Joseph, of the line of David. Out of catastrophe God brings forth new, definitive salvation — not by way of the great and mighty, however; rather, through those of low esteem.

One is struck by the mention of four women: Tamar (v. 3), Rahab (v. 5a), Ruth (v. 5b), and the wife of Uriah (v. 6). They are cited not because they were thought of as sinners and probably not because they were foreigners, but because together, through God's providence, they introduce an irregular element in the genealogy. Thereby Matthew prepares for the altogether extraordinary intervention of God, who willed that the Messiah should be born of the Virgin Mary (Matt. 1:16; 13:55). The four women listed in the genealogical tree are pointers to, or signals of, the miracle of the virginal conception of Jesus, who nevertheless traces his lineage to the line of kings through the Davidic Joseph, and thus can be the bearer of the promise.

Jesus was already recognized as the "Son of David" by the primitive church (Rom. 1:3; cf. Luke 1:27; 2:4); Matthew is giving a particular theological argument for Jewish use, one that does not fit our culture today. Luke offers an altogether different family tree (Luke 3:23-38), which by and large differs from the one given by Matthew, reaches back to Adam, and climaxes in Jesus' divine Sonship.

In many circles "shoot of Jesse" has not lost its fascination today. The Jewish origin of Jesus, proclaimed in the salvific promises of the Old Testament, must never be forgotten in Christianity. Jews, too, can see their "brother" in Jesus (Shalom ben Chorin).

The Birth of Jesus the Messiah (1:18-25)

18 *Now the birth of Jesus the Messiah took place in this way. When his mother Mary had been engaged to Joseph, but before they lived together, she was found to be with child from the Holy Spirit.* 19 *Her husband Joseph, being a righteous man and unwilling to expose her to public disgrace, planned to dismiss her quietly.* 20 *But just when he had resolved to do this, an angel of the Lord appeared to him in a dream and said, "Joseph, son of David, do not be afraid to take Mary as your wife, for the child conceived in her is from the Holy Spirit.* 21 *She will bear a son, and you are to name him Jesus, for he will save his people from their sins."* 22 *All this took place to fulfill what had been spoken by the Lord through the prophet:*
23 *"Look, the virgin shall conceive and bear a son,*
and they shall name him Emmanuel,"
which means, "God is with us." 24 *When Joseph awoke from sleep, he did as the angel of the Lord commanded him; he took her as his wife,* 25 *but had no marital relations with her until she had borne a son; and he named him Jesus.*

18-25   Here we have an "extended footnote" on, or elucidation of, 1:16. We hear a presentation to Joseph of how Jesus' conception has occurred through the Holy Spirit. That presentation is a statement in narrative form of the Christian explanation of the mystery of Jesus' origin. The fact, certain to Matthew and arising from the faith conviction of primitive Christian circles, that not Joseph but the Holy Spirit is Jesus' true father, has already been expressed in verse 18. The "righteous" Joseph's disturbed reflections are altogether put to rest by the revelation that the child in Mary's womb has been conceived by the Holy Spirit (vv. 19-20). The angel goes on to reveal to him that it is a boy, and that he is to give him the name "Jesus" (v. 21). Here Matthew appends a fulfillment quotation (vv. 22-23); this is a prophetically foretold, profoundly meaningful event that includes the virginal conception and is intimately bound up with redemption. The last two verses (vv. 24-25) recount the execution of the divine commission, Joseph's taking of Mary into his home, his respect for her virginity, and the imposition of the divinely chosen name. The manner and arrangement of this Christian faith-narrative forbid us from assuming a historical scene. Revelations in dreams were widespread in the ancient world. Gods such as Serapis, Osiris, and Asclepius appear in dreams and give instruction or advice for the healing of the sick. Matthew adopts Jewish views. God appears to the patriarch Jacob in a dream, from a ladder that reaches to heaven, and gives him a promise (Gen. 28:11-16); later an "angel of God" communicates to him a commission (Gen. 31:11-13). For Judaism angels are frequent intermediaries of revelation; they are also trusted messengers of God for primitive Christianity (e.g., the angels in the story of Jesus' birth [Luke 2:8-15], at Jesus' tomb, at the ascension, and frequently in Acts). In Matthew all divine instructions are communicated through angels in dreams (2:13, 19), and only through dreams (2:12, 22); in Luke (Luke 1:11-20; 1:26-38), by contrast, the angel Gabriel speaks directly to Zechariah and Mary. This manner of presentation is used to convey the truth of an otherwise incomprehensible revelatory event.

Matthew has not composed his material himself, nor has he received it from the Sayings Source, as Luke has (1:26-38), in a different form, but has probably received it from the storehouse of faith memories of Jewish-Christian circles. The concept of the virginal conception by the Holy Spirit is common to both evangelists. Unlike Luke, Matthew finds his addressee not in Mary but in Joseph, who has been identified, as we have seen, as being of the line of David and as the husband of Mary (Matt. 1:16). Joseph's reflections presuppose the relationships of Jewish marriage and Jewish views of life. With the espousal itself (engagement), he is legally Mary's spouse (v. 20); but only after taking her into his house (cf. 25:1, 10) does the marriage ceremony begin. If a bride had sexual relations with another man before the beginning of the marriage ceremony, she was regarded as having committed adultery. Joseph knows of Mary's pregnancy, but he is unwilling to "expose" her — bring her into disrepute. Instead, he intends to hand her her bill of divorce privately, he does not want her to be publicly shamed, and most of all he does not want her to be punished as an adulteress (cf. Deut. 22:23-24).

Why is Joseph called "righteous," or "just"? According to the Jewish view, a "just" person was one who observed the law perfectly. But Joseph is precisely unwilling to deliver Mary over to legal punishment. On the contrary, he seeks to protect her from dishonor. Does he surmise the divine mystery, as many interpreters suppose, and therefore shun marital relations with Mary? But Joseph is as surprised at the angel's announcement as Mary is in Luke. "Just," or "righteous," therefore connotes a good, compassionate man, pleasing to God, as he is seen through the eyes of Christians (cf. Matt. 13:43; 25:37, 46). "Do not be afraid" is a regular element of address in divine appearances (Luke 1:13, 30; 2:10; Matt. 14:27; 28:10; etc.).

The climax of the revelation is the proclamation of the origin of the child from the Holy Spirit. Despite the expression "conceived," any sexual reference is out of the question (as in Luke 1:35). This is totally unlike what occurs in Gentile myths, in which gods have sexual relations with maidens. The concept of a Spirit-begotten virginal conception has its source rather in a Jewish-Hellenistic mentality. Still, a conception by the operation of the Holy Spirit is nowhere else attested (not even for the miraculous births of "sterile women" in the Old Testament). Only in Matthew's added fulfillment quotation is there any question of conception by a virgin (Matt. 1:23). However, generation by the Spirit and virginal conception are closely tied together in the faith view represented by Matthew.

At the same time Matthew seeks to show his readers the significance of the divine child in his narrative. In the giving of the name, which here falls to Joseph (in Luke 1:31, in terms of the text, it is Mary's prerogative), Jesus is called *Yeshua,* a later form derived from the Hebrew *Yehoshua* ("Yahweh is help"), and is thereby presented as the redeemer of his people (cf. Ps. 129:8 in the LXX). It is a Christian interpretation, with Matthean characteristics ("my people" = Israel: 2:6; 4:16; 13:15; 27:25; forgiveness of sins, 9:2, 5, 6; 26:28). The fulfillment quotation, which interprets the proclamation of the angel from a Christian understanding of Scripture, deepens the christological view.

In the Greek translation of Isaiah 7:14, the Hebrew expression *'almâ* (young, marriageable woman) is translated *parthenos* (virgin) and confirms for Matthew Mary's virginal conception. The concept is not concocted from this passage: neither the conception by the Holy Spirit nor Jesus' divine Sonship (Luke 1:35b) springs from it. For Matthew, the name given the child in Isaiah 7:14, Emmanuel, meaning "God with us," acquires a highly important signification: in Jesus God is helping, redeeming, protecting his people (chaps. 8–10;

12:15-20), and, with a view to the new people of God ("*they* shall name him Emmanuel), he is near (18:20) and present with them to the end of the age (28:20). In the church, the old divine covenant is renewed.

24-25 The "implementation formula" (cf. 21:6-7; 26:19) indicates, as often in the Old Testament, the exact fulfillment of the divine commission: Joseph takes Mary into his house (v. 20b) but has no marital relations with her "until she had borne a son" since the child comes from the Holy Spirit (v. 20c), and he gives the boy the name "Jesus" (v. 21). Any further intention concerning his behavior after the birth is therefore not to be inferred from this passage.

A Catena of Narratives from the Early Childhood of the Messiah Jesus (chap. 2)

The second chapter of Matthew's Gospel, which relates a connected series of events *after* Jesus' birth (2:1), and in this narrative unity may already have existed in its essentials before the composition of the Gospel of Matthew (A. Vögtle, *Messias und Gottessohn (zu Mt. 1–2)* [Düsseldorf, 1971], ad loc.), poses considerable difficulties for today's reader, who is accustomed to regard narrative as historical *report*. But as in the case of the genealogy and the revelation in Joseph's dream, this chapter must be interpreted according to its literary genre and the intent of the evangelist. Jewish narrative tradition has certainly had its effect; but Jewish Haggadah or edifying homiletic "midrash" does not fit the narrative form we meet here. Haggadah and midrash are directly attached to biblical texts, while the Christian narrative concerns the history of Jesus — his early childhood — and sets it in the light of biblical statements and Jewish traditions.

The improbabilities for such a "historical" view are the following. (1) The behavior of King Herod: Herod and the priests were actually mutual enemies; he permits the astrologers to go their way without escorts or spies; Flavius Josephus, who describes the reign of Herod the Great in detail, makes no mention of the "event." (2) Jerusalem and the scribes: that all Jerusalem was thrown into a state of excitement has no aftermath in the presentation of the Gospels; Bethlehem as Jesus' birthplace seems hereafter unknown (cf. 13:53-58; 21:11). (3) The star: for its remarkable behavior, which violates the laws of astronomy, see our observations below (on 2:1-2). (4) Comparison with Luke: there is no mention in Luke 2:22, 39 of the flight into Egypt and the later move to Nazareth. Matthew, then, has other than "historical" intentions in his account, and we shall examine them as they occur.

The catena of narratives comprises four units:

1. The astrologers from the East and their homage to the child in Bethlehem (2:1-12)
2. The flight into Egypt (2:13-15)
3. The slaughter of the children in Bethlehem (2:16-18)
4. The return from Egypt and the move to Nazareth (2:19-23)

Each of the latter three units closes with a citation from Scripture bearing on its fulfillment in Jesus' history. In the account of the astrologers, the normative scriptural passage stands in the middle (2:6). Matthew is strongly attached to scriptural references, and this betrays his outlook.

The Visit of the Wise Men (2:1-12)

2:1 *In the time of King Herod, after Jesus was born in Bethlehem of Judea, wise men from the East came to Jerusalem,* 2 *asking, "Where is the child who has been born king of the Jews? For we observed his star at its rising, and have come to pay him homage."* 3 *When King Herod heard this, he was frightened, and all Jerusalem with him;* 4 *and calling together all the chief priests and scribes of the people, he inquired of them where the Messiah was to be born.* 5 *They told him, "In Bethlehem of Judea; for so it has been written by the prophet:*

6 *'And you, Bethlehem, in the land of Judah,*
    are by no means least among the rulers of Judah;
for from you shall come a ruler
    who is to shepherd my people Israel.'"

7 *Then Herod secretly called for the wise men and learned from them the exact time when the star had appeared.* 8 *Then he sent them to Bethlehem, saying, "Go and search diligently for the child; and when you have found him, bring me word so that I may also go and pay him homage."* 9 *When they had heard the king, they set out; and there, ahead of them, went the star that they had seen at its rising, until it stopped over the place where the child was.* 10 *When they saw that the star had stopped, they were overwhelmed with joy.* 11 *On entering the house, they saw the child with Mary his mother; and they knelt down and paid him homage. Then, opening their treasure chests, they offered him gifts of gold, frankincense, and myrrh.* 12 *And having been warned in a dream not to return to Herod, they left for their own country by another road.*

1-12 These verses are difficult to fit into the usual genres (cf. above). They recount, in one continuous narrative, the journey of the astrologers, and are divided into the arrival in Jerusalem (1:1-2), the meeting with King Herod and the scribes (vv. 3-6), Herod's commission (vv. 7-8), the following of the star (vv. 9-10), the homage to the child (v. 11), and the return home by another route (v. 12). Examining the structure of the narrative, however, we recognize still other intentions, especially a christological one: the true King of the Jews, to whom Herod relates so suspiciously and inimically (vv. 2-3) — the Messiah (v. 4); the leader of the people of Israel who comes from Bethlehem, *by no means* a small place (cf. below); the royal child (cf. the gifts) to whom divine worship is due (the homage, v. 11) — is Jesus Christ. There is also an echo of Jesus' relationship with Israel and the Judaism of the time, as there is later in the Gospel of Matthew: he is the promised shepherd of the people of God (v. 6d; cf. 9:36; 10:6), and yet "all Jerusalem" is in a turmoil, together with Herod (v. 3). None of Jerusalem's inhabitants bothers to go to nearby Bethlehem; yet the Gentiles come from afar (cf. 8:10-12). The entire background is one of God's plan and guidance (the star; the finding of the child; the thwarting of Herod's wicked intent by a dream, v. 12).

1-2 "Wise men," originally a designation for Persian priests, here is a general word for astrologers "from the East." They may be from Persia (as in the oldest presentations), Babylonia (Chaldea; cf. Dan. 2:4-5; 4:4-7; 5:7), or Arabia (because of the gifts; but cf. our commentary on 2:11 below). They have observed a star at its "rising," its first appearance (not "in the East," as in the Vulgate), and have concluded that an altogether special King of the Jews has been born. The awaiting of a future, ideal ruler was widespread in antiquity; still, the expectation of the astrologers from the East more likely refers to the oracle of Balaam (Numbers 22–24). The Gentile seer from the Euphrates (Num. 22:5) must bless Israel instead of cursing it (Num. 23:7-8), and says: "A star shall come out of Jacob, and a scepter shall rise out of Israel" (Num. 24:17). This "star oracle" was interpreted in Judaism as referring to the Messiah, in Qumran is presented among the messianic Testimonia (4QTest 9:13), and in CD 7:18-19 is referred to the "student of the Law"; cf. *Testament of Judah* 24:1; etc. True, here the graphic oracle becomes an actual star arising in the heavens and the vision becomes a reality, which is interpreted in its light. But this is the only way for Matthew to explain the astrologers' subsequent behavior, being led to Bethlehem where the star comes to rest over the house of the royal child (Matt. 2:10). Beginning with Johannes Kepler (d. 1630), repeated attempts have been made to find an astronomical explanation of the text, but in vain, since stars do not move from north to southwest (the direction from Jerusalem to Bethlehem) and cannot indicate a precisely delimited location. The star of Bethlehem was neither a supernova (a very bright new star), nor a comet (e.g., Halley's Comet, last seen in 1987, probably also visible in 12 or 11 B.C.), nor, finally, a conjunction of stars. A conjunction of Jupiter and Saturn did occur in 7 B.C., and part of its fascination was owing to its symbolism: Jupiter represents the lord of the world, Saturn was the star of Palestine, and the constellation Pisces represented the end of the age. But this hypothesis of a *conjunctio magna* founders forthwith: the Greek word for the star of Bethlehem denotes a single star. Thus the star is a literary symbol for the way by which God has led the Magi to the newborn king of salvation, who is the "star of Jacob."

The statement in Matthew 2:19 and Luke 1:5 that Jesus' birth occurred during the reign of King Herod the Great (d. 4 B.C.) is reliable. His birth must have occurred some six or seven years before the Christian era, which Dionysius Exiguus miscalculated in A.D. 525.

3-4 The astrologers' question, from which Herod learns of the birth of the Messiah (v. 4), unleashes a general terror — a violent fright such as might be typical in the presence of a divine visitation (14:26). Not only the king is seized with fear, but Jerusalem itself. It is not a matter of fear in the king and hope in the citizenry. Judaism, as Matthew sees it, together with their ruler ("with him"), who is of Idumean origin, and whom Matthew regards as an illegitimate king, resists the thought that the Messiah has now appeared.

5-6 The scribes' response is unequivocal. Bethlehem, from which Jesse (1 Sam. 16:1) and David (1 Sam 17:12, 15) had come, in the region of Ephrath, was expected to be the place of origin of the Messiah as well. Micah 5:2 was the decisive prophecy for Judaism on this point, and had already been directly related to the Messiah by the Targum (the Aramaic interpretation of the Hebrew Old Testament). With a view to a scriptural proof in a Christian interpretation, Matthew introduces certain further accents, such as the insertion of "by no means" (meaning, by no means the least important city) and his closing line. The latter adopts 2 Samuel 5:2, the word of the Lord to David, and combines it with Micah 5:2. Jesus' birthplace identifies him as the awaited saving King, of David's line or progeny. In Jesus, Israel ought to acknowledge its leader and shepherd.

7-8 This scene serves to indicate Herod's hypocrisy, as well as to lay the groundwork for the slaughter of the infants (v. 16). Joseph learns of the hostile king's murderous intent from an angel of the Lord in a dream (v. 13). Thus the astrologers' story is interwoven with the flight into Egypt and the slaughter of the innocents.

9-11 The astrologers hear Herod out (perhaps skeptically) and depart for Bethlehem, only eight kilometers from Jerusalem. The star appears again, and goes "ahead of them," coming to rest over the house in Bethlehem. None of this is to be explained naturally. The miraculous star illustrates God's guidance, which bestows on the wayfarers the fulfillment of their longing and occasions their exceedingly great rejoicing (cf. 28:8; Luke 2:10; 24:52). The "house" in which they find the child "with Mary his mother" (Joseph is not mentioned — which is striking, after 1:18-25), unlike the Lukan presentation, suggests a permanent residence. The "homage" done the child fits his royal station and, according to Eastern custom, is accompanied by full prostration. In Greek Matthew's verb also suggests adoration, the reverence due to God (cf. Matt. 4:9-10; 14:33; 28:9, 17). The presents are gifts of homage for the King of peace (Ps. 72:10-11, 15; Isa. 60:6). Gold and incense suggest especially Arabia. Matthew, however, is concerned not with the origin of the gifts but with streams of "peoples" journeying from afar (Isa. 2:2-3; cf. Isa. 60:5; Mic. 4:1-2 — the pilgrimage of the peoples to Zion). The astrologers are symbols of a journey now being undertaken by the nations, the floods of Gentiles entering the church of Christ (Matt. 28:19). That the presents are three in number is an expression of royal honor, and no conclusion can be drawn as to the number of astrologers, who were later interpreted as representatives of the then known parts of the earth and provided with names (Caspar, Melchior, and Balthasar). The interpretation of the presents (gold for a king, incense for God, and myrrh for burial — see John 19:29), of ancient origin, while profoundly devout in its sentiments, has no basis in Matthew. The royal homage, along with other possible influences (Isa. 60:3b; the cult of Mithras; pictures or illustrations), led to a conceptualization of the Magi as kings. Their relics were reverenced in Constantinople, then in Milan, and finally in Cologne. Already symbolic in Matthew, the story bore rich fruit in the areas of popular piety.

The Escape to Egypt (2:13-15)

13 *Now after they had left, an angel of the Lord appeared to Joseph in a dream and said, "Get up, take the child and his mother, and flee to Egypt, and remain there until I tell you; for Herod is about to search for the child, to destroy him." 14 Then Joseph got up, took the child and his mother by night, and went to Egypt, 15 and remained there until the death of Herod. This was to fulfill what had been spoken by the Lord through the prophet, "Out of Egypt I have called my son."*

13-15 The astrologers' homage is followed by a contrasting scene: the Messiah-King must flee from Herod's persecution. Revealed in its more profound meaning by the fulfillment citation (v. 15), the story is intended not as a biographical event, but, after the fashion of a midrash, as a demonstration of God's protection and guidance of his Son. Against the background of Jewish Mosaic traditions, Jesus is seen as the antitype of the first savior of Israel, whose destiny included a similar element. In the Jewish Mosaic Haggadah, which amplifies the Old Testament account (Exod. 1:15–2:10), there are features that shed new light on the story of the Magi. Pharaoh has a dream and sends for his dream interpreters. Both magi, Jannes and Jambres, interpret the dream as referring to the impending birth of an Israelite boy who will annihilate Egypt *(Targum Pseudo-Jonathan).* Josephus, however, tells a different story: an Egyptian scribe (!) prophesies the same thing, and Pharaoh consequently commands the Egyptian (!) midwives to cast the boy into the Nile and thereby kill him ("Intensification of Murderous Intent," *Antiquities* 2.205-9). The Israelites are "in a hopeless plight"; but, in God's providence, the child is rescued.

The motive of the flight is also present in the case of Moses, but in another fashion. After slaying an Egyptian, Moses, now an adult, flees to Midian (Exod. 2:15), returning to Egypt after the death of "all who were seeking [his] life" (cf. Exod. 4:19). For the Israelites, Egypt was the classic place of refuge in many times of need and peril (1 Kings 11:40; 2 Kings 25:26; Jer. 26:21; etc.). According to a later midrash, Jacob, too, the forebear of Israel, had to flee to Egypt, for fear of his father-in-law Laban.

Finally, the Christian community will recall Israel's deliverance from Egyptian servitude, constantly celebrated and gratefully relived: as God called Israel, his "son," out of Egypt, so now he calls Jesus, his true Son (v. 15). The flight into Egypt becomes a sign of the Messiah-Savior, who surpasses Moses. In him Israel's journey is also fulfilled. Nothing definite is said about the sojourn in Egypt; only in later Christian legend is the locality of Matarea, in the vicinity of Leontopolis, cited. The Matthean recital is concerned only with the flight and the return; nor is any polemical tendency in evidence against Jewish accusations (attested only later) that Jesus had learned sorcery in Egypt. The time period is bounded by the death of Herod: two years are calculated, in accordance with Matthew 2:16; or else three and a half years, in terms of Revelation 12:14 (symbolic interpretation!).

The Massacre of the Innocents (2:16-18)

> 16 *When Herod saw that he had been tricked by the wise men, he was infuriated, and he sent and killed all the children in and around Bethlehem who were two years old or under, according to the time that he had learned from the wise men.* 17 *Then was fulfilled what had been spoken through the prophet Jeremiah:*
> 18 *"A voice was heard in Ramah,*
> *wailing and loud lamentation,*
> *Rachel weeping for her children;*
> *she refused to be consoled, because they are no more."*

16-18 The sanguinary deed of the frenzied Herod, unleashed among the infant boys of Bethlehem and its environs, is like a dark foil to the protection provided by God for his Son in Egypt. It clearly refers once more to the story of

Moses (the cruel sovereign, the murder of the Israelite boys), the prototype of Matthew's unique presentation. The spare recital of the event (v. 16) is again followed by a reflection bearing on Scripture (vv. 17-18), which supplies more profound concepts for the story. At the same time the brief passage forms a bridge between the two stories of Joseph's escape to and return from Egypt with the child and his mother, and nothing further is said about it.

16   The rage and cruelty of King Herod, who has unscrupulously seen to the elimination of all persons dangerous to himself, including his wife and sons, are confirmed by the report we have from Josephus (*Antiquities* 15-17). True, the Jewish historiographer writes nothing about the murder of the children of Bethlehem. The prideful king, whose ruse has failed, feels that the astrologers have made him look ridiculous (cf. Matt. 27:29, 31) and seeks, by giving his command, to slay the male infants of Bethlehem and the surrounding area and thereby destroy the royal child. Having learned the exact moment of his birth from the astrologers (2:7), Herod includes children up to the age of two years. One can only speculate on the number of infants slain: suggestions range from twenty to the symbolic number 144,000 (as in Rev. 14:1-5).

17-18   The fulfillment citation gives the impression of being forced. In the prophecy of Jeremiah (Jer. 31:15), Rachel, the mother of Joseph and Benjamin, raises her voice in Ramah ("height"). She bewails the Israelites' being deported in the Babylonian Captivity. The application to the Bethlehem story is possible only under the presupposition that Rachel's tomb, which was on the way from Bethel to Ephrath(a), some eight kilometers *north* of Jerusalem (Gen. 35:16-19), lay along the road to Bethlehem (*south* of Jerusalem).

The quotation from Jeremiah 31:15 (in the LXX, 38:15) looks at first as if it were giving expression only to the lament over the death of the children. But in the Matthean context, it has a deeper meaning. Rachel, who bewails "her children," stands for Israel, which is seen in its continuity through all generations and in the solidarity of its lot (exile and present event). For Matthew, Israel is the source and sign of the new people of God (cf. Intro., no. 7, above). The Messiah, who has emerged from Israel, takes upon himself the ancient lot (the Babylonian Captivity; see 1:11-12) as well as inaugurating a new one similar to it.

The Return from Egypt (2:19-23)

19 *When Herod died, an angel of the Lord suddenly appeared in a dream to Joseph in Egypt and said,* 20 *"Get up, take the child and his mother, and go to the land of Israel, for those who were seeking the child's life are dead."* 21 *Then Joseph got up, took the child and his mother, and went to the land of Israel.* 22 *But when he heard that Archelaus was ruling over Judea in place of*

his father Herod, he was afraid to go there. And after being warned in a dream, he went away to the district of Galilee. 23 *There he made his home in a town called Nazareth, so that what had been spoken through the prophets might be fulfilled, "He will be called a Nazorean."*

19-23 The concluding link in the chain of events in the story presents not only the return to Judea that has been announced in v. 13 but also the move to Nazareth, and this is what is being emphasized here. The underlying tradition takes cognizance of Jesus' well-known origin in Nazareth in Galilee (3:13; 4:13), and Matthew ascribes great importance to "Galilee of the Gentiles" (4:14-16). Matthew devotes special attention to the destination, Nazareth, through the fulfillment citation (2:23), which he himself has probably introduced.

The first part (vv. 19-21) simply details, in stereotypical fashion, what the reader already knows. The second part (vv. 22-23) bases the prolongation of the journey first of all on external conditions in Judea (v. 22a). After a further warning (v. 22b) Joseph settles in Nazareth, an event that has a deeper sense for Matthew (v. 23). Note the staggered arrangement of the narrative pieces: 2:1-12, 16-18 and 2:13-15, 19-23.

19-21 The sojourn in Egypt comes to an end with the death of Herod the Great (4 B.C.). An orientation in the history of Moses is betrayed by the observation that "those who were seeking the child's life have died" (cf. Exod. 4:19), as well as by the expression "land of Israel," found only here in Matthew (v. 21). Here is the promised, holy land to which Israel is to return from its banishment (Ezek. 20:41-42; cf. Ezek. 7:2; 12:19; 13:9; and passim) and the messianic child from "exile" in Egypt. The old Mosaic exodus is repeated and fulfilled in a new way.

22 Archelaus, son of Herod and designated by the latter as successor to the throne in his last testament, but appointed by Caesar Augustus only as ethnarch of Judea, Samaria, and Idumea, was the equal of his father in prodigality and cruelty, and in A.D. 6, at the entreaty of a Jewish delegation, was deposed by Augustus and banished to Galilee. Joseph has apparently set out for the family's former place of residence, Bethlehem (Matt. 2:11); but out of fear of Archelaus and after a divine warning (here only in a dream), he travels to the district of Galilee and settles in Nazareth. "Israel, Galilee, and Nazareth are an anticipatory indication of Jesus' career, and of the membership in his Church" (R. E. Brown, *The Birth of the Messiah* [Garden City, N.Y., 1977], p. 218). The Matthean community will one day be made up of both Jews and Gentiles, represented by "Galilee" (4:15; cf. 26:32; 28:7, 10, 16).

23 Nazareth, an insignificant town in Galilee (John 1:46) nowhere mentioned in the Old Testament or older Jewish literature, is well attested as Jesus' "hometown," or "native city" (13:54-57; Luke 4:23). The orthographic forms *Nazarēnos* (four times in Mark, twice in Luke) and *Nazōraios* (twice in Matthew, once in Luke, thrice in John, and six times in Acts) are linguistic variants for "from Nazareth" (or "from Nazara," Matt. 4:13; Luke 4:16). But *Nazōraios* is important to Matthew here because he finds a scriptural reference in it. An exact text from the Old Testament cannot be located; nor indeed is Matthew's allusion more precise than "what had been spoken through the prophets." The much discussed possible scriptural basis is sought primarily in two directions: in the "shoot" (Heb. *nētser*, Isa. 11:1, a text interpreted as messianic in Judaism); or in *nazir*, a man dedicated to God whose hair, as a sign of that dedication, is left untrimmed. His prototype is Samson (Judg. 13:5, 7). Compare Samuel (1 Sam. 1:11, and, according to a Qumran fragment, 1:22). The former interpretation is to be preferred because of its proximity to the Emmanuel prophecy (Isa. 7:14).

Here, too, a messianic and christological interpretation is important to Matthew. In Jesus the words of the prophets are fulfilled, and in the Christian understanding they point to Jesus the Messiah. Even in the name of Jesus' home city, a place regarded by the Jews with contempt, this kind of meaning is implied. From inconspicuous Nazareth, the Messiah undertakes his journey (Matt. 4:13) as God's servant, who heals illnesses (8:17) and does not cry aloud (12:19).

BEGINNINGS: JOHN THE BAPTIST, JESUS' BAPTISM AND TEMPTATION, AND EMERGENCE IN GALILEE (3:1–4:16)

From chapter 3 onward, for its temporal and geographical structure Matthew follows the Gospel of Mark, which begins with the emergence of John the Baptist and Jesus' baptism. The original "good news of Jesus Christ" (Mark 1:1) extends from Jesus' baptism to his resurrection. Since Matthew, in 4:17, introduces Jesus' public proclamation (see Intro., p. 2, above), this passage after the "pre-Gospel" can be regarded as a transition — a historical prerequisite for Jesus' proclamation (German Ecumenical Translation, "Preparation for Jesus' Work," 3:11–4:11); in many commentaries it is extended to 4:22. We may distinguish six shorter narrative units: (1) the appearance of John the Baptist on the scene (3:1-6); (2) his preaching of the judgment (3:7-10); (3) the heralding of the Messiah (3:11-12); (4) Jesus' baptism in the Jordan (3:13-17); (5) Jesus' temptation in the wilderness (4:1-11); and (6) Jesus' return to Galilee (4:12-16). Three units treat of John the Baptist (1 to 3), and three of Jesus (4 to 6). The important thing here is Jesus' connection with the Baptist, which in Matthew (as in Mark) is seen entirely against the background of a Christian view of history.

The Appearance of John the Baptist (3:1-6)

> 3:1 *In those days John the Baptist appeared in the wilderness of Judea, proclaiming,* 2 *"Repent, for the kingdom of heaven has come near."* 3 *This is the one of whom the prophet Isaiah spoke when he said,*
>
> *"The voice of one crying out in the wilderness:*
> *'Prepare the way of the Lord,*
>   *make his paths straight.'"*
>
> 4 *Now John wore clothing of camel's hair with a leather belt around his waist, and his food was locusts and wild honey.* 5 *Then the people of Jerusalem and all Judea were going out to him, and all the region along the Jordan,* 6 *and they were baptized by him in the river Jordan, confessing their sins.*

1-6 John, who according to Luke 1:11-17, 57-63, 80 was the son of the priest Zechariah and his wife Elizabeth, who made his home in the mountainous region of Judea, and who himself lived in the wilderness since his youth (Luke 1:80), has entered history under the designation "the Baptist" (so also Josephus, *Antiquities* 18.116). The single baptism administered by John (see below, on v. 5) distinguishes him from the Essenes of Qumran and other "baptism-minded" groups (cf. Bannus, according to Josephus, *Life of Moses* 2, para. 11); there was probably a significant baptismal movement in the region of the Jordan. John the Baptist is a unique personage, a "charismatic prophet" (J. Becker, *Johannes der Täufer und Jesus von Nazareth*) whose proclamation of judgment marks him as a preacher of repentance. In Christian tradition his picture is repainted: he is the forerunner of Jesus, that baptizer in the Spirit (Matt. 3:11-12); he is Elijah returned (17:12); he is the witness to the Son of God come into the world (John 1:6-8, 15).

"In those days," a general biblical time designation (Exod. 2:11; Judg. 18:1; Dan. 10:2; Matt. 24:19, 38), here means approximately A.D. 27-28 (Luke 3:1). The "wilderness of Judea" is the barren, rugged area along the south bank of the Jordan (its mouth at the Dead Sea). Here stands the Qumran settlement as well; John could have lived there only at first, if at all, and then have had to detach himself from that monastic community to follow his own calling. He turns to the people and proclaims a message of his own, probably in the vicinity of a much used ford of the Jordan.

2 According to Matthew, and him alone, John proclaims the same message as does Jesus (4:17). But John the Baptist did not present Jesus' special message of the approaching, and already dawning, Reign of God. The wilderness preacher of penitence did, however, demand "conversion": the abandonment of one's past sinful ways, confession of sins (v. 6), and a life that yielded fruit in conformity with one's conversion (v. 8).

3 John's self-understanding as "one crying out in the wilderness" is historically credible. The scriptural citation of Isaiah 40:3 — which Matthew, unlike Mark 1:2, does not connect with Malachi 3:1 (Matthew presents the latter, which refers to Elijah, in 11:10, borrowing from the Sayings Source) — also plays a role in Judaism, especially at Qumran. The Qumran community regarded itself as the sacred remnant of Israel and settled in the wilderness with an appeal to Isaiah 40:3 (1QS 8:13-14; 9:19-20 — according to the Hebrew division of the text, ". . . in the desert prepare the way of the LORD"). *In* the desert, John calls all Jews indiscriminately (Matt. 3:5, 7-12) to repentance and baptism. Many a motif is connected with the *desert.* The desert is the place of intimacy with God, of prayer, of struggle and temptation (4:1) but also of the hope of Israel's salvation, in remembrance of that time of grace which was the wandering in the desert. Through his person and his preaching, John is shown as the prophet of the last days sent by God (11:7-10).

4 John's food and clothing indicate a man of the wilderness — in the Christian view, one like the prophet Elijah (17:12-13), returning and preparing the way for the Messiah (11:10). His garments recall the prophet from Tishbe, who wore a coat of goat's hair (Matthew: camel's hair) and a leather belt around his waist (2 Kings 1:8). His food — locusts and wild honey — is in keeping with his sojourn in the wilderness and underscores his life of renunciation (see 11:18; Luke 7:33).

5 The desert preacher brings all Jerusalem, Judea, and the "region along the Jordan" (doubtless the reference is primarily to the then thickly settled east bank) under his spell. His baptism required that the Jews "go out" to him. The place shown today as that of John's baptism is almost certainly not the correct one. It disregards the datum in John 1:28: ". . . Bethany across the Jordan" (see John 10:40). Later John took up his baptismal activity farther to the north (John 3:23).

6 The meaning of John's baptism, which was continued by his disciples (John 3:25; Acts 19:3), is to be seen in (1) the once-for-all character of the baptism, (2) its administration by the Baptist, (3) his preaching of the imminent judgment, and (4) the confession of sins. John's baptism is both a sign and an efficacious act protecting from God's judgment by fire (Matt. 3:10b, 12, at the end), but not a sacrament in the Christian sense (in which the Holy Spirit is at work). It is the only chance to escape the judgment of divine wrath. Partial or total immersion in the Jordan doubtless has a symbolic meaning as well — the washing or wiping away of sins, although this would occur only when accompanied by "repentance" (v. 11a), which is shown through the confession of one's sins.

The Proclamation of John the Baptist (3:7-10)

> 7 *But when he saw many Pharisees and Sadducees coming for baptism, he said to them, "You brood of vipers! Who warned you to flee from the wrath to come? 8 Bear fruit worthy of repentance. 9 Do not presume to say to yourselves, 'We have Abraham as our ancestor'; for I tell you, God is able from these stones to raise up children to Abraham. 10 Even now the ax is lying at the root of the trees; every tree therefore that does not bear good fruit is cut down and thrown into the fire."*

7-10   This passage, as is clear from a comparison with Luke 3:7-9 (Sayings Source), is a sermon on the judgment, addressed to the Jews coming for baptism (Luke 3:7a: the crowds). In Matthew, however, it becomes a censure of the Pharisees and Sadducees. Since verses 11-12 are surely addressed to all candidates for baptism and verse 12 appeals once more to the judgment, both passages (in the Source) are intimately associated: the judgment is turned over to the one proclaimed to be "more powerful." Through his introduction of the Pharisees and Sadducees (see 16:1, 6, 11-12), Matthew as redactor has placed his own accent on the text.

7   If we disengage the "sermon on the judgment" from the Matthean viewpoint, we come upon the Baptist's original popular sermon. "Brood of vipers" is an extremely harsh expression, but it becomes comprehensible in view of the coming judgment of God's wrath. The Baptist does not acknowledge the advantage of descent from Abraham (v. 9). Matthew, who repeats "brood of vipers" in 12:34 and 23:33 (again against the Pharisees), thereby creates a tension pointing to 21:25, 32, since there the leaders of the people are said not to have believed John. In his confrontation with contemporary Judaism (see Intro., no. 5, above), Matthew has representatives of both leading groups at the time of Jesus coming to John for baptism, but only with a hypocritical attitude (see v. 9).

8   Baptism calls for "fruit" (Luke: "fruits") in conformity with one's conversion. The frequent image of producing fruit (7:16-20; 12:33; 13:8; 21:41, 43; etc.) here illustrates the seriousness of one's conversion, which must be expressed in deeds (cf. Jer. 17:10). The warning may be addressed to the candidates before their actual baptism (v. 7) or after its reception (v. 6). With his call for a moral conversion, John takes up the preaching of the ancient prophets (Amos 5:23-24; Joel 2:12-13; Isa. 1:10-17; etc.); but there is no more averting of judgment (Amos 5:14-15; Joel 2:14) — only rescue and redemption for the converted.

9   Descent from Abraham, with its sign, circumcision, was a source of pride for all Israelites (John 8:33, 53; Rom. 4:11). It was their guarantee of salvation. According to a widely accepted notion, all who were physically descended from Abraham were to be saved, even if they were sinners, because of Abraham's service to God (Justin, *Dialogues* 140). But John calls this notion radically into question. With the blunt assertion that God could raise up children to Abraham from stones, that is, in his omnipotence raise up a new Israel, Matthew may be going even beyond the Christian devaluation of bodily descent from Abraham (John 8:37-40; Rom. 4:12, 16; 9:7).

10 The Baptist's irreconcilable attitude, which gives the appearance of constituting a breach with the past, is to be explained by his conviction of imminent judgment. He directs everything exclusively to this future but now impending event (J. Becker, *Johannes der Täufer* [Neukirchen, 1972]). The axe is "even now" striking the roots of the trees: the trees are on the verge of falling. The image of the fire in which any tree that fails to bear good fruit is burned is chosen intentionally and appears again in the image found in v. 12. It is an old metaphor for the wrath of God (Pss. 79:5; 89:46) and for the judgment. But a new opportunity for rescue appears: trees with good fruit are not chopped down — these are the people who perform deeds corresponding to their conversion (v. 8), all who have sincerely received the baptism of repentance (vv. 6, 11).

> 11 *"I baptize you with water for repentance, but one who is more powerful than I is coming after me; I am not worthy to carry his sandals. He will baptize you with the Holy Spirit and fire.* 12 *His winnowing fork is in his hand, and he will clear his threshing floor and will gather his wheat into the granary; but the chaff he will burn with unquenchable fire."*

11-12 After the harsh words of the preacher of judgment, we are struck by the new tone with which the Baptist describes his position vis-à-vis the "more powerful one." He places himself completely below him, and regards himself as unworthy so much as to do him a lowly service (v. 11).

11 The "more powerful one" cannot mean the "Messiah" — in the Jewish understanding of the time the Son of David, the ideal king of Israel ("the Lord's Anointed"), who would establish a just and peaceful rule on earth. There were other "messianic" expectations, however. The Moses-like prophet to whom the Israelites were to listen (Deut. 18:15, 18; see Matt. 17:5; John, passim) is likewise to be excluded. Neither can the "more powerful one" be God himself, therefore, as other interpreters would have it, since the metaphor of removing or carrying his shoes would not fit. At most, the figure of the son of man from Daniel 7:13-14 and the imagery of *Ethiopian Enoch* are suggested, because of the judgment aspect (J. Becker, *Johannes der Täufer*). The expression "the more powerful one" remains imprecise and is probably intentionally indeterminate.

John interprets the distinction between himself and the more powerful one to come once more with reference to the baptism he confers. His own baptism is only a baptism "with water" (v. 11a), while that of the awaited one is a baptism "with the Holy Spirit and fire." In the context of the Baptist's preaching, the much discussed double expression can only indicate the strength of the "more powerful one." The opposition between water and fire suggests a "baptism of fire" at the judgment. In the Old Testament God sends down fire on godless, sacrilegious cities (Amos 1:4, 7, 10, etc.), and the fire of the divine wrath melts the house of Israel as does a refining furnace (Ezek. 22:17-22). In the New Testament, the same image is adopted for division, judgment, and testing (Luke 12:49; 17:29; 1 Cor. 3:13-15; 1 Peter 1:7; Rev. 3:18). "Holy Spirit" does not fit here. Was the expression on the lips of the Baptist a double image of "wind" and "fire"? (In Greek the same word is used for "wind" and "spirit.") In any case, chaff that flies before the wind becomes a warning to Israel in Jeremiah 13:24. Both images can be used together (e.g., Mal. 4:1), as Matthew 3:12 suggests. Other scholars suppose that "with the Holy Spirit" is a Christian interpolation in view of Jesus as the one who "baptizes with the Holy Spirit" (cf. Mark 1:8; John 1:33; Acts 1:5; 11:16). But the Baptist would scarcely have proclaimed the "Holy" Spirit as the gift of the expected one to those who have withstood the trial.

12 Judgment also means the division of the good from the wicked (13:40-43; 25:32-33); so John now uses another image, that of the winnowing fork. The grain lying on the threshing floor will be cleaned off by the wind through the work of the farmer. The good grain falls to the ground, while the chaff is blown away. The thought of imminent expectation is continued: the more powerful one is already holding the fork, and striding forth to his work, to clear (future tense) his threshing floor. As in verse 10, the emphasis falls once more on punitive judgment. However, the reception of the good, their acceptance by God (in the Christian view, reception into the Realm of God, 13:30, 43) as well, is here set forth in the same breath. This is where the Christian expectation is concentrated, on Jesus' message of salvation (5:3-12; 6:9-13).

The Baptism of Jesus (3:13-17)

13 *Then Jesus came from Galilee to John at the Jordan, to be baptized by him. 14 John would have prevented him, saying, "I need to be baptized by you, and do you come to me?" 15 But Jesus answered him, "Let it be so now; for it is proper for us in this way to fulfill all righteousness." Then he consented. 16 And when Jesus had been baptized, just as he came up from the water, suddenly the heavens were opened to him and he saw the Spirit of God descending like a dove and alighting on him. 17 And a voice from heaven said, "This is my Son, the Beloved, with whom I am well pleased."*

13-17   Matthew alters the presentation of Jesus' baptism, which he knows in its Markan form (Mark 1:9-11), in two respects. He inserts a conversation between the Baptist and Jesus (vv. 14-15), and he reproduces the words of God not in the second person, as addressed to Jesus, but in the third person. Thus the occurrence that is referred to Jesus becomes a proclamation, although Matthew retains "he [Jesus] saw the Spirit of God descending." This shift is not unimportant for the narrative genre. Even Mark scarcely seeks to describe an "experience" of Jesus; he wishes to characterize a revelatory event that, for the Christian community, was bound up with Jesus' baptism. Matthew goes a step further and sets before the eyes of the community what God wishes to tell it about Jesus on the occasion of his baptism. This is the prelude, intended and inaugurated by God, to Jesus' activity. Its meaning is revealed by God in the descent of the Holy Spirit on Jesus, whom God presents as his beloved Son, with a view to his messianic activity. Not coincidentally from a theological viewpoint, a trinitarian aspect is suggested in Jesus' baptism, an aspect later featured more explicitly in the Matthean baptismal formula (28:19).

13   Matthew's unspecified "then" refers to the time of the emergence of John the Baptist (3:1), whose approach by Jesus Matthew expresses with the same verb ("appeared," "came"). Jesus does come to him with the intention of being baptized — an indication of the route consciously taken by Jesus and a point of departure for the conversation that follows.

14-15   Matthew creates an exchange between the Baptist and Jesus, perhaps to obviate a difficulty that suggested itself to the community of the faithful: the sinless, just Jesus submits to John's baptism, at which time one's sins are normally confessed (3:6). One often meets with apologetic content of this kind in Matthew's Gospel (contrast Matt. 19:17 with Mark 10:18, and Matt. 26:61 with Mark 14:58). To be sure, the question of confession of sins is not directly touched upon. In context, it is enough that John submits to the "more powerful one" (Matt. 3:11); thus he is unwilling (because of who Jesus is) to admit him to baptism. It is presupposed that the Baptist knows Jesus and recognizes him as the "one who is coming"; this is Christian interpretation. "Righteousness" (5:6, 10, 20; 6:1, 33; 21:32), which must be "fulfilled" (cf. 5:17), is Matthew's way of expressing the realization of the divine salvific decree and the will of God. Jesus receives the baptism, but, Matthew is careful to declare, only as the one who is totally committed to the divine will and bound in solidarity with the people. For the Christian community, however, he also becomes the model ("it is proper") for the fulfillment of the justice required by God ("*all* righteousness").

16   The exchange between John and Jesus reinforces the incontestable fact of Jesus' baptism by John, which Matthew cites only with a participle in order to draw all attention to the revelatory event. He recounts the latter essentially as does Mark, but emphasizes it with his customary "behold" (not in the

New Revised Standard Version) and specifies the "Spirit" as the "Spirit of God," and the "splitting" of the heavens as an "opening." The symbolic speech is vivid. The opening of the heavens is not the earmark of simply one revelation among many (Ezek. 1:1; Rev. 4:1); more than this, it foreshadows the salvific revelation (Isa. 64:1) of the Messiah and Son of God (v. 17; see also Luke 2:9-11). From the cavernous heavens Jesus sees the Spirit of God descending upon him — in the Christian understanding the fulfillment of the prophecy that God's Spirit was to rest upon the Messiah in fullness (Isa. 11:2; 61:1; Luke 4:18; John 1:32-33). Thus the voice of God also indirectly becomes an allusion to Isaiah 42:1: upon his Servant, "in whom [he is] well pleased," God bestows his Spirit (cf. Matt. 12:18). The symbol of the dove, which Matthew has taken from Mark, underscores the reality of the descending Spirit, regardless of the origin of the dove motif (cf. H. Greeven, in *Theological Dictionary of the New Testament* [Grand Rapids, 1965], 6:63-68). The decisive thing, however, is the verbal revelation bound up with this graphically depicted event and presented through the voice from heaven.

17   The voice resounding "from heaven" is actually the voice of God, and not, as in the rabbinic presentation of a *bath qol* ("daughter of the voice"), a mere echo of the divine voice. What God proclaims of Jesus is a dense, pregnant statement about him, and reveals the christological understanding of the primitive church. It is uttered against the background of the Servant of God of Isaiah 42:1, although with the significant deviation that, instead of "Servant," the "Son" is spoken of, and the Son is designated not as "chosen," but as "Beloved." Here we probably have the influence of Psalm 2:7, where God adopts the ideal king of salvation (the Messiah) on Zion as his "son." (See the "Western" reading of Luke 3:22.) But this passage in the Psalms, which was important to the primitive church (cf. Acts 13:33, where it is understood as referring to Jesus' resurrection! and Heb. 1:5, with its connections to 2 Sam. 7:14), yields no Christology of adoption, anymore than can the baptismal revelation be understood as an act of adoption. Rather, it is the proclamation of the Messiah, acknowledged by the primitive church as the Son of God (cf. Matt. 4:3, 6; 14:33; 16:16; 17:5; 21:37; 22:42-44; 26:63), who here inaugurates his messianic career. "Beloved" can be a rendering of "chosen," from Isaiah 42:1 (see Matt. 12:18!), and need not be taken as an allusion to the sacrifice of Isaac, Abraham's only, "beloved" son (Gen. 22:2, 12, 16 in the LXX). This typology does not appear in Matthew's Gospel.

Matthew's concentration on the person and work of Jesus, who now goes his way as the obedient servant of God and at the same time as God's Son, is clear from the sequel, the story of the temptations. More forced interpretations, then, are to be avoided. Neither a dispute between John's disciples and the Jesus community (a dispute that does play a role in John's Gospel) nor a foundation for Christian baptism is recognizable in Jesus' baptism. Jesus' baptism at the beginning of his activity remains a unique event of the highest importance for salvation history and Christology (J. Gnilka, *Das Matthäusevangelium* [Freiburg, 1986], I, ad loc., "christological fundamental history").

The Temptation of Jesus (4:1-11)

4:1 *Then Jesus was led up by the Spirit into the wilderness to be tempted by the devil.* 2 *He fasted forty days and forty nights, and afterwards he was famished.* 3 *The tempter came and said to him, "If you are the Son of God, command these stones to become loaves of bread."* 4 *But he answered, "It is written,*

> *'One does not live by bread alone,*
> > *but by every word that comes from the mouth of God.'"*

5 *Then the devil took him to the holy city and placed him on the pinnacle of the temple,* 6 *saying to him, "If you are the Son of God, throw yourself down; for it is written,*

> *'He will command his angels concerning you,'*
> > *and 'On their hands they will bear you up,*
> *so that you will not dash your foot against a stone.'"*

7 *Jesus said to him, "Again it is written, 'Do not put the Lord your God to the test.'"*

8 *Again, the devil took him to a very high mountain and showed him all the kingdoms of the world and their splendor;* 9 *and he said to him, "All these I will give you, if you will fall down and worship me."* 10 *Jesus said to him, "Away with you, Satan! for it is written,*

> *'Worship the Lord your God,*
> > *and serve only him.'"*

11 *Then the devil left him, and suddenly angels came and waited on him.*

1-11 Matthew has taken the story of the temptations from the Sayings Source, following it more closely than does Luke (Luke 4:1-13), and tying it to the baptism as it appears in Mark 1:12-13. It is disputed whether Matthew or Luke maintains the original order of the temptations. In Matthew the temptations build to a climax in an orderly fashion, beginning with hunger, followed by the leap from the pinnacle of the temple as a challenge to God, and ending with the enticement of universal sovereignty. In Luke the temple scene comes last, perhaps because for him, pointedly, Jesus' destiny — precisely the contrary, death — is met in Jerusalem (cf. Luke 9:51; 13:33). The characteristic presentation, describing an inner experience externally and graphically, with the devil's approach in physical form and with changes of place (wilderness, temple, lofty mountain), is not intended to be understood as a perceptible occurrence but to portray a trial undergone by Jesus at the outset of his messianic career. The favorite interpretation, that of visions, is groundless and inadequate since there is no mention of Jesus' "seeing" the occurrence (as there is in Luke 10:18) and the rejection of the tempter is conceived as real. Nor is the main purpose here to set before Christians' eyes an example of how to overcome temptation. This is a *Christ story* bound up with the person of Jesus: it presents him as the Son of God who works in the power of the Holy Spirit since God himself has certified him in his baptism. For the reader of Matthew's Gospel it becomes, together with the baptism, the key to grasping Jesus' emergence and person. The manner of presentation resonates with far-off echoes of the story of the temptation in Paradise; however, the narrative recalls other motifs as well, such as Israel's temptations in the wilderness, Moses' forty-day fast (Exod. 34:28; Deut. 9:9, 18), and Elijah's nourishment by an angel (1 Kings 19:5-8). The application to the seductive power of gluttony, vainglory, and lust for power or possessions, which appeared early in the church, must not be allowed to obscure the christological content. In its historical context, a rejection of the Zealot movement, which strove for the liberation of Israel by force, is not to be excluded from the Sayings Source, nor is it very obviously present.

1   The wasteland, to which Jesus is "led up," may have been the barren region above the Jordan (cf. 3:1), but it also has a symbolic meaning: the place of the evil spirits, of renunciation (11:7), or indeed of nearness to God (as for Moses). The movement of the Spirit that has descended upon Jesus in his baptism is an inner impulse (Mark 1:13: "drove him out"), and not a rapture. The devil, as a spirit contrary to God, confronts the (Holy) Spirit as an opponent. His temptations, which, according to Mark 1:13 par. Luke 4:2, extend over the entire forty days, are presented as the object of the sojourn in the wilderness, but they are portrayed as such only at its end.

2   With the specification "forty days and forty nights," Jesus' fast (not mentioned by Mark) recalls Moses' fast in the presence of God in the revelation to him on Sinai (cf. above). While only an incidental remark, it connects the fast with the nearness of God (consider the service of the angels, v. 11). Ecclesiastical use of the forty days' Lenten fast (in the East since ca. A.D. 400; in the West since 700) transfers the example of Christ to Christians, who are called to repentance.

3-4   The "tempter" (as in 1 Thess. 3:5; cf. 1 Cor. 7:5), usually called "the devil" (*diabolos*, a loanword from the Greek; literally, "slanderer") by Matthew, fastens on Jesus' hunger and challenges him as the "Son of God" to work a miracle: to transform stones into bread. All three temptations are an attack on Jesus' divine Sonship (cf. Matt. 4:6), including the third (v. 9), in which this appellation is dropped, as it must be, in the context of a challenge to worship the devil. "Son of God" cannot be meant in a metaphysical sense; rather, it characterizes the Messiah in the Christian sense (16:16; 26:63), in his union with God the Father, a bond proclaimed by God himself (3:17; 17:5). This "Son of God," who nevertheless can be hungry and have appetites, presented no difficulties for the narrator (cf., however, Heb. 4:14-15), as it later did for the Fathers of the church. The devil seeks to draw Jesus away from the path of obedience, which demands "all righteousness" (Matt. 3:15) and which is displayed in the quiet ministry to human beings performed by the servant of God (12:18-21). But Jesus rebuffs him with words from Scripture (Deut. 8:3b), taken from the context of Israel's wandering in the wilderness. Just as God wished to try Israel for forty years in the desert (Deut. 8:2), and fed them with manna (Deut. 8:3a), so God's Son knows that he gathers strength from any word that comes from God's mouth.

5-7   The devil, too, knows Scripture. He takes Jesus to a high part of the temple (scarcely a "gate installation"; more likely a projection in the wall) and demands that he perform another miracle (cf. 12:38-39; 16:1), which he seductively bases on a scriptural passage promising angelic protection (Ps. 91:11-12). But Jesus rebuffs him again, this time with a citation from the Exodus event (Deut. 6:16). To dare such a challenge would be to scorn the divine holiness, as Israel "tested the LORD" at Massah (Exod. 17:1-7; Num. 20:7-13). Paul also warns against "putting Christ to the test" in this fashion (1 Cor. 10:9); and, as Jesus is being taken prisoner, Matthew has him renounce the protection of angels when it would have interfered with the execution of a divine decree (26:53-54).

8-10   Now the devil drops his mask and offers Jesus (without appealing to Scripture) sovereignty over the world if he will prostrate himself and worship him. The "very high mountain" to whose summit he leads him, from whence he shows him "all the kingdoms of the world," cannot be localized geographically, and, according to widespread scholarly opinion, merely sets the stage (cf. *Syrian Apocalypse of Baruch* 76:3). The "Mount of the Temptation" (called Quarantana since the twelfth century), in the vicinity of Jericho, owes its sacred status to fourth-century hermits, and later became the destination of religious pilgrimages. For Matthew the mount of the diabolical seduction finds its antithesis in the Mount of Transfiguration (Matt. 17:1). Again, on a mountain in Galilee the Risen One reveals the fullness of his power and sends forth his disciples to all peoples (28:16) — a God-created "sovereignty" of an altogether different kind. The abrupt, harsh dismissal of the tempter ("Away with you, Satan!") is once more grounded in words addressed to Israel in the desert (Deut. 6:13); the slightly altered quotation has close connections with the "Hear, O Israel" and the commandment of love of God of Deuteronomy 6:4-5.

11   The ministry of the angels, already cited in Mark 1:13, is conceived first of all — in view of his fast — as that of offering Jesus something to eat (cf. 1 Kings 19:5-7); but the angels also indicate God's protective proximity to his Son, which will embrace him in all of his activity (cf. John 1:51). In the power

of the divine Spirit (Matt. 12:28), Jesus has bound the "strong one," the enemy of God and of human beings, shattering all demonic might (12:29).

Jesus Begins His Ministry in Galilee (4:12-16)

> 12 *Now when Jesus heard that John had been arrested, he withdrew to Galilee.* 13 *He left Nazareth and made his home in Capernaum by the sea, in the territory of Zebulun and Naphtali,* 14 *so that what had been spoken through the prophet Isaiah might be fulfilled:*
> 15 *"Land of Zebulun, land of Naphtali,*
>   *on the road by the sea, across the Jordan, Galilee of the Gentiles —*
> 16 *the people who sat in darkness*
>   *have seen a great light,*
>   *and for those who sat in the region and shadow of death*
>   *light has dawned."*

12-16 This pericope concludes the narrative arch initiated in 3:1, and effects a transition to Jesus' Galilean activity. Matthew has taken the reference to the arrest of the Baptist from the Gospel of Mark (1:14), which he now continues to follow, if in his own arrangement of the material. Thus he at once mentions Capernaum, which for him becomes Jesus' "home" and the center of his intense activity ("his own town," Matt. 9:1). Beyond this, Galilee acquires a profound meaning for Matthew, which he reveals with a fulfillment quotation (vv. 14-16): once "heathen" ("Gentile") Galilee becomes the very region in which God's mercy is unveiled in Jesus' salvific activity (4:23, 24b). After Easter, the appearance of the Risen One is to be granted to the disciples in Galilee (28:7); and it is from a mountain in Galilee that Jesus sends forth his disciples "to all nations" (28:16, 19, using the same word as in "Gentile Galilee").

    12-13 Jesus' return from the Jordan to Galilee seems to be for the sake of escaping imminent danger, as was the case in Joseph's return from Judea to Galilee (2:22). As Joseph then settled in Nazareth (2:23), so Jesus now takes up residence in Capernaum. This correlation no doubt also occasioned the observation, "He left Nazareth" (here spelled *Nazara*; contrast 2:23). For Matthew these moves from one locality to another pertain to salvation history since they are based on God's plan. Capernaum, well established archaeologically ("Nahum's Village," today Tell Ḥûm, four to five kilometers west of the mouth of the Jordan at the Dead Sea), was at the time a rather large settlement (a "city"), a border locality with a toll station (9:9) and a military garrison. Its location "by the sea" (Lake Gennesaret) — at one time in the region of the two northern tribes, Zebulun and Naphtali — enables Matthew to make his connection with the ancient prophecy.

14-16   The fulfillment quotation from Isaiah 8:23b–9:1, like that used in Matthew 2:23, is intended to reveal the background meaning here. Furthermore, the quotation is abbreviated, transferred from its original context in order to be set against a new background and tailored to Jesus' appearance on the scene (cf. "Nazorean," 2:23). In Isaiah the region, fallen under the rule of Tiglath-pileser (cf. 2 Kings 15:29), is promised liberation, light in the darkness, and new respect, through the awaited sprout of Jesse (Isa. 11:1). This land is called "Gentile Galilee" because at that time its native Jewish population was interspersed with large groups of foreigners, Gentiles who had resettled there. The "road by the sea" probably originally referred to the route leading from Damascus westward along the Mediterranean Sea, but here it means the trade route running along Lake Gennesaret to the east. In the Old Testament "across the Jordan" probably means the region along the western side of the Jordan where the tribes of Zebulun and Naphtali lived; but for Matthew's Gospel it will rather be the region east of the Jordan where many Jews also lived at the time of Jesus (cf. 4:25). At that time Galilee was once more completely within the Jewish federation; nor, from the viewpoint of religion, was it one whit "Gentile," or less loyal to the law than the rest of the people. Matthew is thinking of the numerous folk who had been streaming to Jesus from the wider area, "from Galilee" (4:15, 25), upon whom a "great light" arises through the proclamation of the gospel; indeed, Jesus is himself this light, shining in the darkness of death (cf. Luke 1:78-79). But he also foresees the approach of the age of the new people of God, to whom the Gentile peoples will be joined (cf. Matt. 8:11; 28:19).

JESUS' PROCLAMATION AND WORKS OF HEALING (4:17–9:34)

With 4:17 Matthew begins his presentation of Jesus' extensive activity among the Jewish people. Here he follows Mark. Most exegetes think this verse forms a unit with 4:12-16. With its proclamation of the approach of the Reign of God, it stands as a section heading, as it were, over the entire first part of the Gospel, which is then followed by a second part that deals with Jesus' way of suffering and death (16:21). The call of the disciples (4:18-22) is closely connected with Mark 1:16-20 and is indispensable if the disciples are to be Jesus' companions and heralds from the very first. The entire report (4:23-25) finds parallels in Mark 1:39 and 3:7-8, although it is differently shaped. The emphasis lies on Jesus' teaching and proclamation as well as on his cures, both elements being closely connected and then developed by Matthew in succession in the Sermon on the Mount (chaps. 5–7) and through Jesus' works of healing (chaps. 8–9).

The Message of the Kingdom (4:17)

> 17 *From that time Jesus began to proclaim, "Repent, for the kingdom of heaven has come near."*

17   Matthew places Jesus' basic message of salvation — here without the designation "gospel" (but cf. 4:23; 9:35; 24:14) — near the beginning of his Gospel, as does Mark (Mark 1:15), but uses the same words as those of John the Baptist (Matt. 3:2). If he omits the announcement, "The time is fulfilled," this is owing to his view of salvation history; after all, the prophetic promises already begin to be fulfilled (fulfillment quotations!) with Jesus' conception and birth, and John the Baptist, for Matthew, himself belongs to "fulfilled" time. As with John, "repentance" is Jesus' all-inclusive requirement. With the Baptist, of course, repentance and baptism unto repentance are safeguards against the judgment (but cf. 3:2, 8); with Jesus, however, conversion consists in faith in the gospel — in the acceptance of the mercy offered by God (cf. 11:20-21).

The "kingdom of heaven," Matthew's usual expression (33 times), is nothing other than the Reign of God (12:28; 19:24; 21:31, 43). "Heaven" is merely a Jewish circumlocution for God. Thus we must not think of it as the "heaven" to which we hope to go, nor as a visible "kingdom" established by God on earth, nor as the church, although the Reign of God is to be realized in the church. The expression means rather God's royal rule, which is to bring the people of God final peace, salvation, and redemption (Isa. 52:7). The message of the Reign of God is the central, special element that Jesus, as a messenger of joy, a courier, announces as his gospel. The Reign of God is not so much the subject of a teaching as it is an event, one that occurs in the presence of Jesus and through his person. Accordingly, Jesus does not describe it but enables his hearers to appreciate it, especially in the parables (Matt. 13:1-52), as an entity given in grace and characterized by a challenge. Proclaimed by Jesus, it is now bursting in upon us in all its dynamism; but it has yet to attain its complete form, which only God can introduce ("kingdom of the Father," 13:43). Everyone is called to await the Reign of God (cf. the Beatitudes; the "entry" sayings, 5:20; 7:13-21; 18:3; 19:23-24; etc.). The full meaning of the Reign of God is unveiled only as the presentation of the Gospel progresses.

Jesus Calls the First Disciples (4:18-22)

> 18 *As he walked by the Sea of Galilee, he saw two brothers, Simon, who is called Peter, and Andrew his brother, casting a net into the sea — for they were fishermen.* 19 *And he said to them, "Follow me, and I will make you fish for people."* 20 *Immediately they left their nets and followed him.* 21 *As he*

went from there, he saw two other brothers, James son of Zebedee and his brother John, in the boat with their father Zebedee, mending their nets, and he called them. 22 *Immediately they left the boat and their father, and followed him.*

18-22　In this pericope Matthew follows Mark almost verbatim, although with two accents of his own: he calls Simon by his surname, "Peter" (v. 18); and, in the case of the second pair of brothers, he emphasizes their leaving their father (vv. 21 and 22). It is a "typical" account of the calling of disciples — it does not depict a historical situation but devotes its whole attention to the call to discipleship and the reaction of those called. The four disciples whose names are given do not represent a special circle of apostles, although they do stand at the head of the list of apostles (10:2), but all those called to the community of salvation. Matthew does not recount the installation of the circle of the Twelve (Mark 3:13-16a); rather, he presupposes it (Matt. 10:1). His concern is with the notion that "disciples" accompany Jesus in his activity from the beginning, and with depicting the salvation community that Jesus seeks to assemble (cf. 5:1).

　　18-20　The brothers Simon and Andrew are portrayed in the act of fishing. They are casting out their net, which sinks into the depths of the lake and then is drawn up — unlike the "dragnet" (13:47), which is towed behind the boat. Thus we can better understand how they can leave their nets "immediately" (v. 20). The brothers do not wait to see how successful the fishing expedition has been. We must await Luke, who draws on another tradition, to hear of a rich catch of fish (Luke 5:1-11), in the context of the calling of Peter. One must answer Jesus' call to discipleship immediately and decisively, and this must be made clear. In "following" Jesus (Matt. 4:19), those called become "fishers for people." This graphic expression, which Matthew has received from tradition, promises the disciples that they will be assisting Jesus by winning people to the movement that he has initiated. Matthew is surely applying this to the disciples' mission to the "lost sheep of the house of Israel" (10:6) and, after Easter, to all people (28:19). Simon's surname, already given here — although it will be interpreted only in 16:18 — reminds the Matthean community of the authority of Peter, of which they are already aware; but the "first" of the apostles (10:2) is here simply inducted into the community of disciples. Andrew is subordinate to his brother; however, see John 1:40-42. John's different presentation of the summoning of the first disciples does not call the Synoptic pericope into question since it orients its message differently and is composed in a different stylistic genre.

　　21-22　The second pair of brothers, the sons of Zebedee, are seen together, already in their boat, mending their nets, "with their father Zebedee" (v. 21; absent in Mark 1:19); thus verse 22 states that they left their father

Zebedee and followed Jesus. The slight shift of emphasis vis-à-vis Mark brings out more forcefully that following Jesus can, as here, imply the surrender of one's current calling and blood relatives (cf. 19:29). Jesus' disciples enter a new "family" (12:49-50). This is understood as a matter of principle, without a demand for the same renunciation on the part of all community members. But there must be a readiness to renounce earthly goods and to separate oneself from one's family, if necessary (cf. 10:34-37). Those who respond to Jesus' call with perfect obedience, keeping nothing back, can also accept the demands of the one who delivered the Sermon on the Mount; and only in conjunction with them is Jesus able to assemble the people that God intends to form.

Jesus Ministers to Crowds of People (4:23-25)

23 *Jesus went throughout Galilee, teaching in their synagogues and proclaiming the good news of the kingdom and curing every disease and every sickness among the people.* 24 *So his fame spread throughout all Syria, and they brought to him all the sick, those who were afflicted with various diseases and pains, demoniacs, epileptics, and paralytics, and he cured them.* 25 *And great crowds followed him from Galilee, the Decapolis, Jerusalem, Judea, and from beyond the Jordan.*

23-25   The summary of coming developments, consisting of "teaching" and "proclamation" (the Sermon on the Mount) and discrete instances of healing (chaps. 8–9), is presented in two stages. First we hear a general statement of Jesus' activity throughout Galilee and the spread of his reputation to Syria itself (vv. 23-24a). Then, by way of specification, we have cures of all diseases and a following consisting of crowds from all parts of the Holy Land (vv. 24b-25). This Matthean composition (using Mark 1:39; 3:10; 3:7-8) is pregnant with conclusions concerning Matthew's particular viewpoint.

23-24a   Teaching, proclamation, and healing are distinguished, and yet they are closely bound together (just as in 9:35). Jesus' teaching in "their synagogues" betrays a certain distancing from Judaism (cf. 10:17; 12:9; 13:54; 23:34). Still, the "teaching" itself remains one of Jesus' essential activities and reveals the fullness of his power (7:28-29; 21:23; cf. 22:16, 33), especially when reinforced by his mighty deeds (13:54-56). The "proclamation of the good news" lays the accent on the special message of the Reign of God (4:17; 10:7; 24:14) but is to be seen in conjunction with Jesus' teaching activity (11:1). Jesus' "teaching" applies the proclamation to his hearers (cf. 5:2 and the Beatitudes). But the cures, too, are "proclamation in deeds." Word and deed go hand in hand and bring to light the irruption of the Reign of God (11:4-5). "Syria" (cited only here in Matthew) must have meant not the Roman province (Luke 2:2; often in

43

Acts), but, to a Jew, the areas adjacent to Galilee. This is how far Jesus' renown extends, but it is intended to underscore the power of his activity only throughout "Galilee."

24b-25 Matthew continues to devote special attention to the cures (8:16-17, with fulfillment quotation). All of the illnesses enumerated here, including that of the "demoniacs," are mentioned again in the later healing accounts. Unlike Mark 3:10 ("many"), Matthew says that *"all"* of those troubled with diseases were healed (qualified in 13:58, "because of their unbelief").

The list of areas in verse 25 seems at first blush to broaden the extent of Jesus' work beyond "Galilee"; but this list is not intended — despite the strong Hellenization of the "Ten Cities" (the Decapolis, southeast of Lake Gennesaret) — to indicate that any of Jesus' activity was performed on behalf of non-Jews (10:5b-6 is explicit to this effect). Strikingly, Idumea (in the South), and the "typically" Gentile cities of Tyre and Sidon (in the North), which Mark names (Mark 3:8), are omitted by Matthew. The great crowds thronging to Jesus from the Ten Cities, Jerusalem and Judea, and the land east of the Jordan represent the people of Israel, to whom Jesus is sent and to whom he brings his message. The places listed (with Jerusalem in the middle!) represent the biblical land in which the people lived, in its ideal (real in David's time) extent. "At the moment of Jesus' programmatic discourse, all of the Israel of the Fathers must be present, or, better, must be represented" (G. Lohfink, *Wie hat Jesus Gemeinde gewollt?* [Freiburg, 1982]). If until now the sick, whom Jesus heals, are in the spotlight, this has been in token of the hope that the people of God (in Greek, *laos*) fulfilled: "The LORD will turn away from you every illness" (Deut. 7:15). Great crowds "followed" Jesus, this time not in utter commitment, as had the disciples who had been called, but with goodwill and a desire to hear his word (cf. 5:1).

The Sermon on the Mount (chaps. 5–7)

The Sermon on the Mount, localized by Luke to a "level place" ("Discourse in the Field"), is a Matthean composition, applying, with Luke 6:20-49, material drawn primarily from the Sayings Source, or Quotations ("Logia") from Jesus (Q, for *Quelle*, "source"). Matthew, however, expands this into a "programmatic discourse." As Jesus' manifesto of the Reign of God, it is directed to the people of God to be gathered from Israel and shaped by Matthew into an address relevant to his community, the new people of God that has emerged from Israel (21:43). In its call to put into practice the morality that God now makes possible, and requires, these words span all ages and are a constant challenge to the church to actualize God's liberating dominion in this world, under the image and aegis of the coming Reign of God. While constantly spurring to action, Jesus' extreme or radical demands must not be "watered down," or restricted to particular persons or groups. They are addressed to the entire people of God, who as such are to hear and follow Jesus' words, however utopian they may appear today. But the demands are supported by the promise of the Reign in its perfection and by the power of God's dominion already making its appearance. In the implementation of God's will, which Jesus proclaimed (and actually carried out), the dawn of the Reign of God is dynamically fulfilled in these very times. All things are possible when one trusts in God the Father, whose love and mercy pervade the entire Sermon on the Mount.

The structure of the discourse is disputed. Matthew's version adopts a great deal of material from Q, the Source of Quotations of Jesus (which Luke uses elsewhere), besides employing much of his own material. Easily recognizable, after the introduction, with its Beatitudes (5:3-12) and metaphors of salt and light (5:13-16), is the passage concerning the "greater righteousness" (5:17-48), along with the following one concerning the piety that that righteousness requires (6:1-18). Then the community is enjoined to undivided service of God, one that surmounts earthly cares (6:19-34), and receives other admonitions for its life (7:1-12). This passage, however, is the least transparent. Finally, the saying concerning the narrow gate and the warning against false prophets and enthusiasts make clear the urgency of the situation (7:13-23). The conclusion of this discourse consists (as in Luke) of the parable of the construction of a house (7:24-27), which once more issues in an urgent call to action. In the center of the Matthean Sermon on the Mount, not coincidentally, is the "Our Father" (6:9-13). We shall forgo a precise dissection and proceed by taking up the familiar segments.

The Beginning of the Sermon on the Mount (5:1-19)

The Beatitudes (5:1-12)

5:1 *When Jesus saw the crowds, he went up the mountain; and after he sat down, his disciples came to him. 2 Then he began to speak, and taught them, saying:*

3 *"Blessed are the poor in spirit, for theirs is the kingdom of heaven.*

4 *"Blessed are those who mourn, for they will be comforted.*

5 *"Blessed are the meek, for they will inherit the earth.*

6 *"Blessed are those who hunger and thirst for righteousness, for they will be filled.*

7 *"Blessed are the merciful, for they will receive mercy.*

8 *"Blessed are the pure in heart, for they will see God.*

9 *"Blessed are the peacemakers, for they will be called children of God.*

10 *"Blessed are those who are persecuted for righteousness' sake, for theirs is the kingdom of heaven.*

11 *"Blessed are you when people revile you and persecute you and utter all kinds of evil against you falsely on my account.* 12 *Rejoice and be glad, for your reward is great in heaven, for in the same way they persecuted the prophets who were before you."*

1-2 The "crowds" are the persons who have thronged together from all corners of the land (4:25) and who represent the people of Israel about to hear the message and teaching of Jesus. The "mountain" is not identified more precisely (today the "Mount of the Beatitudes" is not far from Capernaum) and should be understood typologically: as Moses ascended the mountain of God to proclaim God's revelation and law to the children of Israel (Exod. 19:3; 24:18; 34:1-2), so Jesus now ascends "the mountain" to present his message, along with the demands of God, which go beyond the old law. The disciples who approach him do not represent a privileged group but are the people who have been called (Matt. 4:18-22) and are open to his word, with whom all the people are to identify. The later interpretation of the church, so frequently heard, distinguishing the "perfect," who are enjoined the loftiest requirements, from the people, who are called to repentance (a two-level ethic), is untenable. The Sermon on the Mount is addressed to all alike, as evidenced in 7:28, and its teaching is set forth with authority (7:29). Jesus "teaches" (seated, like the scribes) God's word and will to the disciples and the people, as indicated by the biblical expression "opening his mouth" (Exod. 4:12, 15; Num. 22:28; Ezek. 3:27; etc.). Jesus' ultimate instruction climaxes in the love that knows no measure (5:44-48) and challenges all believers to love (Thomas Aquinas). It is also from a mountain in Galilee that, after the resurrection, Jesus enjoins his disciples to teach and urge obedience to his commandments (28:20).

3-12 The Beatitudes, which in their core (i.e., the first three) refer to Jesus, represent a familiar stylistic usage in the Old Testament and Judaism that can either bear a more sapiential stamp or be directed toward the future (the "apocalyptic" variety). Jesus' Beatitudes are to be grouped with the latter type. Not only do they direct our gaze toward the future (Isa. 30:18; 31:9 in the LXX; 32:20; etc.), however; in the framework of his message of the Reign of God (cf. 5:3, 10), they also inspire human beings even now with the certainty of God's mercy. Originally a proclamation of salvation to everyone in the audience with eyes to see and ears to hear (cf. Matt. 13:16-17), the Lukan version emphasizes Jesus' concern for the actual poor, hungry, and weeping, while Matthew stresses the moral attitude thereby demanded. Thus Matthew's expanded series becomes an urgent appeal to respond, in attitude and activity, to Jesus' promises. Divine grace, moral requirements, and promises form a unity. The Beatitude concerning the persecuted (Luke 6:22; Matt. 5:10, 11-12) has become timely now (and is even present in Q). The number of Beatitudes adopted from the tradition is doubled in Matthew, so that there are eight, perhaps as a result of the tradition of his community. Their numbering as eight is not to be questioned (vv. 3-10): the lengthier promise for the persecuted (vv. 11-12), of special importance to Matthew (cf. also the Beatitude of the peacemakers, 5:9, 44), sounds out of place in the series (v. 10). The newly added Beatitudes are formulated in the spirit of Jesus, in loyalty to his teaching. In Matthew the Beatitudes are formulated in the third person; in Luke they are addressed to the audience, in the second person. It is difficult to say what their original form was.

3   The Beatitude of the poor, which in Luke refers to the needy of the earth, is interpreted by Matthew as applying to all who know their poverty before God and who, in every need, place their trust in God alone. Thus he adds, "in spirit." This "piety of the poor" has deep roots in the Old Testament (cf. Pss. 34; 37; 69:33-34; etc.), and has an entire history of its own. In Jesus' time, many among the people were moved and inspired by it (cf. the Magnificat, Luke 1:46-55). Jesus proclaims the message of salvation to the poor (Luke 4:18, following Isa. 61:1; see Matt. 11:5; Luke 7:22). The members of the Qumran community, too, regarded themselves as the "poor" or "humble," at times with the addition "of spirit" (1QM 14:7; 1QH 14:3) or "of grace" — an expression of their conviction of their election ("community of the poor," 4QpPs 37). Jesus does not restrict his summons to salvation to a "sacred remnant" in Israel, but addresses all in Israel who are conscious of their human wretchedness and who surrender to the divine mercy.

4   The sorrowful are precisely the poor (compare Isa. 61:2 with the verse just before it). They are the lowly and humble (Ps. 33:18 in the LXX; see 1QH 18:14-15) — all who groan under the burden of sorrow and guilt and who look to God alone for their "comfort" (Isa. 49:13). For God is the guarantor of the promise expressed in the passive voice, "They will be comforted." God's "comfort," which turns sorrow to gladness, is a familiar concept, especially in the promises in the Old Testament and in Judaism whose fulfillment is awaited for the future (Isa. 40:1-2; 66:13; *Syrian Apocalypse of Baruch* 44:7; etc.), and here refers to the dawning Reign of God (cf. Luke 2:25; 16:25).

5   The "meek," too, or the gentle, are precisely the "poor" and the "sorrowful." The Greek expression is a Septuagint translation of 'ănāwîm, the poor, and the Beatitude echoes Psalm 37 (LXX 36):11: "The meek shall inherit the land, and delight themselves in abundant prosperity." Psalm 37 was important to the Qumran community (4QpPs 37): it claimed the "inheriting of the land" for itself, as "the community of his elect" (4QpPs 37 2:5; 3:5). The Matthean Be-

atitude understands the same verse as referring to the Reign of God, and is a universal call to salvation of all who await peace and happiness from God and who are "humble" and gentle (cf. 11:21; 21:5). It is not a specific appeal for the renunciation of violence, but it does carry the connotation of peaceful behavior (cf. v. 9). The first three or four Beatitudes are distinguished in Greek by their identical consonantal sounds, their alliteration (the letter *pi* — perhaps a development of the Greek-speaking community.

6 The Beatitude of the hungering, which in Luke 6:21 refers to the physically hungry, is spiritualized by Matthew and at the same time set in a larger context with the addition of "for righteousness." Now the "hunger" is that of the poor and afflicted for the all-embracing righteousness that God, or his Messiah, will establish (Isa. 11:4; Jer. 23:5-6; 33:15-16; see Matt. 12:20). It is to this yearning for salvation that the interpolation "and thirst" refers, which is absent from the promise itself. In the background are the experiences of the wandering in the wilderness (Ps. 107:4-9) as well as the provision of manna and water from the rock, which point, typologically, to the approaching of salvation (Pss. 78:24-25; 105:40-41; Isa. 48:21). The satisfaction of hunger and thirst pertains to the hope of Israel (Isa. 49:10; 65:13), but even in the Old Testament it is transferred to a longing for the word of God (Amos 8:11) and for wisdom (Prov. 9:5; Sir. 24:21; 51:24). The expression chosen by Matthew, "righteousness," connects the salvation given by God with the behavior required of human beings (Matt. 3:15; 5:20; 6:1, 33). Divine graciousness and a morality surpassing all previous "righteousness" are, under the Reign of heaven, indivisible. At the same time the still hidden appeal to what is demanded of human beings suddenly channels the train of thought below to the second set of four Beatitudes, which addresses moral striving more powerfully.

7 All-embracing mercy is demanded, as God shows it even now (Luke 6:36; Matt. 18:33). God wills mercy, not ritual sacrifices (Matt. 9:13; 12:7) — a thrust at a legalistic, formalized Judaism (23:23). Jesus hears the cry of the sick and those who despair of mercy (9:27; 15:22; 17:15; 20:30-31), and he has compassion for an abandoned people (9:36; 14:14; 15:32). Partisans of the needy and abandoned belong to the blessed of the Father and will find mercy at the judgment (25:31-46).

8 Purity of heart is not reducible to a particular virtue (such as chastity) but requires what is demanded from visitors to the temple (Psalms 15 and 24: "Torah liturgies"): "clean hands and pure hearts" (Ps. 24:4). It is a matter of actions that proceed from a sincere heart — especially truthful speech, keeping one's word, dealing honestly with one's neighbor (Ps. 15:2-5), and conduct oriented to God's trustworthiness, goodness, and fidelity (Psalm 26; Mic. 6:8). Jewish piety is likewise the source of the promise of beholding God. The primordial "vision of the face of God" on the occasion of a visit to the temple later

became the expectation that the souls of the just would behold God in the heavenly paradise (*Apocalypse of Abraham* 29:20; *4 Ezra* 7:98; etc.; P. Billerbeck and H. L. Strack, *Kommentar zum Neuen Testament*, 4 vols. [Munich, 1922-28], 1:205-15). The concept was adopted by primitive Christianity (1 Cor. 13:12; 1 John 3:2; Rev. 22:4), and refers in Matthew and in Revelation 22:5 to the coming Reign of God. This Beatitude had a profound impact on the early church, especially on those fathers whose inspiration was Greek, frequently in connection with Matthew 13:16-17 and 1 Corinthians 2:9.

9   The Beatitude of the peacemakers is Matthew's own, although it is related to James 3:18. The meaning of "peace" here is the usual biblical one: a comprehensive, salutary condition. "Peaceable" would be too weak a translation of the word used here for the persons to whom the Beatitude is addressed. The word denotes an active concern for peace, as God wills it and as Jesus embodies it (Matt. 21:4-5). To create this peace means to seek to propagate among humans the peace proclaimed by God (Luke 2:14), in conformity with the Reign of God throughout the world, even among the Gentiles (Isa. 2:4; Mic. 4:3). The more immediate addressees are the community of disciples, who are to renounce retaliation (Matt. 5:38-42) and force of arms (26:52-54), be open to reconciliation (5:23-26), and even love their enemies and pray for their persecutors (5:44-48). The expected status of children of God, which sounds forth as early as Hosea 1:10-11 (in the LXX: "They shall be called 'sons of the living God'") and, based on that text, is found in *Jubilees* 1:24-25 (cf. also Wis. 2:16-18; 5:5), once more is a salvific aspect of God's Reign; in primitive Christianity it is understood as the full realization of the status of children of God already bestowed, and it is linked in 1 John 3:1-2 to the vision of God. The Beatitude is a signpost for today's peace movement, provided it is understood in its original historical context.

10   Persecution "for righteousness' sake" — on account of one's fidelity to Jesus Christ and his gospel — had actually been experienced by the Matthaean community (Matt. 10:23; 23:34). This Beatitude asks the community to accept that, and to pray for their persecutors (5:44). Urgent as this was for the community at that time, in order to comply with Jesus' ultimate demand, that of love of enemies, it is still valid for all times and situations. To have been persecuted (perfect tense) will be a mark of Jesus' disciples (10:22, 24-26) if they are to share in the coming Reign of God. The power of the gospel is shown in persecution, and discipleship, or following Jesus, is put to the test (10:38-39; 16:24-25; John 15:20; 1 Peter 1:6-7; 3:13).

11-12   Matthew takes this Beatitude in the second person plural, as he has it from Q (cf. Luke 6:22-23), joins it to his series, and adapts it to the community of his time ("revile," "persecute," "slander"). Jesus' disciples undergo the same persecutions as the prophets, God's spokespersons par excellence in the Old Testament. Thus the Christ community takes its place in salvation history and meets with the same lot as does its Lord (see 2:13, 16-18; 21:33-39; 23:37-38). The historical scene of the murder of the prophets (22:6; 23:34-36) is taken over from the historical work of the Deuteronomist. Jesus, too, the "prophet from Nazareth in Galilee" (21:11, 46), experiences rejection in his home city (13:57) and suffering and death in Jerusalem. For his sake (Luke's "for the sake of the Son of Man") the disciples must endure the same, but they may expect a "reward in heaven" (with God) as well. In the certitude of this fulfillment, they can, even now, rejoice and "be glad" — an expression of the beatification already dawning (Acts 2:46; 1 Peter 1:6, 8; 4:13; Rev. 19:7).

Salt and Light (5:13-16)

13 *"You are the salt of the earth; but if salt has lost its taste, how can its saltiness be restored? It is no longer good for anything, but is thrown out and trampled under foot.*

14 *"You are the light of the world. A city built on a hill cannot be hid.* 15 *No one after lighting a lamp puts it under the bushel basket, but on the lampstand, and it gives light to all in the house.* 16 *In the same way, let your light shine before others, so that they may see your good works and give glory to your Father in heaven."*

13-16 Following the words to the persecuted community, we encounter a series of logia on the value and enlightening power of the community in the world, composed by Matthew himself. However, the portrayal of the ideal becomes a demand as well: thus must you be and act if you would glorify your Father in heaven with your good works (v. 16). Matthew has taken his images essentially — that is, for the logia of the salt and the light — from Q (cf. Luke 14:34-35; 11:33), adding a quotation of his own concerning the city on the mountain (5:14b) and thereby assembling originally independent metaphors into a single appeal to the disciples. This grouping of logia, unique from the standpoint of form criticism, is addressed not to an inner circle (apostles, preachers, or teachers), but to the entire people of God. It is an image for the later church (cf. Vatican II, *Lumen Gentium*, art. 9).

13 The address in the second person is attached to the expanded Beatitude of the persecuted (vv. 11-12). The metaphor of salt is to be understood in terms of the flavor added by salt (cf. Mark 9:50; Luke 14:34). Other interpretations (a slab of salt in the oven, a fertilizer) are far-fetched; casting it out and seeing people trample it illustrates only the worthlessness of unusable salt. The loss of savor, which is impossible with pure salt, may represent the admixture of salt from the Dead Sea or other adulterations. A transferred meaning — wisdom, proclamation, or readiness for sacrifice — is not definitely implied. Perhaps the original intent was a threat against Israel or its leaders (21:43). Together with the image of the lamp, it is an appeal to the community of disciples to bear witness to the gospel, in the midst of a world still averse to it, by living a life in conformity with Jesus' instructions.

14-15 The image of the light of the world is familiar throughout Judaism, where it is applied to Israel, Jerusalem, and the Torah, as well as to the righteous and teachers of the law as exemplars. Now the light of the world is the community of Jesus' disciples, perhaps in conscious opposition to unbelieving Judaism. The "city on a hill" must not be understood as Jerusalem (*the* city of God). Like a city visible from a distance, the community is to attract persons by its exemplary life.

The logion concerning the lamp, which ought to be on a lampstand, doubtless spoken by Jesus in a concrete situation, is taken up by the Synoptics in various situations. It refers to the proclamation of the gospel (Mark 4:21; Luke 8:16 — perhaps the original intent), or to Jesus (Luke 11:33; see John 8:12; 9:5), or, here in Matthew, to the community. The original situation of the image is unclear: Is the bushel basket (used for measuring wheat) to be seen as a snuffer, or only as a hiding place (Mark 4:21; Luke 8:16: ". . . or under a bed")? The drastic expression is intended only to emphasize that the lamp ought to be placed on a lampstand. For Matthew, who visualizes a one-room dwelling, the lamp is to give light "to all in the house"; for Luke, who is thinking of a house with a vestibule, it shines for "all who enter" (a mission situation).

The "good works" (in Matthew otherwise only in 26:10) are not the Jewish works of the law ("fulfilling the law"), and yet they call to mind works of mercy (so called by the Jews as well; see 25:31-46). Here we have general primitive Christian usage (Eph. 2:10; pastoral letters; Heb. 10:24; 13:21; etc.). A misunderstanding of the expression as "righteousness of works" is thereby excluded — the works should lead only to the praise of God (who also makes them possible). "Your Father in heaven" is named here for the first time — the One with whom all the thinking of Jesus' disciples originates and toward whom all their activity is directed (5:45; 6:9 — the "Our Father").

The Law and the Prophets (5:17-19)

17 *"Do not think that I have come to abolish the law or the prophets; I have come not to abolish but to fulfill.* 18 *For truly I tell you, until heaven and earth pass away, not one letter, not one stroke of a letter, will pass from the law until all is accomplished.* 19 *Therefore, whoever breaks one of the least of these commandments, and teaches others to do the same, will be called least in the kingdom of heaven; but whoever does them and teaches them will be called great in the kingdom of heaven."*

51

17-19   Matthew begins the discourse on the morality, piety, and sense of community required of Jesus' disciples, which extends to 7:12, with some basic statements about the validity of the law. But the three verses are difficult to understand given this arrangement. The basic idea is that the law must be "fulfilled"; but what does this mean? According to verse 18, not the slightest part of the law must be neglected "until all is accomplished," which suggests fulfillment in terms of salvation history (but see below on v. 18). The next verse places the emphasis on action. Is the law to be "fulfilled" in its entire scope? But a literal meaning is contradicted by the subsequent antitheses, as well as by Jesus' own conduct. Apart from the first dictum (v. 17), which Matthew may himself have composed, the evangelist is obviously committed to received formulas. There is a parallel to verse 18 in Luke 16:17 (Q). Verse 19 is peculiar to Matthew, who may have received it from the Jewish-Christian tradition. The "law and the prophets" are still in force, but they must be "fulfilled," brought to completion, and implemented, in a new fashion. There must be no question of a new "law" handed down by Jesus.

17   Here the evangelist warns against a misinterpretation of Jesus' coming, just as he does in 10:34. Now the person of Jesus comes into perspective: the community is to hold exclusively to Jesus' self-awareness and instructions. The "law and the prophets" (cf. 7:12) denote the Old Testament in its moral prescriptions (22:40) but also in its promises (11:13). "Abolish" (literally, "dissolve") means "render invalid"; "fulfill" may express an activity in full conformity with the divine will (it does not occur with this sense elsewhere in Matthew, but see Gal. 5:14; Rom. 13:8). The frequent use of "fulfill" in the sense of salvation history (fulfillment citations), however, also suggests that Jesus introduces fulfillment into the question of the law. Perhaps Matthew seeks to connect the two meanings in his particularly rich expression.

18   The "letter," the *iota,* is the smallest letter in the Greek alphabet. The "stroke of a letter" doubtless means an embellishment on a letter — a graphic expression for the least prescription of the law (see v. 19), a figure of speech consciously exaggerated to emphasize the unconditional validity of the law as long as the world shall endure. Matthew adds, ". . . until all is accomplished," a turn of phrase that in Mark 13:31 (= Matt. 24:34) refers to the inauguration of the eschatological occurrences. Jesus' words will not pass away (cf. Matt. 24:35), and this includes his words concerning the law: they are to be complied with and realized "to the end of the age" (28:20).

19   The astonishing declaration that anyone abolishing one of these least commandments will be the least in the Reign of heaven probably does not mean that he or she will nevertheless still have a place in it, but places such a person in stark contrast with those who actually practice what they preach. The contrast powerfully stresses the actual practice of a teaching and makes any "greatness" in the Reign of God (18:1; 20:26; 23:11) dependent on it (cf. 7:21; 23:3). Far from still having a "least" place reserved for them in the Reign of God, they will be excluded from that Reign by the Lord of the judgment (7:23; 25:12; 25:41-46).

The entire series of logia is marked by the Jewish-Christian confrontation with the Jewish understanding of the law — in dependence and exemption alike — and thus must not be invoked as evidence that the Judaism approved by Jesus was simply one of total acceptance of the law; but it is also a warning that Jesus is to be distinguished from the ancient people of God. As the prophets engaged in a critique of the practice of the law, so did Jesus: with him everything converges on the surpassing commandment of love (5:45-48; 7:12; 22:37-40).

"Greater Righteousness": Antitheses (5:20-48)

The thematic statement of verse 20 is illustrated and developed in individual commandments — in six "antitheses," as they are called. However, this series of antitheses, which Matthew alone presents, contains declarations whose content is to be found in Luke (from the Sayings Source) as well: the prohibition of divorce (Luke 16:18), the principle of nonretaliation (Luke 6:29-30), and the commandment to love one's enemies (Luke 6:27-29, 32-36), together with the verses on litigation (Luke 12:57-59). There can be no doubt of the origin of the content of this material with Jesus, but Matthew has introduced the antithetical form here, secondarily. The other antitheses, which have no substantial parallel in Luke, may have come from Jesus himself ("primary antitheses"). Still others suggest a form created by the Jewish-Christian community, or by the evangelists themselves.

Using the same formulation in verses 21 and 33 (with "Again . . ." in the latter instance), Matthew composes two series of three antitheses each (showing his predilection for the number three; see Intro., p. 4). He adds further material to certain antitheses: to the first, the pronouncement on reconciliation (vv. 23-24) and the logion on the judicial adversary (vv. 25-26); to the second, the exhortation on the removal of bodily members (cf. Mark 9:43-48; Matt. 18:8-9). In terms of the weight of the content, we can distinguish between antitheses that render Old Testament commandments more stringent (first and second antitheses) and those that "abrogate" them (third antithesis through the sixth). A climactic order is to be observed; but the entire series is unified with the same "But I say to you . . . ," pronounced with sovereign authority.

Introduction (5:20)

> 20 *"For I tell you, unless your righteousness exceeds that of the scribes and Pharisees, you will never enter the kingdom of heaven."*

20 "For" connects this verse with the logion unit just completed (vv. 17-19); but the comparative, "exceeds," already indicates the antitheses that explain the "more" for which Jesus calls. The "righteousness" required of Jesus' disciples (see 3:15; 5:6, 10) is to surpass that of the scribes and Pharisees. Matthew's frequent double expression (7 times) betrays the opposition to the Judaism led by Pharisaic teachers of the law after A.D. 70 (recital of woes, chap. 23). In Jesus' time, there were Sadducean teachers of the law as well; but even then the "brotherhood" of the Pharisees, with their teachers, was influential. The discourse concerned with "entering the kingdom of heaven," only in Matthew in this place, is akin to that of Mark (9:47; 10:15, 23-25); in adopting the concept, Matthew has strengthened it (7:21; 21:31; cf. the images of 7:13-14; 22:12-13; 25:10-12; 8:12; 25:30). Originally an image for entry into the promised land, then into the temple as well (Torah liturgies; see 5:8), it is here carried over to sharing in the Reign of God. This verse sets the antitheses in the perspective of that reign.

Concerning Anger (5:21-26)

> 21 *"You have heard that it was said to those of ancient times, 'You shall not murder'; and 'whoever murders shall be liable to judgment.' 22 But I say to you that if you are angry with a brother or sister, you will be liable to judgment; and if you insult a brother or sister, you will be liable to the council; and if you say, 'You fool,' you will be liable to the hell of fire. 23 So when you are offering your gift at the altar, if you remember that your brother or sister has something against you, 24 leave your gift there before the altar and go; first be reconciled to your brother or sister, and then come and offer your gift. 25 Come to terms quickly with your accuser while you are on the way to court with him, or your accuser may hand you over to the judge, and the judge to the guard, and you will be thrown into prison. 26 Truly I tell you, you will never get out until you have paid the last penny."*

21-22 "Ancient" refers to earlier generations, old Israel, which received the Sinaitic revelation (the Decalogue). Jesus elevates the proscription of murder (Exod. 20:13; 21:12; Deut. 5:17) to a prohibition against anger. The rhetorical expression, "But I say to you," present in all the antitheses and addressed to the disciples (the word "you" is in the plural), cannot be explained as a stock phrase used in rabbinical disputations over the interpretation of Scripture; rather, it brings Jesus' teaching to expression "in full authority" (see 7:29). Jesus sets his understanding of the divine will in emphatic opposition to the literal meaning of the Decalogue. By now, even in Judaism anger has become reprehensible — an incitement to murder, and, indeed, something that brands anything approaching it (Billerbeck, *Kommentar zum Neuen Testament,* 1:276-82). In terms of content, Jesus is scarcely saying anything new. But he strikingly and emphatically raises to the status of obligations for the salvation community matters not expressly commanded or literally formulated in the Torah — for a community that is to understand itself as one of siblings ("brother or sister"). What is meant by "judgment" is, for the moment, undetermined. It becomes clearer in what follows. It is unlikely that it refers to the local court which is outranked by the High Council (the highest Jewish court) and then by the divine judgment (the fires of hell).

Verse 22a is a thesis statement, somewhat like a "topic sentence," implying what follows. The climaxing reproaches, "fool" and "godless person" (proved to be such), show the limits to which anger drives a person and how it is to be assessed. The "council" only illustrates the gravity of the fault. For Jesus, the divine judgment looms over all anger, insult, and injury to brothers or sisters (cf. 6:14-15; 18:35; 25:41), and this, despite the "steps" peculiar to Matthew here, is what his presentation means to say. "Righteous anger" lies outside his purview.

23-24 Anger is kindled by a perception of offense — by insult and hostility. Thus this pronouncement culminates in the positive demand of reconciliation with one's enemies. Probably it was originally joined ("So . . .") to something else in the tradition, in turn standing entirely against a Jewish background, as is shown by the picture of offering a gift. Regardless of whether the gift is a sin offering or a peace offering, the one offering it is seeking peace with God; but — and this is the sense of the pronouncement — without reconciliation with one's sibling, fellowship with God is impossible. The other person's guilt is simply not in question; it suffices that "your brother or sister has *something against you.*" Observance of the commandment of love far surpassed the implementation of ritual prescriptions (9:13; 12:7; Mark 12:33-34).

25-26 Matthew takes a parable that had originally been eschatological (Luke 12:57-59) and uses it to convey a warning to the people of his community to come to an understanding with any judicial adversary. The situation is critical when one is haled into court on account of an unpaid debt: conviction and imprisonment threaten. Guilt is presupposed (v. 26), as in the parable in 18:21-35 (cf. 18:34). This emergency ("Come to terms quickly . . . ," v. 25) implies an intensification vis-à-vis the ritual image of verses 23-24. From imprisonment, as in 18:35, the mind moves to the thought of divine judgment. The basic demand, as before, is reconciliation with one's neighbor, the primacy of love.

Concerning Adultery (5:27-30)

27 *"You have heard that it was said, 'You shall not commit adultery.'* 28 *But I say to you that everyone who looks at a woman with lust has already committed adultery with her in his heart.* 29 *If your right eye causes you to sin, tear it out and throw it away; it is better for you to lose one of your members than for your whole body to be thrown into hell.* 30 *And if your right hand causes you to sin, cut it off and throw it away; it is better for you to lose one of your members than for your whole body to go into hell."*

27-30   A second example of the radical character of Jesus' requirements is taken from the area of history. Matthew has joined the caution against coveting another's wife with the pronouncement concerning bodily members that lead astray — which originally had a broader application, equivalent to our expression "cause to stumble" (Mark 9:43-48), but which here is applied to sexual desire ("eye," "hand").

27-28   Here the introduction is shorter. The prohibition against adultery is once more taken from the Decalogue (Exod. 20:14; Deut. 5:18). It is surprising that Jesus contrasts his prohibition against coveting the wife of another (whose marriage the lecher violates "in his heart") with the Decalogue, since Deuteronomy 5:21 itself forbids coveting one's neighbor's wife. Lewd glances have been proscribed in Job 31:1 and Sirach 9:3. Jesus' judgment is no stricter than that of quite a number of rabbis (Billerbeck, *Kommentar zum Neuen Testament*, 1:299-301). Just as with anger, then, Jesus is demanding nothing new with respect to content. Is his intent to reemphasize the divine will in the face of lax practice? to protect women from sexual harassment? Within the framework of the other antitheses, this passage emphasizes surmounting a legalistic attitude; it is a matter of a demand by God that pierces to the innermost self (the heart). Here, too, divine judgment ("hell," vv. 29-30) looms for the one who sins in secret.

29-30   These verses express an exaggeration, in keeping with Jesus' extremely graphic style of speech (cf. 7:3-5; 19:12c, 24). As the sexually promiscuous are liable to be taken off to a place of punishment, so also hell (Gehenna, derived from the dismal valley of Hinnom outside Jerusalem) is not meant as a literal place of fire (see 3:12; 5:22), but is cited in order to indicate the gravity of the decision, taken in the presence of God. The correlate remains unspoken: the person who resists temptation will surely enter the Reign of God (Mark 9:47).

Concerning Divorce (5:31-32)

31 *"It was also said, 'Whoever divorces his wife, let him give her a certificate of divorce.'* 32 *But I say to you that anyone who divorces his wife, except*

*on the ground of unchastity, causes her to commit adultery; and whoever
marries a divorced woman commits adultery."*

31-32   Owing to its kinship with verses 27-30 (adultery), Matthew has seized
upon a logion from tradition (Luke 16:18, probably from Q, in addition to the
dispute of Mark 10:2-9; Matt. 19:3-9) and (secondarily) molded it into an antithesis. In this way he formally sets Jesus' command over against words of
Scripture (Deut. 24:1), although in 19:8 he explains the latter as a "concession"
on Moses' part. This is the only one of the antitheses in which we observe a sovereign injunction of Jesus going beyond, indeed contradicting, Scripture. This
also occurs, however, in the Jewish understanding of the Torah (cf. below).
Thus it is all the more surprising to see the addition by Matthew, and by him
alone, of "except on the ground of unchastity" (cf. also 19:9), in which he seems
to relativize the prohibition once more — a topic of animated discussion even
today.

    31   The introduction here is even briefer than the one in verse 27 (with-
out "You have heard . . ."). The quotation is from Deuteronomy 24:1, but it is
actually abridged. The directive that the husband who wishes to dismiss his
wife because he discovers "something objectionable" in her must present her
with a bill of divorce was originally intended as a protective measure for the
wife, but, owing to variations of interpretation of "unchastity," had led to lax divorce practice. Many exegetes suppose that this is what motivated Jesus to issue
his prohibition of divorce. But his prohibition cannot be understood solely in
terms of consideration for disadvantaged women: he also forbids a divorced
woman to remarry (v. 32c), which, humanly speaking, would have been a relief
for such a woman. Jesus' decision is grounded in his conception of the divine
will for marriage.

    32   This prohibition is formulated (more clearly than in Luke 16:18) al-
together according to Jewish matrimonial legislation. Generally only the husband was legally entitled to secure a divorce (while Greco-Roman law, in terms
of which Mark 10:11-12 is formulated, accorded the right of divorce to a wife as
well), and this only by way of dismissal with a bill of divorce. Adultery was one
man's breaking into the marriage of another who had a legal claim to his wife. A
wife who was unfaithful to her husband committed this delinquency in that she
permitted the perpetration, with her, of this offense on the part of another man
against the legitimate rights of her husband. This explains the peculiar formulation in verse 32b: "causes her to commit adultery." The fault is that of the husband who dismisses his wife. Here it is presupposed that the dismissed wife is
forced by the divorce to wed another husband. But Jesus holds all such dismissal to be impermissible; thus he considers the first marriage to be still in
place. The severe Essene community, appealing to Genesis 1:27, forbade one

man "to take two wives in his lifetime" (CD 4:21; see, for the King, 11QTemple 57:17-19). Not being dependent on Qumran, nor working from the same legal perspective, Jesus transcends both to reach back to the original will of God.

Of the numerous attempts to solve the riddle of the "unchastity" clause, only two are generally regarded as holding a great deal of promise today. The first consists of an interpretation of the "unchastity" as referring to illegitimate marriages between near relatives *(zĕnûth)*, which was intolerable for Jewish Christians, and which (in mixed communities) Gentile Christians are to avoid as well (cf. Acts 15:20, 29). The second interpretation would be that of an actual exception for the case of adultery. The Greek expression for "unchastity" can also have the meaning of "adultery."

The first interpretation lies in the area of Jewish thought but does not fit well with the Matthean formulation. The second supposition must be taken seriously for Jewish-Christian communities, since in Jewish thought it was a sacred duty to dismiss adulteresses. By doing so one sought precisely to comply with the divine will. At all events, the Matthean unchastity clause along with Jesus' unqualified prohibition of divorce threw primitive Christian (here Jewish-Christian) communities into great difficulties (for Gentile communities, see 1 Cor. 7:10-16). Jesus had made his determination solely in accordance with the holy will of God, without regard for its practical realization in this world — the basic problem of the Sermon on the Mount!

Concerning Oaths (5:33-37)

> 33 "Again, you have heard that it was said to those of ancient times, 'You shall not swear falsely, but carry out the vows you have made to the Lord.' 34 But I say to you, Do not swear at all, either by heaven, for it is the throne of God, 35 or by the earth, for it is his footstool, or by Jerusalem, for it is the city of the great King. 36 And do not swear by your head, for you cannot make one hair white or black. 37 Let your word be 'Yes, Yes' or 'No, No'; anything more than this comes from the evil one."

33-37 The second group of antitheses ("Again . . .") begins with the same lengthy introductory formula as in verse 21. The structure is not homogeneous, and it betrays an evolution of the text in tradition. The three prohibitions referring to God are followed by a ban on swearing by one's own head (v. 36). After the prohibitions comes the strict commandment of truthful speech without an oath (v. 37). In the motivation for such conduct (vv. 34b-35), one is struck by use of scriptural citations, which occur in no other place in the entire series. Matthew draws on Jewish-Christian tradition, perhaps apart from the conclusion (v. 37b). Nor need Jesus reject the prohibition of the oath in the strict sense, which, of course, is foreign to the Old Testament. A parallel in conduct is to be found in James 5:12.

33 There is no formal prohibition of perjury in the Decalogue, but there is in Leviticus 19:12, in an appeal to keep the Name of God holy. The second clause, which deals with the fulfillment of a promise made to God (vow), is a fresh construction from various Old Testament passages (Num. 30:3; Deut. 23:21-23; Ps. 50:14). The vow goes very far back into Israel's history, and involved calling upon Yahweh ("As Yahweh lives . . ."). The religious meaning of the oath and the vow is also shown by the fact that Yahweh himself swears, by himself (Gen. 22:16; Exod. 32:13; Amos 6:8; 8:7; etc.), for blessing or for a curse. One must attend to this religious background when considering Jesus' prescription.

34-35 Jesus' words are unequivocal: "Do not swear at all." The argumentation presents an exalted picture of God as Lord of heaven and earth (Isa. 66:1; see Pss. 11:4; 103:19). Swearing "by Jerusalem" (or, in terms of the Greek preposition, "facing Jerusalem"; the direction one faced while praying?) is otherwise unknown. The "city of the great King" (Ps. 48:2) testifies to Israel's faith that God dwelt, and was enthroned, on Zion, in Jerusalem (Ps. 78:68-69). Will God not be excellently honored through such oaths?

36 The motivation here is of a different kind. The familiar oath by one's own head, frequently practiced even outside Israel, shows the inability of the human being to change anything by an oath. By way of graphic illustration, the coloring of the hair is mentioned, doubtless alluding to one's age. Such oaths were often connected with self-cursing (cf. 26:74), and were intended to corroborate an assertion. The hierarchy descends from the "sacred oath" (especially vows) to assurances, guaranteed by an oath, in the human area.

Appropriately, the positive commandment is added here to restrict oneself to the simple Yes or No. The double statement demands unqualified truthfulness; see James 5:12, where the same requirement is formulated more crisply and authentically. That Matthew 5:37a has the same sense is shown by the addition (v. 37b), which attributes all else to evil or the evil one (see 6:13 for the masculine; see also 13:19, 38; John 8:44). James 5:12 warns of God's judgment. Paul says that Christ Jesus was not "Yes and No," but only "Yes" (2 Cor. 1:19). The prohibition against swearing presents great difficulties. There was criticism of the oath in Hellenism on various grounds, as well as in Hellenistic Judaism (Philo, *On the Decalogue* 92-95) and at Qumran. The rabbis sought to protect the divine name by paraphrase and understatement (cf. Matt. 23:16-22). Frivolous and superfluous oaths were demonstrably frequent. But Jesus' wholesale prohibition of the oath must not be referred exclusively to such abuses; they were at most its occasion. The antithesis is as sharply formulated as the prohibition against divorce. Still, the prohibition against swearing was not received in the same way; the history of its effect is confused. Paul repeatedly calls God to witness (Rom. 1:9; 2 Cor. 1:23; Phil. 1:8; 1 Thess. 2:5). The early church took the prohibition seriously (even the military oath); since the early Middle Ages, the church has used the oath, as it does today. Jesus' absolute requirement is to be explained by his proclamation of the Reign of God: where God holds sway, with his truth and fidelity, those who belong to his community ought to deal with one another in the same way. Earthly relationships (even in court) are no longer in focus: only God's new order has validity, hard though it may be to observe that order in this world. Once more, the basic problem of the Sermon on the Mount!

Concerning Retaliation (5:38-42)

> 38 *"You have heard that it was said, 'An eye for an eye and a tooth for a tooth.' 39 But I say to you, Do not resist an evildoer. But if anyone strikes you on the right cheek, turn the other also; 40 and if anyone wants to sue you and take your coat, give your cloak as well; 41 and if anyone forces you to go one mile, go also the second mile. 42 Give to everyone who begs from you, and do not refuse anyone who wants to borrow from you."*

38-42 This antithesis, from admonitions that Luke connects (Luke 6:29-34) with love of enemies, is molded by Matthew in such a way that it likewise leads to the commandment of love of enemies. This has special importance for him, and, like the first antithesis (against anger) and the fourth (against swearing), is constructed both negatively and positively. We observe that v. 42 goes beyond the summons to give and to lend — granted, with the application of elements from the Lukan text (Luke 6:30, 35). Inasmuch as no bases are offered for the required behavior, an understanding of the sense of this antithesis is especially difficult and has led to extremely diverse interpretations, with far-reaching consequences for practical conduct.

38-39a The shorter opening formula, once more (as in vv. 27 and 43), introduces a principle that in Exodus 21:24, Leviticus 24:20, and Deuteronomy 19:21 is formulated for the right of equal retribution (the so-called *ius talionis*). Matthew sets forth this view of the law, which itself was intended to prevent legitimate retribution from becoming revenge, before he gives us the traditional words of Jesus. He sees the new element as "do not resist" the one who injures you.

39b-41 The three cases here (the third, v. 41, is absent from Luke) are all of the same nature: not resisting the evil that one suffers but, on the contrary, giving in to what is demanded, and even more. The first case hypothesizes an act of physical violence bringing about a grave insult. The blow on the right cheek ("right" is absent from Luke), which could be inflicted by a right-handed person only with the back of the hand, perhaps suggests a particularly weighty insult. In the second example, that of seizure through judicial process, one is struck by the order of things: shirt — coat. In the East a coat was especially important for protection against the cold of night and, in a case of its retention as a pledge, had to be returned to a poor person before sunset (Exod. 22:25-26; Deut. 24:13). Luke, who follows the reverse order (Luke 6:29), is probably thinking of assault and robbery. The third example refers to forced service of the kind frequently imposed by Roman soldiers on the population in the Palestine of that day (cf. Matt. 27:32). The examples use the second person singular (as in 5:23-24, 25-26) but are not to be understood as applicable only to relations between humans; they address the community of disciples in its confrontation with a violent, evil environment. One need scarcely ask the "reason" for such behavior: the shame of the other, a change of attitude, the conquest of violence by nonviolence (so that the latter becomes a "weapon" against a regime of violence), and so forth. Paul demands that evil be overcome by good (Rom. 12:17-21) — in the earliest commentary on the words of the Sermon on the Mount.

42 The positive injunction to give to one who asks, and not to turn away from a person who wishes to borrow something, is loaded with the same kind of radicalism and in Luke is even more trenchant: ". . . do not ask for them again" (Luke 6:30). This, too, contradicts common sense and ordinary behavior. At its core, such a love of neighbor itself contains something of love of enemy, with which Luke connects it.

This antithesis, too, is understandable only in the framework of the proclamation of the Reign of God — which, with the goal, the coming order of salvation, on the horizon, posits requirements for the present that can be realized, if at all, only with difficulty amid the realities of this earth. This state of things can and ought constantly to provoke new stimuli for behavior (cf. Paul on lawsuits, 1 Cor. 6:7). Matthew is thinking especially of life in the community (see 5:23-24) and its conduct in a situation of persecution (see 5:11-12; see also 1 Peter 2:20-23; 3:14; 5:9).

Love for Enemies (5:43-48)

> 43 *"You have heard that it was said, 'You shall love your neighbor and hate your enemy.' 44 But I say to you, Love your enemies and pray for those who persecute you, 45 so that you may be children of your Father in heaven; for he makes his sun rise on the evil and on the good, and sends rain on the righteous and on the unrighteous. 46 For if you love those who love you, what reward do you have? Do not even the tax collectors do the same? 47 And if you greet only your brothers and sisters, what more are you doing than others?*

Do not even the Gentiles do the same? 48 *Be perfect, therefore, as your heavenly Father is perfect."*

43-48   The command to love one's enemies is the climax, and at the same time the summary, of all of the requirements arising in the antitheses. The call to transcend all previous righteousness, found in Matthew 5:20, sounds forth once more (v. 47). God, in whose name Jesus makes his authoritative pronouncements ("But I say to you"), now enters the scene as the heavenly Parent (see 5:16), as we see from the allusions to the divine judgment (vv. 22, 26, 29-30), enlisting persons and making promises. The concluding admonition, formulated by Matthew in such a way as to imply the others (v. 48), is not only coupled with v. 45 but also closes the entire series of antitheses. The structure is tighter than Luke's (Luke 6:27-28, 33-36) since it is composed entirely in a balanced bipolarity. The antithesis (vv. 43-44) is followed immediately by a glance at the Father in heaven, with the two wisdom motifs of sunshine and rain (v. 45) and the attending exhortations (vv. 46-47) to rise above ordinary behavior (as seen in tax collectors and Gentiles), and this generates the concluding admonition (v. 48). Matthew is as faithful to the primitive document Q in his wording of individual sayings as Luke is in his ordering of those sayings. Matthew has shaped the antithesis himself, just as he has changed Luke's "merciful" (Luke 6:36) to "perfect" (Matt. 5:48).

43   The scriptural citation (Lev. 19:18) concerns only the first part of this verse and cannot of itself serve for the antithesis, since Matthew adopts it positively in the chief commandment (Matt. 22:39). And so he adds, by way of contrast, ". . . and hate your enemy." The latter is nowhere to be found in the Old Testament, nor is it anywhere in the rabbinic texts (at most, hate the evildoer). In particular, the Qumran community ("to love all children of light, . . . but to hate all children of darkness," 1QS 1:9-10; but see 1QS 10:17-18), let alone Judaism across the board, would scarcely have accepted the antithesis in Matthew's view. Nowhere does Judaism attain the breadth of Jesus' commandment of love (Luke 10:29-37).

44-45   Matthew concentrates the four-part Lukan form of the commandment into a double proposition, in which the summons to pray for one's "persecutors" (Luke has "for those who abuse you") is striking. Matthew has his troubled community's sufferings in mind (see 5:10). The motive, to become "children of your Father in heaven," reminds us of the promise to the peacemakers (5:9). Hence the coming recompense (Luke 6:35) is in view rather than present adaptation to God's way of living, although the imitation of God is addressed in what follows. Matthew adopts the wisdom motif of the goodness of the God who creates (Job 5:10-11; Ps. 145:9; Wis. 11:23-24; Sir. 18:11), but only by way of support of a love that goes beyond all bounds and includes enemies as its object. There are similar propositions in Stoic philosophy, but only as a result of the concept of world reason at work throughout the cosmos (Seneca, *On Favors*, 4.26.1). Love of enemies is to be found in other religions and schools of thought as well. But the biblical concept of God goes deeper. Here the imitation of God is rightly beyond reach, but it is an urgent motif in Judaism (see v. 48).

46-47 Giving greater clarity to love of enemies, which does not stop at natural love (v. 46) and the bond of brothers and sisters (v. 47), these verses urge the new — the "greater" righteousness (5:20), the element in Jesus' requirements that transcends customary measurements and appraisals. Ordinary behavior is demonstrated by reference to the tax collectors, a despised status, and to the "Gentiles," the non-Jews, contemned by the members of Israel. This Jewish attitude lingered on in the Jewish-Christian community (18:17), although Jesus himself took a different stance toward both groups.

48 We read in the holiness code, "You shall be holy, for I the LORD your God am holy" (Lev. 19:2; see 11:44). Such a requirement, issuing from the being of God, was seen in Judaism as the comprehensive "imitation of God," unattainable and paradoxical as it was. Matthew uses the expression "perfect," which in the biblical understanding denotes the complete fulfillment of God's will (Gen. 6:9; Deut. 18:13), flawless observance of the law (the latter especially at Qumran). For Matthew, perfection is realized in following Jesus (19:21). Thus the "fulfillment" of the law (5:17) in the (Jewish-)Christian community is further clarified: the divine commandments are affirmed, but their exposition is that of Jesus, who surmounts a legalistic understanding and exposes their proper sense. Perfection is not (as it is in the Greek understanding) the highest degree attainable in a striving for virtue, but holistic integration into the way shown by Jesus for reaching the Reign of God. Love of enemies, demanded of all Christians, is an expression of Jesus' supreme requirement — and is practicable as well in the thought of the early church, by God's mercy (Luke 6:36) and the power of the Holy Spirit (Rom 8:2-4). It is not feeling and gushing emotion, but must pass the test of conduct and activity in all areas: in personal encounter as well as in the realm of the social, between the community and its neighbors near and far.

The Right Attitude before God the Father (6:1-18)

This passage is connected with the previous one, which has dealt with "greater righteousness" (5:17-48). The keyword "piety" (6:1) is what brings about the connection. Behavior toward human beings must be shown and tested in relation to one's attitude toward God. By way of illustration, three exercises dear to Judaism (Tob. 12:8: prayer, fasting, mercy and righteousness) are adduced, although in another order. Prayer shifts to the middle, and Matthew, through his insertion of the "Our Father" (6:9-13), forcefully places it before the eyes of his community, which still has its ties with Jewish piety. Indeed, Matthew makes prayer the center of the entire Sermon on the Mount. Jesus' image of God shines forth in all of the admonitions, each of which is constructed as a unit: God is the good Father who demands good, who sees all that occurs in darkness and will one day requite it. In contrast to a sham, external piety, we receive positive stimuli for the religious life — a Magna Charta of true piety.

Concerning Almsgiving (6:1-4)

6:1 *"Beware of practicing your piety before others in order to be seen by them; for then you have no reward from your Father in heaven.*

2 *"So whenever you give alms, do not sound a trumpet before you, as the hypocrites do in the synagogues and in the streets, so that they may be praised by others. Truly I tell you, they have received their reward.* 3 *But when you give alms, do not let your left hand know what your right hand is doing,* 4 *so that your alms may be done in secret; and your Father who sees in secret will reward you."*

1-2 Private philanthropy (there were practically no organized social services) has always been highly esteemed by the Jews (Billerbeck, *Kommentar zum Neuen Testament*, 4:536-58). "Alms," a loanword from the Greek expression for "compassion" *(eleēmosynē)*, must not be just some small gift, but was subject to the assessment of one's own fortune (cf. Mark 12:41-44). Jesus does not attack almsgiving, but only its abuse on the part of "hypocrites" — not identified by Matthew here, as they are in the recital of the woes (Matt. 23:13-15), with the scribes and Pharisees. The performance of acts to be "praised by others," described with the exaggeration, "sound a trumpet before you" (no such actual behavior has been established), serves only for self-glorification and forfeits any recompense from God.

3-4 In sharp contrast ("But you . . ."), Jesus calls for action in secret. The instruction to the effect that the left hand must not know what the right hand is doing is an exaggeration and therefore means not that a good deed ought to be unconscious, but more likely that one ought to keep silent about it. God's reward comes at the final judgment (16:27; 25:34-40); the recompense (5:12, 46; 10:41-42), however, will be given not because of desert, but out of the Father's goodness (20:8-15).

The warning not to do good for the sake of appearances is found among rabbis and Stoics as well, among the latter for the sake of conscience. Jesus' words tie all human mercy to the mercy of the Father (5:48), and promise precisely that mercy in return (5:7).

Concerning Prayer (6:5-15)

5 *"And whenever you pray, do not be like the hypocrites; for they love to stand and pray in the synagogues and at the street corners, so that they may be seen by others. Truly I tell you, they have received their reward.* 6 *But whenever you pray, go into your room and shut the door and pray to your Father who is in secret; and your Father who sees in secret will reward you.*

7 *"When you are praying, do not heap up empty phrases as the Gentiles do; for they think that they will be heard because of their many words.* 8 *Do not be like them, for your Father knows what you need before you ask him.*

9 *"Pray then in this way:*
Our Father in heaven,
    hallowed be your name.

10 *Your kingdom come.*
Your will be done,
    on earth as it is in heaven.

11 *Give us this day our daily bread.*

12 *And forgive us our debts,*
    as we also have forgiven our debtors.

13 *And do not bring us to the time of trial,*
    but rescue us from the evil one.

14 *For if you forgive others their trespasses, your heavenly Father will also forgive you;* 15 *but if you do not forgive others, neither will your Father forgive your trespasses."*

Verses 5-6 are structured in exact correspondence with the words about almsgiving; verses 7-8 draw attention to the Gentiles (see 5:47), with whose wordy (v. 7) and pestering (v. 8) prayers to God the prayer taught by Jesus (vv. 9-13) is then contrasted. Of special importance to Matthew in the "Our Father" for his community is the forgiveness to be granted to brothers and sisters (18:21-35), which he especially urges in the lines immediately following the prayer (6:14-15). The particular kind of prayer enjoined on Jesus' disciples is that of a gaze directed toward the Father and that of the prayer of Jesus.

5-6   Among the Jews the preferred place of prayer was the synagogue (the temple in Jerusalem). However, the regular private morning, noon, and evening prayers could be said anywhere, even on the street or in a public square. As with almsgiving, exhibitionism is censured since it serves self-glorification. Praying in one's room, endorsed in Elisha's conduct before the raising of the dead boy (2 Kings 4:33), is chosen to establish a contrast with public prayer. The intent is not to define a place of prayer but to shed light on the right way to pray (cf. John 4:21, 24). One who prays in secret finds God the Father. Community prayer, presupposed in the "Our Father," is not thereby excluded. Jesus knows both kinds of prayer (cf. Mark 1:35; Luke 4:16).

7-8   "Heaping up empty phrases," whose Greek original is very rare, is the foolish speech, wordy and yet empty, with which the Gentiles seek to gain God's attention (cf. 1 Kings 18:26-29). A similar "rush on God," an all-too-human attempt at manipulation, is forbidden Jesus' disciples (addressed here in the plural once more). But is not prayer superfluous if God the Father knows what we need before we pray for it? Such cold calculating misses the point of prayer to Jesus' God-who-is-Father. God himself desires the asking, the knocking (Matt. 7:7), that is, an expression of trust and dedication, one that corresponds to the gifts God has intended (6:31-32). In prayer the bond to the Father grows more intimate. Praise, thanksgiving, and petition come together in the certainty of being heard.

9-13   Despite its resemblance to Jewish prayers, the "Our Father" remains the altogether special prayer that Jesus taught his disciples. In a shorter form, it is handed down, other than in the Sermon on the Mount, in Luke 11:2-4. The longer version, in Matthew, may have originated with its use in his community. Over against Luke, three expansions attract our attention: the addition of "in heaven" to "Our Father"; the third petition, "Your kingdom come"; and the addition to the last petition: "but rescue us from the evil one." Externally, there are seven petitions in Matthew and five in Luke; but in terms of inner content, there are three basic "prayer wishes" before the four actual "petitions" for the earthly, historical existence of Jesus' disciples. Precisely this connection between an urgent call concerning the coming Reign of God and a concern for the actualization of its effectiveness in our world is characteristic of Jesus' prayer. The urgency of the coming of the Reign, in the face of the needs and threats to salvation that still exist until God introduces his perfect Reign, is of utmost importance to Jesus. In this prayer Jesus draws all of his followers into his own relationship with God, and shares his message with them.

9   The image of God as father, which has its motherly traits as well (Isa. 49:15; 66:13), goes back very far in Israel (Hos. 11:1-4), and they relied on it for their hope (Hos. 1:10; *Jubilees* 1:24-25). In Israel's prayers, trust and awe are intertwined ("our Father," "our King"), in acknowledgment of their distance and guilt. In his Jewish-Christian mentality, Matthew has retained these words (adding "in heaven"; or "heavenly," 5:16, 45, 48, etc.). Jesus himself used the trusting and familiar form of address, *Abba* (Mark 14:36), which has so profoundly marked primitive Christianity (cf. Gal. 4:6; Rom. 8:15). It is presupposed in the "Our Father" as well (Luke 11:2), and permeates the entire prayer. Yes, there is complete trust, but the exalted sovereignty of God remains. His name shall be "hallowed" — made great, shown by God himself in his self-designation as the mighty one (Ezek. 36:23; 38:23; 39:25), as it is worded in the

opening "petition." The Jewish Kaddish as well, the prayer that the "Our Father" particularly resembles, begins: "Exalted and hallowed be his great name in the world, which he has created according to his will." In the Johannine "hour" of the Mount of Olives, Jesus prays, "Father, glorify your name" (John 12:28).

10 How and in what way is the Father to show his power and glory? By having his Reign come! This is the central "petition" of this "kingdom prayer," here directed toward the coming Reign of God. In this it is close to the Jewish Kaddish, the prayer that, after praise of the divine name, likewise expresses this petition — although for Israel, emphatically — and this "in haste and dispatch." Jesus includes this in his message (Matt. 4:17), but sees God's Lordship already powerfully arising in his proclamation of salvation and his mighty deeds (11:4-6; 12:28; 13:17). Just so are the disciples to pray for the perfection of the Reign, to be introduced by God alone (cf. 20:23), which will at last put an end to all earthly torment and need. Uttered in the oppressive situation of this world (vv. 11-13), the "Our Father" draws its strengthening and consoling power from its image of the ultimate goal — which, meanwhile, calls for earnest effort and struggle on the part of the disciples (5:17-48; 10:34-39). It is no simple "pie in the sky," then, or "utopian hope." The explanatory petition, that God's will should be realized, emphasizes the wish for God's implementation of the divine plan, "on earth as it is in heaven." "Heaven and earth" can stand for the whole world (5:18; 11:25; 24:35; 28:18), but it can also counterpoise the divine and human realms (5:34-35; 16:19; 18:18; 23:9). Because of the "as . . . so," the latter is more likely. As God reigns from his throne in heaven (among the angels) (5:34; 18:10, 14; 23:22), so is he to realize his will on earth as well. In their own need, disciples are to utter this prayer as their master has (on the Mount of Olives, 26:39). Beyond this, it will have occurred to Matthew that the community will be required to do the will of God through their moral efforts (7:21; 21:28-31). But in the framework of the "Our Father," especially the "your" petitions, the emphasis is on God's rendering his will effective through the establishment of the divine dominion.

11 The second part of the prayer, with its "us" petitions (vv. 11-13), reflects Jesus' concerns in the light of his disciples' existential situation, and shows his realistic appraisal of the current age. This part as well is without direct correspondence in Jewish prayers. The petition for bread refers to our dependence on nourishment. The petition for forgiveness sees our spiritual existence, our personal existence, as threatened by sin and guilt. The petition for preservation from the tempting might of the evil one has our whole historical being in view. The series of petitions builds to a crescendo in its concern for the salvation of all human beings, the entire human race.

The petition for bread is recorded differently in Luke and in Matthew (Luke, ". . . our daily bread"; Matthew, "Give us this day"), including the word *epiousios,* whose derivation is disputed but which probably has the sense of "necessary." The petition is not a metaphorical reference to the repast in the future Reign of God (cf. Luke 14:15), or to the spiritual bread of God's word (Matt. 4:4), or to the Eucharist, on the model of the manna. These are all beautiful early applications of the petition to the religious life, and all of this may harmonize very well in today's liturgy. But the original meaning must not be lost in the shuffle: Jesus was thinking of the daily nourishment we need. Bread (in flat cakes) was baked daily and was indispensable (some three loaves for a satisfying meal; see Luke 11:5-8). Jesus fed the hungering people (Matt. 14:15-21; 15:32-39) and spoke of the Father's concern (6:26; 7:11), but he was also outraged at the hard-heartedness of the rich (Luke 16:19-21). Trustful as we may be of a Father who knows what we need (Matt. 6:8, 32), we should nevertheless ask him for what is necessary for life (7:7-11). But those who pray this petition may not sidestep their duty to feed the hungry (25:35, 42).

12 Jesus proclaims the pardon of "debts" (Luke, "sins") as a demonstration of God's grace (18:23-27). He himself releases the paralytic from the bonds of his sins before he heals him bodily (9:2), and one of the signs he proclaims is that he receives "tax collectors and sinners" into his community (9:9-13). But his disciples as well can fall into sin ("trespasses," 6:14-15), and need the Father's forgiveness again and again. Sin diminishes and destroys fellowship with God but also fellowship among human beings. Mutual forgiveness, which is extremely important to Matthew (18:21-22), is included in the petition for forgiveness from God. We should *have* forgiven the one who stands guilty before us when we ask the Father for forgiveness (the present tense in Luke expresses constant readiness to do so). This corresponds to the spirit of Jesus (5:23-24), whose whole life was a battle with sin as the power of destruction and whose death became for the church a guarantee of the "forgiveness of sins" (26:28).

13 The petitions climax in a cry for protection from the power of the evil one, a power that operates in temptations and thereby threatens our salvation. God cannot lead into temptation (James 1:13). The expression is a Semitism and means: do not permit us to fall into temptation (cf. 1 Cor. 10:13). "Temptation" denotes not only the acute situation to arise before the end of the age (24:11-13); it is at work throughout all history. But it means not simply any temptation in which Christians are to prove themselves (James 1:12). This petition bears on the constantly threatening attack of the evil one, which outstrips human strength, as Matthew's expansion makes clear ("but rescue us . . ."). The evil one as God's adversary (13:39), or the evil that lurks in human hearts (12:35; 15:19), can and should be defeated in prayer (26:41). Jesus' pessimistic outlook on this "evil and adulterous generation" (12:39; 16:4) cannot shake his confidence in the mightier power of God (cf. 12:28-29); that power is to be summoned in urgent prayer to the Father. (The added doxology, to be found in many manuscripts of Matthew as well as in the *Didache,* or "Teaching of the Twelve Apostles," is an early addition, originating in the prayer of the church.)

14-15   Matthew's typical moral admonition of his hearers (5:16; 18:35), urging them to mutual forgiveness, is formulated here (as in 18:35) as a condition. However, as the parable of the unmerciful servant shows (18:23-34), God displays a boundless readiness to forgive, while expecting human beings to do likewise. What we have here is community catechesis for those already baptized (cf. Col. 3:13; Eph. 4:32).

Concerning Fasting (6:16-18)

> 16 *"And whenever you fast, do not look dismal, like the hypocrites, for they disfigure their faces so as to show others that they are fasting. Truly I tell you, they have received their reward.* 17 *But when you fast, put oil on your head and wash your face,* 18 *so that your fasting may be seen not by others but by your Father who is in secret; and your Father who sees in secret will reward you."*

16-18   Apart from the legally enjoined fast day of the Feast of Atonement (Lev. 16:29-31; Num. 29:7) and other special occasions, fasting was also done as a private exercise of piety (twice weekly; see Luke 18:12). The Jewish-Christian community had obviously retained this custom, which continued to be observed in the ancient church as well (*Didache* 8:1 specifies Wednesdays and Fridays, while the weekly Jewish fast was on Mondays and Thursdays). Jesus himself defends his disciples when they fail to fast as do John's disciples and the Pharisees (Mark 2:18-19 and pars.). The tension between this report and the usage presupposed here is to be explained by Jewish-Christian practice, which deviated from Jesus' own conduct; but the differing senses of the two passages must be also attended to. Jesus was not expressly forbidding fasting, but was defending his disciples' failure to fast by pointing to the dawning age of salvation.

16-18   Fasting is the third example of right behavior before God. Its position following prayer may be due to the fact that fasting was frequently practiced in order to reinforce prayer (cf. Acts 13:2-3; 14:23; and the addition in certain manuscripts of Mark 9:29 and Matt. 17:21). In our passage his concern is only the matter of behavior while fasting. Again (as with almsgiving and prayer), and with the same graphic description, the pompous strutting of "hypocrites" is set over against the discreet acts of those who seek God. Throughout, Jesus insists on religious motivation and corresponding conduct in the sight of fellow human beings. Christians still obliged by Jewish piety ought to be sensitive to this, and Jesus' teaching holds for today's religious practice as well. Fasting out of health considerations is another matter altogether.

Undivided Service to God and the Quest for His Reign (6:19-34)

Following these comments on the three exercises of piety, Matthew introduces further sayings that urge dedication of every aspect of the life of Jesus' disciples to the service of God as the most important thing. It is a Matthean composition, as we see by comparing the scattered material of Luke and the Lukan Sermon on the Mount. Opposition to an absorption in the earthly, such as laying up treasure on earth (6:19-21), service of Mammon (v. 24), and anxious concerns (vv. 25-34), is predominant. It is in this context that the difficult logion in Matthew concerning the eye (vv. 22-23) is to be understood. The first three declarations (6:19-24) climax in the admonition to be undividedly devoted to God; the more extended treatment, concerning cares, in the call to seek first God's Reign and God's righteousness (v. 33). The supposition that Matthew intends this petition to be a continuation of the petition for bread in the "Our Father" (as he does in 7:1-5 with the petition for forgiveness) is uncertain. More likely he seeks to expand the tie with God, sought in piety, to all areas of life. Here his position on possessions and acquisitions is paramount; Jesus has often warned of the dangers of wealth.

In Luke the logion on the storing up of wealth (Luke 12:33-34) comes at the end of the discourse on useless concern (Luke 12:22-31), while in Matthew the logion (6:19-21) precedes the discourse (6:25-34). Meanwhile, in Luke 11:34-35 the graphic statement concerning the eye occurs in a different context, and the logion concerning divided service (Luke 16:33) comes in a lengthier passage on dealing with earthly goods. Matthew combines these logia, and has them immediately precede the discourse on anxiety, connecting them closely with it. Thus everything here is a unit.

Concerning Treasures (6:19-21)

19 *"Do not store up for yourselves treasures on earth, where moth and rust consume and where thieves break in and steal; 20 but store up for yourselves treasures in heaven, where neither moth nor rust consumes and where thieves do not break in and steal. 21 For where your treasure is, there your heart will be also."*

19-21 The importance of earthly and heavenly treasures is vastly different. Warnings about the ephemeral quality of wealth (cf. Luke 12:16-20) are abundant in the wisdom literature (Prov. 23:4-5; Eccl. 2:18-19; 6:2; Sir. 11:19; etc.) — indeed, they are linked with the admonition to store up treasure with God (Sir. 29:10-12). Judaism saw the looming judgment of God (*Ethiopian Enoch* 94:7-9; 97:8-10), and was anxious to amass a treasure of good works with God (*4 Ezra*

7:97; *Syrian Apocalypse of Baruch* 14:12; *Slavonic Enoch* 50:5; similarly with the rabbis). Jesus picks up the train of thought (so also Matt. 19:21), but does not cite the judgment; instead he directs our gaze toward God, in whom the human heart should rest (v. 21).

The Sound Eye (6:22-23)

22 *"The eye is the lamp of the body. So, if your eye is healthy, your whole body will be full of light; 23 but if your eye is unhealthy, your whole body will be full of darkness. If then the light in you is darkness, how great is the darkness!"*

22-23 The eye may be pure, or it may be evil. The metaphors of "light" and "lamp" (Matt. 5:14-16) are susceptible of a variety of interpretations. In this logion it is difficult to conceive of Matthew making a comparison between the bodily organ (healthy and diseased eye) and a spiritual organ that we would have (the "light in you," often understood as the soul, reason, or conscience). Instead we have a graphic image of what persons are capable of and how they ought to act. Thus the epithets modifying "eye" may express moral conduct — the "healthy" eye uprightness and purity of heart (*Testament of Issachar* 3:2-6; 4:1-6; *Testament of Benjamin* 6:4-7), the "unhealthy" eye resentment, jealousy, and greed (Matt. 20:15). Christ's disciples (here addressed in the singular) should not allow themselves to be seduced into evil (in context, into greed), but should safeguard their purity of heart (5:8); otherwise they will find themselves plunged into great darkness, separation from God. The "light in you" refers to fellowship with God and to the God-given inclination to good, which a human being can lose (cf. 12:35; 15:19; 24:48-49).

Serving Two Masters (6:24)

24 *"No one can serve two masters; for a slave will either hate the one and love the other, or be devoted to the one and despise the other. You cannot serve God and wealth."*

24 Service to God and service to Mammon are irreconcilable. Legally, a Jew might have two masters; but this pronouncement makes no reference to the fact (the word "slave" does not occur). It is a piece of popular wisdom, transferred to the service of God. Granted, "hate" and "love" can be understood relatively, as loving less or more (compare Matt. 10:37 with Luke 14:26); but here they are intended to mark a radical dichotomy — "either . . . or. . . ." Serving God and serving Mammon are incompatible. "Mammon" means money and goods, all of one's property, and appears here as an anti-God, an idol, enslaving people unless they are utterly devoted to uncompromising service of God — the clearest rejection of dedication to earthly gain (softened in Luke 16:9, 11).

Do Not Worry (6:25-34)

25 *"Therefore I tell you, do not worry about your life, what you will eat or what you will drink, or about your body, what you will wear. Is not life more than food, and the body more than clothing?* 26 *Look at the birds of the air; they neither sow nor reap nor gather into barns, and yet your heavenly Father feeds them. Are you not of more value than they?* 27 *And can any of you by worrying add a single hour to your span of life?* 28 *And why do you worry about clothing? Consider the lilies of the field, how they grow; they neither toil nor spin,* 29 *yet I tell you, even Solomon in all his glory was not clothed like one of these.* 30 *But if God so clothes the grass of the field, which is alive today and tomorrow is thrown into the oven, will he not much more clothe you — you of little faith?* 31 *Therefore do not worry, saying, 'What will we eat?' or 'What will we drink?' or 'What will we wear?'* 32 *For it is the Gentiles who strive for all these things; and indeed your heavenly Father knows that you need all these things.* 33 *But strive first for the kingdom of God and his righteousness, and all these things will be given to you as well.*

34 *"So do not worry about tomorrow, for tomorrow will bring worries of its own. Today's trouble is enough for today."*

25-34 The beautiful but easy to misunderstand (and often misunderstood) expansion on trust is not "didactic poetry" sentimentally contemplating nature but an admonishing discourse in wisdom motifs drawn from creation, such as Jesus adduces elsewhere as well (Matt. 5:45; 10:29-31; and the growth parables). Its purpose is not to deter from labor but to commit all of one's strengths and abilities to the Reign of God, without cowardly anxieties (v. 30) but rather with full confidence in God the Father (v. 33). This signification, and the fact that the discourse is addressed to the disciples (and not to human beings as such, in their economic situation), keep the text from seeming at all strange. A justifiable provision for the societal area and a concern for others are not under consideration. The almost identically worded discourse transmitted by Luke (Luke 12:22-31; but using "ravens," v. 24, and without "first") comes from the Sayings Source. The two passages came to be understood as an encouragement for the disciples themselves and for their traveling ministry, undertaken in the most extreme poverty (Luke 10:4-9; Matt. 10:7-13), although Matthew applies it to the entire community of disciples. The passages abide as a testimonial of Jesus' love for creation and his care for human beings, as well as for the "simple life," which he himself led with his disciples. Let us consider some particular points.

25 Biblical anthropology sometimes distinguishes "life" (Gk. *psychē* for Heb. *nephesh*) and "body," but each can also stand for the entire person (see Matt. 10:28). The human being as such (the person) is more than nourishment and clothing.

26-28 The negative assertions concerning "toil" when it comes to the birds or the flowers of the field ("lilies" is not necessarily the correct specification) are only for the purpose of illustrating human effort, which contributes nothing without God's care.

27 It cannot really be determined whether what is meant by the Greek word *hēlikia* is bodily stature or length of life. The second (as in the German Ecumenical Translation) is more probable; the import, however, is the same.

30 The much loved conclusion, which moves "from the lesser to the greater," emphasizes human beings' greater worth, and, correspondingly, God's greater care for them (7:11; see 10:31). "Of little faith," here the original expression (Luke 12:28), in Matthew frequently becomes a vocative for the disciples, as well as an epithet for the faithful to come (8:26; 14:31; 16:8; 17:20).

32 The "Gentiles" are those (non-Jewish) persons outside the community of disciples who have not (yet) grasped Jesus' character and manner of word and work (cf. 5:47; 6:7; 18:17).

33 Two things strike us in this climactic verse of Matthew: (1) the injunction to seek God's Reign "first" (absent from Luke), the urgent task, which in the community does not altogether exclude other concerns; (2) the addition of ". . . and his [God's] righteousness," which points the disciples to what is demanded of them, the performance of "good works" (see 3:15; 5:6; 5:16, 20; 6:1). "Striving for" God's Reign includes efforts for God and for the human community.

34 This addition concerns burdensome preoccupation about the future. "For tomorrow," in contrast to today, denotes that which will impose itself painfully in the future.

34b-c This statement merely presents buttressing motives drawn from experience. The pessimistic-sounding final observation expresses a realism that only lends increased urgency to the petition for bread in the "Our Father."

Instructions for a Community of Siblings (7:1-12)

The following passage, in which various ingredients from tradition are thrown together, seems to be addressed especially to the Christian community as a fellowship of brothers and sisters. In favor of this interpretation are the admonition not to pass judgment on the "brothers" (vv. 1-5) and the summons to trustful prayer (vv. 7-11). Puzzlingly, the remark about the dogs and pigs (v. 6) suddenly appears in the middle. The "golden rule" (v. 12) reaches beyond the community to all people and concludes the main part with the Matthean parenthesis, "the law and the prophets" (5:17 and 7:12b), preceded by a summarizing clause that offers a formal, ever applicable rule for behavior. Thus the community is again reminded of its responsibility for the world around it (cf. 5:16).

Judging Others (7:1-5)

> 7:1 *"Do not judge, so that you may not be judged.* 2 *For with the judgment you make you will be judged, and the measure you give will be the measure you get.* 3 *Why do you see the speck in your neighbor's eye, but do not notice the log in your own eye?* 4 *Or how can you say to your neighbor, 'Let me take the speck out of your eye,' while the log is in your own eye?* 5 *You hypocrite, first take the log out of your own eye, and then you will see clearly to take the speck out of your neighbor's eye."*

1-2 All judgment in the sense of condemnation (Luke 6:37) must reckon with the judgment of God. Nothing is said here about secular jurisdiction; Matthew has the community in mind, to which, as a holy community, he does ascribe the authority to expel sinners, but only in extreme cases, when all attempts to move the sinful member to conversion have been in vain (18:15-18). Most importantly of all, he insists on actual forgiveness (18:21-22), and this is what he has in mind here as well. The "measure" of judgment can be understood negatively (measurelessly severe) or positively (merciful), once more in view of God's conduct at the judgment; but it is an admonition concerning the divine retribution (5:26; 12:36; 18:27, 34-35). The image of the "measure" (of grain) originally referred (Luke 6:38) to giving and being given to (by God), but is transferred by Matthew to judging and being judged (while in Mark 4:24 it had received a different application still).

3-5 The exaggerated image of the speck and the log, intended to shock (as in Matt. 19:24), calls for forbearance with one's sibling, and reproves arrogance ("You hypocrite!"), but it is not intended to exclude all reprimand of siblings (18:15). Only self-examination, however, and one's own improvement confer the right to administer that reprimand and generate the correct attitude toward one's sibling, now finding himself or herself in sin.

Profaning the Holy (7:6)

> 6 *"Do not give what is holy to dogs; and do not throw your pearls before swine, or they will trample them under foot and turn and maul you."*

6   Here is a puzzling pair of propositions (the dogs and the swine), all the more so in view of the connected warning (lest one be trampled, then mauled). Obscure as the original sense is, in the Matthean context the passage may have been a call to the defense of their sacred goods. Does it have to do with their liturgy, after the fashion of the subsequent reference to prayer (7:11)? The *Didache* appeals to this verse in support of the exclusion of the unbaptized from the Eucharist (9:5). In the Old Testament, "what is holy," "that which is holy," is meat offered in sacrifice (Exod. 29:33; Lev. 2:3; etc.), and "dogs" (like swine) becomes in Judaism a metaphor for Gentiles (cf. Matt. 15:26-27). Stated in climactic progression, the meaning is that that which is most precious (pearls; cf. 13:45-46) is not to be surrendered to the scornful (swine; cf. 8:30-32). That could have destroyed the community as a sacred fellowship. Is this an expression of the self-awareness of the Jewish-Christian community? Interpretations supposing concrete references, be these of "the holy" (as referring to wisdom utterances, the gospel, the Eucharist) or of "dogs" and "swine" (villains, Gentiles, apostates), are scarcely sound ones.

Ask, Search, Knock (7:7-11)

> 7 *"Ask, and it will be given you; search, and you will find; knock, and the door will be opened for you.* 8 *For everyone who asks receives, and everyone who searches finds, and for everyone who knocks, the door will be opened.* 9 *Is there anyone among you who, if your child asks for bread, will give a stone?* 10 *Or if the child asks for a fish, will give a snake?* 11 *If you then, who are evil, know how to give good gifts to your children, how much more will your Father in heaven give good things to those who ask him!"*

7-11   The kinship of this series of logia with the "Our Father" is unmistakable, and is even clearer in Luke 9:13, in a framework of instructions for prayer (Luke 11:13). With its invitation to ask, to seek, and to knock, it issues a summons to a prayer that is sure to be heard, one whose favorable reception is guaranteed in verse 8 itself. The argumentation in verses 9-11 begins with the concept of God as Father, and reinforces the certainty of a hearing with the conclusion "from the smaller to the greater." The examples selected, bread and fish (the most important sources of nourishment) in Matthew and fish and an egg in Luke, must not cause one to fix one's gaze on earthly and material gifts. What the heavenly Father, of a goodness far exceeding that of human fathers (who are called "evil," in comparison with God), seeks to give his children is "good" *simpliciter.* This can include spiritual goods (Luke: the Holy Spirit). The spectrum of the gifts of God lies along a broader horizon. Jesus' absolutely profound, personal conviction of God's power and will to hear prayer that is offered in belief and trust is evinced in many another utterance (Mark 9:23; 11:24; Matt. 17:20; 18:19; 21:22; Luke 11:5-8; 18:7).

The Golden Rule (7:12)

12 *"In everything do to others as you would have them do to you; for this is the law and the prophets."*

12 Widely acknowledged in many cultures and religions, the Golden Rule had become known in Palestinian Judaism as well, ever since Hillel, an older contemporary of Jesus, had cited it for a Gentile as a compendium of the Torah. One must not attribute too much importance to the more familiar negative formulation, "as you would *not* have . . . ," in contradistinction to Matthew's positive rule: in the Hellenistic-Jewish *Letter of Aristeas,* which is even older, both components are joined (§207). The kinship of the Golden Rule with the commandment of love (Lev. 19:18), which, with its "as yourself," likewise presents a maxim for conduct, is important. Luke places the Golden Rule in the context of love of enemies, and Matthew understands it as the quintessence of Jesus' precepts, which go beyond those of the old law and which he, too, regards as reaching their climax in the commandment of love. Love for brothers and sisters and love for enemies, the Golden Rule and the greatest commandment, go hand in hand for Matthew. His concern for his community is that it express its love in action, beyond the confines of the community, among all people, as occurs with the love they have experienced, and continue to experience, at God's hands (Matt. 25:31-46).

Concluding Admonitions (7:13-29)

Like the introduction to the Sermon on the Mount (5:1-16), the finale turns to the community in the midst of the world — more powerfully now, however, in view of the difficulties emerging from its concrete situation. The way to the Reign of God is difficult (vv. 13-14): false prophets confuse the community (vv. 15-19); enthusiasts and gossips are within their very ranks (vv. 21-23); the decisive thing is to build on solid ground, as the concluding parable warns (vv. 24-27). The four units, of which the second and third are more closely connected with each other, are intended to set us on the path to which Jesus points.

Through and through, they display contrasts: good tree, bad tree; the one who cries, "Lord, Lord," the one who does God's will; rocky ground, sandy soil. The criterion of the good is effort, exertion, fruitfulness, the discharge of God's will (or conformity of practice with the words of Jesus). All the emphasis falls on the test of action.

All of the logia, like the concluding comparison, draw on Q. In Luke's Sermon on the Mount, however, one finds only the words concerning good and bad trees (Luke 6:43) and the saying "Lord, Lord" (Luke 6:46), along with the comparison to the construction of a house (Luke 6:48). Luke sets the logia of the narrow door (Luke 13:24) and of the exclusion of evildoers (Luke 13:26-27) in another context. Matthew has recombined and reworked this material (Matt. 7:13-14, 19, 21), tailoring it to the situation of his community (vv. 13a, 15, 22).

The Narrow Gate (7:13-14)

> 13 "Enter through the narrow gate; for the gate is wide and the road is easy that leads to destruction, and there are many who take it. 14 For the gate is narrow and the road is hard that leads to life, and there are few who find it."

13-14 The image of the narrow door (Matthew, gate), with which, in Luke 13:24, Jesus issues his summons to effort, in Matthew is broadened to the double image of gate and road and to include the opposition of wide and narrow, easy and hard. The goal is the same, however: to enter into "life," that is, to attain entry into the Reign of God (v. 21). Doubtless both images are so closely connected for Matthew that mention of the "road" at once suggests, at the end of that way, the "gate" through which one enters into life or perdition. Since tradition prioritized the door or gate, Matthew will have introduced the teaching of the two ways because his concern is with the "way of righteousness" (21:32; see 3:15) by which one can reach that goal. Way — path, route — was a familiar metaphor for lifestyle (even in Hellenism — Heracles at the crossroads), but its most vigorous expression is in the Old Testament (Deut. 11:26-28; 30:15-18; Jer. 21:8) and Judaism (Qumran, the rabbis). In primitive Christianity the two-ways teaching was adopted and developed more thoroughly (*Didache* 1-5; *Barnabas* 19-20; Hermas, *Mandates* 6). The "many" and the "few" are not intended to indicate the relative number of the redeemed and the damned (a redactional question in Luke 13:23, but one that elicits no response): with a view to experience, they become a warning and admonition. In the Greek the "hard" way can also indicate the harassments besetting those who walk the way that leads to "life."

A Tree and Its Fruit (7:15-20)

> 15 *"Beware of false prophets, who come to you in sheep's clothing but in-wardly are ravenous wolves. 16 You will know them by their fruits. Are grapes gathered from thorns, or figs from thistles? 17 In the same way, every good tree bears good fruit, but the bad tree bears bad fruit. 18 A good tree cannot bear bad fruit, nor can a bad tree bear good fruit. 19 Every tree that does not bear good fruit is cut down and thrown into the fire. 20 Thus you will know them by their fruits."*

15-20 False prophets and beguiling spirits were frequently the object of ad-monition in the post-apostolic period, and not only with regard to the end of the age (Mark 13:22; Matt. 24:11, 24) but to the present as well (Acts 20:29-30; 1 Tim. 4:1-3; 2 Tim 4:3-4; Titus 1:10; 1 John 4:1-4; etc.). The comparison with wolves that break into a herd of sheep (Acts 20:29; John 10:12; *Didache* 16:3; Ignatius, *To the Philadelphians* 3:2; etc.) takes up the familiar motif of the en-mity between the wolf and the lamb (Isa. 11:6; 65:25; Sir. 13:17; Aesop's Fables; etc.) that also underlies Matthew 10:16. "Wolves in sheep's clothing," however, is a unique metaphor here. Since they come to the community ("to you," plu-ral), they are possibly wandering missionaries, for whom *Didache* 11–13 estab-lishes criteria and very strict rules. Nothing is said of their teaching. The crite-rion of the good or bad fruits (v. 17), resumed in 12:33, suggests a morally questionable attitude or praxis. A more precise identification with other move-ments (antinomianism, Zealotism, Pharisaism) is not possible. Luke may have other corrupters in view in 6:39 ("blind guiding the blind" = Matt. 15:14), and still others in using this same criterion of good and bad fruits (Luke 6:43-45). The touchstone can be struck in many ways — even today.

Concerning Self-Deception (7:21-23)

> 21 *"Not everyone who says to me, 'Lord, Lord,' will enter the kingdom of heaven, but only the one who does the will of my Father in heaven. 22 On that day many will say to me, 'Lord, Lord, did we not prophesy in your name, and cast out demons in your name, and do many deeds of power in your name?' 23 Then I will declare to them, 'I never knew you; go away from me, you evildoers.'"*

21-23 Matthew has revised the "Lord, Lord" logion (Luke 6:46) to suit him-self (Matt. 7:21), and in 7:22-23 he has oriented it eschatologically. Obviously he is expanding its scope to include partisans of the false prophets or other per-sons in the community. They, too, appealed to prophetic (Spirit-filled) speech, indeed to the exorcism of demons and other miracles, which they allegedly wrought "in the name" of Jesus, the power of Jesus. The *aggiornamento* is betrayed by a comparison with Luke 13:26-27, where the rejected (members of Israel) appeal to their association with the earthly Jesus. Matthew refuses to be impressed by signs and wonders that seducers, too, can perform (24:24); he ignores the tradition of the "foreign exorcist" (Mark 9:38-41; Luke 9:49-50), with its open, broad-minded attitude. For him, moral observance is the only thing that counts. The judgment, with its elimination of the immoral and unmerciful (Matt. 13:41-43; 22:11-13; 25:11-12; 25:41-46), will also be the judgment of the community. The "evil-doers" (German Ecumenical Translation, "transgressors of the law") are not those who spurn the Jewish law but those who fail to respond to the demands of the Sermon on the Mount (the same expression occurs in Matt. 13:41). "Lawlessness" connotes a wicked hardening of the heart (24:12), indeed ultimate evil (cf. 2 Cor. 6:14; 2 Thess. 2:3, 7; 1 John 3:4). "I never knew you" is a Jewish formula, not of excommunication, but of vehement rejection of one or more of its members on the part of any community (also occurring in 25:12), an expression of exclusion from the Reign of God.

Hearers and Doers (7:24-27)

> 24 "Everyone then who hears these words of mine and acts on them will be like a wise man who built his house on rock. 25 The rain fell, the floods came, and the winds blew and beat on that house, but it did not fall, because it had been founded on rock. 26 And everyone who hears these words of mine and does not act on them will be like a foolish man who built his house on sand. 27 The rain fell, and the floods came, and the winds blew and beat against that house, and it fell — and great was its fall!"

24-27 Still set in an eschatological context of the judgment (vv. 21-23), the parable presented here tenders its admonition in the form of a particular occurrence, making it a "parable" in the proper sense of the word rather than simply a comparison involving regular natural occurrences (as with the parables or comparisons of growth). Originally one of the "crisis parables," which warn of imminent catastrophe (the great Flood, Matt. 24:37-41; breaking into a house at night, 24:43), it is elevated by Matthew to the level of an admonitory discourse with a wisdom ring (wise/foolish; see the parable of the virgins, 25:1-12, and of the steward, 24:45-51). The Matthean intent is recognizable in the framing sentences, verses 24a and 26a: Jesus' words — *these* words, namely, those of the Sermon on the Mount — are not only to be heard but also to be done! We meet the same tendency in the parable of the two sons (21:28-31), although without the motif of judgment.

Concluding Formula (7:28-29)

> 28 *Now when Jesus had finished saying these things, the crowds were astounded at his teaching,* 29 *for he taught them as one having authority, and not as their scribes.*

28-29   The narrative conclusion of the Sermon on the Mount harks back to the introduction (5:1), but it clarifies that all of this has been addressed to the crowds. Like the disciples, everyone in the audience is called to follow Jesus, including, for Matthew, after Easter, the Gentile peoples (28:19). The throngs are "astounded" at Jesus' teaching (as in 22:33), as later are Jesus' fellow Nazarenes (13:54) and the disciples (19:25). Jesus' "authority" is also experienced in his mighty deeds (13:54), as we see in chapters 8 and 9 that follow. This fullness of power in Jesus' earthly life receives its light from the all-embracing authority of the Risen One (28:18). The concluding remark (v. 28a) refers to the five discourses (cf. Intro., no. 1); and with vv. 28b-29, taken verbatim from Mark 1:22, Matthew is back in line with Mark. Jesus descends from the mount of the sermon (Matt. 8:1) like Moses from the mount of the revelation of God and is followed by great throngs, a picture of the new people of God that is charged with a promise.

Jesus' Salvific Works, Especially in Cures and Deeds of Power (8:1–9:34)

Immediately following this authoritative discourse Matthew devotes two chapters to a portrayal of Jesus' mighty deeds on behalf of human beings' salvation. The works of power gathered here are, strikingly, if we count them up, ten "miracles" or "wonders," largely cures, but also the calming of a storm on the lake (Matt. 8:23-27). It remains unsure whether the "ten count" is intentional; whether the series is meant as a counterpart to the ten plagues of Egypt is even less certain, as there is no direct indication to that effect. They are signs of the time of salvation, as the response to John the Baptist (11:4-6) indicates. The same unit comprises the proclamation of the gospel to the "poor." Other material is brought into this chronicle as well, such as the view of the Gentiles thronging from East and West (8:11-12), the words concerning discipleship (8:18-22), the dinner at the home of the publican (9:9-13), and the question of fasting (9:14-17).

Matthew has gathered the material for this presentation primarily from Mark, but also with certain elements from Q. The Markan line is recognizable in Matthew 8:2-4, 14-17, 23-27, 28-34; 9:1-8, 9-13, 14-17, 18-26. However, Matthew does not follow the Markan arrangement slavishly: he presents the calming of the storm, the healing of the possessed man from Gerasa, and the raising of the daughter of Jairus, and adds to the register of healings that of two blind persons and a possessed mute (9:32-34), in order to report that all the promises cited in 11:4-5 have been fulfilled. From a geographical standpoint, Matthew establishes a framework in terms of the area of Capernaum (8:1, 5, 14), the crossing to the east bank (8:18, 28) — sparsely populated by Jews — and Jesus' return to "his own town" (9:1) and that populous area on the northwest bank of the lake (without further local specifications).

Jesus Cleanses a Leper (8:1-4)

8:1 *When Jesus had come down from the mountain, great crowds followed him;* 2 *and there was a leper who came to him and knelt before him, saying, "Lord, if you choose, you can make me clean."* 3 *He stretched out his hand and touched him, saying, "I do choose. Be made clean!" Immediately his leprosy was cleansed.* 4 *Then Jesus said to him, "See that you say nothing to anyone; but go, show yourself to the priest, and offer the gift that Moses commanded, as a testimony to them."*

1-4 Matthew has abbreviated the story of the healing of the leper, which in Mark (1:40-45) is recounted in more detail and without specification of place, to Jesus' conversation with the leper, and, in his "descent from the mountain," transferred it to the vicinity of Capernaum (8:5). In Matthew a single encounter with the victim of the illness, isolated from other human beings, seems to have taken place not far from the throngs (v. 1), as a result of which tension arises (v. 4a). The community is meant to feel itself addressed as well, not primarily with a view to cleansing from sins (which does not come up before 9:1-8) but comprehensively — in terms of complete healing and sanctification. Matthean peculiarities are "knelt," the same expression, with the connotation of "worship," as in 2:8, 11; 4:9-10, and the omission of any citation of Jesus' emotions or of any aftermath (Mark 1:45). Against Matthew's communitarian background, the proof they need may have an accusatory sense (cf. 8:10); a missionary intent, however, is just as likely (cf. 10:18; 24:14).

Jesus Heals a Centurion's Servant (8:5-13)

5 *When he entered Capernaum, a centurion came to him, appealing to him* 6 *and saying, "Lord, my servant is lying at home paralyzed, in terrible distress."* 7 *And he said to him, "I will come and cure him."* 8 *The centurion answered, "Lord, I am not worthy to have you come under my roof; but only*

speak the word, and my servant will be healed. 9 *For I also am a man under authority, with soldiers under me; and I say to one, 'Go,' and he goes, and to another, 'Come,' and he comes, and to my slave, 'Do this,' and the slave does it.'"* 10 *When Jesus heard him, he was amazed and said to those who followed him, "Truly I tell you, in no one in Israel have I found such faith.* 11 *I tell you, many will come from east and west and will eat with Abraham and Isaac and Jacob in the kingdom of heaven,* 12 *while the heirs of the kingdom will be thrown into the outer darkness, where there will be weeping and gnashing of teeth."* 13 *And to the centurion Jesus said, "Go; let it be done for you according to your faith." And the servant was healed in that hour.*

5-13   Matthew has taken the story of the healing recounted here from Q; it also appears in Luke (Luke 7:1-10) and, in another form, in John (John 4:46-53). In view of the Sermon on the Mount, it takes on a special meaning for Matthew as an anticipatory reference to the calling of the Gentiles. He has inserted the logion of the streaming of the peoples from East and West (Matt. 8:11-12) into a context different from Luke's (Luke 13:28-30). He has also concentrated the narrative on the conversation between the centurion and Jesus (rather than with the leper), and omitted the (perhaps authentic) intervention of the Jewish elders (Luke 7:3-6). Jesus' direct encounter with the centurion is important to him, while Luke has "friends" intervene once more (Luke 7:6, surely redactional). The circumstances are historically credible. The "long-distance cure," which in John becomes even more remarkable, is not especially emphasized; the faith of the non-Jew of the story is salient.

5-10   Following immediately upon the connecting remark by which Matthew maintains his framework (8:5a), we have the centurion's approach to Jesus (as in 8:2) with the request that he heal his "servant" (or, according to the Greek, "child," "lad"), who has fallen seriously ill ("paralyzed"; see Matt. 4:24; in John 4:52 the victim of a fever). One of Herod Antipas's garrisons was stationed in the border locale of Capernaum and probably consisted of Syrian mercenaries. Jesus expresses his readiness to come and heal the servant (scarcely to be understood as a question). The commandant of a company of a hundred soldiers, who is familiar with the Jewish prohibition against entering the home of a Gentile, asks, in his military mentality, only that Jesus utter a word of command to the demon of the illness. Jesus acknowledges the officer's great faith (cf. 15:28), which puts Israel to shame.

11-12   This interpolated logion dovetails with the prophecy of the pilgrimage of the peoples to Zion (Isa. 2:2-3 = Isa. 60:3-4; Jer. 3:17; Mic. 4:1-2; Zech. 8:20-22; etc.) and of the festival meal on God's mountain (Isa. 25:6-8). A Gentile share in the community of the patriarchs (Luke: and prophets) in the future Reign of God stands in sharp contrast to the profile of an unbelieving, excluded Israel. In Luke 13:28 these are Jesus' contemporaries, who have turned a deaf ear to his message, and in Matthew they are the "heirs of the kingdom," those actually called (cf. Matt. 13:38) — an unheard-of provocation for the Judaism of that time, but one of which we must recognize Jesus capable. The "outer darkness" (the depths of the underworld, or the space outside the well-lighted festival hall; cf. 22:13; 25:30) and the "weeping and gnashing of teeth" (used by Matthew five additional times) are images of damnation and of the reaction of the damned. Exclusion from the Reign (see 7:23), missing the way Jesus indicates (see 7:13-14), is the greatest of disasters, the heaviest of punishments.

13   The Gentile captain, however, is saved by his faith, and the healing of his servant, which is immediately verified as having occurred at once, is the warranty and sign of it (9:6-7, 22).

Jesus Heals Many at Peter's House (8:14-17)

> 14 *When Jesus entered Peter's house, he saw his mother-in-law lying in bed with a fever;* 15 *he touched her hand, and the fever left her, and she got up and began to serve him.* 16 *That evening they brought to him many who were possessed with demons; and he cast out the spirits with a word, and cured all who were sick.* 17 *This was to fulfill what had been spoken through the prophet Isaiah, "He took our infirmities and bore our diseases."*

14-17   Taking the two small units here from Mark 1:29-34, Matthew has abbreviated them but then expanded them by way of fulfillment citations (v. 17). The healing of Peter's mother-in-law (vv. 14-15), an altogether credible element in the tradition at hand (the house of Peter, with his marriage presupposed; the crisp presentation), for Matthew constitutes a further example of healings from various diseases. As for the activity of healing in the evening (v. 16), which in Mark occurs at Sabbath's close, he emphasizes the expulsion of demons, doubtless because he has passed over Mark's detailed exorcisms (Mark 1:23-26). In all of these healings he sees the fulfillment of the scriptural promise of Isaiah 53:4 regarding the Servant of God. For Matthew, Jesus is the Servant of God (cf. Matt. 12:18-21) who takes away our sufferings and illnesses (to be understood here in this way, without allusion to his expiatory suffering). The christological accents of the past here blend in perfect harmony: healing mercifully and mightily, Jesus executes the salvific will of God.

Would-Be Followers of Jesus (8:18-22)

> 18 *Now when Jesus saw great crowds around him, he gave orders to go over to the other side.* 19 *A scribe then approached and said, "Teacher, I will follow*

you wherever you go." 20 *And Jesus said to him, "Foxes have holes, and birds of the air have nests; but the Son of Man has nowhere to lay his head."* 21 *Another of his disciples said to him, "Lord, first let me go and bury my father."* 22 *But Jesus said to him, "Follow me, and let the dead bury their own dead."*

18-22   Jesus withdraws from the rush and press of the throngs, just as in Mark 1:36-38 and 6:31. The portrayal of the situation is *pro forma:* in each case, both of the persons who approach Jesus before the departure for the further shore — in verse 19 a scribe (in Luke 9:57 an indeterminate "someone"), two verses later "another of the disciples" (differently in Luke 9:59) — merely serve to frame the two logia on discipleship (in Luke 9:61-62 followed by a third), although with a look ahead to the later community. The disciples' failure on the occasion of the storm on the lake (Matt. 8:26) stands in contrast to the demanding character of Jesus' call to discipleship. It is intended to convey Jesus' sovereignty and demands.

19-20   Willingness and words in themselves are not enough (see 5:19). All who are fascinated by Jesus' teaching and power to heal must stand before the hard demands of Jesus' example. This is illustrated by the logion of the "Son of Man": Jesus, God's Servant (see 8:17), is at the same time the altogether sovereign Son of Man (see 9:6, etc.). He may scandalize (11:19; 16:21-23). Discipleship means sharing his poor and onerous life.

21-22   Here we have one of the most trenchant of the logia of discipleship. In Judaism the duty to ensure and participate in one's parents' burial was a supreme duty of filial piety. Jesus' paradoxical expression, to let the "dead" (spiritually dead) bury their own dead, must have sounded extremely scandalous to Jewish ears. At most, Jeremiah 16:5-7 and Ezekiel 24:15-24 are comparable. With the great prophets, Jesus violates law and pious custom — not, however, as a prophetic sign but rather as a result of unconditional discipleship for the sake of the Reign of God (cf. also the logion in Matt. 19:12c). An original testimonial to Jesus' radicalism!

Jesus Stills the Storm (8:23-27)

23 *And when he got into the boat, his disciples followed him.* 24 *A windstorm arose on the sea, so great that the boat was being swamped by the waves; but he was asleep.* 25 *And they went and woke him up, saying, "Lord, save us! We are perishing!"* 26 *And he said to them, "Why are you afraid, you of little faith?" Then he got up and rebuked the winds and the sea; and there was a dead calm.* 27 *They were amazed, saying, "What sort of man is this, that even the winds and the sea obey him?"*

23-27 By way of its attachment to the logia of following or discipleship (cf. the disciples "following" in v. 23), by way of the conversation with the disciples, now shifted back to the middle, and by way of the expression "of little faith," the narrative that Mark and Luke hand down elsewhere becomes in Matthew an express history of discipleship that, together with the words on discipleship, is intended to take the community aback. As for genre, what we have here is not properly a "nature miracle," anymore than is any other of the miracles of this type. We ought to speak of a "miracle of rescue," which shows Jesus' power (v. 27) at work to protect those who belong to him (28:20b, "I am with you") but also summons them to full belief.

Matthew has omitted the presentation in Mark, with its richer color, preferring instead the exchange with the disciples before the "rebuke" of the wind and the waves (German Ecumenical Translation, "he threatened"). The mention of "the men" (v. 27) is striking since Jesus is alone with the disciples. In Mark and Luke, the disciples speak with one another about Jesus' commanding might. It is a "choral ending," as in 9:31 and 15:31; Matthew is thinking of "the men," as in 5:16 he is thinking of those standing without. The familiar later application of the ship to the church buffeted by the storm of earthly concerns does enjoy a purchase in Matthew. The most important thing for him is the defeat of all "little faith" (see 6:30) in the church. The same intent stands behind the scene with the sinking Peter (14:31).

Jesus Heals the Gadarene Demoniac (8:28-34)

> 28 *When he came to the other side, to the country of the Gadarenes, two demoniacs coming out of the tombs met him. They were so fierce that no one could pass that way.* 29 *Suddenly they shouted, "What have you to do with us, Son of God? Have you come here to torment us before the time?"* 30 *Now a large herd of swine was feeding at some distance from them.* 31 *The demons begged him, "If you cast us out, send us into the herd of swine."* 32 *And he said to them, "Go!" So they came out and entered the swine; and suddenly, the whole herd rushed down the steep bank into the sea and perished in the water.* 33 *The swineherds ran off, and on going into the town, they told the whole story about what had happened to the demoniacs.* 34 *Then the whole town came out to meet Jesus; and when they saw him, they begged him to leave their neighborhood.*

28-34 Matthew has taken this story, so utterly strange to us today, from Mark 5:1-20, but has radically abbreviated it (from twenty verses to seven). The Decapolis was a Hellenistic ten-city alliance that lay southeast of Lake Gennesaret. Whatever be the origin of the account played out in the Decapolis, Matthew has maintained all of the essentials: the particularly serious disease (insanity), which led to residence in "the tombs" (Matt. 8:28), the encounter of the possessed persons with Jesus (v. 29), the expulsion of the demons into the herd of swine and the destruction of the swine in the waters of the lake (vv. 30-32), the swineherds' report in the city, and the request of the citizenry that he leave their neighborhood (vv. 33-34). The peculiarities in Matthew are two possessed persons instead of Mark's one (cf. our Intro., p. 4); "suddenly" (v. 29); "at some distance" (v. 30); "the whole town came out" (v. 34), and indeed "to meet Jesus," as if to a celebration. In Mark the conclusion (Mark 5:18-20) resembles the ending in the account of the cleansing of the leper (Mark 1:45). Here there are certain Markan tendencies that Matthew does not adopt (missionary activity in Gentile territory).

28a   As in the case of all the Synoptics, the geography in the manuscripts shifts: from Gerasa (the best-known city, although a two days' journey from the lake) to Gadara, best known from Matthew (two hours from the lake), to Gergesa on the southeastern shore of the lake. Topographically, the last named, on a cliff over the lake, is questionable, to say the least.

28b   Tombs, like other desolate places, were the preferred dwelling places of demons. The harassment of "passersby," with cries and the tremendous power of possession, are portrayed in greater detail in Mark 5:3-5.

29   The conjuring, parrying calls, in Mark with the use of names, are restricted by Matthew to "Son of God." Jesus' true rank (see Matt. 3:17) is appealed to by the devil (4:3, 6) and acknowledged by the demons (cf. Mark himself, earlier, 3:11), but known by the disciples only in faith (Matt. 14:33; 16:16). Until the appointed time of their final annihilation, the demons hope to find a dwelling in the swine (for Jews, contemptible beasts).

32   But the demons forthwith accompany the swine into the annihilating precipice (an image of the underworld).

34   The Gentile denizens of the city are first impressed by the swineherds' report, but when they see Jesus they ask him to leave their area. In Matthew such deeds of might outside Galilee are exceptions (cf. 15:21-28), radiations of his activity as addressed to Israel (see 4:24-25; 10:5b-6).

The entire event is intended to illustrate the power with which Jesus is invested to defeat evil (12:23-30). Other questions (possession of animals? the devil tricking or being tricked?) are neither here nor there, as are misunderstandings of mental illness as possession.

Return to Capernaum and Further Deeds of Healing (9:1-34)

After the return to the densely populated northwest shore of the lake, we hear of further activity on Jesus' part. This time, however, it includes not only miracles of healing but encounters and conversations as well, which for Matthew belong to Jesus' salvific activity. As for genre, the healing of the cripple, the banquet at the house of the tax collector, and the question of fasting in Mark 2:1-22 (in the same order) should be designated "conversations of conflict," while Matthew has used them as simple reports of Jesus' activity. The remaining conflictual conversations (Mark 2:23–3:6), however, are transferred by Matthew to a later passage containing such confrontations (Matt. 12:1-14; see our Intro., no. 1). Alongside healing of diseases, the inner meaning of Jesus for people's salvation — deliverance from sin and guilt (Matt. 1:21), the new age of joy — now comes under consideration. At every step one must keep in mind the evangelist's bond with tradition.

Jesus Heals a Paralytic (9:1-8)

> 9:1 *And after getting into a boat he crossed the sea and came to his own town.*
>
> 2 *And just then some people were carrying a paralyzed man lying on a bed. When Jesus saw their faith, he said to the paralytic, "Take heart, son; your sins are forgiven." 3 Then some of the scribes said to themselves, "This man is blaspheming." 4 But Jesus, perceiving their thoughts, said, "Why do you think evil in your hearts? 5 For which is easier, to say, 'Your sins are forgiven,' or to say, 'Stand up and walk'? 6 But so that you may know that the Son of Man has authority on earth to forgive sins" — he then said to the paralytic — "Stand up, take your bed and go to your home." 7 And he stood up and went to his home. 8 When the crowds saw it, they were filled with awe, and they glorified God, who had given such authority to human beings.*

1-8 Matthew follows Mark's presentation but omits the description of the opening of the roof of the house and the lowering of the cripple before Jesus. Otherwise there are slight abbreviations and stylistic alterations, until the final sentence (cf. below). The tie between forgiveness of sins and healing is retained, as is the confrontation with the scribes. The tension, already recognizable in Mark, between a healing account and the controversy over the forgiveness of sins is frequently traceable to two different traditions. However, although the internal crevices and cracks are not to be overlooked, we will have to conclude that there was a single act on Jesus' part, and one with a character of its own. He promises the cripple forgiveness by God (v. 2), but the scribes understand this as the usurpation of a divine right (v. 3; clearer in Mark 2:7). The community recognizes here the authority of the Son of Man (v. 6a) and has Jesus himself utter this basic enunciation. For Matthew that pronouncement is grounded in the authority of the Resurrected One (28:18). In terms of the authority given by

God to "human beings" (9:8) — only Matthew has it this way — he is thinking of the authority given to the disciples or the community for healing (10:8) and the forgiveness of sins (16:19; 18:18).

The Call of Matthew (9:9-13)

> 9 *As Jesus was walking along, he saw a man called Matthew sitting at the tax booth; and he said to him, "Follow me." And he got up and followed him.*
> 10 *And as he sat at dinner in the house, many tax collectors and sinners came and were sitting with him and his disciples.* 11 *When the Pharisees saw this, they said to his disciples, "Why does your teacher eat with tax collectors and sinners?"* 12 *But when he heard this, he said, "Those who are well have no need of a physician, but those who are sick.* 13 *Go and learn what this means, 'I desire mercy, not sacrifice.' For I have come to call not the righteous but sinners."*

9-13   Even pre-Markan tradition has this pericope in its spliced form, from two originally independent pieces of tradition: the call of the tax collector (v. 9), and the banquet at the home of the tax collector (vv. 10-13). Thus the impression arose that the tax collector was giving a farewell banquet to which many of his colleagues had come; but where it was taking place is uncertain: "in the house," says Matthew, or "in his house," says Mark, which leads many to think it might be Jesus' house, and finally, in Luke, in the house of Levi. The punch line of the story is recognizable in Jesus' utterance concerning the healthy and the ill (v. 12), emphasized in Matthew (v. 13a) by way of a verse from Scripture (Hos. 6:6), whose complete fulfillment is presented in Matthew 8:13b.

9   There was a tax or toll station at Capernaum, at the frontier of Herod Antipas's region (see 8:5). The Jews despised tax collectors, who collected taxes and tolls under a supervisor (cf. Luke 19:1-10), as "sinners" because of their frequent dishonesty as well as because of their traffic with Gentiles. Like the fishers at Lake Gennesaret (4:18-22), the tax collector at once ("he got up") abandoned the toll station at Jesus' call — a typical story of the call to discipleship (see 8:19-22). Matthew changes the original name, Levi (used in Mark and Luke), to "Matthew" since he is thinking of a member of the circle of the "twelve apostles" (10:3). This identification is historically doubtful (cf. our Intro., no. 4).

10-13   As early as verse 10, the theme of Jesus' mercy toward sinners is addressed; after all, the story is about a banquet given by a tax collector. Sinners, including, for Matthew, prostitutes (21:32), stand for all the despised groups in the Judaism of the day. Consciously ordering them here, Matthew names, after the teachers of the law (9:3), the Pharisees (9:11), who supervised life according to the law, and, later, the disciples of John (9:14) with their question of fasting. Responsibility is distributed, but Jesus enjoys sovereign exaltation over all Jewish authorities. A meal shared in common is the expression of full community, here the sign of acceptance into fellowship with God (cf. 8:11). In God's name Jesus turns to sinners, as the utterance (heard in Hellenism as well) concerning the sick and the well (v. 12) and then that about Jesus' mission (v. 13b) demonstrate. Jesus' invitation goes out to all (11:28; 22:1-10), if to sinners only conditionally. Matthew inserts a citation from Scripture that places the accent on the mercy willed by God (see 5:7), reserving criticism of worship until 12:7. The tax collector's banquet, with Jesus' part "pregnant with signs," is a sure testimony to his attention to the despised and to sinners.

The Question about Fasting (9:14-17)

> 14 Then the disciples of John came to him, saying, "Why do we and the Pharisees fast often, but your disciples do not fast?" 15 And Jesus said to them, "The wedding guests cannot mourn as long as the bridegroom is with them, can they? The days will come when the bridegroom is taken away from them, and then they will fast. 16 No one sews a piece of unshrunk cloth on an old cloak, for the patch pulls away from the cloak, and a worse tear is made. 17 Neither is new wine put into old wineskins; otherwise, the skins burst, and the wine is spilled, and the skins are destroyed; but new wine is put into fresh wineskins, and so both are preserved."

14-17 Following the Markan line, Matthew now broaches — fittingly, after the tax collector's banquet — the question of fasting. A verbal confrontation in Mark, including a key utterance of Jesus (an "apothegm"), namely, concerning wedding guests who do no mourning, becomes in Matthew another incident ("Then disciples came to him . . .") in the sketching of Jesus' activity. For the rest he closely follows Mark, who attaches to the question of fasting two originally independent verbal pictures of the "old" and the "new."

14-15 In Matthew the only inquirers are John's disciples (cf. Mark 2:18), who approach Jesus once again in 11:2-3 (Q). It is precisely to them that what is new in Jesus' activity must be pointed out (11:4-6, 11). The wedding guests ("sons of the bridal chamber") are a reliable image of Judaism. Their joyful celebration is not compatible with "fasting," an expression of sorrow and penitence (see 6:16-18). A view of the time when the bridegroom "is taken away from them," a reference to Jesus' death, is an interpolation on the part of the transmitting community. It suited Matthew because he knew of the future custom of fasting in the Jewish-Christian community (see 6:16-18). Jesus' pronouncement basically draws attention to the time of salvation that has dawned with him (no mourning) and passes over the special question of the practice of fasting. After Jesus' death a new situation emerges, which occasions a variety of responses.

16-17   In the present context both pictorial utterances stress the new element, which is incompatible with the old. Matthew emphasizes that new wine is *preserved* in new containers (at the end of v. 17), by which he implies the continuing validity of the new teaching of Jesus that surpasses the old (5:20), without denying its connection with the Old Testament revelation (5:17; 13:52).

A Girl Restored to Life and a Woman Healed (9:18-26)

> 18 *While he was saying these things to them, suddenly a leader of the synagogue came in and knelt before him, saying, "My daughter has just died; but come and lay your hand on her, and she will live." 19 And Jesus got up and followed him, with his disciples. 20 Then suddenly a woman who had been suffering from hemorrhages for twelve years came up behind him and touched the fringe of his cloak, 21 for she said to herself, "If I only touch his cloak, I will be made well." 22 Jesus turned, and seeing her he said, "Take heart, daughter; your faith has made you well." And instantly the woman was made well. 23 When Jesus came to the leader's house and saw the flute players and the crowd making a commotion, 24 he said, "Go away; for the girl is not dead but sleeping." And they laughed at him. 25 But when the crowd had been put outside, he went in and took her by the hand, and the girl got up. 26 And the report of this spread throughout that district.*

18-26   These two interconnected miracles, a raising from the dead and the healing of a serious disease, which Mark himself presents in this compact form, are inserted by Matthew into his continuing narrative (v. 18a). The account is condensed (almost two-thirds shorter than in Mark). Despite remarkable departures — the father's arrival after his daughter has already died, the healing of the hemorrhaging woman only after Jesus' utterance — Matthew's presentation is to be recognized as redactional work on his part. In addition to certain stylistic peculiarities ("suddenly came in . . . knelt before him . . ." [v. 18], "take heart . . ." [v. 22], "go away" [v. 24]), we have the closing remark of verse 26 (see 4:24); Matthew also omits the command not to report the event (cf., however, 9:30). For him the raising of the dead was important for the response to the Baptist (11:5), and the healing of the hemorrhaging woman for the meaning of faith.

18   The "leader of the synagogue" — in Mark the synagogue leader Jairus — was an influential Jew in the anonymous locale. His belief in the possibility of raising the dead may have been based on the deeds of the prophets Elijah (1 Kings 17:17-24) and Elisha (2 Kings 4:32-37). A belief in the raising of the dead is to be found at that time in Judaism and Hellenism alike.

20-22 Mark's detailed, graphic account of the woman healed by touching Jesus' garment (Mark 5:27-34) is abbreviated by Matthew to the woman's magical notion of touching Jesus' cloak; but he has the cure itself happen through Jesus' words. For Matthew the faith of the woman, who approaches Jesus only from a distance, is doubtless comparable to the faith of the centurion of Capernaum (8:8; here, too, "only"). In the healing utterance (v. 22), Jesus emphasizes this faith, which is the exact opposite of magic and gets its power through trust in him. The Greek expression for "healing" is reminiscent of the redemption of the entire person (cf. also Luke 7:50).

23-25 As in Mark, Jesus tells the flute players and professional mourners to leave. But Matthew does not mention the parents, nor Jesus' guides. Everything is focused on Jesus' sovereign conduct. The pronouncement, "The girl is not dead but sleeping," adopts the common image of the sleep of death but applies it metaphorically to the announcement of her restoration to life. This "sleep of death" is such only in appearance: Jesus calls the girl back from death to life (cf. 2 Kings 4:31, 35). An understanding of Jesus' words as denoting death merely in appearance is completely off track. The wonder is recorded briefly (v. 25), with a note as to the spreading reputation of Jesus' deeds after this climax (v. 26).

Jesus Heals Two Blind Men (9:27-31)

> 27 *As Jesus went on from there, two blind men followed him, crying loudly,* "Have mercy on us, Son of David!" 28 *When he entered the house, the blind men came to him; and Jesus said to them, "Do you believe that I am able to do this?" They said to him, "Yes, Lord."* 29 *Then he touched their eyes and said,* "According to your faith let it be done to you." 30 *And their eyes were opened. Then Jesus sternly ordered them, "See that no one knows of this."* 31 *But they went away and spread the news about him throughout that district.*

27-31 This cure of two blind men, again spun into the narrative fabric (v. 27) without a direct parallel in Mark and Luke, is obviously reported by Matthew with 11:5 in mind ("the blind receive their sight . . ."). It may be that the same verse also explains the number of blind men in the story, two. The pericope is striking in virtue of its kinship with the healing of the blind men of Jericho (20:29-34, following Mark 10:46-52): the same expression for "crying loudly," the same call of entreaty, "Have mercy on us, Son of David," the same "touching of their eyes." The striking conclusion (Matt. 9:30b-31) is strongly reminiscent of Mark 1:43-45 (the "stern" prohibition against reporting the event, the spreading report of the event). The peculiarities can be explained by redactional intent: the "house" Jesus enters recalls 8:14, 9:10, and 9:23 and serves to set a scene separate from the crowd. Jesus' question concerning their belief carries forward the theme of faith (8:10, 13; 9:2, 9, 22). The prohibition against reporting the healing, which Matthew has avoided until now, and its nonobservance by the ones healed are understandable after the remark of 9:26 (note: "throughout that district"). After these many wonders, the spread of Jesus' renown is unstoppable. The supposition is justified, then, that Matthew has formed this pericope from available pieces of tradition. This makes sense for a depiction of Jesus's salvific activity and is permissible in the narrative technique of the time. In view of the well-attested healing of the blind men of Jericho, one need suspect no scandal.

Jesus Heals One Who Was Mute (9:32-34)

> 32 *After they had gone away, a demoniac who was mute was brought to him.* 33 *And when the demon had been cast out, the one who had been mute spoke; and the crowds were amazed and said, "Never has anything like this been seen in Israel."* 34 *But the Pharisees said, "By the ruler of the demons he casts out the demons."*

32-34 Likewise, the pericope on the mute person possessed by a demon betrays Matthew's own hand, as its kinship with 12:22-24 (par. Luke 11:14-15) shows. There Jesus drives a demon out of a person who is blind and mute, which occasions wonderment in the crowd and suspicion among his adversaries. Our pericope is constructed exactly the same way, except that after the healing of the blind men Matthew speaks of only one mute (as does Luke, 11:14). The healing of the blind and the dumb belongs to the prophetic fulfillment of Matthew 11:5. The choral ending praises the God of Israel, just as in 15:31. Jesus is the shepherd and redeemer of God's people (see 1:20-21; 2:6). The Pharisees suspect Jesus of a compact with the leader of the demons, a theme that will be taken up again only later (12:22-29).

THE DISCIPLES AS JESUS' MESSENGERS: THE DISCOURSE AT THE SENDING OF THE DISCIPLES (9:35–11:1)

After presenting Jesus' salvific proclamation, with its deeds — summarized, once more, in 9:35 — Matthew broadens his view to include the disciples' share in Jesus' activity. They are already "laborers" in their earthly activity, and Jesus summons them to the "harvest" (9:36-38). At the same time, however, they are representatives of the future missionaries of the church. First, Matthew presents the circle of the "twelve apostles," by name (10:1-5), and then fashions a missionary discourse to the disciples (10:5-42) that, against a background of the first dispatch, also tells later missionaries (cf. 10:40-42) everything important for their own mission. It consists not only of instructions for missionary work (10:5-16) but also of warnings of persecution (10:17-25), encouragement to fearless profession (10:26-33), and admonitions to loyal discipleship (10:34-42). Like the Sermon on the Mount, it is a composed discourse, which Matthew emphasizes with the concluding formula (11:1) about its being instruction for the "twelve disciples."

It can be seen that the passages just indicated are individual logia skillfully woven together by Matthew, also from the material of tradition. The list of apostles is based on Mark 3:16-19, where they appear in the same order. For the missionary discourse itself (Matt. 10:7-16), Matthew combines material transmitted in Mark 6:8-11 (par. Luke 9:3-5) and in Luke 10:3-12 (the mission of the "seventy"). He takes the declaration regarding persecution (Matt. 10:17-25) essentially from the eschatological discourse (Mark 13:9-13). The invitation to fearless confession (Matt. 10:26-33) originates with Q (Luke 12:2-9), and the subsequent admonitions are likewise brought together from various utterances in Q. Throughout (some elements, including material peculiar to Matthew, can be clarified only separately), we are aware of a conscious concern to address the situation of the Matthean community.

The Harvest Is Great, the Laborers Few (9:35-38)

> 35 Then Jesus went about all the cities and villages, teaching in their synagogues, and proclaiming the good news of the kingdom, and curing every disease and every sickness. 36 When he saw the crowds, he had compassion for them, because they were harassed and helpless, like sheep without a shepherd. 37 Then he said to his disciples, "The harvest is plentiful, but the laborers are few; 38 therefore ask the Lord of the harvest to send out laborers into his harvest."

35-38 Jesus' activity is summarized (v. 35) for the sake of the tradition: Jesus wants to make his disciples participants in that activity. A broad impact on the people requires co-workers, both to show compassion to the throngs left in the lurch by the Jewish leaders (v. 36) and to bring in the great harvest (vv. 37-38). For this purpose Matthew makes use of two utterances from different places in the tradition, one from Mark 6:34 and the other from Q, which Luke uses at the beginning of his lengthier missionary discourse (Luke 10:2).

36   The image of sheep without a shepherd is frequently used in the Old Testament to depict the need of the people (1 Kings 22:17; Ezek. 34:5; Zech. 10:2), but also to indicate a shepherd chosen by God — in Numbers 27:17 Joshua and in Ezekiel 34:11-24 the true shepherd through whom God himself gathers and leads his flocks. Mark 6:34 also alludes to this messianic shepherd who takes pity on the people before feeding the crowd; and Matthew, who further dubs the people as "harassed and helpless" (German Ecumenical Translation, "weary and exhausted"), understands the shepherd in the same way (cf. Matt. 11:29-30).

37   In the Old Testament the harvest is more frequently an image of the judgment (Isa. 17:5; 27:12; Joel 3:13; cf. Matt. 3:12; 13:30, 39; Rev. 14:15), and more rarely one of the time of salvation (Ps. 126:6). Here it refers to the present "harvest time," when God's dominion is proclaimed and the people of God are gathered together (cf. John 4:36-38). In this sense it is an expression of the time of joy ushered in by Jesus (cf. Matt. 9:15). God is the "Lord of the harvest"; one must ask him for more workers to bring in the messianic harvest. A similar picture (of the wine harvest), if with other points to make, underlies Matthew 20:1-16. Its intention is that the community discern a challenge to pray for preachers.

The Twelve Apostles (10:1-4)

> 10:1 *Then Jesus summoned his twelve disciples and gave them authority over unclean spirits, to cast them out, and to cure every disease and every sickness.* 2 *These are the names of the twelve apostles: first, Simon, also known as Peter, and his brother Andrew; James son of Zebedee, and his brother John;* 3 *Philip and Bartholomew; Thomas and Matthew the tax collector; James son of Alphaeus, and Thaddaeus;* 4 *Simon the Cananaean, and Judas Iscariot, the one who betrayed him.*

1-4   Matthew presumes the establishment, by this time, of the circle of the Twelve (Mark 3:14-15), and speaks at once of the transfer of sovereign authority to them, in which he includes not only the expulsion of demons but the healing of all sufferings and ills (Matt. 4:23; 9:35). The twelve disciples, who represent the twelve tribes of Israel (19:28), are at once designated as the twelve *apostles* (cf. Luke 6:13), although this way of speaking is only a post-Easter one (Acts; 1 Cor. 12:28; 15:7). The Twelve, established by the earthly Jesus, are for Matthew (as even more clearly for Luke) the connecting link with the post-Easter heralds of the gospel sent forth by the risen Lord (Matt. 28:16, "the eleven disciples"). At the same time the horizon is broadened to include those sent forth in the future, too (cf. Eph. 2:20; 4:11).

Matthew alters the list of names he has received from Mark 3:16-19: the imposition of Simon's epithet, which he first justifies only in Matthew 16:18 and here simply presupposes, he omits, like those of the sons of Zebedee. Simon Peter is singled out by the modifier "first" (cf. Intro., no. 6); Matthew places the two brothers, Peter and Andrew, appropriately, at the head of the list in 4:18-22; Matthew is characterized as a "tax collector" (see 9:9) and listed after Thomas. The names of the members of the circle, of varied origin, were important to the primitive church (Acts 1:13, 26; Rev. 21:14).

The Mission of the Twelve (10:5-16)

5 *These twelve Jesus sent out with the following instructions: "Go nowhere among the Gentiles, and enter no town of the Samaritans, 6 but go rather to the lost sheep of the house of Israel. 7 As you go, proclaim the good news, 'The kingdom of heaven has come near.' 8 Cure the sick, raise the dead, cleanse the lepers, cast out demons. You received without payment; give without payment. 9 Take no gold, or silver, or copper in your belts, 10 no bag for your journey, or two tunics, or sandals, or a staff; for laborers deserve their food. 11 Whatever town or village you enter, find out who in it is worthy, and stay there until you leave. 12 As you enter the house, greet it. 13 If the house is worthy, let your peace come upon it; but if it is not worthy, let your peace return to you. 14 If anyone will not welcome you or listen to your words, shake off the dust from your feet as you leave that house or town. 15 Truly I tell you, it will be more tolerable for the land of Sodom and Gomorrah on the day of judgment than for that town.*

16 *"See, I am sending you out like sheep into the midst of wolves; so be wise as serpents and innocent as doves."*

5-16 After a logion peculiar to Matthew alone (vv. 5b-6), there follows, with a new discourse ("Go . . . proclaim . . ."), concrete instruction for the behavior of those sent forth, which betrays certain Matthean accents. Verse 16b is likewise peculiar to Matthew alone.

5b-6 The prohibition against going to the Gentiles, or into a locality of Samaria, stems from the Jewish-Christian community, whose tradition Matthew is echoing. Jesus can scarcely have been of such a harsh mind (cf. 8:28-34; Luke 9:52-56); but the restriction of the object of missionary activity to the "lost sheep of the house of Israel" does correspond to his sense of mission (see 4:23-25; 15:26). Matthew maintains this view for Jesus' earthly activity, but opens the door for the mission to the Gentiles through the missionary mandate of the Risen One (28:19). In his conceptualization of salvation history he can reconcile the two (see 2:1-11; 8:11-12). His community is already composed of former Jews and Gentiles (cf. lntro., p. 5); however, he seeks to maintain a historical preference on the part of Jesus (15:24) and of Jesus' assistants (10:6). The image of the "lost sheep" (not a mere part of Israel; an explanatory genitive) takes up the picture underlying 9:36 as well; cf. also the "wandering" or "scattered" sheep (Isa. 53:6; Jer. 23:2-3; Ezek. 34:12; Zech. 13:7). "House of Israel" is an old expression for the people of God (Exod. 16:31; 2 Sam. 1:12; Jer. 31:31; Acts 2:36; Heb. 8:8, 10).

7-8 Jesus' messengers are to preach what he himself preached (see 4:17). The nearness of God's Reign is shown in cures, which are enumerated in greater detail by Matthew than by Mark. Their therapeutic power is given to the disciples through Jesus' authority, as we learn from the short sentence found only in Matthew: "Freely you have received, freely give." But this power also requires strong faith on the part of the disciples (17:16, 19-20). Healing without remuneration leads at once to the theme of frugality.

9-10 The strict prescriptions for the outfitting of the missionary ambassadors, already present in Mark 6:8-9, become even more so, as in Luke 9:3. Especially, they shall *earn* (by the cures they effect?) no money (in descending order: coins of neither gold, nor silver, nor copper). But not only that: they may not take sandals or staff along, which in Mark are permitted as indispensable paraphernalia. On the other hand, as in Luke 10:7, they are permitted to accept food and drink. The rule, "Laborers deserve their food [in Luke: 'wages']," has its echo in Paul (1 Cor. 9:9-14). As in Luke 10, the concrete instructions allow us a glimpse of primitive Christian wandering missionaries, who set out in the most extreme poverty but who could expect to be supported by the people who received them. Later these words fired the hearts of Francis of Assisi and his companions.

11-13 Rules for entering a locality and a house follow (in Luke in the reverse order). First the messengers are to ascertain who in a given locality is "worthy" to lodge them. Reception of preachers is a mark of distinction, because it goes hand in hand with acceptance of the gospel. The greeting of peace upon entry into a house (or among a family) appears as a gift of blessing overflowing to the receiver (cf. Gen. 27:27-29, 38-40), indeed, as a force that, upon being declined, turns back upon the greeter. For the Bible, "greeting" is a great and holy thing (cf. Luke 1:28-29, 40-41). The primitive missionaries are aware of their charismatic power.

14-15 Rejection of the ambassadors, however, bodes ill for a house or city. As a sign of it, the preachers of the gospel are to shake the dust from their feet, a symbolic gesture understood as entailing breach of communion (Acts 13:51; cf. Acts 18:6). This carries a great deal of weight since it is the gospel ("your words") that these persons are rejecting. And so a threat follows, citing the exemplary fate of the sinful cities of Sodom and Gomorrah (Gen. 19:28-

29). It comes from Q, and Matthew repeats it in the cry of woe over the cities of Galilee (Matt. 11:23-24; cf. also Luke 17:28-29).

16 The danger threatening persons sent among those hostile to them is portrayed with the image of sheep among wolves (see 7:15). Luke places this utterance of warning at the very beginning of the missionary discourse (Luke 10:3), but Matthew sets it here in order to make a transition to the next passage. The craftiness of serpents and the simplicity of doves are proverbial, as, for example, in a midrash to the Song of Songs (Song of Sol. 2:14). Matthew's interpolation is not a rule of conduct to be observed literally (by contrast, cf. 10:19-20), but prescribes that, no matter what human prudence may be applied, the sincerity and integrity willed by God must be present as well (see 5:8; cf. Rom. 16:19; Phil. 2:15).

Coming Persecutions (10:17-25)

17 *"Beware of them, for they will hand you over to councils and flog you in their synagogues; 18 and you will be dragged before governors and kings because of me, as a testimony to them and the Gentiles. 19 When they hand you over, do not worry about how you are to speak or what you are to say; for what you are to say will be given to you at that time; 20 for it is not you who speak, but the Spirit of your Father speaking through you. 21 Brother will betray brother to death, and a father his child, and children will rise against parents and have them put to death; 22 and you will be hated by all because of my name. But the one who endures to the end will be saved. 23 When they persecute you in one town, flee to the next; for truly I tell you, you will not have gone through all the towns of Israel before the Son of Man comes.*

24 *"A disciple is not above the teacher, nor a slave above the master; 25 it is enough for the disciple to be like the teacher, and the slave like the master. If they have called the master of the house Beelzebul, how much more will they malign those of his household!"*

17-25 Until verse 22, Matthew follows the Markan version of the eschatological discourse, then inserts a pronouncement of his own (v. 23), attaching a basic utterance to be found in Luke 6:40 as well. He oversteps the situation of the disciples at the time of Jesus considerably. Persecutions by Jewish groups (vv. 17, 23), as well as judicial proceedings presided over by the Romans (v. 18), are taken into account. The disciples' lot will resemble their master's, and this is also an encouragement, like the promise of the assistance of the Holy Spirit when on trial (v. 20). Even strife that disturbs the family for the gospel's sake and betrayal on the part of one's closest of kin must not shake Christ's emissaries (vv. 21-22). Despite the missionary label, it is the entire community (as in the eschatological discourse) that is being addressed. Precisely at the time of the evangelist, the Matthean community is exposed to a variety of persecutions and slanders (see 5:11-12). "Persecution for righteousness' sake" (see 5:10), however, is a badge of discipleship, and entails the promise of sharing in the Reign of God.

17-18 After a transition to connect v. 16 (cf. the "wolves") with what follows, in the form of an urging (v. 17b) to be on their guard, the disciples are apprised of Jewish punitive measures (scourging in the synagogues; cf. 2 Cor. 11:24), which will be imposed by local tribunals (not by the great Sanhedrin in Jerusalem). But they will also be denounced before Roman governors and puppet kings. Matthew probably understands the witness the disciples will bear before them (before these judges, surely not the Jewish courts) and the "Gentiles" (a larger audience) in a missionary sense (cf. Mark 13:10, which Matthew omits here).

19-20 The advocacy of the Holy Spirit in a court of law is an early, well-attested utterance (also in Q; cf. Luke 12:11-12 and the echo in John 15:26-27). With Luke, Matthew says "how or what you are to say," cites (only Matthew) "the Spirit *of your Father*," and thereby recalls the heavenly Father's care for Jesus' disciples (see 6:26). His Spirit gives them the right words, and speaks through them.

21-22 One is struck by the warning that the disciples are to be delivered up to tribunals by immediate relatives, even in the face of a possible death penalty (cf. John 16:2). This concept, formulated here as in Mark 13:12, adopts the prophecy from Micah 7:6, a passage cited almost literally in Q (Matt. 10:35-36; cf. Luke 12:53). Being the object of hatred for Jesus' name's sake as a sign of discipleship is even more powerfully set forth in John (John 15:18-25). "Enduring to the end" includes the possibility of martyrdom (Rev. 13:10). And so, "rescue," or "redemption," means not preventing the disciples from being haled before the courts, but acquittal in the divine court and entry into eternal life (Matt. 10:28; 16:25).

23 The origin and meaning of this peculiarly Matthean logion are disputed, but it stands in close connection with 10:5b-6. The Jewish-Christian tradition is unmistakable. According to the meaning of the words, the point is not missionary preaching but persecution and flight; yet they are stated against a background of the activity of wandering Jewish-Christian missionaries. They meet with resistance, are persecuted, and are to flee from one city to another (cf. 23:34). The admonition to flee may seem surprising, but it is a concrete directive based on experience (cf. v. 17a). The promise, introduced by the Amen formula (not always a sign of Jesus' immediate voice), that they will not have gone through the cities of Israel (in Palestine; see 2:21; 4:25; 9:33; 10:6, their mission) before the Son of Man would come (in the parousia) is a consolatory motif for these very hard-pressed missionaries as well as an indirect threat against their persecutors (cf. v. 15). Taken in itself, Jesus' utterance would indicate a determinable moment for his imminent expectation of the Reign of God; other logia suggest the contrary (24:32, 46, 50; 25:13; Luke 17:20). And so we are dealing with a time-conditioned prophecy, which set forth Jesus' imminent expectation in conformity with the historical situation and which Matthew adopted against the background of 10:5b-6. We may not conclude, with Albert Schweitzer, to an erroneous expectation of an imminent parousia on Jesus' part, nor is the logion open to apologetic dilution in terms of Jesus' coming at Easter, at Pentecost, or the like. For that matter, "updated" applications and interpretations of Jesus' words are to be observed elsewhere (cf. also 16:28; 24:34).

24-25   Immediately following verse 23 comes this utterance about disciples and their teacher (utilized differently in Luke 6:40), a slave and his master (only in Matthew; but cf. John 13:16; 15:20), as another encouragement not to allow oneself to be disconcerted by persecution. Likewise in Judaism we find the proverbial expression, "It is enough for the disciple to be like his master," referring to God and those serving him. For Jesus' disciples, this means following their Lord, namely, Jesus, in all things (Matt. 10:38-39). This holds true as well for scorn and abuse, as Matthew interprets it in view of 9:34 and 12:24. If Jesus calls the disciples "those of his household," that is, slaves, they can still become conscious of their close community with their master (cf., by contrast, 10:36).

Whom to Fear (10:26-33)

> 26 "So have no fear of them; for nothing is covered up that will not be uncovered, and nothing secret that will not become known. 27 What I say to you in the dark, tell in the light; and what you hear whispered, proclaim from the housetops. 28 Do not fear those who kill the body but cannot kill the soul; rather fear him who can destroy both soul and body in hell. 29 Are not two sparrows sold for a penny? Yet not one of them will fall to the ground apart from your Father. 30 And even the hairs of your head are all counted. 31 So do not be afraid; you are of more value than many sparrows.
>
> 32 "Everyone therefore who acknowledges me before others, I also will acknowledge before my Father in heaven; 33 but whoever denies me before others, I also will deny before my Father in heaven."

26-33   The next passage, taken directly from the Sayings Source (Q) (Luke 12:2-9), is inserted by Matthew for encouragement after the instructions concerning persecution: "So have no fear of them" (Matt. 10:26a). He seizes especially on the utterances of verses 28-31, enveloped as they are by this challenge (vv. 28, 31). The remaining discursive units, concerning what is not hidden (vv. 26-27) and profession of Jesus (vv. 32-33), are drawn into this context. Small

Matthean alterations (v. 29, "your Father"; vv. 32-33, "my Father in heaven") underscore this, and bring the passage up-to-date for the disciples and for the Matthean community.

26-27 The common Synoptic expression of v. 26 (in synonymous parallelism), which is handed down in double form (also in Mark 4:22 and Luke 8:17), was open to a variety of applications. Luke ties it to a warning against hypocrisy (Luke 12:1). In the Matthean context the instruction it issues is for forthright preaching. Rooftops were the place where public announcements were made.

28 Unlike 6:25, where "life" *(psychē)* and body are placed in tandem and have the same meaning, this utterance distinguishes between "body," which human beings can kill, and "soul" *(psychē)*, which they cannot kill. But this distinction, possible in the Judaism of the time, connotes no separation between body and soul (dualism) but only the belief that the human being bears a deeper life (see Matt. 10:39) within than the corporeal (Luke, "Human beings can then do no more"). Through his judgment God is able to cast the entire human being into the ruin of hell (cf. Isa. 8:12-13; 4 Macc. 13:14-15). That this would be Satan, lord of hell, rather than God is improbable since "human beings" and "God" form the antithesis. Also, God is to be feared; but, for the true disciple, the threat of divine judgment becomes the announcement of loving divine concern in the very next logion.

29-31 The comparison with the sparrows, who do not fall to the ground, dead, except by the will of God the Father (scarcely "fall into a snare"), and God's care for the disciples shown through it are reminiscent of 6:26-30. It is the same argument "from the smaller to the greater." Two sparrows were sold for one penny at that time. That even the hairs of the head are counted (protected) illustrates God's loving concern.

32-33 This logion, originally appearing apologetically in Luke 12:8-9, is seen by Matthew from a different viewpoint, the post-Easter one: the Son of Man is directly identified with Jesus. Originally referring to Jesus as the Son of Man and Judge, the utterance here is applied by Mark 8:38 and Luke 9:26 as a threat against those who would deny Jesus. For Matthew, in context, it is an encouragement to public, steadfast confession of Jesus. Instead of speaking of the angels of God, he speaks of "your" or "my Father in heaven." In so doing, he sets human beings and God in sharper opposition and at the same time indicates, with "Father," the latter's special protection and future reward.

Not Peace, but a Sword (10:34-42)

34 *"Do not think that I have come to bring peace to the earth; I have not come to bring peace, but a sword.*

35 *For I have come to set a man against his father,*
  and a daughter against her mother,
  and a daughter-in-law against her mother-in-law;
36 *and one's foes will be members of one's own household.*
37 *Whoever loves father or mother more than me is not worthy of me; and whoever loves son or daughter more than me is not worthy of me;* 38 *and whoever does not take up the cross and follow me is not worthy of me.* 39 *Those who find their life will lose it, and those who lose their life for my sake will find it.*

  40 *"Whoever welcomes you welcomes me, and whoever welcomes me welcomes the one who sent me.* 41 *Whoever welcomes a prophet in the name of a prophet will receive a prophet's reward; and whoever welcomes a righteous person in the name of a righteous person will receive the reward of the righteous;* 42 *and whoever gives even a cup of cold water to one of these little ones in the name of a disciple — truly I tell you, none of these will lose their reward."*

34-42 The utterance concerning the division among one's next of kin (vv. 34-36) stands as a link between the foregoing passage about fearless profession and the next one on following Jesus to the very surrender of one's life. Like the following, this discursive unit stems from the Sayings Source, from which Luke as well cites it, if in a different place. To appropriate effect, the strife among family members is set in opposition to a discipleship that, for Jesus' sake, sets at naught the tie to father or mother, son or daughter (v. 37). Then Matthew uses (vv. 38-39) the logion cited by Mark, after the first prediction of the passion according to the tradition, on taking up one's cross and on losing one's life and finding it — a high point in the instruction on discipleship. Since these utterances apply to all of Jesus' disciples (16:24-25, following Mark 8:34-35), the purview expands to the entire community. This is even more clearly revealed in the succeeding logion, which deals with welcoming preachers and a reward for such support (Matt. 10:40-42). In this way Matthew assigns to his community a share in the task of the envoys, just as, along with the envoys, they have been addressed throughout the missionary discourse.

34-36 As in 5:17, to prevent a misinterpretation of his mission Jesus speaks of the struggle that breaks out in families because of his coming. He is to bring not "peace," but the "sword" (in Luke 12:51, "division"). This sounds like a correction of his message of peace (see 5:9), but it actually stands in a different context of meaning. The gospel has dividing power as well, surrendering none of its acuity "for the sake of dear peace." What Micah 7:6 portrays as a lamentable decline of behavior and morality among the people now appears as an inescapable consequence of the decision for or against the gospel. Verse 36 is added by Matthew according to the Micah citation.

37   Matthew softens the sharper, Semitic logion formula ("hate") to a form more understandable to the reader of Greek. Jesus does not necessarily require that his disciples surrender natural love for their kin, but only when such love stands in the way of discipleship. He does not speak of the wife; this must have been an addition on Luke's part; however, Matthew, too, knows that celibacy for the sake of the Reign of God can come up as a question to the disciples (19:12). Readiness to surrender one's life (Luke) is not yet mentioned by Matthew since he now cites the logion of verse 39, which Luke sets forth elsewhere (Luke 17:33).

38   A twofold tradition has given the logion of taking up one's cross (in Mark and Q) this appropriate place, after the first prediction of Jesus' passion (Mark 9:31 and pars.), to which an early tradition had already attached the utterances of taking up one's cross and surrendering one's life. However, the words concerned with taking up one's cross (Matthew) or carrying one's cross (Luke) are more briefly formulated in Q, without the interpretative addition, ". . . let him deny himself," and without the Lukan "daily" (Luke 9:23). What the cross will have meant on *Jesus'* lips is disputed: a reference to the familiar form of capital punishment, or to the sign, pregnant with meaning, inscribed on the forehead of those loyal to God according to Ezekiel 9:4-6, which had the form of a cross (Hebrew *tau*). The Christian community surely applied it to Jesus' cross, which the disciples who follow him are to take upon themselves.

39   This paradoxically formulated logion, whose wording is changed in Luke 17:33 and is further interpreted in John 12:25 ("keeps it for eternal life"), is an original logion that mightily moved the primitive church and reveals Jesus' understanding of existence and of human beings. The life that people live upon earth is not the whole and true life that they have from God and one day are to fulfill in God. Human existence is invested more deeply (Matt. 6:25) and has always been connected with God, the source of all life. Human beings can destroy physical life, but cannot rob anyone of the true one (10:28). A person who loses earthly life "for Jesus' sake" will find it with God, namely, in a newer, indestructible way. In the Matthean context this becomes a promise to Jesus' messengers: it is the reward hidden away in their hard lot (cf. 19:29).

40-42   A consolation for the hard-pressed preachers is their welcome at the hands of other persons (see 10:10b-11), a strengthening of their assimilation of the thought that they are envoys of Jesus and thereby of God. The positive/negative formulation of the logion in Luke (10:16) seizes upon the Jewish rule of the envoy: those sent are as the sender (cf. John 13:20). Matthew speaks only of welcome (believing and hospitable) and the reward that will fall to the welcomers. "Prophet" and "righteous person" are two different expressions for people of God (1 Kings 17:24; 2 Kings 4:9), and Matthew uses them together elsewhere as well (Matt. 13:17; 23:29). Concretely he is surely thinking of the wandering missionaries (23:34-35). Even the "little ones" are simple disciples of Jesus (see 18:6, 10, 14), as a good deed "to one of these little ones" shows. The word of encouragement for the envoys is a word of summons to the community to treat them well.

Concluding Formula (11:1)

> 11:1 *Now when Jesus had finished instructing his twelve disciples, he went on from there to teach and proclaim his message in their cities.*

1 Now Matthew closes this commissioning speech for the "twelve disciples" with the same concluding formula with which he ended the Sermon on the Mount for the throngs (7:28). Jesus' own "teaching and proclaiming" (4:23; 9:35) goes further; but the outlook on the time to come is open.

CONVERSATIONS AND CONFRONTATIONS (11:2–12:50)

The next passage gathers quite a variety of material, in part from the Sayings Source (John the Baptist, 11:2-19; the cities of Galilee, 11:20-24; the cry of jubilee, 11:25-27; the sign of Jonah, 12:38-42; the logion on relapse, 12:43-45), in part from Mark 2:23–3:35. In addition, we have Matthew's own material on the call of the Savior (11:28-30) and a longer fulfillment citation (Servant of God, 12:17-21). The Matthean composition is inserted between the discourse on the disciples' mission (chap. 10) and the parabolic discourse (chap. 13). Matthew's intent may have been to put his oar in the water where the waxing discussion on Jesus, his person, and his work (cf. Intro., no. 1) was concerned. Christologically, Jesus is represented as the promised Messiah (11:4-6), the comforting Savior (11:28-30), the silent Servant of God (12:18-21), the Son of David (12:23), and the one greater than the prophets and kings (12:41-42). For unbelievers he becomes an obstacle and the source of judgment.

Jesus and John the Baptist (11:2-19)

This tradition unit, adopted from the Sayings Source and extensively consonant with Luke 7:18-35, betrays primitive Christian reflection on the relationship between Jesus and John. It also affords a glimpse of Jesus' appraisal of the Baptist (esp. 11:7-9) as well as of Jesus' own self-understanding, which that early tradition took up and interpreted. The Matthean notion of the Baptist's role

(3:1-3) becomes more clearly recognizable (Elijah; 11:14). The following threads, at first partially divided from one another, can be distinguished in the tradition: (a) the Baptist's inquiry and Jesus' response (Matt. 11:2-6); (b) Jesus' opinion of the Baptist (11:7-11); (c) the Baptist's position in salvation history (11:12-15); (d) the parable of the playing children (11:16-19).

Messengers from John the Baptist (11:2-6)

2 *When John heard in prison what the Messiah was doing, he sent word by his disciples* 3 *and said to him, "Are you the one who is to come, or are we to wait for another?"* 4 *Jesus answered them, "Go and tell John what you hear and see:* 5 *the blind receive their sight, the lame walk, the lepers are cleansed, the deaf hear, the dead are raised, and the poor have good news brought to them.* 6 *And blessed is anyone who takes no offense at me."*

2-3 The Baptist's inquiry, so frequently called into question as a historical fact, is altogether understandable in Matthew's framework since John proclaims the one "who is to come" (see 3:11), but specifies him as the imminent executioner of divine judgment (3:12). That resembles neither Jesus' works (4:23-24) nor the image Matthew paints of his person (12:19-20). A merely pedagogical interpretation of the Baptist's attitude is to be avoided; "doubt" on John's part stands in conflict with John 3:28-30. "What the Messiah was doing," which, alongside the cures, includes preaching to the "poor" (Matt. 11:5), is a discursive formation created from a Christian perspective. The Baptist's arrest, which Mark 1:14 places even before Jesus' appearance on the public scene (but cf. John 3:22-23), is presupposed by Matthew, although he does not relate it until 14:3-4.

4-6 Jesus' reply, the important thing for the community delivering the tradition, lists his works briefly, in terms of texts from Isaiah (29:18-19; 35:5-6; 61:1), as the fulfillment of Israel's ancient hopes for salvation. This appeal of Jesus to the prophecy from Isaiah (cf. also Luke 4:18) is well grounded in Jesus' self-understanding (cf. Matt. 13:16-17). For Jesus, the healings that take place are a sign of the irruption of God's Reign (12:28). The cures enumerated, which, according to chapters 8 and 9, are meant to be taken literally and not metaphorically, mount until they finally reach the raising of the dead (see 9:23-25) and preaching to the poor (see 5:3-6). As a result "hearing" receives the emphasis (11:15; 13:9, 16-17, 43). The beatitude (v. 6) applies to the believer who is not scandalized at the appearance of the unexpected Messiah — a warning cry for the later believer as well (cf. 13:21, 57; 24:10; 26:31).

Jesus Praises John the Baptist (11:7-19)

> 7 *As they went away, Jesus began to speak to the crowds about John: "What did you go out into the wilderness to look at? A reed shaken by the wind? 8 What then did you go out to see? Someone dressed in soft robes? Look, those who wear soft robes are in royal palaces. 9 What then did you go out to see? A prophet? Yes, I tell you, and more than a prophet. 10 This is the one about whom it is written,*
>
>> *'See, I am sending my messenger ahead of you,*
>> *who will prepare your way before you.'*
>
> 11 *Truly I tell you, among those born of women no one has arisen greater than John the Baptist; yet the least in the kingdom of heaven is greater than he. 12 From the days of John the Baptist until now the kingdom of heaven has suffered violence, and the violent take it by force. 13 For all the prophets and the law prophesied until John came; 14 and if you are willing to accept it, he is Elijah who is to come. 15 Let anyone with ears listen!*
>
> 16 *"But to what will I compare this generation? It is like children sitting in the marketplaces and calling to one another,*
>
> 17 *'We played the flute for you, and you did not dance;*
>> *we wailed, and you did not mourn.'*
>
> 18 *For John came neither eating nor drinking, and they say, 'He has a demon'; 19 the Son of Man came eating and drinking, and they say, 'Look, a glutton and a drunkard, a friend of tax collectors and sinners!' Yet wisdom is vindicated by her deeds."*

7-11 Jesus' positive attitude toward John the Baptist, not to be doubted where John's work of baptism in the Jordan is concerned (see 3:13-17), nor indeed for the time of his own public appearance, which notably differed from that of the Baptist's preaching, is attested elsewhere (21:25-32) but here is handed down in striking words. He has acknowledged the immovable preacher of repentance, no "shaken reed" (v. 7; cf. 3:7-10), and clad accordingly in his ascetic garb (v. 8; cf. 3:4). Further, he regards him not only as do the people, as a prophet (14:5; 21:26), but as someone still greater (v. 9). The connecting Scripture citation from Malachi 3:1 is itself a reflection on the part of the transmitting community (cf. Mark 1:2, appearing in Matthew in Matt. 3:3). The promised messenger of God, who in Malachi 4:5 is Elijah, through a change in the pronoun ("before *you*," singular; for *you*, singular) becomes the forerunner of the Messiah, Jesus. The expression "greatest among human beings" (Semitical, "born of women") is not to be written off as inauthentically from Jesus even if in the sequel, the "least in the kingdom of heaven is greater than he [John]" sounds more like a production of the community. But both lines of verse 11 belong together antithetically. What is meant is that, with all of his human greatness, John cannot measure up to anyone belonging to the Reign of God as a disciple of Jesus. The Baptist is not thereby excluded from the coming Reign of God but only relativized in his meaning for salvation history. The "smallest" is not Jesus himself but the one who becomes his disciple (see 10:42). The exclusively Matthean expression reflects Jesus' consciousness of having brought that which is "new" (see 9:16-17).

12-15   Here Matthew inserts the "violence logion," which Luke 16:16 transmits differently. The wording in Q is uncertain, and the original sense vague. Is a threat to God's Reign on the part of violent persons meant, or, metaphorically, an assault by persons of goodwill? The Matthean wording, "the violent take by force," unlike the Lukan, suggests the former. In the context of a subsequent passage, Matthew may have in view the growing enmity toward Jesus; but a positive understanding of the "violent" is also possible against a background of the popular movement set afoot by John and Jesus' assembling of Israel. Matthew's concern here, as the key sentence (v. 13; in Luke the initial sentence) shows, is primarily the role of the Baptist. "All the prophets and the law" is a reference to ancient times with their prior indications of the time of salvation, but which John already opens ("until," exclusively). As a preacher at the initial stage of God's Reign (3:2) and the forerunner of the Messiah (11:10), he himself belongs to the time of salvation. Matthew connects the Baptist more closely with Jesus and the dawn of the time of salvation than does Luke. In verse 14 Matthew interprets him according to the citation in verse 10 as Elijah, whose return is expected (cf. 16:14; 17:10-11). In order to recognize John as Elijah returned, however, one must have the eyes of faith ("if you are willing to accept it"), as is underscored by the call to listen (v. 15).

16-19   This originally independent piece of tradition combines a "parable" or comparison and its application to the Baptist and to Jesus. The complaint of the present generation, raised not only here but frequently (12:39-42, 45; 16:4; 17:17), arises from its aversion to John and Jesus alike, thereby bringing John and Jesus into closer connection, despite their differences in conduct. In the Matthean context (11:20-24) the growing criticism of and aversion to Jesus become clear throughout; but the pericope (parallel to Luke 7:31-35), adopted from Q with respect to Jesus' behavior and applied to John, carries its own weight.

16-17   The similitude of the children playing may presume the following situation: the children at play have invited others to play with them, but can recruit them neither for a wedding game nor for a funeral game. So, afterward, they reproach them. Their audience remains stubborn and unmoved. According to another interpretation, the children sitting in the marketplace become angry that the children at play have stubbornly refused to "dance to their flutes" and have sung no dirges. Verses 18-19 suggest the latter interpretation. A mutual struggle between the children (cf. Luke) is scarcely what is meant.

18-19 The image of dancing and mourning is applied to John and Jesus in the opposite order. John is explained as mad because of his asceticism ("possessed"; cf. John 7:20; 8:48-49; 10:20), while Jesus, the "Son of Man" (see 8:20), is criticized as a glutton and a drunkard (cf. Deut. 21:20). Underlying the reproach are Jesus' meals with "tax collectors and sinners" (see 9:10). The crass expressions used reflect denunciations in leading Jewish circles and are actually traceable to Jesus' days on earth. But over against this stubborn generation, God with his wisdom holds fast, as Jesus' deeds of salvation attest (cf. 11:2). Luke speaks of "children" of wisdom, which is likely more original; after all, he speaks of believing persons in contrast to this evil generation (cf. the "minor," "under age," in 11:25). The wisdom of God is actualized in Jesus (cf. 11:28-30).

Cries of Woe, of Jubilee, and of the Savior (11:20-30)

The complex of these three cries may be a conscious Matthean ordering, to show what varied reactions Jesus' works' provoke but also the constancy of his messianic endeavor as he is again and again disappointed by the unbelief of the cities of Galilee but gladdened by the receptivity of simple persons of a childlike faith, whom he continues to woo with merciful love. The cry of woe and that of jubilee, originally belonging to the missionary address of the Sayings Source (Luke 10:13-15, 21-22), are mutually complementary. Matthew has inserted the call of the Savior, which Luke does not offer, from an unknown source. For Matthew it corresponds in a certain sense to the pronouncement on the Servant of God (12:16-21), after confrontations with opponents. Throughout, and despite all his difficulties in having his message accepted, Jesus keeps faith with his self-understanding and mission.

Woes to Unrepentant Cities (11:20-24)

20 *Then he began to reproach the cities in which most of his deeds of power had been done, because they did not repent.* 21 *"Woe to you, Chorazin! Woe to you, Bethsaida! For if the deeds of power done in you had been done in Tyre and Sidon, they would have repented long ago in sackcloth and ashes.* 22 *But I tell you, on the day of judgment it will be more tolerable for Tyre and Sidon than for you.* 23 *And you, Capernaum,*

will you be exalted to heaven?

No, you will be brought down to Hades.

For if the deeds of power done in you had been done in Sodom, it would have

107

remained until this day. 24 But I tell you that on the day of judgment it will be more tolerable for the land of Sodom than for you."

20-24   Historically speaking, the three named cities were the main centers of Jesus' activity. The fact that, along with Capernaum and Chorazin, otherwise nowhere mentioned, Bethsaida, cited by Matthew only here (cf., however, Mark 6:45; 8:22; John 1:44; 12:21), is addressed suggests the old tradition as a source. The contraposition with Gentile cities, or with the notoriously sinful Sodom, betrays a tendency like that of 8:10-12 (also from Q). Capernaum marks the climax. The stylistic form of the "woe" has its origins in prophetic address.

  20-22   Chorazin, today but a field of rubble with the ruins of a synagogue, lies two miles northwest of Capernaum (Khirbet Kerazeh). Bethsaida ("house of fish") is probably the Bethsaida-Julias repeatedly mentioned by Flavius Josephus, east of the Jordan, near its mouth in Lake Gennesaret. The fishing village where Jesus healed the blind person (Mark 8:22-26) later disappeared, perhaps in silt from the Jordan. The judgment with which Jesus threatens these cities because they "did not repent," that is, did not receive his gospel (see 4:17), is not their historical disappearance but the last judgment. The Phoenician cities of Tyre and Sidon were thought of as typically Gentile or pagan cities (cf. 15:21-28). The comparison with them is meant only to emphasize the guilt of the Galilean cities. The proclamation of the judgment here is not an irrevocable sentence of damnation, but is in the stylistic form of a prophetic threat and warning.

  23-24   As Capernaum has been more graced by Jesus' works, so is it threatened with more profound perdition, in an image (from heaven to Hades) that in Isaiah 14:13-15 proclaims the deepest abasement of the King of Babel for having thrown down a challenge to God. Matthew has introduced the comparison with the sinful city of Sodom only by way of adaptation to verses 21 and 22 (cf. Matt. 10:15). The woe logia bear witness to Jesus' prophetic style of speech, which threatens hard-necked unbelief with the judgment (cf. further 12:41-42). Matthew heightens this in his additions. In other logia of the tradition, however, Jesus keeps the door to conversion open (Luke 13:1-5, 6-9).

Jesus Thanks His Father (11:25-30)

> *25 At that time Jesus said, "I thank you, Father, Lord of heaven and earth, because you have hidden these things from the wise and the intelligent and have revealed them to infants; 26 yes, Father, for such was your gracious will. 27 All things have been handed over to me by my Father; and no one knows the Son except the Father, and no one knows the Father except the Son and anyone to whom the Son chooses to reveal him.*

28 *"Come to me, all you that are weary and are carrying heavy burdens, and I will give you rest. 29 Take my yoke upon you, and learn from me; for I am gentle and humble in heart, and you will find rest for your souls. 30 For my yoke is easy, and my burden is light."*

25-27   The stylistic genre of the first two verses here (vv. 25-26) is that of a prayer of praise and thanksgiving; verse 27 consists of Jesus' self-declaration with respect to his fullness of power and his relation to the Father. However, the two logia are bound together by the concept of revelation and addressed to the receivers of the revelation. The revelation of the Father to "infants" is more fully clarified through Jesus' self-witness. The logion unit reveals a high ("Johannine") Christology, which is remarkable for the Sayings Source. Jesus' self-declaration is grounded in his consciousness of his unique proximity to God the Father and in the fullness of power of which he is the recipient, but it also includes the Easter experience of those who have formulated it.

25-26   Jesus' address to the Father (see 6:9) is expanded in the praise of God, whose genre is so well illustrated by the praise and thanksgiving songs of the Qumran community (the *Hodayot*), where we have the Jewish form of address, "Lord of heaven" (Tob. 7:17). Here is the speech of faith in God's creation, universal dominion, and historical works, as often appears in Jewish prayers, a faith in which Jesus, too, has been reared (cf. 5:35, 45; 6:26). But the pronouncement concerning the revelation to the immature extends into the present, the time of Jesus' work. What is the content of this revelation, which remains unspecified ("these things"; literally, "this")? After all, no concrete situation is named. One thinks of the "secret of the kingdom" (Mark 4:11; cf. Matt. 13:11), of the fullness of power received by Jesus (Matt. 11:27a), of the mystery of his Messiahship, and so on. In any case, it must be something that only believing eyes and ears recognize in Jesus' works (13:16-17): the "infants" are none other than the "little ones" (see 10:42), those whose belief is childlike (18:3, 6), the humble (23:12), who do not insist on their own knowledge and wisdom. The antithesis to the "wise and intelligent" is striking, given the fact that in Judaism it was precisely to them that a higher understanding of revelation was ascribed. But Isaiah 29:14 speaks of God's paradoxical conduct, proclaiming that the wisdom of the wise passes away, and the discernment of the discerning disappears (adopted by Paul in 1 Cor. 1:19). The poor and downtrodden, whom Jesus declares blessed (Matt. 5:3-5), who open themselves to his message, are "infants" as well, in comparison with the "wise" of the time, the scribes, who shut their ears to it. This experience on Jesus' part (and on that of his messengers) forms the background, as the cry of the Savior (vv. 28-30) confirms. Emphatically invoking his "Father," Jesus endorses (v. 26) this salvific plan of God. "Your gracious will" (a Semitic and rabbinic figure) indicates the comprehensive divine decree, which Jesus knows and fulfills (cf. v. 27, "to whom the Son chooses").

27   What his Father has "handed over" to Jesus is comprehensive fullness of power ("All"). The old question whether this is a matter of a transmission of revelation alone or simply of salvific power is, in terms of 28:18, to be decided in favor of the latter alternative. Jesus is no "hand down" of schoolish tradition (as in rabbinism), but the sovereign and absolutely unique transmitter and fulfiller of the divine salvific will. His earthly work shows this in his words and deeds of unlimited might (7:29; 9:6, 8), as does, and to perfection, his post-Easter missionary commission. For Q and its writer, the two are indivisibly connected, probably according to its presentation of the "Son of Man" (see 10:32-33), and Matthew makes this thought his own (10:23; 13:37, 41; etc.). The expression is reminiscent of the transmission of dominion to the "son of man" according to Daniel 7:13-14. But the Son of Man is now the "Son" to be found on earth, who stands in an exclusive relationship with the Father. "The Son" becomes a title for Christ (cf. 24:36), as it does in verse 27b-c, where one could scarcely see the comparison with the relationship of an earthly father to his son. "Knowing the Son" means grasping his position and commission in God's salvific plan, which is hidden from everyone else. "Knowing the Father" means having insight into God's secret salvific plans (P. Hoffmann, *Studien zur Theologie der Logienquelle* [Münster, 1972]). Now the reader understands the revelatory function that falls to the Son alone, as well as the revelation given to "infants" by the Father — through the Son.

28-30   In terms of style, Jesus' invitation here is quite close to that of Sirach 51:23-27 (cf. Sir. 24:19), and even the image of the yoke and the promise of rest are to be found there. But in terms of the content of this double logion, which initiates and lays out his promise of repose (v. 28), with the invitation to take up his yoke in verses 29-30, Jesus speaks not of his divine wisdom but of his teaching and instruction, and indeed in forthright opposition to the scribes, who lay such heavy burdens upon people (23:4). The image of the yoke is taken from the figure of the porter, who laid the heavy wood on his neck and shoulders. In Judaism it was used to convey a willing, gladsome acceptance of the Torah; to cite the "Hear, O Israel" (the *Shema;* cf. Mark 12:29) means "to take the yoke of the rule of heaven upon oneself." But what had been understood by Israel as a gift of God and admonishment for life, the law (cf. Psalm 119), had through the interpretation of the scribes (rabbinism counted 613 commandments) become an oppressive burden (cf. Matthew 23). The invitation to those "who are weary and carrying heavy burdens" is reminiscent of the Beatitudes. What the invitees are to "learn" are not Jesus' gentleness and humility but his admonitions, *because* he is "gentle and humble in heart." He, too, imposes a yoke, but a bearable one. That seems to stand in contradiction with the extreme

110

demands of the Sermon on the Mount; but when we observe the antithesis to rabbinic exposition of the law, we see that the two can go together for a Jewish-Christian community. The later church rightly found the solution to the tension in the love required by Jesus, whose demands are without limit but which exerts no pressure, only freedom and gladness. "Find rest for your souls" means not peace of mind but, using biblical speech (Isa. 28:12; Jer. 6:16), the satisfaction of the salvific longing of the entire human being (cf. 1 Peter 1:9; Heb. 3:11–4:11). Wisdom's invitation is transferred to Jesus.

Confrontations with Opponents (12:1-21)

Now Matthew takes up two pieces of the Markan collections of the material concerned with contention: the plucking of grain on the Sabbath (12:1-8) and the healing of the man with the withered hand (12:9-14), both being conflicts about the Sabbath. Then, after a brief transition, he employs a relatively lengthy fulfillment citation concerning the Servant of God (12:15-21). In this way he consciously places Jesus' healing activity in confrontation with the growing criticism and enmity of opponents. At the same time he interprets Jesus' appearance on the scene in the light of the passage from Isaiah. The same complex of intent is recognizable in the next passage (12:22-50).

Plucking Grain on the Sabbath (12:1-8)

12:1 *At that time Jesus went through the grainfields on the sabbath; his disciples were hungry, and they began to pluck heads of grain and to eat. 2 When the Pharisees saw it, they said to him, "Look, your disciples are doing what is not lawful to do on the sabbath." 3 He said to them, "Have you not read what David did when he and his companions were hungry? 4 He entered the house of God and ate the bread of the Presence, which it was not lawful for him or his companions to eat, but only for the priests. 5 Or have you not read in the law that on the sabbath the priests in the temple break the sabbath and yet are guiltless? 6 I tell you, something greater than the temple is here. 7 But if you had known what this means, 'I desire mercy and not sacrifice,' you would not have condemned the guiltless. 8 For the Son of Man is lord of the sabbath."*

Matthew changes the familiar narrative of Mark 2:23-28 *(q.v.)* as follows: he mentions the disciples' "hunger" and thereby paves the way for the pronouncement on "mercy" (Matt. 12:7). By using the example of David, he avoids mentioning the name of the high priest, which was Ahimelech and not Abiathar

(1 Sam. 21:1-6). Instead, additionally, in Matthew 12:5 he alludes to the instruction in the Torah that the priests should prepare and offer the sacrifice of the lamb even on the Sabbath (Num. 28:9-10) — despite the Sabbath rest. Thus he proceeds from the example of David to an express commandment. Matthew himself adds, "Something greater than the temple is here" (Matt. 12:6), an allusion to Jesus' exalted being (cf. 12:41-42). Then, before adopting the sentence, already present in Mark, "The Son of Man is lord of the sabbath" (Matt. 12:8), he inserts the expression from Hosea, which he has already cited in 9:13, that God desires mercy, not sacrifice (12:7). This construction pictures the evangelist as the scriptural expert at work, profiling Jesus as the perfect observer of the will of God in the Old Covenant (see 5:17-20). Accordingly, he has omitted Mark 2:27. A rejection of Jewish worship across the board cannot be concluded from the passage.

The Man with a Withered Hand (12:9-14)

9 *He left that place and entered their synagogue;* 10 *a man was there with a withered hand, and they asked him, "Is it lawful to cure on the sabbath?" so that they might accuse him.* 11 *He said to them, "Suppose one of you has only one sheep and it falls into a pit on the sabbath; will you not lay hold of it and lift it out?* 12 *How much more valuable is a human being than a sheep! So it is lawful to do good on the sabbath."* 13 *Then he said to the man, "Stretch out your hand." He stretched it out, and it was restored, as sound as the other.* 14 *But the Pharisees went out and conspired against him, how to destroy him.*

9-14 The last Markan controversy to be adopted by Matthew here revolves around a healing on the Sabbath. Matthew molds Mark's scene (*q.v.*) more emphatically as a confrontation with Pharisees in the rabbinic tradition. The Pharisees begin at once with the question as to permissibility (v. 10), while Jesus holds another example up to them (v. 11) and draws the conclusion — contrary to legalistic exposition — that it is permissible "to do good" (v. 12) on the Sabbath. Then, appropriately, Matthew recounts the cure (v. 13) and, as in Mark, the reports on the Pharisees' determination to see to Jesus' death. The mind-set is the same as with the plucking of the ears of grain: Jesus places compassion over a strict construction of the law even if this entails the mortal enmity of the guardians of the law.

As with the healing of the leper (8:3), Matthew omits any mention of Jesus' emotions (Mark 3:5). Drawing a sheep from a pit into which it has fallen on the Sabbath (cf. Luke 14:5) is a piece of classic casuistry, and was disputed in the schools (Billerbeck, *Kommentar zum Neuen Testament,* 1:629-30). Jesus regards the need of the poor man with his single sheep and maintains that help should be allowed even on the Sabbath. He stresses mercy and behaves accordingly with the man with a withered hand. This conceptualization of fulfillment of the law is not only important to the Jewish-Christian community but remains forever normative.

God's Chosen Servant (12:15-21)

15 *When Jesus became aware of this, he departed. Many crowds followed him, and he cured all of them,* 16 *and he ordered them not to make him known.* 17 *This was to fulfill what had been spoken through the prophet Isaiah:*

18 *"Here is my servant, whom I have chosen,*
my beloved, with whom my soul is well pleased.
I will put my Spirit upon him,
and he will proclaim justice to the Gentiles.
19 *He will not wrangle or cry aloud,*
nor will anyone hear his voice in the streets.
20 *He will not break a bruised reed*
or quench a smoldering wick
until he brings justice to victory.
21   *And in his name the Gentiles will hope."*

15-21 Jesus' return and his healing activity among the crowds are endowed by Matthew with a causal connection to the intent of his opponents to see him put to death (v. 15a). Jesus seeks to avoid all sensationalism and open conflict — hence, too, his prohibition against publicizing his cures (v. 16). Matthew abbreviates Mark's lengthy composite report (Mark 3:7-12; see, however, Matt. 4:25) and instead uses a fulfillment quotation to highlight Jesus' behavior. The Servant of God — for Matthew also the "Beloved Son" (see 3:17) — was already interpreted in messianic terms in the Targum (Aramaic translation). The citation from Isaiah 42:1-4, a fresh translation following the Hebrew text (instead of the LXX), is intended to subject the Messiah to a Christian understanding. Hence the accent falls on his quiet, compassionate deeds, as in the case of the "Son of David" (cf. Matt. 9:27; 12:23; 20:30-31). The Old Testament itself personifies, in the Servant of God, "Yahweh's establishment of justice in an astonishing act of grace" (W. Zimmerli), and Matthew reinforces these traits with his sketch of Jesus' activity of healing. Jesus will "not wrangle or cry aloud" (v. 19), and this is his motive for withdrawing from his opponents. "He will not break a bruised reed" and "he will not quench a smoldering wick" are images of Jesus' love for sinners. "Bringing justice to victory" (v. 20c) is reminiscent of the promise to the poor, the mourning, and the powerless, who await their justification and rescue from God. But Matthew also adopts (vv. 18, 21) the perspective of the Gentiles, for whom the Servant of God will be a "light" (Isa. 42:6; 49:6); after all, the peoples of the Gentiles, too, have their hope fulfilled through this Messiah (see 4:15; 8:11; 24:14; 28:19).

Imputation of Complicity with the Devil, Demand for Signs — Jesus' Majesty and His New Family (12:22-50)

Now the attacks of the opponents intensify. Jesus is even accused of being in league with the devil, and unbelief is shown in the demand for an unusual sign. But Jesus refutes the abuse in a lengthy discourse and thus demonstrates his superiority and majesty. He breaks his ties with his own family and looks on his audience as his new family. Put together and developed by Matthew, the passage is a high point in Jesus' confrontation with the people of his time; but it also affords a glimpse of the evangelist's intention for his time and environment. The great composition of 12:22-37, collected and shaped from Mark and the Sayings Source, should be handled as a unit. It is connected to the demand for a sign, and to Jesus' response (12:38-42). A more external link ("this evil generation") in terms of the image of the return of impure spirits comes as a warning against relapsing (12:43-45, from Q). Matthew concludes the entire passage with the visit of Jesus' relatives (which he takes from Mark) and his pronouncement concerning his new family (12:46-50). As in 12:15-21, his positive tone is worthy of note.

Jesus and Beelzebul (12:22-32)

> 22 Then they brought to him a demoniac who was blind and mute; and he cured him, so that the one who had been mute could speak and see. 23 All the crowds were amazed and said, "Can this be the Son of David?" 24 But when the Pharisees heard it, they said, "It is only by Beelzebul, the ruler of the demons, that this fellow casts out the demons." 25 He knew what they were thinking and said to them, "Every kingdom divided against itself is laid waste, and no city or house divided against itself will stand. 26 If Satan casts out Satan, he is divided against himself; how then will his kingdom stand? 27 If I cast out demons by Beelzebul, by whom do your own exorcists cast them out? Therefore they will be your judges. 28 But if it is by the Spirit of God that I cast out demons, then the kingdom of God has come to you. 29 Or how can one enter a strong man's house and plunder his property, without first tying up the strong man? Then indeed the house can be plundered.

30 *Whoever is not with me is against me, and whoever does not gather with me scatters.* 31 *Therefore I tell you, people will be forgiven for every sin and blasphemy, but blasphemy against the Spirit will not be forgiven.* 32 *Whoever speaks a word against the Son of Man will be forgiven, but whoever speaks against the Holy Spirit will not be forgiven, either in this age or in the age to come."*

22-32 The very length of this passage shows the evangelist's interest in this confrontation, which was probably current with Judaism at the time in question. The frequently heard designation "Jesus' defense" fails to do the content full justice: we find important self-declarations here as well, like the words concerning the "strong man" (v. 29) and, especially, the climactic sentence on the bursting in of the Reign of God through Jesus' expulsion of demons (v. 28). An ancillary theme is the unforgivable sin of "blasphemy against the Spirit" (vv. 31-32).

22-24 As a vehicle for Jesus' discourse, Matthew makes use of the healing of a person who is blind, deaf, mute, and thought to be possessed, scarcely a different case from the one in 9:32-34. Even in that instance the people and the Pharisees reacted differently, as they do here. Now the stakes are higher. The sufferer is blind, deaf, and dumb. The crowd, beside itself, wonders whether Jesus is perhaps "the Son of David" (the Messiah). The Pharisees render their allegation more specific: he expels devils through Beelzebul ("lord of the house," originally a designation for a Phoenician god). This is the art of storytelling. Luke, too, records the healing of a possessed deaf mute here (11:14).

25-27 Jesus sees through their wicked thoughts and refutes their malicious suspicions with a clear argument: a principality, a city, or a family divided within itself cannot stand. Beelzebul, here equated with Satan, cannot seek to destroy his own crown. The demons' tie with Satan (see 4:10) comes from Jewish demonology: harmful spirits, especially fomenters of disease, were identified with evil angels. Jesus is accused of having received the power of exorcism from their leader and accused of connections with him. The notions are a product of their time and thus nonessential. But Jesus uses them, and applies them to a positive explanation of his healing power (v. 28). His dispute with the Jewish exorcists (v. 27) is surprising since it theatens his pronouncement (v. 28) in its particularity. Perhaps it comes from the controversy between Jewish Christians and their Jewish opponents.

28 The reason why this statement, which Jesus may well have uttered, is so important is that it brings his preaching of the Reign of God into such intimate relation with his expulsion of demons (cf. Mark 1:39; 6:7, 12-13). Jesus' cures and exorcisms are signs of the actual dawn of the Reign of God. The Greek for "the kingdom of God is come to you" leaves no doubt that a present event is meant — granted, not that the Reign of God is already here to the full but that its forces now pierce the present and are already visible and effective in Jesus' activity. This present condition of the Reign of God, coming from God and available to experience in Jesus' saving deeds, is the special thing about Jesus' *basileia* or Lordship (see 4:17). It becomes clearer as it unfolds in Jesus' parabolic sermon (chap. 13). In Luke 11:20 we read: "If it is by the *finger* of God that I drive out demons," which is certainly the original wording. When Matthew says, ". . . by the *Spirit* of God," he is making an indirect reference to the one "upon whom my Spirit" will rest in the prophecy of the Servant of God (12:18), as well as laying the groundwork for the imputation of "blasphemy against the Spirit" (v. 31).

29-30 The comparison of the breaking of the "mightier one" into the house of the strong man (also Mark 3:27) illustrates Jesus' victory over the lord of the demons. The very fact of such a casual use of a picture in which the paradigm for Jesus commits a criminal act means that Jesus must have used it. The subsequent "doublet" of v. 30 (from Q; cf. Luke 11:23) brings Jesus' claim and demand to forceful, uncompromising expression. "Gather," it is true, well fits his collecting of the people of God, but the sentence as a whole must have been added by way of commentary on the original tradition. Just the opposite formula (in the plural), "Whoever is not against us is for us," is found in Mark 9:40 and Luke 9:50, after the pericope on "exorcists that are strangers," which Matthew passes over. Such general logia are variously applicable. Each of our two strict meanings finds its application in Jesus' conduct: uncompromising insistence where the demands of his mission are concerned, and tolerance toward persons whose faith is accompanied by goodwill (cf. Matt. 10:5-6 with 15:21-28). Doubtless there is profit to be drawn here for the endeavors of ecumenism.

31-32 The unforgivable sin of "blasphemy against the Spirit" enjoys a formal coupling with Jewish thinking. In spite of their tendency to relegate sinners to the interim place of punishment but then to assign them a place in God's future world, or God's acquittal in the last judgment, they still drew up a list of those definitively excluded (Mishnah *Sanhedrin* 10:1-3). An example would be the generation of the great Flood. This explains Matthew's expression here, absent from the other Gospels, "either in this age or in the age to come" (v. 32), which actually only underscores "not be forgiven." Behind the double expression, however, stands not Jewish speculation, but the Christian conceptualization of sins "against the Holy Spirit." Those who ascribe the workings of God's Spirit to the spirit of Satan, insofar and so long as they hold this attitude, exclude themselves from salvation. This is a stubborn refusal of God's forgiveness, offered to all by Jesus Christ (cf. 13:13-15). Jesus' universal message of salvation, which promises all sinners God's forgiveness, is not called into question (see 9:10-13). But a believing acceptance of the gospel — conversion, in other words — is necessary (21:31-32). Difficulties beset the second sentence (v. 32; Luke 12:10), which explains blasphemy against the "Son of Man" as forgivable. Does one who speaks against the "Son of Man" not blaspheme the Holy Spirit as well? But in this distinction it is evidently the earthly, lowly Son of Man who is meant (cf. 8:20; 11:19), whose power in the Spirit is not altogether clear. Those who recognize this power through the expulsion of demons (v. 28) and ascribe the workings of the Holy Spirit to Satan do sin against the Holy Spirit. Another explanation offered is that the time of Jesus' earthly activity is being contrasted with the post-Easter time of the Spirit, so that we would be dealing with utterances of charismatic prophets. The sense in which the sentence is used in Q is less than transparent. At all events, Matthew is using verse 32 only to reinforce verse 31. The later church reckoned six sins against the Holy Spirit — presumption, despair, rejection of known truth, and so on.

A Tree and Its Fruit (12:33-37)

33 *"Either make the tree good, and its fruit good; or make the tree bad, and its fruit bad; for the tree is known by its fruit.* 34 *You brood of vipers! How can you speak good things, when you are evil? For out of the abundance of the heart the mouth speaks.* 35 *The good person brings good things out of a good treasure, and the evil person brings evil things out of an evil treasure.* 36 *I tell you, on the day of judgment you will have to give an account for every careless word you utter;* 37 *for by your words you will be justified, and by your words you will be condemned."*

33-37 Matthew has appended these verses against *evil speech* partly from already used image and utterance material (v. 33; cf. 7:16-20), partly from other material from the Q tradition (vv. 34b-35) and partly from his own imagery (v. 34a) with its cry of outrage, "You brood of vipers!" (see 3:7; 23:33 and the final verses, 36-37). The words are sharply polemical and are addressed to those who speak with evil and blasphemous intent. The "careless" word (v. 36) intensifies the warning: one is accountable even for these. Or is it a scornful word that is meant (cf. Sir. 23:15)? Verse 37 (in the second person singular) sharpens responsibility for all speech. James 3:1-12 is a lengthier disquisition on the might of the tongue, with a wisdom motif. Christians, too, especially teachers in the communities, must be on their guard against a misuse of speech.

The Sign of Jonah (12:38-42)

38 *Then some of the scribes and Pharisees said to him, "Teacher, we wish to see a sign from you."* 39 *But he answered them, "An evil and adulterous*

generation asks for a sign, but no sign will be given to it except the sign of the prophet Jonah. 40 *For just as Jonah was three days and three nights in the belly of the sea monster, so for three days and three nights the Son of Man will be in the heart of the earth.* 41 *The people of Nineveh will rise up at the judgment with this generation and condemn it, because they repented at the proclamation of Jonah, and see, something greater than Jonah is here!* 42 *The queen of the South will rise up at the judgment with this generation and condemn it, because she came from the ends of the earth to listen to the wisdom of Solomon, and see, something greater than Solomon is here!"*

38-42 The demand for an unusual sign, a "sign from heaven" (cf., e.g., Matt. 4:5-6), is handed down in different forms: in Mark 8:11-12 (par. Matt. 16:1, 4) and in the Sayings Source (Luke 11:29; cf. also John 2:18; 6:30). Jesus' answer, however, citing the sign of Jonah, is found only in Q. Jesus has rejected the call for a certifying sign, a call issuing from unbelief, for a magical wonder. For him the cures and deeds of power that he performs are signs of God, but they require believing eyes. (John expressly calls them "signs.") Luke 11:31-32 takes the comparison with the Queen of the South and the inhabitants of Nineveh from the "sign" form of the utterance; Matthew has appended these originally independent words more closely to the "Jonah sign" by changing their order.

38-40 The "evil" (Matt. 17:17) and "adulterous" generation (cf. 11:16) is called "adulterous" here too, certainly metaphorical, in terms of the image of Yahweh's "marriage" with Israel, which the people constantly violated by infidelity (Jer. 3:6-10; Hos. 2:4-7; 4:15; 5:3-4). The "sign of Jonah" is almost certainly not Jonah's preaching unto repentance (Jonah 3), although it is often so interpreted. Rather, it is Jonah's person (genitive of apposition), or, more precisely, his rescue from the belly of the sea monster (Jonah 2), which, according to Jewish exposition, became known to the inhabitants of Nineveh. The point of comparison is rescue from death by God. But in Jesus' mouth it remains a riddle for the audience. According to Luke 11:30, it must refer to the parousia if anything: Jonah's "reappearance" becomes an image for the "reappearance" of the Son of Man (A. Vögtle, *Messias und Gottessohn*, ad loc.). Then it is too late for faith, and this sign is not what the Jews are demanding, but a sign from God in an entirely different sense. Matthean (or that of Jewish-Christian tradition before him) homiletic interpretation has expounded God's redemption according to Jonah 1:17 ("three days and three nights in the belly of the sea monster") in terms of Jesus' resurrection after his sojourn in the realm of the dead ("in the heart of the earth"). The utterance concerning the sign of Jonah is related to Jesus' declaration before the High Council (Matt. 26:64), in which Jesus threatens his judges with his prompt justification at the hands of God and his coming with power.

41-42   These two identically constructed utterances had already been associated with and attached to the sign of Jonah in the Sayings Source (in the same order as in Luke). As to genre, they are akin to the cries of woe over the Galilean cities (11:20-24): the absence of conversion leads to judgment. This time the Queen of Sheba (1 Kings 10:1-13) and Nineveh with its readiness for repentance (Jonah 3:3-10) — both from heathendom — are shaming examples for "this generation" of stubbornly unbelieving Jews. But the two pronouncements still have a positive point: Jesus is more than Solomon, more than the prophet Jonah. Here is a clear sign of the coming time of salvation and its dawning with Jesus (Matt. 16:16) — as well as a call, however, to come to faith in Jesus, whom God has sent. Christologically, the series of Jesus' self-declarations continues (cf. 12:6, "Something greater than the temple is here"). He surpasses the mighty prophet (v. 41) and the wise king: he is the Messiah (v. 23, "David's Son") in a unique sense.

The Return of the Unclean Spirit (12:43-45)

> 43 "When the unclean spirit has gone out of a person, it wanders through waterless regions looking for a resting place, but it finds none. 44 Then it says, 'I will return to my house from which I came.' When it comes, it finds it empty, swept, and put in order. 45 Then it goes and brings along seven other spirits more evil than itself, and they enter and live there; and the last state of that person is worse than the first. So will it be also with this evil generation."

43-45   The stylistic genre of this peculiar "narrative," told in terms of the demonology of the time, is that of a parable. The entire portrayal seeks to warn against a relapse: the point (v. 45a-b) is clear. The Sayings Source appends the graphic portrayal of the return of an unclean spirit, with a throng of demons, into the abandoned "house," now all "swept and put in order," to the dispute over Jesus' expulsion of demons (Luke 11:24-26). Matthew, who has appended other material as well, especially the call for signs, holds it up to "this evil generation" (v. 45c, which he adds), and thereby skillfully dovetails Jesus' reprimand of the scribes and Pharisees (12:38-39). Once more we glimpse the confrontation of his primitive community with Judaism: they would be well advised to be on the watch for worse things to come.

The portrayal, found almost verbatim in Luke and Matthew, corresponds to Jewish attitudes: the wasteland as a favorite stopping-off place for demons (cf. Mark 5:5; Matt. 8:28), the comparison of the possessed to "houses," "seven" as the number of completeness, the evil workings of this multitude. Jesus' exorcisms drive the evil spirit out forever, but here a possible case, not a standard one, is recounted, in order to warn of a relapse. "Relapse is not inevitable, unavoidable, then, but blameworthy" (J. Jeremias, *The Parables of Jesus* [New York, 1972], ad loc.). The portrayals of demons here are tied to a moment in history; the warning is still valid.

The True Kindred of Jesus (12:46-50)

> 46 *While he was still speaking to the crowds, his mother and his brothers were standing outside, wanting to speak to him.* 47 *Someone told him, "Look, your mother and your brothers are standing outside, wanting to speak to you."* 48 *But to the one who had told him this, Jesus replied, "Who is my mother, and who are my brothers?"* 49 *And pointing to his disciples, he said, "Here are my mother and my brothers!* 50 *For whoever does the will of my Father in heaven is my brother and sister and mother."*

46-50   The pericope on the visit of Jesus' nearest kin follows the conversation about Beelzebul even in Mark (Mark 3:31-35), and this in a context suggesting a skeptical attitude on the part of these relatives (cf. Mark 3:20-21). Luke places the pericope (Luke 8:19-21) after the parabolic discourse, apparently on account of the theme of right hearing (cf. Luke 8:18). Matthew suppresses the intent of the relatives to seize Jesus and return him by force (Mark 3:21): he is concerned only with the new "family" that Jesus is gathering around him.

46-47   Now Matthew identifies Jesus' audience once more as the throng of people (last so called in Matt. 12:23), and, following his words against the Pharisees, once more points to willing hearers. The crowd are standing so closely together that Jesus' mother and brothers (whose names are finally given only in 13:55, *q.v.*) cannot reach him, but try to "speak" to him, as the neutral expression has it.

48-50   Jesus distances himself from his relatives according to the flesh (v. 48), thereby paving the way for the words that interest Matthew and his community: Jesus points to his disciples (Mark: those sitting around him) and declares the one who does the will of his Father in heaven (7:21) to be his brother, his sister, and his mother. The list — which includes his sisters, not previously referred to — is that of the new family of God whom Jesus is gathering about himself (cf. 19:29; clearer in Mark 10:30). No disparagement of Jesus' mother is implied; on the contrary, the climactic position in a list is at the end, so that "and mother" here suggests rather Jesus' special appreciation of Mary. Jesus' utterance is of prime importance for the community's self-understanding. The outlook is as positive as it was in 12:15-21!

THE PARABOLIC DISCOURSE (13:1-53)

After Jesus' confrontations with opponents, which already demonstrate a division among Jesus' contemporaries, the parabolic discourse — the third of Jesus' great discourses — posits a basic clarification: Jesus' central preaching about the Reign of God (4:17) is the decisive event that exposes belief and unbelief. The required decision produces a division into those who understand and those who do not, the impenitent (13:10-15). Matthew surely has in view the detachment of the Christian community from Judaism in his time.

The "growth parables" illustrate the dynamic bursting in of God's Reign in Jesus' works: the seed is broadcast and ripens, despite all obstacles, ready to harvest and in final form. The fact that they are recounted by Jesus demonstrates that this God-given event is bound up with his person.

The parabolic sermon is not a "teaching" *concerning* the Reign of God; rather, the Reign of God *itself* becomes a "speech event" — a quantity that makes a demand and that succeeds when accepted by its audience. The expression "to teach" is avoided. Matthew has only "speaking in parables" (13:3, 10, 13, 34), or the "presentation" of a parable (13:24, 31). In Jesus' words the Reign of God, in metaphorical address or "parables," when linked with his saving deeds becomes a real quantity. Now it is living reality, and now its nature can become known. Its inauguration is now, in Jesus' appearance on the scene; but it strains toward its future fulfillment and perfection.

Matthew uses material from Mark (the parable of the sower and its interpretation, and the parable of the mustard seed), Q (the parables of the mustard seed and the leaven), and special sources (the parables of the weeds among the wheat, the treasure and the pearl, and the dragnet), all of which he has taken up, combined and redacted in his own fashion. Part of the application to the community has been from tradition, while part of it has been created by Matthew himself (13:36-43, 49-50). All told, then, we have seven parables of the Reign of God (only in the parable of the sower is the phrase not explicitly used as such). Matthew recounts them not uninterruptedly, however, but with the insertion, after the first parable, of a reflection on speaking in parables (13:10-17), following Mark's example, and especially including an important redactional decision regarding the dividing of the audience in two: the first part of the parabolic discourse is addressed to the crowds (13:1-35, with the interruption for the disciples in 13:10-23); the second part is emphatically intended for the disciples alone (13:36-52). The concluding formula of the address is found in 13:53.

The division of the discourse is extremely helpful when it comes to grasping Matthew's understanding of the discourse as a whole. Speaking in parables before the crowds is a way of using veiled speech, which explains the lack of understanding and belief and includes apologetic accents vis-à-vis Judaism. Before the disciples, who represent the later church, the parables become an un-veiling, revealing discourse, which only believers grasp.

Parabolic Discourse before the People (13:1-35)

The parables gathered here are all "growth parables." They use images from nature (sower, mustard seed), although they associate these images with human conduct (weeds among the wheat, leaven). Through the natural event, in which God's creative might is at work, they demonstrate the God-given event of the dawning Reign that will one day reach its goal, but do so only in "image and likeness." Thus they become a riddle (Heb. *māshāl*) for outsiders (13:11). The parables are presented to the crowds, altogether publicly, on the shore of the lake. They call everyone, the totality of the people of Israel (see 4:23-25), to hearing and understanding (13:9). But according to the Matthean presentation, the representatives of the people show themselves to be already turned off; the people reveal that they are unsure. It is precisely into this situation that the discourse concerning the Reign of God is inserted, although one could have expected it as Jesus' basic message before the Sermon on the Mount. The nature of the "discourse in parables" is confided to the disciples in the intervening passage (13:10-17) and is underscored by the evangelist in the observation with which this part concludes (13:34-35).

The construction betrays the pattern used in Mark 4. Changes worthy of note (other than in wording) are the insertion of the logion of the blessed eyes and ears (Matt. 13:16-17); the omission of the chain of logia of Mark 4:21-25 (but with the adoption of Mark 4:25 in Matt. 13:12); the replacement of the parable of the grain that grows without cultivation (Mark 4:26-29) with the parable of the weeds among the wheat (an intentional alteration; see our explanation); the complement of the parable of the mustard seed with that of the leaven (Matt. 13:33, from Q); and the addition of a fulfillment quotation (13:35).

The Parable of the Sower (13:1-9)

> 13:1 *That same day Jesus went out of the house and sat beside the sea.* 2 *Such great crowds gathered around him that he got into a boat and sat there, while the whole crowd stood on the beach.* 3 *And he told them many things in parables, saying: "Listen! A sower went out to sow.* 4 *And as he sowed, some seeds fell on the path, and the birds came and ate them up.* 5 *Other seeds fell on rocky ground, where they did not have much soil, and they sprang up quickly, since they had no depth of soil.* 6 *But when the sun*

rose, they were scorched; and since they had no root, they withered away.
7 *Other seeds fell among thorns, and the thorns grew up and choked them.*
8 *Other seeds fell on good soil and brought forth grain, some a hundredfold,*
some sixty, some thirty. 9 *Let anyone with ears listen!"*

1-9 Matthew has taken the framework of the parabolic discourse from Mark, but he ties it more closely with what has gone before ("that same day," "house"; cf. 12:46). The "beach" has no symbolic significance (as it does, e.g., in the Sermon on the Mount).

The first parable to be recounted, followed in 13:18-23 by an interpretation formed only in the primitive church, although early, raises some questions: (1) Is it a parable of the Reign of God, or is it meant to describe only the experiences of a "sower," a preacher? But the central message of the Reign of God is presupposed, at least by Matthew (cf. "the word of the kingdom," 13:19). The words of Jesus himself will have borne on the same object when it comes to an efficacious word (cf. Isa. 55:10-11). (2) Is the "sower" Jesus, as the "undaunted" broadcaster of God's word? But the sower is referred to only at the beginning and then fades into the background, while the seed takes center stage. The primitive church's christological interpretation (13:37) has in Jesus no more than a concealed point of departure. Jesus gives precedence to his message of God and God's Reign over his own person but he is nevertheless included in that message as its proclaimer. (3) What would be the right name for the parable? To call it the parable "of the Sower" would miss the main point. Then what about "of the Different Kinds of Soil"? But the enumeration does not come into play when the point is being made (not even for the rich yield), and one must not allow oneself to be influenced by the (secondary) interpretation subsequently made in terms of the various human groups in 13:19-23. "The Broadcast Seed" would be better since, even according to the other parables of growth, the present inconspicuous beginning is contrasted with the coming glory. (4) Are the relationships portrayed to be understood as realistic, taken from the way farming was done at the time (before contour plowing!), or is an unusual experience being related? In terms of soil quality in Galilee (shallow earth above stony soil, abundance of thorns and thistles, downtrodden paths) and farming practices, the portrayal is not impossible, but it is surely only of marginal applicability where daily occurrences are concerned. The "exaggerations" are accents consciously placed by Jesus on his proclamation of the Realm, which emphasizes God's unexpected conduct. (5) Are we to conclude that there were a special situation and intention in Jesus' activity? If what is in view is the present moment, with its difficulties and obstacles, the story does fit into the framework devised by Matthew; but it is impossible to say anything more precise.

The sense of the parable on Jesus' lips, a sense seen in light of such varied interpretations, or held to be no longer ascertainable, could be, in a framework of his proclamation of the Reign, this: the sowing has succeeded. God's powers are at work, and God will reach his goal despite all obstacles. Perhaps Jesus also seeks to meet the objection that nothing of the Reign of God can as yet be observed. The broad portrayal of the "failure" and then of the great yield is also conditioned by the narrator, namely, through the use of triadic style. In the parable, the Reign of God comes into words as God's deed and promise, as a wonderful, God-wrought occurrence. But it also becomes a call to trust the message and let oneself be seized by it. The finale, with its call to hearing (v. 9), seems to have been bound up with the narrative early. The primitive church understood that the parable called for concrete application according to the situation of the times.

A particular Matthean change vis-à-vis Mark is the descending order in the amount of yield: "a hundredfold, or sixty, or thirty" (the reverse of the Markan enumeration). Is Matthew thinking that his community does not always bear full fruit (cf. 21:43) and that God causes *enough* fruit to grow despite any failure?

The Purpose of the Parables (13:10-17)

> 10 *Then the disciples came and asked him, "Why do you speak to them in parables?"* 11 *He answered, "To you it has been given to know the secrets of the kingdom of heaven, but to them it has not been given.* 12 *For to those who have, more will be given, and they will have an abundance; but from those who have nothing, even what they have will be taken away.* 13 *The reason I speak to them in parables is that 'seeing they do not perceive, and hearing they do not listen, nor do they understand.'* 14 *With them indeed is fulfilled the prophecy of Isaiah that says:*
> *'You will indeed listen, but never understand,*
> *   and you will indeed look, but never perceive.*
> 15 *For this people's heart has grown dull,*
> *   and their ears are hard of hearing,*
> *   and they have shut their eyes;*
> *   so that they might not look with their eyes,*
> *   and listen with their ears,*
> * and understand with their heart and turn —*
> *   and I would heal them.'*
> 16 *But blessed are your eyes, for they see, and your ears, for they hear.* 17 *Truly I tell you, many prophets and righteous people longed to see what you see, but did not see it, and to hear what you hear, but did not hear it."*

10-17 Following the Markan line, Matthew interrupts the discourse to the people and has the disciples, who are doubtless thought of as being in the boat with Jesus, ask about the meaning of the discourse in parables. Matthew has conformed the passage to the situation, as well as to his own intent, more closely than has Mark. Larger alterations are the insertion of verse 12, from Mark 4:25; the addition of the literal citation from Isaiah 6:9-10, from the Septuagint, in vv. 14-15; and the appending of the Q logion, which Luke 10:23-24 also has, concerning the blessed eyes and ears. Functionally the change from "in order that" in Mark 4:12 to "the reason is" in Matthew 13:13 is significant. If we consider the perfect tenses of the citation in verse 15, the text created by Matthew may have been more explicitly directed against Jewish unbelief as the community experienced it at the time of the evangelist.

10-11 In Jesus' answer to the disciples' question, the difference in formulation between Mark and Matthew is striking: "To you it has been given to know the secrets of the kingdom of heaven" (worded as in Luke 8:10). Is this only a clarification? Is the plural, "secrets," used only because of the plurality of parables? But the "knowing" refers more acutely to the more profound faith understanding of the community. The fundamental "secret of the kingdom of God" (Mark 4:11) is surely its presence in Jesus' activity. Nevertheless, further insights flow from it that are more emphatically revealed (cf. v. 51, "Have you understood all this?") in the second part of the discourse, the part intended for the community.

12 Here, in the Matthean perspective, this utterance is added, with its wisdom tone, like material found in Judaism (cf. Billerbeck, *Kommentar zum Neuen Testament,* 1:660-62). When taken in isolation, it is extremely easy to misunderstand today (because of our endorsement of capitalism?). But strange as it may sound in the earthly realm, it is intended to denote God's own praxis (note the passive voice). God gives persons who have faith understanding ever deeper insights, while those who close their minds are left in extreme spiritual poverty.

13 Matthew assumes that this lack of understanding of the parables will characterize those who are not disciples, and establishes why the meaning does not dawn on them: they experience the salvific event beginning in Jesus, but close their eyes and ears. They are at fault here, and this is why everything is offered them in mystifying speech. In themselves, parables in Judaism serve for clarification and illustration, and this must have been how it was with Jesus at first. But the primitive church "thought things over," Mark in theological reflection (God's plan and disposition) and Matthew in historical application. The case is similar to those in Acts 28:25-28 and John 12:37-43. The unbelief of the majority of Jews was a puzzle and stumbling block for the primitive church (cf. also Paul in Romans 9–11), which sought to grasp this theologically with a view to God's thoughts.

14-15   The primitive church sought and found the most light shed on God's plans in the Old Testament — here in the prophecy of Isaiah 6:9-10. Mark's indirect citation of this passage is developed by Matthew by the addition of a direct quotation of the prophet's declaration — strikingly, according to the Greek Bible (the LXX), unlike the typical "fulfillment quotations." Many commentators suppose that this quotation, which is used in other ways as well, is a later addition to the evangelist's text; but it can also have been adopted with an eye to the interpretation in Matthew 13:19-23 (cf. "heart," "hear and *learn*"). At all events, it brings the "hardening of this people's heart," which renders all understanding and conversion impossible, even more emphatically to expression. The last part of the quotation ("so that they might not . . .") is also difficult to interpret as envisaging any possibility of conversion, as Jewish scribes expounded it according to the Aramaic text ("let it be, then . . ."). Matthew sees the fulfillment of the prophecy in a hardening of the heart that has already occurred. In Jesus' very appearance on the scene, in his concealing parabolic discourse, a judgment is passed. But it is not said to be a definitive judgment; nor does this painfully mysterious pronouncement (any more than 27:25) give anyone the right to place God's everlasting curse and judgment on the Jewish people.

16-17   Matthew emphatically contrasts the seeing and understanding of Jesus' disciples with the hardening of the Jewish majority (*"your* eyes . . ."). Moreover, he has shifted to the present passage the logion handed down by Luke in another context (Luke 10:23-24) and slightly changed it. From the very outset he calls the disciples' eyes blessed *because* they see, and (going beyond Luke 10:23) their ears *because* they hear. He is concerned with an understanding hearing of the parables. In the two-line saying from tradition (Matt. 13:17), accented by the Amen formula, he writes, instead of the certainly older "prophets and kings," "prophets and righteous people," probably owing to his predilection for the word "just," or "righteous," which he also predicates of the Old Testament people of God (23:35). Jesus' original utterance relates to the time of salvation as fulfilled in his works (cf. 12:41-42); for Matthew it is verified as well in the preaching of God's Reign, when grasped in belief and understanding.

The Parable of the Sower Explained (13:18-23)

18 *"Hear then the parable of the sower.* 19 *When anyone hears the word of the kingdom and does not understand it, the evil one comes and snatches away what is sown in the heart; this is what was sown on the path.* 20 *As for what was sown on rocky ground, this is the one who hears the word and immediately receives it with joy;* 21 *yet such a person has no root, but endures only for a while, and when trouble or persecution arises on account of the word, that person immediately falls away.* 22 *As for what was sown among*

thorns, this is the one who hears the word, but the cares of the world and the lure of wealth choke the word, and it yields nothing. 23 *But as for what was sown on good soil, this is the one who hears the word and understands it, who indeed bears fruit and yields, in one case a hundredfold, in another sixty, and in another thirty."*

18-23 The interpretation of the parable of the sower (as Matthew designates it in v. 18) is an early church application, which shifts the center of gravity of the original kingdom parable. In the figure of the sower, the primitive Christian preachers are now addressed; after all, the fate of the seed is broadly and concretely described in the varied receptions of the "word of the kingdom" by the hearers. Here the preaching mission of the primitive church is presumed, as we see from the expressions customary in instructional address. Everything is tailored to "bearing fruit" (v. 23) in persevering faith and moral conduct, even though the rich harvest of fruit originally meant the arrival of God's Reign. A similar shift from eschatology to parenesis (instruction for those already baptized) is also to be observed in, for instance, the utterance concerning the judicial adversary (see 5:25-26). But since what is in mind here is the future expectation, the parenetic application is not unjustified, although it is abbreviated; still it is applicable to the present out of pastoral concerns. The *Sitz im Leben* need not be especially the preaching to new converts. The whole community is addressed: all have an instructional sermon, preachers have an impact on the fruit to be harvested, and the good are encouraged to persevere in their ways.

18 The emphatic "you" (plural) makes clear that it is the believing community that is being addressed.

19 Matthew omits Mark's "The sower sows the word" (Mark 4:14), since it is a matter of human beings as seed. He at once shifts the focus to "anyone [who] hears the word of the kingdom." The German Ecumenical Translation sets forth the correct relation between word and hearer when it reads that the word (the seed) has fallen "here" (v. 19), or "this is the one who . . ." (vv. 20, 22, 23), on the ground described. The sown word is subject to the reception of its hearers. The first case, portrayed in v. 19, has primary significance inasmuch as "understanding" is the underlying condition (contrast v. 23), and the negative effect is ascribed to the "evil one." But the evil one (the devil) can also work through evil human beings (Matt. 13:28, 38-39).

20-21 The second case, that of the seed sown on stony soil, connects well with the comparison in 13:5-6, and explains the prompt refusal of the hearer in whom the seed is able to strike but shallow roots. These cheerful persons presently bubble with enthusiasm, which, come persecution, promptly subsides. The reference to persecution (already in Mark) is acceptable to Matthew in his community situation (see 5:10).

22   The third case, that of the seed that has fallen among thorns, addresses a widespread concern in the primitive Christian teaching. For earthly cares, being caught up in this world, cf. Luke 21:34 and 1 Corinthians 7:32-34; for the "lure of wealth" ("unrighteous Mammon") cf. Matthew 6:19-21; 1 Timothy 6:9-10, 17; James 1:10-11; 5:1-3. Both warnings are prominent in Jesus' preaching and are taken over in the Matthean Sermon on the Mount (cf. false concerns, 6:25-34; gathering of treasures, 6:19-21; service of Mammon, 6:24).

23   Matthew sees the good soil, with its rich yield of fruit, as presented by the person who hears *and understands* the word — takes it to heart (v. 19) and puts it to work in such a way that it bears fruit in action. We recognize Matthew's thrust toward the deed, toward moral conduct (5:19; 7:21; 13:41; 21:43; etc.). The yield of fruit is once more listed in graded order, as in 13:8.

In the later church, an allegorizing approach to the present material resulted in frequent exaggerations and became arbitrary, especially for the three-level yield of fruit (e.g., Augustine: martyrs, virgins, married). The application in the primitive church, restricted to Jesus' instruction, should not be overstepped.

The Parable of Weeds among the Wheat (13:24-30)

24 *He put before them another parable: "The kingdom of heaven may be compared to someone who sowed good seed in his field; 25 but while everybody was asleep, an enemy came and sowed weeds among the wheat, and then went away. 26 So when the plants came up and bore grain, then the weeds appeared as well. 27 And the slaves of the householder came and said to him, 'Master, did you not sow good seed in your field? Where, then, did these weeds come from?' 28 He answered, 'An enemy has done this.' The slaves said to him, 'Then do you want us to go and gather them?' 29 But he replied, 'No; for in gathering the weeds you would uproot the wheat along with them. 30 Let both of them grow together until the harvest; and at harvest time I will tell the reapers, Collect the weeds first and bind them in bundles to be burned, but gather the wheat into my barn.'"*

24-30   If Matthew offers this parable *instead* of the parable of the seed that grows of itself (Mark 4:26-29), having had to take it from a separate tradition, the reason for his preference must be that it contains a stronger appeal to his audience: Be good seed! The new beginning in v. 24 suggests that, to the mind of Matthew, this parable, like the next two (vv. 31-33), is presented to the people (vv. 31-33), so that "before them" refers to the same audience as it does in Matthew 13:3. The *disciples* are then offered an interpretation, the community being mentioned only in the second part of the address (vv. 36-43).

The parable is applied to the division between good and evil persons at the end of the age. The narrative is quite suggestive of the Palestinian milieu: such cases of the pollution of a planting by enemies may actually have occurred. It affords a glimpse into Jesus' thinking: the good seed is broadcast — all are invited to participate in the Reign of God. Jesus does not restrict the seed to a "holy remnant" (as does the Qumran community), but does take the resistance and power of the evil one realistically. The judgment upon those who do not repent (cf. 11:20-24), and their final separation (24:40-41; 25:32-46), find expression elsewhere in his preaching as well.

24 The introduction to the parable, which does not compare the Reign of God with the sower but only seeks to tell a revealing story about it, is to be found in the same form again in 18:23 and 22:2 (and is related to 25:1), each time in parables from Matthew's own sources.

25-26 The weeds represent darnel, whose sprouts greatly resemble wheat. Only its black spikes distinguish it from the latter.

27-29 The slaves' first question (v. 27) aids in its interpretation; the second (v. 28) is understandable in context — weeds were customarily uprooted — but here it likewise serves the purpose of the parable (v. 30).

30 "Collect the weeds first" is to be explained in the light of the practices of the time. Once the scythe begins to swing, darnel and wheat both fall to the ground, but first the darnel is collected and bundled, to be burned later as fuel. The order of the narrative is the same as that of the interpretation in verses 41-43, although Matthew is eager to warn of the sentence to be pronounced on the wicked at the end of days. As for "weeping and gnashing of teeth," see 8:12; 13:50; 22:13; 24:51; 25:30. The image of the barn has already been used in the preaching of John the Baptist (3:12). The positive outlook is consonant with Jesus' salvation message.

The Parable of the Mustard Seed (13:31-33)

> 31 He put before them another parable: "The kingdom of heaven is like a mustard seed that someone took and sowed in his field; 32 it is the smallest of all the seeds, but when it has grown it is the greatest of shrubs and becomes a tree, so that the birds of the air come and make nests in its branches."
>
> 33 He told them another parable: "The kingdom of heaven is like yeast that a woman took and mixed in with three measures of flour until all of it was leavened."

31-33 These two parables (from Q, soon becoming one double parable, Luke 13:18-21) recount the actions of a man and a woman, with each story setting forth the same thought. The parable of the mustard seed — which Mark, too,

offers (Mark 4:30-32), in another form, without the mention of the sower —
has been synthesized by Matthew from Mark ("the smallest of all the seeds")
and the version in Q. Mark's textual form is more primitive. Secondary traits in
Luke and Matthew are: the mustard *plant* becomes a *tree*, and the birds not only
find a haven in its shadows but actually build their nests in its branches. The intent of the statement, however, lies along the same lines in Matthew as in Q: the
contrast between the invisible beginning and the wonderful end. The connection between the mustard seed and the leaven calls for the same interpretation
of the two parables. Accordingly, the earlier application of the mustard seed to
the intensive, and the leaven to the extensive, growth of God's Reign, popular as
it was, is to be rejected. By no means may the Reign of God be equated with the
church, so that the external development (mission) and internal (spiritual)
penetration of humanity would be indicated. This is also contradicted by historical experience. Is the church today an all-embracing "tree" and leaven for
humanity? Matthew portrays not an organically progressing "development"
but an astounding event for those of his time, pointing to the mysteriously
working powers of God. The relationship, then, has to do with the Reign of
God preached by Jesus — the present bursting in of God's Reign in Jesus' deeds
as a promise and guarantee of the perfected Reign of God. Thereby both parables become sources of encouragement to all who take refuge in God's Rule and
of confounding to those who despise it.

31   The person who sows the mustard seed in his field (Luke: his garden) is reminiscent of the sower of 13:3 and the lord of the manor of 13:24, but
comes in for as little recognition as does the protagonist in the parable of the
sower. Only in the post-Easter church does he become a more explicit symbolic
figure for Jesus.

32   The tiny mustard seed was proverbial in Judaism as well: mustard
plants were also raised as vegetables. Once mature, the plant could become
wooden. With "tree," however, the interpretation strikes a chord with the citation from Daniel 4:10-12 (cf. Ezek. 17:23; 31:6). The citation will have been
grafted on in early interpretation. Originally an image for a universal kingdom
of peoples, the tree in which the birds build their nests becomes a promise to
the early community that the peoples will flock to it (see Matt. 8:11) in Matthew and a promise of the conversion of the Gentiles in Luke (cf. Matt. 28:19).

33   This parable, too, bears a Palestinian coloration. Three *seahs* of flour
(almost ten and a half gallons) constituted a not unusual measure (Gen. 18:6),
but a large one in comparison with the amount of leaven. The fullness of the
leavened mass portrays the great size of the Reign to come.

Conclusion (13:34-35)

> 34 *Jesus told the crowds all these things in parables; without a parable he told them nothing.* 35 *This was to fulfill what had been spoken through the prophet:*
>   *"I will open my mouth to speak in parables;*
>   *I will proclaim what has been hidden from the foundation of the world."*

34-35 Matthew emphatically applies Mark's conclusion of the parabolic discourse (Mark 4:33-34) and uses it as the ending of the speech before the throngs. He also uses a fulfillment quotation to underscore the meaning of such an address, as he does in Matthew 13:13-15: for those who fail to understand it is mystifying, although originally it was meant to reveal God's ways. After all, in the quotation from Psalm 78:2 the psalmist seeks to declare the "secret sayings from of old," the "glorious deeds of the LORD, and his might" (Ps. 78:4). His standing is that of a "prophet," and this has occasioned the inauthentic addition of "Isaiah" in older manuscripts. Jesus' preaching of the Reign of God is grounded in God's work in creation and history.

Parabolic Discourse to the Disciples (13:36-53)

Inspired by Mark 4:34b ("He explained everything in private to his disciples"), in this second part of the parabolic discourse, from which the throng is excluded, Matthew presents first an interpretation of the parable of the weeds for the later community (vv. 36-43), then the parables of the treasure and pearl and of the dragnet (vv. 44-50), and, finally, a redactional conclusion of the address for the disciples (vv. 51-52). Verse 53 is the sign-off for the entire parabolic discourse. The intentional restriction of the audience of the second part to the community of disciples is not to be overlooked and betrays Matthew's concern: community members can and should understand Jesus' words and take them to heart (cf. v. 51). The three new parables, fashioned from a special tradition, certainly were originally intended for the whole people, but with Matthew and his community they gain a different meaning.

Jesus Explains the Parable of the Weeds (13:36-43)

> 36 *Then he left the crowds and went into the house. And his disciples approached him, saying, "Explain to us the parable of the weeds of the field."* 37 *He answered, "The one who sows the good seed is the Son of Man;* 38 *the*

field is the world, and the good seed are the children of the kingdom; the weeds are the children of the evil one, 39 *and the enemy who sowed them is the devil; the harvest is the end of the age, and the reapers are angels.* 40 *Just as the weeds are collected and burned up with fire, so will it be at the end of the age.* 41 *The Son of Man will send his angels, and they will collect out of his kingdom all causes of sin and all evildoers,* 42 *and they will throw them into the furnace of fire, where there will be weeping and gnashing of teeth.* 43 *Then the righteous will shine like the sun in the kingdom of their Father. Let anyone with ears listen!"*

36-43 This passage not only contains unmistakable indications of the primitive Christian kerygma or proclamation, similar to the interpretation of the parable of the sower, but bears the stamp of Matthew, in style and train of thought as well as in other ways. Perhaps the evangelist has himself put the explanation together, as it rather closely follows the pattern of 13:19-23. He could, however, have depended instead on the community's oral tradition. The second half (vv. 40-43) is, in terms of genre, a mini-"apocalypse." A framework consisting of seven allegorical interpretations of individual images provides the vehicle for the apocalyptic depiction that ensues, but that depiction displays additional traits of its own (the Reign of the Son of Man and the Reign of the Father). The community, living as it does between the time of the resurrection and of the return of the Son of Man, ought to apply Jesus' parable, which had been focused on the eschatological event, to its own situation in its own time and draw conclusions appropriate for its conduct (v. 43, "Let anyone with ears listen!"). The present time of God's Reign is presupposed in the parable and its interpretation, but is set forth more trenchantly and in a more differentiated fashion. The eschatological perspective is retained, but without heavy accents on imminent expectation. Verses 37-39 are allegorizing, but such an exposition has its legitimacy for a believing community. It contributes to the latter's concept of its relationship to the world (the power of the evil one) and to its Christian self-understanding (good and evil persons in its own ranks).

36 By "house" Matthew means the house that Jesus has left before his discourse on the lakeshore (13:1), doubtless the house in Capernaum (8:14; 9:10). It is a symbol of the inner realm of the community in contrast to what is "out there" (10:14; 12:46-47).

37 For the identification of the sower as the Son of Man, cf. 9:6; 11:19; 12:8, 32. In a post-Easter focus, the earthly Jesus is himself the "Son of Man" (12:40; 16:13; 17:9, 12, etc.).

38 One is struck by the identification of the field as the "world," but it corresponds to Matthew's universalist view (cf. 5:14; 18:7; 26:13 — here with Mark). The devil thinks he can lord it over "all the kingdoms of the world"

(4:8); however, the Son of Man scatters the good seed throughout that world. The seed, here as in 13:19-23, is persons (not the word of God), and is divided into "children of the kingdom" and "children of the evil one," that is, of the devil. In 8:12 the "heirs of the kingdom" were the invited, but recalcitrant, members of the ancient people of God; here Matthew applies the expression, his own, to the good members of God's new people.

39   The "devil" is Matthew's favorite term for the "evil one" (13:19), the enemy of God (see 4:1-11; 25:41). Similarly, the "end of the age," in Greek, is the "fulfillment of the time of the world," a special Matthean expression (as also in 13:40, 49; 24:3; 28:20). The angels have already played a role in the eschatological event in the primitive Christian tradition (Mark 8:38; 13:27), and Matthew includes them in the image of the harvest, namely, as executors of the judgment (cf. 25:31).

40-42   The apocalyptic depiction assumes traditional traits: the harvest as an image of judgment (see 9:37-38), the sorting out of the wicked, and burning in the fire of judgment; cf. John the Baptist's preaching (see 3:10, 12). As a new element we have the exclusively Matthean discourse on the "kingdom of the Son of Man." Inasmuch as the field where the Son of Man has scattered his seed is the world, this Reign cannot be equated with the church. The church belongs to it, but the Son of Man maintains a comprehensive dominion, even over evil persons, in however concealed a form. Now these are openly eliminated by the angels. With an eye to the community, Matthew includes Christians who constitute stumbling blocks — those who lead others into sin (18:6-7), "evil-doers" (7:23; 24:12). The unworthy in the church are excluded from the perfected Reign of God (22:11-14), especially when they have set at naught the commandment of love (25:31-46). The might of the evil one, which penetrates the church itself and which will actually grow in intensity at the end of the age (24:12), is for Matthew a badge of the present world, a constant admonition to watchfulness (24:42; 25:13; 26:41) and sobriety (24:49-50).

43   That the "just" (10:41; 13:17; 25:37) shine like the sun is an image motif that we find in the Old Testament itself (Judg. 5:31; 2 Sam. 23:3-4; Dan. 12:3), here as in Wis. 3:7 referring to the last judgment. The Reign of the Father (cf. 26:29), the perfected Reign of God, is the goal for which the church on earth longs ("Your kingdom come," Matt. 6:10), but it stands in conjunction with the present "kingdom of the Son of Man," which rushes toward this goal. The Son of Man receives the righteous into the Father's Reign (25:34), thereby accomplishing his mission. The theocentric approach (20:23), which evinces Jesus' subordination to the Father, was maintained by the entire primitive church (cf. Luke 22:29-30; 1 Cor. 15:28).

Three Parables (13:44-50)

> 44 "The kingdom of heaven is like treasure hidden in a field, which some-
> one found and hid; then in his joy he goes and sells all that he has and buys
> that field.
>
> 45 "Again, the kingdom of heaven is like a merchant in search of fine
> pearls; 46 on finding one pearl of great value, he went and sold all that he had
> and bought it.
>
> 47 "Again, the kingdom of heaven is like a net that was thrown into the sea
> and caught fish of every kind; 48 when it was full, they drew it ashore, sat
> down, and put the good into baskets but threw out the bad. 49 So it will be at
> the end of the age. The angels will come out and separate the evil from the
> righteous 50 and throw them into the furnace of fire, where there will be
> weeping and gnashing of teeth."

44-46   The first two parables, which we find only in Matthew, are intimately
related but need not originally have constituted a double parable. The great
treasure and the pearl of surpassingly great worth surely picture the value of the
Reign of God that transcends all else. But where does the emphasis fall? On the
finding of this treasure and the great gladness that the discovery occasions? Or
on the striving to gain the treasure discovered? Both times we hear that the
finder "sells all that he has." The motif of joy over what has been discovered is
found only in the parable of the treasure but is presupposed for the parable of
the pearl as well. A person's gladness over the share he or she has been granted
in the Reign of God echoes in the images of the festival feast or wedding banquet (22:2, 9; 25:10). However, one must also seek the Reign of God (6:33). For
Matthew the two elements coincide. The parable of the treasure in the field illustrates the overwhelming, beatifying experience of finding God's Rule but
also represents one's readiness to surrender all else. The merchant is offered the
once-in-a-lifetime chance to buy an extraordinary pearl. He, too, "finds" it, and
then spares no effort to obtain it. With his eye on the community Matthew is
thinking especially of total commitment to the priceless Reign of God once it
has been recognized.

44   The man who finds the treasure buried in a field, perhaps a pot of
silver coins, is a poor farmhand, to whom the field does not belong. To keep his
discovery secret he "hides" it — buries it once more — and purchases the field
with everything he has. As the owner of the field, he does not behave unlawfully
in taking the treasure as his own. True, he makes no inquiries concerning the
original owner. "There is no reflection upon legality; it is only portrayed how
the average person behaves" (J. Jeremias, *The Parables of Jesus*, ad loc.). Overcome with joy, the man acts impulsively.

45-46   In contrast to the farmhand, here we are dealing with a wholesaler already fully engaged in a search for beautiful pearls. Especially splendid pearls commanded high prices. He too, however, is extremely fortunate to find the precious pearl, and he also gives up everything else to possess it. Both parables may bear on the calling of the disciples: discipleship derives from the grace of God, but it also requires prompt decision and full commitment (cf. 4:18-22; 8:18-22; 19:27-29).

47-50   This parable is often seen as a parallel to that of the weeds. The application (vv. 49-50) does correspond to the interpretation given in 13:41-42. But this application has been added only by Matthew, with his frequent threats in terms of judgment. In Jesus' preaching the accent lay on the "gathering." Jesus used his kingdom kerygma in an attempt to gather in the members of the ancient people of God, but now learns that both good and evil join his movement. He may have used the parable to express a warning that only the good, those who accept and comply with his demands, will attain to the Reign of God (cf. 7:13-14; Luke 13:24). Availing himself of the resemblance to the parable of the weeds, Matthew makes this one, too, a warning for the community. The community, too, harbors unworthy and untested persons (Matt. 22:10, 11-13; 25:41-46). And so he warns: Beware lest you fall into the fires of judgment!

Treasures Old and New (13:51-53)

> 51 *"Have you understood all this?" They answered, "Yes."* 52 *And he said to them, "Therefore every scribe who has been trained for the kingdom of heaven is like the master of a household who brings out of his treasure what is new and what is old."*
>
> 53 *When Jesus had finished these parables, he left that place.*

51-52   The question addressed to the disciples shows Matthew's concern to lead the members of his community to a right understanding and authentic fruitfulness (see 13:23). Here the presentation and application of the parable are important, and for this task the Christian "scribe" now comes into focus as well. He must himself be a teacher instructed about God's Reign, and he must be a disciple of Christ willing and able to turn teaching into action (see 5:19). Here we are afforded a glimpse of the self-concept maintained by the evangelist and other teachers and "catechists" at work in the community (23:10). They are aware of being altogether under obligation to the community under the one true teacher, Christ (23:8), but have the important function of instructing the community through a transmission of Jesus' tradition and Jesus' exposition of the Bible (cf. the fulfillment quotations) in the light of faith in Christ. Such a biblical scholar is compared to a householder who brings forth "what is new and old" from his store. The order is striking: the message of Christ must ever be repeated, applied to each current situation, and maintained in its renewing force (19:16-17), and yet it remains the same salvation proclamation brought by Jesus himself. Other commentators interpret "old" as the ancient "law and prophets," which Jesus came to fulfill (5:17). Emphasis is laid on what has dawned in Jesus and his preaching and must continue to be preached. We are in the presence of a verbal signpost for a right understanding of the transmission of the faith.

53 Here we have a stereotyped "sign-off" for the entire parabolic discourse (cf. 7:28; 11:1; 19:1; 26:1). Any indication of the audience to whom it is addressed is omitted here, by contrast with 7:28 and 11:1, inasmuch as Matthew has distinguished the audiences of the parables (13:2-3, 34-36).

JESUS' FURTHER ACTIVITY, AMID MOUNTING OPPOSITION (13:54–14:36)

After the great parabolic discourse, Matthew presents another account of Jesus' activities, much as he does after the Sermon on the Mount, reporting his wondrous cures (chaps. 8–9) This arrangement corresponds to the procedure invoked in his writings generally. But the very first pericope, on his rejection in Nazareth (13:54-58), brings out a definite emphasis: Jesus' appearance on the scene arouses increasing opposition. The threatening nature of the situation is seen in the behavior of the tetrarch Herod, regional ruler of Galilee, who has John the Baptist beheaded (14:1-12). For Matthew, the Baptist is closely connected with Jesus (see 3:13; 4:12; 11:18-19). His preaching receives no hearing with the leaders of the people (21:25, 32), and his death presages the same fate for Jesus (17:12-13). Hence Jesus withdraws after word of John's death (14:13 — in Matthew only). But the throngs follow him into the desolate region where the great feeding occurs (14:15-21). As in Mark, Jesus' appearance to the disciples on the waters of the lake is appended here (14:22-33). After the crossing, Jesus again encounters a large crowd, in Gennesaret, and heals the sick (14:34-36). Matthew has adopted the entire narrative complex from Mark, but without the framework of the disciples' dispatch and return. With the Christophany on the lake, he favors his community with still more lights of his own. His narrative bent is characterized by an emphasis on Jesus' going ahead with his salvific work despite growing rejection and threat. Many people continue to flock to him, and he has compassion on their need (14:14) and heals their sick (14:36).

The Rejection of Jesus at Nazareth (13:54-58)

> 54 *He came to his hometown and began to teach the people in their synagogue, so that they were astounded and said, "Where did this man get this wisdom and these deeds of power?* 55 *Is not this the carpenter's son? Is not his mother called Mary? And are not his brothers James and Joseph and Simon and Judas?* 56 *And are not all his sisters with us? Where then did this man get all this?"* 57 *And they took offense at him. But Jesus said to them, "Prophets are not without honor except in their own country and in their own house."* 58 *And he did not do many deeds of power there, because of their unbelief.*

54-58 In Mark 6:1-6, Jesus' rejection in Nazareth is recorded by way of intentional contrast with his cures in Mark 5. If Matthew offers the narrative after the parabolic discourse, it is because he seeks to illustrate the division following Jesus' preaching of God's Rule, the hardening of the hearts of unbelievers (13:14-15). Jesus is spurned precisely in his native city — for Matthew a sign of his rejection by his own people, the Jews. His nearer compatriots take offense at him because of his family, and refuse to believe in him although he is so close to them. This dark riddle of Jewish unbelief is unraveled only in light of the lot of a prophet: Israel has persecuted and slain other prophets as well (23:35-37). The "prophet from Nazareth in Galilee" (21:11) is rejected in his native city. The varying presentations of this event in Mark and Matthew on the one hand, and Luke 4:16-30 on the other (a programmatic scene at the inception of Jesus' activity), like the traces of the same in John 4:44 and 6:42, suggest a historical occurrence but without supplying indications as to time.

54 As in other synagogues (4:23), Jesus "teaches" in the synagogue of Nazareth — preaches his messages and expounds the will of God, as the reader knows from the Sermon on the Mount (cf. 5:2; 7:28-29). Along with the "wisdom" contained in his messages, Jesus' miraculous deeds are named, of which the Nazarenes can only have heard (cf. Luke 4:23). Both hurl them to the heights of astonishment, but not the astonishment of faith. The question, "Where did this man get this wisdom and these deeds of power?" must have made them think of God; but they "trip over the ordinary" — Jesus' origin, which is all too familiar to them.

55-56 The enumeration of Jesus' relatives, which Matthew takes from Mark, is intended to elucidate the scandal of Jesus' origin. At the end Matthew repeats, "Where then did this person get all this?" (v. 56, not in Mark). Does Matthew wish to be even more emphatic in calling the attention of his readers, who know of Jesus' origin from the Holy Spirit (1:18-25), to the Nazarenes' lack of understanding? And Matthew's alteration of the Markan version of the question, "Is this not the carpenter?" to "Is this not the carpenter's *son*?" can be explained by the fact that Jesus' townsfolk are ignorant of the mystery of his origin. Matthew has already mentioned Jesus' relatives in 12:46-47; now his mother and brothers are actually named, and his sisters are mentioned — not a few for Matthew since he adds, "all." This list, taken from tradition, presents difficult questions. Are these natural brothers and sisters of Jesus, younger sons and daughters of the marriage of Joseph and Mary? Or are they Joseph's children from a previous marriage, as many of the fathers of the church, and the Eastern Orthodox Church today, hold? Or cousins, a widespread view in Catholic exegesis? Now it is true that in the Semitic languages more distant relatives can be called "brothers"; but in order to clarify the nearer relationships, to ascribe Jesus' "brothers," whose names we are given, to a particular father (Clopas for Simon and Jude) or a particular mother (Mary for James and Joseph; cf. Matt. 27:56 with variants in Mark 15:40), as Blinzler does (*Lexikon für Theologie und Kirche*, 2nd ed. [Freiburg im Breisgau, 1957-65], 2:714-17), is not a very satisfying solution. Even some more recent Catholic exegetes incline toward the prevailing Protestant view that tradition spoke of Jesus' actual brothers and sisters. But is this tradition historically reliable? Probably even Matthew was not better informed on the matter. It would present serious difficulty for the Catholic notion of Mary's perpetual virginity. The question is in need of still further discussion, both hermeneutically and dogmatically.

57 "Taking offense" ("stumbling block"), of which 11:6 already warns, is tripping over the person of Jesus, a disclosure of unbelief. (The German Ecumenical Translation adds, "and rejected him.") For Matthew and his community the word has an extremely harsh sound (cf. 13:21; 18:6; 24:10). Loss of salvation threatens culpable unbelief and the tempting of others to apostasy from the faith (18:7). The words about a prophet not being honored in his country and family ("house") are not on record anywhere as a proverb; they adopt the (Deuteronomical) view of the fate of the prophets in Israel.

58 The observation in Mark 6:5, "He *could* work no deed of power there," is softened by Matthew ("He *did* not do many deeds of power there"), but brings out the reason more strongly: ". . . because of their unbelief." The reference is to healing the sick (Mark), which belongs to the image of the Savior of the people (Matt. 14:35-36; 15:30-31). Jesus steadfastly rejects unbelief, something that demands unusual signs (see 12:38-39). Jesus' healing power presupposes believing trust (9:22).

The Death of John the Baptist (14:1-12)

14:1 *At that time Herod the ruler heard reports about Jesus; 2 and he said to his servants, "This is John the Baptist; he has been raised from the dead, and for this reason these powers are at work in him." 3 For Herod had ar-*

rested John, bound him, and put him in prison on account of Herodias, his brother Philip's wife, 4 because John had been telling him, "It is not lawful for you to have her." 5 Though Herod wanted to put him to death, he feared the crowd, because they regarded him as a prophet. 6 But when Herod's birthday came, the daughter of Herodias danced before the company, and she pleased Herod 7 so much that he promised on oath to grant her whatever she might ask. 8 Prompted by her mother, she said, "Give me the head of John the Baptist here on a platter." 9 The king was grieved, yet out of regard for his oaths and for the guests, he commanded it to be given; 10 he sent and had John beheaded in the prison. 11 The head was brought on a platter and given to the girl, who brought it to her mother. 12 His disciples came and took the body and buried it; then they went and told Jesus.

1-12   Unlike its parallel in Mark, this passage is intended by its author to constitute a single unit. While Mark 6:14-16 also brings forward popular opinions concerning Jesus and, in retrospect, blends in the key idea of the beheading of John the Baptist, Matthew speaks only of Herod's sentence (vv. 1-2), then offers a condensation of the story of the Baptist's execution (vv. 3-11), and has his death reported to Jesus by the disciples (v. 12). Matthew's extended presentation raises a difficulty: Herod's judgment upon Jesus (v. 2) supposes John's death, which is recounted only later, but whose report is not an explanatory retrospective, as it is in Mark. Rather, it is an account focusing on Jesus' activity. According to Matthew, Jesus withdraws to a forsaken locale as he hears of John's death (v. 13). The discrepancy reveals Matthew's intent: after Jesus' rejection in Nazareth, the threat posed by the ruler of Galilee — in close connection with the rejection ("at that time") — is to be presented. Jesus must fear a destiny similar to John's. Matthew writes not out of historical interest but out of dramatic intent: the antagonistic forces of unbelief and worldly might are now out in the open.

1-2   Herod (Antipas), the youngest of the sons of Herod the Great (2:1), to whom, after the latter's death, the government of Galilee and Perea has been entrusted, is introduced here, along with his official title of tetrarch ("ruler of a fourth," used for vassal princes of the Romans). In this story taken from Mark, however, he is popularly referred to as "king" (v. 9). In his mentality and conduct, he passed for a Jew. With his notion that Jesus was John the Baptist risen from the dead, he adopts a view current among the people (cf. Mark 6:14) that makes an impression on him on account of Jesus' wonders, of which he has heard. Judaism held the possibility of a return from the dead, including that of former prophets; and especially, in terms of Malachi 4:5-6, a return of Elijah was expected (see Matt. 16:14; 17:10-11). The thought of a reincarnation of John the Baptist in Jesus, however, corresponds only to popular fancy, and if

Herod expresses it to his courtiers it is because of qualms of conscience over John's beheading. The passage cannot be cited in favor of the currency of a doctrine of reincarnation, nor for a Jewish-Christian belief in the resurrection of the dead in the present world. The resurrection of Jesus, who does not return to an earthly life, was attested by the primitive church as a unique, special occurrence through which God initiated the eschatological awakening of the dead (cf. 27:52-53).

3-11   Matthew's radical abbreviation of Mark's account of how John's execution had come about (cf. Mark 6:14-29) has been much discussed in view of the tangentiality and divergence he demonstrates in comparison with the reports of Flavius Josephus (*Antiquities*, bk. 18, nos. 116-19). The Jewish historiographer fails to mention the banquet, Salome's dance, or Herod's oath. He attributes the Baptist's execution to political motives: Herod feared that the Baptist's prestige might drive the people to an uprising. As a place of execution, he cites the fortress of Machaerus (on the eastern bank of the Dead Sea); the banquet scene would better fit the residence in Tiberias. Thus, historically a great deal remains murky. But a public indictment of Herod's adultery with the wife of his half-brother Philip (not the tetrarch Philip) is altogether plausible on the lips of the uncompromising preacher of repentance. Such marriages were forbidden in Leviticus 18:16; 20:21. Herod's oath would not actually have bound him morally to commit the bloody deed; as the presentation suggests, however, not this, but concern for his own standing, and political calculation, supplied the thrust — an example of misuse of power that Jesus castigates (Matt. 20:25).

12   John's burial at the hands of his disciples (permitted by Herod?) is his justification and vindication by God, as well as, to some extent, a parallel with Jesus' (27:57-60). The report to Jesus, of course, is only a redactional parenthesis by Matthew.

Feeding the Five Thousand (14:13-21)

> 13 Now when Jesus heard this, he withdrew from there in a boat to a deserted place by himself. But when the crowds heard it, they followed him on foot from the towns. 14 When he went ashore, he saw a great crowd; and he had compassion for them and cured their sick. 15 When it was evening, the disciples came to him and said, "This is a deserted place, and the hour is now late; send the crowds away so that they may go into the villages and buy food for themselves." 16 Jesus said to them, "They need not go away; you give them something to eat." 17 They replied, "We have nothing here but five loaves and two fish." 18 And he said, "Bring them here to me." 19 Then he ordered the crowds to sit down on the grass. Taking the five loaves and the two fish, he

looked up to heaven, and blessed and broke the loaves, and gave them to the disciples, and the disciples gave them to the crowds. 20 *And all ate and were filled; and they took up what was left over of the broken pieces, twelve baskets full.* 21 *And those who ate were about five thousand men, besides women and children.*

13-21 The feeding of a great multitude in the wasteland, reported by all four evangelists — by Matthew and Mark in a second report with other details (feeding of the four thousand; see 15:32-39), impressed the primitive church deeply and awakened various kinds of associations: with the people of God in the wilderness (Mark 6:40), with Jesus' last supper and how the blessing and distribution suggested the celebration of the Eucharist, and thus also with the Eucharist itself (but cf. below, on v. 19). The tradition had a special christological interest in Jesus' behavior and actions since it thrust his messianic compassion on the people and his sovereign conduct (strongest in John) front and center. Thus the reports are enriched with many different kinds of motivation, nor are the historical relationships (place, time, circumstances) fully transparent. To be sure, the depiction of a wondrous event is intended; but the long-attested expression "multiplication of the loaves" ought to be avoided. What is narrated does not, genre-wise, fit only the category of a "miracle of distribution," and if it is falsely implied that it does, then, against our modern scientific background, it paints a picture of a suspension of the laws of nature. For biblical thought, it was an extraordinary deed of God's grace, like the provision of manna in the wilderness (cf. John 6:31), which is actually surpassed by Jesus. The New Testament presentation will have been influenced in its form by the prophet Elisha's feeding of a hundred men with twenty loaves of barley (2 Kings 4:42-44): "They shall eat and have some left." Jesus is the bestower of still greater gifts; and yet the receivers, too, have their significance: in this gathering, in which, in addition to thousands of men, Matthew mentions women and children, the ancient people of God come into a new light. The twelve baskets filled up with the leftover pieces of bread recall the twelve disciples (10:1), the representatives of the Israel of the end time (19:28). The image that this great feeding offers may be intended to conjure up a vision of the Christian community bound together with its Lord, by whose gifts it lives.

But to what extent Matthew seeks to bring such symbolic allusions and backgrounds to expression is difficult to say. By comparison with Mark, whose report he abbreviates, he exhibits, if less sweepingly than usual, a striking sobriety here, which, yes, many commentators view as liturgical solemnity. In the context of his presentation, what Matthew is trying to do is to demonstrate Jesus' continued salvific activity despite unbelief (Nazareth) and despite the threat from without (Herod).

13 For the chronological connection with the death of John the Baptist, see above on 14:1-2. The location of the great feeding, shifted only by Luke to Bethsaida, at the mouth of the Jordan on Lake Gennesaret (on account of Mark 8:22, which Luke overlooks?), is disputed. Most scholars hold that the less thickly populated east bank (toward the north) is the place from which Jesus returns to the other side, to Gennesaret (Matt. 14:34), after the nocturnal crossing. Others hold that it is the west bank, thinking of Tabgha ("seven springs"), for example, a little over a mile southwest of Capernaum, where today the lovely "Church of the Multiplication of the Loaves," with its ancient Byzantine mosaics, stands. The New Testament permits no unambiguous localization; the east bank, however, may have the advantage.

14 Jesus' "compassion" is not simply a matter of a person's being touched; it is messianic mercy, as the expression "sheep without a shepherd" evinces (Mark 6:34). Matthew skips it here since he already has it in 9:36. Unlike Mark, Matthew speaks not of Jesus' teaching but of his healing the sick. Healing activity and the distribution of the loaves are equally signs of the mercy of God that radiates in Jesus.

16 The Matthean "They need not go away" doubtless means that Jesus wants to keep with him the people who have gathered. The shepherd cares for his flock.

19 The description of the prayer of blessing, with the breaking of the bread and its distribution to the disciples, corresponds in some ways to Jesus' gestures at the institution of the Eucharist (26:26), up to the "looking up to heaven" (exclusively). True, the main verbs in the feeding are "blessed" and "gave to the disciples," while in the Supper they are "broke" and "said." Jesus' actions can be explained equally well from Jewish table customs. Striking, to be sure, is the fact that Matthew fails to mention the distribution of the fish. Whether he seeks to allude by way of background to the last supper and the celebration of the Eucharist is uncertain. Rather just the reverse, readers ought to be reminded of the feeding of the people by the Supper event. A common table with Jesus is also present in a special way in his institution at the last supper, and points ahead to the last fulfillment in the Reign of God, namely, the drinking of the wine (26:29), which has no parallel in the great feeding.

Jesus Walks on the Water (14:22-33)

22 *Immediately he made the disciples get into the boat and go on ahead to the other side, while he dismissed the crowds.* 23 *And after he had dismissed the crowds, he went up the mountain by himself to pray. When evening came, he was there alone,* 24 *but by this time the boat, battered by the waves, was far from the land, for the wind was against them.* 25 *And early in the*

142

morning he came walking toward them on the sea. 26 *But when the disciples saw him walking on the sea, they were terrified, saying, "It is a ghost!" And they cried out in fear.* 27 *But immediately Jesus spoke to them and said, "Take heart, it is I; do not be afraid."*

28 *Peter answered him, "Lord, if it is you, command me to come to you on the water."* 29 *He said, "Come." So Peter got out of the boat, started walking on the water, and came toward Jesus.* 30 *But when he noticed the strong wind, he became frightened, and beginning to sink, he cried out, "Lord, save me!"* 31 *Jesus immediately reached out his hand and caught him, saying to him, "You of little faith, why did you doubt?"* 32 *When they got into the boat, the wind ceased.* 33 *And those in the boat worshiped him, saying, "Truly you are the Son of God."*

22-33   The genre of the narrative to follow, ordinarily referred to as Jesus' walking on the water, is epiphany — divine appearance, so that "Christophany" would be a better heading. The same genre includes God's appearances to Moses (Exod. 3:1-6; 19:9; 33:18-23), Elijah (1 Kings 19:11-13), and others — prophets (in visions and auditory representations) (see Isaiah 6; Ezek. 1:4-28; etc.). The possibility and reality of a god assuming visible form was widely entertained in antiquity. The Bible, however, because of its belief in God, is extremely reticent when it comes to describing this kind of revelation. In Jesus' baptism (see Matt. 3:17), as in his transfiguration (17:5), God is revealed in the voice from heaven. Of course, the transfiguration ought rather to be designated a Christophany, given the radiance of the divine glory streaming from the person of Jesus there, and the transfiguration is closely related to Jesus' manifestation to the disciples during the night. The best elucidation of these Christophanies, however, is found in the appearances of the Resurrected One, in which persons worthy of such experiences "see" Jesus in his divine mien and might (28:9-10, 17-18). This Easter faith is the vehicle of, and precisely Matthew's model for, Jesus' appearance on the lake, as the conclusion (14:33) shows in a special way.

The Matthean presentation of the Christophany stays very close to Mark 6:45-51a in Matthew 14:22-27, 32, but departs from his interpretation of the attitude of the disciples as recorded in Mark 6:51b-52, and most strikingly. In Mark the disciples are entirely without understanding. Their hearts are hardened. In Matthew they worship Jesus as the Son of God. This, besides the characteristics of the genre of the portrayal at hand, is a further index of the evangelist's creative arrangement, which prohibits him from seeking to reconstitute the nocturnal event on the lake historically. The presentation in John 6:16-21 is again different. In Luke, who omits the passage that runs in Mark from 6:45 to 8:26, the story is not to be found. Solidly rooted in tradition, the account emerges from an experience of the disciples that is not open to verification. Again, as a "Christ story," resting on the disciples' faith in the light of the Easter experience, the Christophany on the lake again has a lofty meaning: after all, in the middle of the account stands the sovereign, encouraging, "Take heart, it is I; do not be afraid" (v. 27), a self-revelation on Jesus' part that is firmly grounded in the person and conduct of the earthly Jesus as well.

In Matthew, and only here, another story about Peter (vv. 28-31) is appended to these words of Jesus. It will have sprung from the Matthean community's oral tradition, although its language betrays the hand of the evangelist. The Matthean community is conscious of its bond (cf. Intro., no. 6) to this chief of Jesus' disciples (see 10:2). In this scene, which illustrates faith and doubt, Peter is a pedagogical paradigm for the community that was probably applied in catechesis. Thus the genre of this piece is to be designated as instructional narrative. Looking at this genre, we see that the scene is not to be confused with (unhistorical) legend.

22-23 Jesus constrains the disciples to push off with the boat, and he withdraws from the people. He seeks silence, in prayer. The "mountain" escapes localization and probably has a symbolic meaning: nearness to God (see 5:1; 15:29; 17:1). No destination is assigned for the disciples' crossing (Mark 6:45, toward Bethsaida; John 6:17, to Capernaum). Eventually they put ashore in Gennesaret (14:34).

24 During the crossing the disciples' boat comes into distress. Motifs present in the "storm on the lake" are, strikingly, besides the "waves" (8:24), the cry, "Lord, save me!" in the scene with Peter and the reproach of Peter's lack of faith (cf. 14:30-31 with 8:25-26). An epiphany genre would be possible even without this datum; but the two are closely tied together in the tradition and give the narrative its special character.

25 Only in the fourth watch of the night (from three to six o'clock in the morning) does Jesus come to the disciples, "walking on the sea." This treading across the waves is not the chief declaration of the passage and ought to be interpreted not in a concrete, realistic way but in the sense of a sign in the framework of a Christophany. In the Old Testament and Judaism (especially at Qumran), the power of water is an image of menace and might (Pss. 18:16; 32:6; 69:2; etc.); but God is their Lord (Ps. 77:19: "Your way was through the sea, your path through the mighty waters"). Mark 6:48 even says that Jesus "intended to pass them by," an allusion to Yahweh's "passing by" Moses (Exod. 33:22) and Elijah (1 Kings 19:11-12). Matthew omits this; but it is not needed in order to show Jesus' divine sovereignty and aid.

26-27 The disciples' bewilderment and outcry correspond exactly to Jesus' response: it is he, and no ghost; they ought to have trust, not fear. But more is hidden beneath the surface of this presentation. The sovereign "It is I" (in the Greek, "I am") is not merely a formula of identification, but divine self-revelation, in the same way that Yahweh so often presents himself in the Old Testament (and even more clearly in the Gospel of John). God's protective nearness is communicated in Jesus' appearance. In Isaiah 43:1-3 God speaks: "Do not fear. . . . For I am the LORD your God, the Holy One of Israel, your Savior." The disciples' rescue is expressed, in narrative form, through Jesus' entering the boat and the cessation of the storm (v. 32). With that the epiphany ends.

28-31 But Matthew first inserts the scene with Peter. Matthew's hand is discernible in the words he applies: "commanded," "the water," "sinking," "little faith," "doubt." To believers Jesus grants a share in his might, to the doubting and "sinking" he reaches out his hand. The community is hereby to be encouraged to an undoubting faith (17:20; 21:21; cf. 28:17) and to strong trust in time of need. After all, the ship with the disciples, as in the storm on the lake (see 8:23-27), is an image of the church to come.

32-33 The reference to the community explains the prostration (worship; see 2:11) and the profession of the disciples in the boat. The full profession, "Truly you are the Son of God," is for Matthew the response the Christophany calls for from the believing community. The disciples' profession attains the same height as Peter's in 16:16, with the sole difference that Peter addresses Jesus as the Messiah as well. Although the confession of Peter in 16:17 is labeled a special revelation of the Father, Matthew apparently senses no tension. Both times he seeks to let the profession to God's Son sound forth, but each time for a different reason: after the Christophany it is an expression of liturgical praise (with worship!); at Caesarea Philippi it is an explanation of the Christian conception of the Messiah.

Jesus Heals the Sick in Gennesaret (14:34-36)

34 *When they had crossed over, they came to land at Gennesaret.* 35 *After the people of that place recognized him, they sent word throughout the region and brought all who were sick to him,* 36 *and begged him that they might touch even the fringe of his cloak; and all who touched it were healed.*

34-36 Matthew brings the narrative passage to a conclusion with a compendious report, following Mark, on healings of the sick. We have already seen compressed reports of Jesus' cures in 4:23-24, 8:16, and 9:35. The one at hand proceeds by degrees: from all the environs the sick are brought and, by merely touching the tassel of his cloak, healed. Still another condensed report, enumerating many kinds of diseases, then follows in 15:29-31. We see how much Jesus' healing activity, in which the prophetic promises were fulfilled (see 11:5), meant to the primitive church (even in Mark).

34 This text sees Gennesaret as a locality. An ancient "Kinneret," from which the lake may have gotten its name, lay on the Tell el-Oreme, in the region of Gennesar, a fertile strip of land southwest of Capernaum. It is possible that a place called Gennesaret existed there, although it is not mentioned elsewhere in the New Testament (or by Josephus). According to variant readings, however, the region of Gennesar may have been meant.

35-36 The transporting of the sick from all over the region indicates Jesus' uninterrupted power of attraction; nor does he withdraw from people. Healings through touch, even the mere touch of his garment, are based on the idea of a communication of power like that of the case of the woman with the hemorrhage (see 9:20-21).

CONFRONTATION WITH JEWISH GOVERNING CIRCLES ON THE OCCASION OF FURTHER ACTIVITY AMONG THE PEOPLE (15:1–16:12)

The division in Israel over Jesus' doctrine and activity intensifies. Jesus conducts a discussion with the Pharisees and scribes on the validity of God's commands and Jewish tradition (15:1-9), along with an instruction by Jesus to the people on "clean" and "unclean" (15:10-20) and a more detailed and explicit explanation for the disciples. Matthew has taken this complex of addresses from Mark 7:1-23, but has reorganized it redactionally for his established ends. Then, like Mark, by way of contrast with the Jewish failure to understand, he tells the story of a Gentile woman with her great faith (15:21-28). Still, such a deed on Jesus' part, reaching out beyond Israel, remains an exception. The subsequent condensed report of healings of the sick (15:29-31) refers once more to an area on or near Lake Gennesaret. Unlike Mark, Matthew avoids giving the impression of a restless wandering into Gentile territory (cf. Mark 7:24–8:26). Thus the "feeding of the four thousand" (Matt. 15:32-39) is to be thought of as being done in a region near Lake Gennesaret. Following Mark, Matthew takes over this tradition, a variant on the feeding of the five thousand (Matt. 14:13-21), in order to present, as in the preceding passage, the uninterrupted thronging of the people to Jesus, and Jesus' compassion to them. But then his opponents step back into the scene, this time Pharisees and Sadducees, with the demand of a sign from heaven (16:1-4). Their resentful ruses and hostility are brought out even more sharply in Jesus' dialogue with his disciples on bread and leaven (16:5-12). With this the passage returns to the opposition between the governing Jewish echelons and Jesus. The groundwork is thus laid for Jesus' question as to who persons hold him to be, and the confession of Peter, in 16:13-20.

The Tradition of the Elders (15:1-20)

15:1 *Then Pharisees and scribes came to Jesus from Jerusalem and said,*
2 *"Why do your disciples break the tradition of the elders? For they do not wash their hands before they eat." 3 He answered them, "And why do you break the commandment of God for the sake of your tradition? 4 For God said, 'Honor your father and your mother,' and, 'Whoever speaks evil of father or mother must surely die.' 5 But you say that whoever tells father or mother, 'Whatever support you might have had from me is given to God,' then that person need not honor the father. 6 So, for the sake of your tradition, you make void the word of God. 7 You hypocrites! Isaiah prophesied rightly about you when he said:*

8 *'This people honors me with their lips,*
   but their hearts are far from me;
9 *in vain do they worship me,*
   teaching human precepts as doctrines.'"

10 *Then he called the crowd to him and said to them, "Listen and understand: 11 it is not what goes into the mouth that defiles a person, but it is what comes out of the mouth that defiles." 12 Then the disciples approached and said to him, "Do you know that the Pharisees took offense when they heard what you said?" 13 He answered, "Every plant that my heavenly Father has not planted will be uprooted. 14 Let them alone; they are blind guides of the blind. And if one blind person guides another, both will fall into a pit." 15 But Peter said to him, "Explain this parable to us." 16 Then he said, "Are you also still without understanding? 17 Do you not see that whatever goes into the mouth enters the stomach, and goes out into the sewer? 18 But what comes out of the mouth proceeds from the heart, and this is what defiles. 19 For out of the heart come evil intentions, murder, adultery, fornication, theft, false witness, slander. 20 These are what defile a person, but to eat with unwashed hands does not defile."*

1-20 Matthew has taken these discourses on the pure and impure from Mark 7:1-23 and reordered them redactionally, giving them a clearer construction. The Pharisees and scribes reproach Jesus for spurning the "tradition of the elders" regarding ritual washing of the hands; Jesus counters at once with the concrete example of the oath of corban, by which teachers of the law would "nullify" a divine commandment (Matt. 15:1-6). Appropriately, the quotation from Isaiah on empty reverence of God (vv. 8-9) follows. In Mark these two pieces are reversed; Matthew has a better order for the concepts, and a sharper confrontation. Matthew divides Jesus' enigmatic pronouncement before the people and the succeeding instruction to the disciples (Mark 7:14-23) more crisply: Jesus' words to the people (vv. 10-11); a conversation with the disciples on the Pharisees' wrong attitude, not open to conversion, a Matthean insertion (vv. 12-14); and a response to Peter's intervention in the form of an explanation of the enigma for the disciples, which reshapes the catalogue of burdens in terms of the Decalogue (vv. 15-20). The new listing directs our gaze more powerfully to the Matthean community.

1-6 Matthew omits Mark's explanation (Mark 7:3-4) of the Jewish prescriptions for purity, with which his community was surely familiar. The "tradition of the elders" refers to the exposition of the "law of Moses from Sinai" by the ancient scribes. This oral tradition was ascribed the same binding force as was the written law. According to Rabbi Akiba (d. ca. A.D. 135), tradition was a "fence" around the Torah ('*Abot* 3:13). Jesus' criticism was important to Matthew. He sets the Decalogue in relief elsewhere as well (cf. Matt. 19:17c; indirectly, 15:19) and emphasizes the internal, ethical observance of the commandments (cf. the antitheses in 5:21-48). The Jewish Christians in his community had perhaps stopped short of the prescriptions of purity (cf. 23:3); but Matthew requires observance of the "weightier matters of the law," justice, compassion, and fidelity (23:23).

Jesus answers the accusing question of the Pharisees and scribes with a counterquestion, as in a rabbinical disputation: "Why do you break the commandment of *God* for the sake of your tradition?" By way of evidence, he names the commandment, esteemed especially highly in Judaism, concerning honor to one's parents; the promise of long life for keeping it (Exod. 20:12) corresponds to the threat of death for its violation ("cursing" one's parents, Lev. 20:9). But when offspring demanded the right to use their patrimony to "dedicate it to God" (the oath of the corban), according to the exposition of the scribes the parents had no claim to it and were simply left in the lurch. This nullifies "the word of God" for the sake of human tradition and, along with the prohibition of divorce (19:3-9), occasions Jesus' most emphatic criticism of Jewish practice of the law. For the sake of service to God, the scribes prevent the service to persons demanded by God. For Jesus, love for God is evinced in love for neighbor (22:34-40).

7-9 And so, fittingly, the quotation from Isaiah 29:13 follows, criticizing liturgical worship, which Matthew takes over (slightly altered) from Mark in the Septuagint version. The passage reproaches human doctrines and statutes. But more than this, fruitless worship accompanied by a refusal to behave morally is branded as lip service. On the contrary, God wants human beings' hearts, their inner selves, their sincerest cast of mind and dedication to deed. This corresponds to other words of Jesus (5:28; 6:21; 12:34) and at the same time paves the way for his instruction of the disciples (15:18-19).

10-11 Jesus addresses words to the whole people that sound like a riddle (*māshāl*), although in Matthew it suggests its own solution: "What goes *into the* *mouth, . . .* what comes *out of the mouth.*" Originally meant more comprehensively and focused more sharply on the antithesis between "inner" and "outer," the expression has the basic meaning of judging people according to their "inner" and "outer" sides. For the biblical understanding of the totality of the human being, there is no separating the two; but the decisive element is the inner one, the heart, from which a person's actions are guided.

12-14 These verses of Matthew (without corresponding material in Mark) betray the current polemics with the Pharisees. The latter regard themselves as God's "plantation," or "planting" (see *Psalms of Solomon* 14:2-3: "The Lord's Paradise, the trees of life therein, are holy. And their planting is firmly rooted forever"). But they are under threat of judgment: they shall be uprooted. John the Baptist makes a similar threat: any tree that fails to bear good fruit will be felled (Matt. 3:10). Matthew takes the appended expression, concerning "blind guides of the blind" (v. 14), from the Sayings Source (cf. Luke 6:39). The reproach of blindness permeates the anti-Pharisaic recital of woes as well (Matt. 23:16 and frequently).

15-20 As in 18:21 and 19:27 (cf. 17:24; 26:40), Peter steps forward as spokesperson for the disciples — Peter the leader and apostolic authority for the Matthean community. Jesus' response, which does not spare the disciples the censure of failure to understand, establishes a more precise correspondence with the enigma of verse 11. Because of the theme of impurity (v. 20), only evil things are named as coming from the heart; in other declarations, the heart appears as the source of good thoughts as well (6:21; 12:34-35; cf. 5:8; 13:19; 22:37). The listing of the evil deeds in terms of the Decalogue is significant (see above). If we add the commandment cited in verse 4, to honor one's parents, all of the commandments of the second tablet are presented, including even the reference to "false witness," absent from Mark. The expression "slander" at the end is doubtless another derogatory utterance against Jesus' opponents, who defame him (12:31, 34, 36).

The Canaanite Woman's Faith (15:21-28)

21 *Jesus left that place and went away to the district of Tyre and Sidon.* 22 *Just then a Canaanite woman from that region came out and started shouting, "Have mercy on me, Lord, Son of David; my daughter is tormented by a demon."* 23 *But he did not answer her at all. And his disciples came and urged him, saying, "Send her away, for she keeps shouting after us."* 24 *He answered, "I was sent only to the lost sheep of the house of Israel."* 25 *But she came and knelt before him, saying, "Lord, help me."* 26 *He answered, "It is not fair to take the children's food and throw it to the dogs."* 27 *She said, "Yes, Lord, yet even the dogs eat the crumbs that fall from their*

masters' table." 28 *Then Jesus answered her, "Woman, great is your faith! Let it be done for you as you wish." And her daughter was healed instantly.*

21-28   This story, taken over fom Mark, is an example of Jesus' generosity and breadth of spirit, as contrasted with the narrow-mindedness of the Pharisaic teachers of the law. Although Jesus is aware that his mission is restricted to Israel (cf. 10:5b-6), he makes an exception for the Gentile Canaanite woman and heals her seriously ill (possessed) daughter. By having her call out to Jesus as "Son of David," Matthew nevertheless brings the Gentile woman into proximity with Jewish tenets (cf. 9:27; 12:23; 20:30-31). He recounts the story considerably differently from Mark, who opens a clearer horizon for the mission to the Gentiles (Mark 7:27: "Let the children be fed *first*"). Matthew's presentation need occasion Jewish Christians no scandal if they understand — as with the centurion of Capernaum — that Jesus does not shut himself off from the great faith that a Gentile man or woman may demonstrate.

21-22   As in 4:12, 12:15, and 14:13, the expression "went away" sounds as if Jesus sought to escape the persecutions of his adversaries; but it may simply be Matthew's style. "Tyre and Sidon" is an Old Testament designation for typically Gentile territory (Isa. 23:1-4; Jer. 25:22; etc.). Just so, Matthew will designate the woman a "Canaanite" (instead of Mark's "Syrophoenician") since he is thinking of Israel's contrast to Canaan. The precise region is not given: ". . . from that region" may refer to the word "woman" or to "came out." In the latter case, Jesus is doubtless thought of as being not so very far to the north. As in Mark 7:24, the encounter takes place in a house, and Jesus, as a Jew, avoids entering a Gentile house (cf. 8:8).

23-24   Matthew has formed these two verses himself. Jesus pays no heed to the woman's loud cries: he makes no response. The approaching disciples could be supporting the woman's plea because she is disturbing them with her cries; Jesus' response in verse 24 would then make more sense. Still Jesus refuses. But only the Greek verb used in Luke 13:12 means "set free from an ailment"; the one used in Matthew means quite simply, "send away." Accordingly, the disciples' request here is difficult to understand as an endorsement of the woman's plea. Jesus' answer can then be understood as a refusal to address the woman (cf. v. 23a). But Jesus' harsh-sounding expression is deliberately inserted by Matthew in order to bring to expression the principle of 10:6: Jesus' mission is restricted to Israel.

25-26   Jesus does give an answer to the woman's insistent plea now, as she falls to her knees. It is a clear rejection, coupled with a graphic comparison. The "children" of the house, who must not be deprived of bread — the grace given by God — refers to the "lost sheep of the house of Israel." "Dogs" in Jewish literature is invective for "Gentiles" (see 7:6), but "whelps" need not be so meant. The expression can simply be being used in the image of the house community since the Jews had house dogs. Then the picture indicates a difference between the children and the dogs, but without the odious connotation.

27-28   In her retort the woman seizes upon the image and turns it to her advantage. Behind the ready wit with which she requests, in any case, the "crumbs" that fall from the table, we recognize the earnestness of her plea: she does recognize Israel's precedence, but she appeals to Jesus' goodness and mercy. Now Jesus no longer refuses, but acknowledges, as with the centurion of Capernaum (8:10), the woman's great faith. This is an instruction for Jewish Christians, but a promise for Gentile Christians as well (cf. 8:11). The image of Jesus as God's merciful servant, in whom even the "Gentiles hope" (12:21), is thereby verified once more.

Jesus Cures Many People (15:29-31)

> 29 *After Jesus had left that place, he passed along the Sea of Galilee, and he went up the mountain, where he sat down.* 30 *Great crowds came to him, bringing with them the lame, the maimed, the blind, the mute, and many others. They put them at his feet, and he cured them,* 31 *so that the crowd was amazed when they saw the mute speaking, the maimed whole, the lame walking, and the blind seeing. And they praised the God of Israel.*

29-31   Soon enough, Jesus returns once more to Lake Gennesaret. Matthew omits the peculiar route (by way of Decapolis) indicated in Mark 7:31. He likewise passes over the healing of a deaf-mute (Mark 7:32-36), perhaps because he has already reported similar cures in 9:32-33 and 12:22, or else because the practice of healing the deaf and dumb (then also the blind person, Mark 8:22-26) appears to him to be inappropriate for Jesus. Instead, he sets forth another condensed report (see 14:35-36), which presents persons with various infirmities. It is the last of such compendia. If these persons then praise "the God of Israel," we may by no means conclude that they are from Gentile territory. Rather, it is precisely Jesus' efficacy among the people of God that is being brought out, through which the prophetic promises are being fulfilled (11:5). This is Matthew's substitute for Mark 7:37, "He [the God of Israel] has done everything well." Israelites as such can also praise him, as the God of the people of the covenant (cf. Isa. 29:23; Pss. 41:13; 72:18; 106:48; Luke 1:68).

Feeding the Four Thousand (15:32-39)

> 32 *Then Jesus called his disciples to him and said, "I have compassion for the crowd, because they have been with me now for three days and have*

nothing to eat; and I do not want to send them away hungry, for they might faint on the way." 33 The disciples said to him, "Where are we to get enough bread in the desert to feed so great a crowd?" 34 Jesus asked them, "How many loaves have you?" They said, "Seven, and a few small fish." 35 Then ordering the crowd to sit down on the ground, 36 he took the seven loaves and the fish; and after giving thanks he broke them and gave them to the disciples, and the disciples gave them to the crowds. 37 And all of them ate and were filled; and they took up the broken pieces left over, seven baskets full. 38 Those who had eaten were four thousand men, besides women and children. 39 After sending away the crowds, he got into the boat and went to the region of Magadan.

32-39 This second feeding, which Matthew takes from Mark 8:1-10, must be regarded as a doublet in the history of the tradition for the same occurrence; otherwise the disciples' protestations would be unexplainable, following their experience of the first feeding; and, of course, the situation is strikingly similar in each recital. The inconsistent numerical data are of no consequence in the narrative style of the time, especially since the divergent presentation indicates the same structure, which corresponds to a miracle of distribution. In Luke the story is absent since he omits the entire passage Mark 6:45–8:26. John, for his part (John 6:1-15), offers only one report of a feeding, which contains traces of both the Markan and Matthean narratives. If Mark and Matthew, in the address regarding the bread and the leaven, make reference to both feedings (Matt. 16:9-10 and par.), this is because of both of the stories previously told, which reinforce Jesus' reproaches. It is not essential, however, to distinguish them as discrete historical occurrences.

Unlike Mark, Matthew attaches his feeding of a multitude directly to the healings of the sick (Matt. 15:29-31). All the less than with Mark, then, can the report be taken as addressed to the Gentiles. As with the healings of the sick, here Jesus is once more delineated as the merciful Savior of the people: before the feeding of the five thousand as well, Matthew spoke of healings of the sick (14:14). There is a new tension here in that Jesus energetically seizes the initiative (15:32). Some features (the smaller numbers, the blessing of the fish as well) could indicate an earlier stage of the tradition; other things, however, such as Jesus' accentuated role, the crowd's longer wait (three days), and the expression used for giving thanks *(eucharistein)*, point rather to a more reflective narrative style, one even more strongly marked in John.

32 Unlike the way in which it is presented in 14:14, Jesus' compassion here is occasioned by the great length of time the people have managed to hold out in the desert place (v. 33) and the danger that they might collapse en route to their homes. Symbolical interpretations, such as of the three days as referring to the practice of fasting, or of divine ministrations after three days (Gen. 40:12-13; Josh. 1:11), are uncertain. Matthew stresses Jesus' intent to send the persons home in good health. He omits Mark's observation, ". . . some of them have come from a great distance"; for Matthew, they are all from the vicinity of the lake (v. 29).

In the preparation for the feeding, Jesus' disciples are included only incidentally. Their question, "Where are we to get enough bread?" is a narrative figure indicating Jesus as the provider (cf. John 6:5-7).

36-38 The blessing of the bread, its distribution to the people by the disciples, the multitude having its fill, and the leftover pieces are all recounted in a manner similar to that of the first feeding. Mark's separate blessing and distribution of the fish are abbreviated by Matthew and absorbed into the treatment of the bread (v. 36). With his "meal of fish," Mark could be implicitly alluding to the Eucharist (cf. John 21:9-13); but this is not Matthew's concern. In listing the participants, again he mentions women and children along with the men. For Matthew the scene is an image of the community that gathers around Jesus and receives his gifts.

39 The destination assigned for the crossing in Mark 8:10 ("Dalmanutha"), as well as in Matthew ("Magadan," according to the best reading), is puzzling. Many scholars hold "Magdala" as the correct solution, as do not a few manuscripts. This locality, whose existence is attested in the New Testament in the person of Mary of Magdala but which is otherwise unmentioned, lay on the west bank, at the place where the lake reaches furthest to the west, and where the plain of Genesar, to the north, begins. This is also consonant with the indication after the first feeding (Gennesaret; see 14:34).

The Demand for a Sign (16:1-4)

16.1 *The Pharisees and Sadducees came, and to test Jesus they asked him to show them a sign from heaven.* 2 *He answered them, "When it is evening, you say, 'It will be fair weather, for the sky is red.'* 3 *And in the morning, 'It will be stormy today, for the sky is red and threatening.' You know how to interpret the appearance of the sky, but you cannot interpret the signs of the times.* 4 *An evil and adulterous generation asks for a sign, but no sign will be given to it except the sign of Jonah." Then he left them and went away.*

1-4 After the picture of the Messiah among the people, distributing more of God's gifts of salvation, Matthew directs his gaze once more toward Jesus' adversaries. These now approach him more demandingly. Jesus rebuffs them (vv. 1-4) but then also warns the disciples about them (vv. 5-12). Matthew ties all of this more closely together than does Mark and, in doing so, achieves a narrative crescendo and climax. He has already reported (12:38-39) a demand for signs in material from the Sayings Source; he keeps that in view, as the formulation, "no sign . . . *except the sign of Jonah*" (v. 4) indicates. But he sharpens the second demand for a sign through certain additional features: the troublesome ones are now Pharisees *and Sadducees,* presenting a united front of otherwise adversarial groups in upper Jewish circles. The Sadducees (namely, the high priests) are the actual promoters of, those responsible for, Jesus' death (cf. 16:21; 20:18; 21:15; and often; then in the trial). They demand "a sign *from heaven,*" and put Jesus *to the test* (as in Mark). Jesus repulses them just as before, upbraiding them as "an evil and adulterous generation" (see 12:39).

Textually uncertain verses 2b-3 speak of "signs of the times" and are a parallel to Luke 12:54-56 (Q). The expression denotes altogether other "signs" than the unusual signs already demanded, namely, the divine signs recognizable in Jesus' activity. The time is one of crisis, of decision, with desirable (rain or fine weather) or undesirable (heat or storm) weather signs. But Luke's context already emphasizes the warning signs. Nor in Matthew, where other weather observations are named, is it otherwise. The choice of different images in the parallel tradition of Matthew and Luke (from Q) is not unusual (compare Matt. 7:9-10 with Luke 11:11-12), but it is striking — perhaps an indication that the Matthean verses are original. The thought itself is clear: what is possible for people to do in the realm of nature ought also to hold for their ability to judge the signs set forth by God in Jesus' activity.

The Yeast of the Pharisees and Sadducees (16:5-12)

> 5 When the disciples reached the other side, they had forgotten to bring any bread. 6 Jesus said to them, "Watch out, and beware of the yeast of the Pharisees and Sadducees." 7 They said to one another, "It is because we have brought no bread." 8 And becoming aware of it, Jesus said, "You of little faith, why are you talking about having no bread? 9 Do you still not perceive? Do you not remember the five loaves for the five thousand, and how many baskets you gathered? 10 Or the seven loaves for the four thousand, and how many baskets you gathered? 11 How could you fail to perceive that I was not speaking about bread? Beware of the yeast of the Pharisees and Sadducees!" 12 Then they understood that he had not told them to beware of the yeast of bread, but of the teaching of the Pharisees and Sadducees.

5-12 In the appended scene with the disciples, Jesus warns of the "yeast" of the Pharisees and Sadducees — a frequent image in Judaism for bad thoughts and "evil urges" (differently in the parable of 13:33). The disciples are caught up in anxiety about earthly bread, and only through their conversation with Jesus are they led to a different understanding. In context, Matthew's concern is to show the dangerous mind-set of the political and social leaders, which threatens Jesus. But in addition he seeks to warn the disciples, and with them the later community, and encourage them once more to faith. The historical level — the increasing danger for Jesus — is connected with the current one — confrontation with unbelieving Judaism — and becomes a teaching for all of Christianity: all weakness of faith is to be overcome by constant watchfulness against the activities of the powers of evil.

Over against Mark's presentations, the following differences are striking. The warning is not against the Pharisees and Herod (Mark 8:15) but against the Pharisees and Sadducees, who form a united front in Matthew 16:1: it is against their "teaching" that the warning is issued (16:12). In Mark the disciples are altogether uncomprehending — their hearts appear stubborn and closed, while in Matthew their faith is characterized as "weak" (v. 8) but they finally understand what Jesus wishes to tell them. The disciples' lack of understanding belongs to Mark's redactional objective (in a context of the "messianic secret"; cf. 6:52). Matthew, on the other hand, seeks to overcome all "little faith" in his community (6:30; 8:26; 14:31), and is concerned with an "understanding" of Jesus' teaching and preaching (see 13:23, 51).

5 Matthew may understand the situation such that Jesus first goes to Magadan/Magdala (15:39) alone (unlike Mark 8:10: "with his disciples"), and that the disciples now follow. But he may also take it for granted that the disciples were present at the demand for a sign, and are represented as landing again only in a figure of narrative style. The situation is nonessential; the important element is the opposition between the disciples and the Pharisees and Sadducees.

9-10 The allusion to the two feedings is not an argument for the historicity of the second feeding (15:32-39) but is merely consonant with the Matthean presentation, which Matthew has in almost the same words as Mark. Jesus seeks to lead the disciples beyond a concern for earthly bread (cf. 6:25-33).

The interpretation of the "yeast" as referring to the "teaching" of the Pharisees and Sadducees may seem surprising since the two Jewish groups were in disagreement on important doctrinal issues (especially with reference to the resurrection of the dead; cf. 22:23-33). But Matthew is not thinking of particular teachings; he is only pointing up a general contest with Jesus' "teaching," which marks and defines the disciples' community as it does Matthew's (7:28-29; 22:16, 33; 28:20). Matthew likewise has his sights set on the later community: whoever would be loyal to Jesus' teaching must reckon with seduction, slander, and persecution (see 5:11).

155

THE CONFESSION OF PETER:
THE CRITICAL POINT FOR THE FAITH-UNDERSTANDING
OF THE COMMUNITY (16:13-20)

Peter's Declaration about Jesus (16:13-20)

> 13 *Now when Jesus came into the district of Caesarea Philippi, he asked his disciples, "Who do people say that the Son of Man is?"* 14 *And they said, "Some say John the Baptist, but others Elijah, and still others Jeremiah or one of the prophets."* 15 *He said to them, "But who do you say that I am?"* 16 *Simon Peter answered, "You are the Messiah, the Son of the living God."* 17 *And Jesus answered him, "Blessed are you, Simon son of Jonah! For flesh and blood has not revealed this to you, but my Father in heaven.* 18 *And I tell you, you are Peter, and on this rock I will build my church, and the gates of Hades will not prevail against it.* 19 *I will give you the keys of the kingdom of heaven, and whatever you bind on earth will be bound in heaven, and whatever you loose on earth will be loosed in heaven."* 20 *Then he sternly ordered the disciples not to tell anyone that he was the Messiah.*

13-20   With the scene at Caesarea Philippi, Matthew concludes the first part of his presentation of the Gospel (see Intro., p. 2). The importance he ascribes to this pericope is shown by the fundamental reorganization he imposes on Mark's presentation here (Mark 8:27-30). Mark's concern is the messianic question; Matthew's, from the very outset, is who the "Son of Man" is (Matt. 16:13) — that is, a true understanding of the person of Jesus in Christian belief. Accordingly, Simon Peter's answer is the full christological profession: "You are the Messiah, the Son of the living God" (v. 16). Jesus solemnly acknowledges this profession as correct by declaring Peter fortunate and blessed for having had this revealed to him by the Father in heaven (v. 17). While the Christ revelation could be regarded as complete at this point, Matthew nonetheless adds a special tradition that contains a promise for the church and that ascribes to Peter a special role (vv. 18-20). A similar connection between Christ and the church is found in the great concluding scene after Easter (28:16-20), this time as authorization, commission, and promise of protection by the Risen One. As far as the community of disciples (the church) is concerned, the promise of 16:18-20 now becomes a commitment for the authority of the Risen One to see to realization: the powers of death shall not overcome the church since its Lord (the "Son of Man"), now come into his power, is with it always, even to the end of the age. True, in the final post-Easter scene Matthew does not repeat Peter's special authorization and the promise made to him, his function as the Rock. But the special words of Peter here, which have had enormous influence in history, and with which, to our day, exegetes (for a historical understanding) and theologians (for the theological and ecclesial consequences) are so intensely involved, ought not cloud our awareness that the promise to Peter is set against the horizon of Easter. This is shown not only by the promise that the church will endure but also by the declaration concerning binding and loosing, with its parallel in Matthew 18:18 and (on Easter day!) John 20:23.

The promise addressed to Peter has ties with Peter's special meaning for the Matthean community (see Intro., p. 8). The tradition of the three statements concerning the building of the church on Peter the Rock, the authority of the keys, and the binding and loosing, which are combined into a single declaration, certainly reaches back to the Matthean community. After all, this important passage is inserted by Matthew right into the scene in which Peter's messianic profession is uttered, and has left traces neither in Luke 9:20 nor in John 6:69. Granted, Luke 22:31-32 and John 21:15-17 essentially register that Peter has Jesus' special assurance and commission, John in connection with an appearance of the Risen One. These testimonials, which may have been tied to the fact of the first appearance of the risen Lord to Peter (cf. 1 Cor. 15:5; Luke 24:34), have a significance for the "question of Peter" that is not to be overlooked. They forbid us to regard the Matthean tradition as altogether isolated special material of the Matthean community. But that community has composed the words addressed to Peter out of its self-concept as a Petrine community and its Easter faith in Christ, and Matthew has inserted them at this suitable place, at the peak of Jesus' earthly activity, in a fitting manner. We shall have to restrict ourselves here to their elucidation against the background indicated, and cannot broach the question of Peter in all of its scope.

13 The specification of place, Caesarea Philippi, is solidly anchored in tradition (Mark). Ancient Paneas (today Bāniyās), standing in honor of Pan, god of shepherds, was dismantled by Philip, one of Herod the Great's sons, and named Caesarea. Lying at the sources of the Jordan, it bore the surname Philippi ("of Philip") to distinguish it from Caesarea on the sea (so also in Josephus). In Matthew Jesus comes only "into the district" (Mark: "to the villages") of Caesarea Philippi, where a Jewish minority still lived at the time of the Jewish War (Josephus, *Life of Moses* 13). Here was the northern frontier of the land settled by the Jews. Jesus' question to his disciples, the only question uttered by Jesus regarding a judgment of his person, makes good sense and enjoys historical credibility, here on the frontier and at this point in the narrative.

Matthew introduces into Mark's simple question the title "Son of Man," which does not occur in Mark before the first prediction of the passion (Mark 8:31). The members of the Matthean community are to take notice of the designation, so meaningful for them (see Intro., no. 7), and know that they themselves are called to respond to the Son of Man, as yet unrecognized in earthly terms (11:19; cf. 8:20) but wielding full authority (9:6; 12:8) and one day to return (10:23; 13:41; 16:27; and frequently). In their name Peter solemnly responds to him in terms of the authentic and adequate profession.

14 The popular opinions cited by the disciples coincide with the ones listed in Mark, except that Matthew adds "Jeremiah." For "John the Baptist," see 14:2; Elijah's return was expected, in terms of Malachi 4:5-6, before the "day of the LORD," that is, before the appearance of the Messiah (cf. Matt. 17:10-13). Why Matthew singles out Jeremiah among the ancient prophets whose return was awaited is a matter of conjecture. Jeremiah was the prophet of downfall, but one who "prays much for the people and the holy city" (2 Macc. 15:14, in a vision of the high priest Onias), who might kindle hope for freedom. After the recital of inadmissible popular opinions, the disciples are pointedly questioned regarding their own belief. "Simon Peter" makes the response. The double appellation anticipates the interpretation of the second element, already cited in the call of the apostles (Matt. 4:18) and their listing (10:2). Otherwise Matthew uses (except in 17:25) exclusively the Greek expression Peter, which has now become Simon's personal name.

The Petrine profession fully expresses the material indicated in the conversation concerning the sonship of David (22:41-45) and only inquired about by the high priest (26:63): Jesus is "the Messiah, the Son of the living God." "Son of God" is Jesus' unique dignity, attested by God himself (see 3:17; 17:5). Jesus claims it for himself in his cry of jubilation (11:27: "the Son"), and the disciples pay it homage after the Christophany on the lake (see 14:33). The Bible speaks of the "living God" in contrast to false gods (2 Kings 19:4, 16; Isa. 37:4, 17; Dan. 6:21; 2 Cor. 6:16; 1 Thess. 1:9), or to express his reality and life-creating power (Hos. 1:10; 2 Cor. 3:3; 1 Tim. 3:15; Heb. 3:12; and often; cf. Matt. 22:32). The expression is a profession of Jesus as the one standing with God in fullness of life, and as the vessel of salvation on the strength of that fullness, surely in virtue of his anticipated resurrection.

The beatitude uttered by Jesus contains, in Aramaic form, Simon's patronymic ("Jonah"), which in John 1:42 and 21:5-17 reads "John." The use of the patronymic was a common form of personal address, and here is a prelude to Jesus' imposition of Simon's new surname. "Flesh and blood" is the Semitic expression for natural humanity, to which God's act of revelation is here emphatically contrasted. The beatitude is the parenthesis that ties Peter's profession to the imposition of the new name and to the promise made to Simon Peter.

18 Just as Jesus bestows a new name to Simon, which cannot be fixed with respect to time (cf. Mark 3:16; John 1:42), he does so to the sons of Zebedee as well (Mark 3:17). In Simon's case, it meant calling him by the Aramaic *Kepha'* (stone, rock), which was adopted by Greek-speaking primitive Christianity in its Greek form, *Kēphas* (as always in Paul, except Gal. 2:7-8), or else actually translated, as *Petros*. True, doubt is sometimes thrown on the giving of a second name by the earthly Jesus, but without very good grounds. It is also the image of the building of Jesus' church on Peter the Rock. The foundation of the church, in this image, is not Peter's faith, or Jesus' messianic dignity, but the person of Peter himself. Abraham, too, the forebear of the ancient people of God, is once called a "rock" (Isa. 51:1-2). The image of a building (or a plantation) as referring to the community occurs repeatedly in the Qumran manuscripts (1QS 8:5-9; 9:6; 11:8; 1QH 6:26; 7:9) In 1QH 6:24-26, a solidly built city, founded on rock, protects from the power of chaos and the "gates of death." This last expression is found in the Old Testament itself (Isa. 38:10; Job 38:17; Wis. 16:13). "The powers of the underworld" (literally, "the gates of Hades") therefore designate, in the passage under our consideration, the annihilating power of death, not, for instance, Satan and his realm. An allusion to the sacred rock in Jerusalem, which in a later Jewish representation was regarded as the rock stopping up the passage to the underworld, is uncertain.

The word *ekklēsia* (the community or church) may be from the Old Testament *qāhāl*, or from another word (such as Qumran's *sodh*, or *'edah*). The *ekklēsia* is God's holy community — although not, as at Qumran, a separatist community, the "sacred remnant" of Israel, but *Jesus'* community, embracing *all* of the "lost sheep of the house of Israel" (see Matt. 10:6; 15:24), an "open" community, that receives everyone who follows Jesus' call. The view to the future ("I will build my church") includes the Gentiles, called after Easter. Once more we note the Easter horizon, although the style of speech and the symbolism indicate a Palestinian Jewish origin. The building of the church announced by Jesus is the sequel to his history — to his earthly activity and specifically his crucifixion and resurrection.

19a A second image brings to expression the fullness of authority given to Peter. The one possessing the "keys" (the bundle of keys) in a house or palace exercises the right and power of the person in charge of the house (cf. Isa. 22:20-22). The reference here is to the Reign of God, into which candidates seek to come (cf. the "entry sayings": Matt. 5:20; 7:13, 21; and often) — not to "heaven" (Peter as doorkeeper of heaven) but to the perfected Reign of God, toward which Christ's disciples are headed. Peter exercises his authority on earth (cf. 16:19b) in harmony with Jesus, who remains the Lord of his church. Polemically, we read, against the scribes and Pharisees, that they lock people out of the Reign of God, themselves failing to enter and hindering those who would (23:13). Keeping to the teaching of Jesus (28:20) and the fulfillment of the "righteousness" demanded by him (see 5:19-20) are therefore presupposed. Peter must urge the community to do this (cf. Luke 22:32; John 21:15-17).

19b A third pronouncement, containing the expression "binding and loosing," shows that we are dealing with a genuine fullness of authority conferred on Peter. "Binding" and "loosing" are technical rabbinical terms for "forbidding" or "declaring permitted," as well as for the imposition or lifting of a ban or excommunication. The "power of the keys" of verse 19a is thereby precisely expressed: through preaching the will of God, a preaching that obliges its hearers and includes a judgment as to the fulfillment or nonfulfillment of that divine will (sacred doctrinal and juridical authority), the authorized agent opens the door to the Reign of God or shuts it off. The Matthean community drew on this for its disciplinary authority (cf. 18:15-17 with 18:18). The authority conferred by God or Jesus comes to expression through the fact that these decisions on earth will be sanctioned by God ("in heaven"). A variation, referring to the forgiveness of sins or the withholding of that forgiveness, is the Risen One's declaration in John 20:23. The order of the words, ending with "loosing," while it is the order used in Jewish tradition, in Matthew may mean an emphasis on that loosing: Jesus came to call sinners, not the righteous (Matt. 9:13).

For the relationship of this fullness of authority conferred on Peter to the plural formulation in 18:18, see that verse. Whether and how the three statements, combined in 16:18-19, were bound together in the (Jewish-Christian) tradition adopted by Matthew is disputed in scholarship. Rarely are they recognized as declarations of the earthly Jesus. But since the messianic question was placed in a historical scene at Caesarea Philippi, the community, and the evangelist with it, could explain the Petrine profession, which at first seems to be an inadequate messianic profession (Mark 8:29-30), in the light of the faith of Easter, as well as bring out Peter's primacy. For Matthew, Peter is the guarantor of the Jesus tradition and the community's authorized teacher.

20 Jesus' prohibition against speaking to anyone of his messianic dignity is taken over from Mark 8:30. Its sense for Matthew as well is the avoidance of a false understanding of the Messiah in the situation of the time. Jesus does see persecution on its way at the hands of the civil and religious leadership, and wishes to offer no false points of attack. He will go to Jerusalem and death, but according to God's plan and disposition (Matt. 16:21). With this announcement of his suffering to come, the material set forth by Matthew in 16:21-23 ("From that time on . . .") opens the second major division of his Gospel.

THE WAY TO JERUSALEM (16:21–20:34)

First Prediction of Jesus' Passion and Resurrection: Instructions for the Disciples (16:21–17:21)

Jesus Foretells His Death and Resurrection (16:21-23)

> 21 *From that time on, Jesus began to show his disciples that he must go to Jerusalem and undergo great suffering at the hands of the elders and chief priests and scribes, and be killed, and on the third day be raised.* 22 *And Peter took him aside and began to rebuke him, saying, "God forbid it, Lord! This must never happen to you." 23 But he turned and said to Peter, "Get behind me, Satan! You are a stumbling block to me; for you are setting your mind not on divine things but on human things."*

21 This prediction of the passion, death, and resurrection of the Son of Man, taken over from tradition, is presented by Matthew as Jesus' revelation to the disciples of an event founded in God's mysterious decree. It is a necessary complement to the profession in 16:16: "You are the Messiah, the Son of the living God." Contrary to all Jewish expectation, the Christian Messiah "must" go the way of suffering and death — according to early interpretation, including Matthew's, "in accordance with the scriptures" (1 Cor. 15:3; cf. Matt. 21:42; 26:54, 56). However, neither this nor the meaning of Jesus' death as an atonement ("for our sins") is as yet expressed in the old formula (for Matthew see 20:28; 26:28). Rather, it is a look to the past, by the believing community, on the route traversed by its Messiah since Easter, as shown in the last expression, "and be raised on the third day."

By contrast with Mark 8:31-33, the following changes are worthy of note. (1) Instead of Jesus "began to teach them," Matthew says that Jesus began to "show," to "demonstrate" (German Ecumenical Translation, "to explain"), to the disciples. Matthew reserves "teaching" for Jesus' public discourses; this is instruction for disciples. (2) Matthew sets in relief Jesus' ascent to Jerusalem, where prophets meet their fate (Matt. 23:37). (3) The prediction of the passion is somewhat abbreviated (omitting "be rejected"), and the proclamation of the resurrection is altered — conformed (as also by Luke 9:22; 13:32) to the more usual primitive Christian form, "raised on the third day" (often in Paul). While there is no material difference between "rise" and "be raised," the latter expression places a stronger accent on the activity of God. Being put to death by human beings stands in contradistinction to being raised by God (so, too, in Acts 3:15; 4:10; 5:30; 10:40). Those responsible for Jesus' passion are, as in Mark, the three groups in the Sanhedrin: the elders, the chief priests, and the scribes, whom Matthew binds more closely together by omitting the repetition of the article.

The announcement of the suffering and resurrection of the Son of Man has, especially in view of the "must" (Gk. *dei*), the character of a prophetic apocalypse (cf. Matt. 17:20; 24:6). It was through Jesus' resurrection that the primitive church became aware of the change of direction that God had willed, the shift from the preaching of God's dominion of grace to this new salvific path of the atoning death, which had brought God's mercy to its goal in another fashion (cf. 26:28), and the church shaped it into the present prediction at an early date. As the primitive church looked back at Jesus' words at the last supper, it was sure that Jesus had recognized this determination on his Father's part, instead of being attached beyond all bounds to the proclamation of the Reign of God (cf. 26:29). That gave it the right to place the announcement of the passion and resurrection at the beginning of Jesus' route to death, although the disciples were unable to digest it at that particular moment.

22-23   Peter attempts to dissuade Jesus from the thought of the passion, even more trenchantly than in Mark, that is, in direct address (v. 22b). "God forbid" is a free rendering of the variously interpreted Greek turn of phrase, certainly correct in sense. Despite having been favored with a revelation of Jesus' divine Sonship (16:17), Peter is a human being and remains the prisoner of human thoughts. Jesus rebuffs him sharply: Peter has become a tempter, as Satan once was in the wilderness (4:10: "Away with you, Satan!") — indeed, a stumbling block, perhaps a conscious paradox recalling Peter's having had conferred upon him the function of being a rock for the church (16:18). Nor is this the only instance of Peter's appearing, precisely in Matthew, in this contrast between divine summons and human weakness (cf. 14:28-31). Thus he becomes the prototype of the disciple suspended between the two poles of believing obedience and overestimation of self, and an admonitory notice to the community not to swerve from the path God has shown it.

The Cross and Self-Denial (16:24-28)

> 24 *Then Jesus told his disciples, "If any want to become my followers, let them deny themselves and take up their cross and follow me. 25 For those who want to save their life will lose it, and those who lose their life for my sake will find it. 26 For what will it profit them if they gain the whole world but forfeit their life? Or what will they give in return for their life?*
>
> 27 *"For the Son of Man is to come with his angels in the glory of his Father, and then he will repay everyone for what has been done. 28 Truly I tell you, there are some standing here who will not taste death before they see the Son of Man coming in his kingdom."*

24-25 The logia on taking up the cross and finding or losing one's life have already been introduced by Matthew, according to the Q tradition, in 10:38-39 — there in a context of the persecution that preachers will have to expect. Here the same words are addressed once more to the disciples according to the Markan tradition, repeating Mark 8:34-35 almost verbatim. Here, however, they are not relevant to Jesus' mission commandment (Matt. 10:5; 11:1) but are addressed to Jesus' disciples as such — that is, to the entire community of disciples. The addressees in Mark 8:34 ("the crowd with his disciples") and Luke 9:23 ("to all") clarify the horizon: for Matthew Jesus' disciples also represent the entire later community of faith. All Christians must follow their Lord on the way of the cross (for an explanation, see Matt. 10:38). What this means is further interpreted in this text by "let them deny themselves." The cross to be taken up by the disciple (Luke 9:23: "daily"), which indicates suffering and death, presupposes total self-sacrifice for the sake of belonging wholly to Christ. Renunciation of the world, of earthly goods, honor, and power, may be included; but the decisive thing is the rejection of one's own ego in order to be totally dedicated to God (as was the crucified Jesus). The words added as a basis for such renunciation, on saving and losing one's life (Matt. 16:25), promise those who lose their lives for Jesus' sake "finding" (Matthew's word, just as in 10:39) life with God.

26 The saying on gaining the world and suffering the loss of life, originally a distinct logion warning against striving for possessions and once again connected with what has preceded by the use of the conjunction "for," has precisely the same meaning. This wisdom saying, which employs an image from the life of a laborer (earning and loss of earning), means more than the insight that, at death, the human being must leave possessions and wealth behind; against the background of the passive turn of phrase ("lose") stands God, the one who requires the giving of an account (cf. Luke 12:20), the judge of the useless life of such persons; at bottom, they judge and nullify themselves. The logion is influenced by Psalm 49, in which those who boast of their riches are answered with: "Truly, no ransom avails for one's life; . . . the ransom of life is costly, and can never suffice" (Ps. 49:7-8). "Like sheep they are appointed for Sheol; Death shall be their shepherd. . . . But God will ransom my soul from the power of Sheol, for he will receive me" (Ps. 49:14-15). A failed life presents itself before the judgment seat of God as futile and useless (cf. Matt. 10:28); a life bound up with God, by contrast, finds its fulfillment.

27-28 The threatening words concerning the Son of Man as the one who punishes, recorded in Mark 8:38b, are omitted by Matthew since he has already presented them, according to the Q tradition, in 10:33; but he is more explicit concerning the coming of the Son of Man in the exaltation of his majesty, in that he appends a quotation from Scripture (Ps. 62:12). Each human being's requital according to his or her deeds — a thought solidly rooted in belief in Yahweh (cf. even Paul, Rom. 2:6) — is now applied to the evil *and* the good. Along with the series of logia for those who take up their cross, Matthew's concern is also with the reward of Jesus' true disciples (cf. 13:43; 25:46). The logion in this respect (v. 28), unlike the one in Mark 9:1, seems to confirm this. The prophecy here adopted, that "some standing here" will not taste death (an Old Testament idiom) until they see the Son of Man coming "in his kingdom" (Mark: "with power"), is explained in Mark in terms of an urgent expectation on the part of the community, which in Matthew is no longer so palpable (despite 10:23). Logia of this type, stressing the imminence of the parousia, have indeed been included by Matthew in his Gospel (again in 24:34), but only to give encouragement, admonition, and comfort. The coming of the Son of Man in *his* glory belongs to the Matthean idiom (13:41) and to Matthew's own representation of the glorious appearance of the Son of Man (19:28; 25:31). Verse 28 is indeed part of the series of sayings in 16:24-28, but it also forms a transition to the pericope of the transfiguration, which brings Jesus' eschatological appearance in glory before the eyes of certain fortunate disciples by anticipation.

The account of Jesus' transfiguration, a Christophany in its style genre (appearance of Jesus in divine glory), like the walking on the water (see 14:22-27), is characteristically modified by Matthew vis-à-vis Mark 9:2-10. In Matthew Moses comes before Elijah (vv. 3, 4, in contrast to Mark), Jesus' appearance enjoys a stronger christological concentration (v. 2), and the divine voice (as in Jesus' baptism; see 3:17) adds: ". . . with him I am well pleased." Peter's role becomes more positive (Mark 9:6 is omitted), and that of the disciples, for all of their numinous fright, becomes one of reverence and worship (vv. 6-7). Matthew makes the most of the Mosaic typology with his symbolic features (the very high mountain, the six days, and the bright cloud).

The Transfiguration (17:1-13)

17:1 *Six days later, Jesus took with him Peter and James and his brother John and led them up a high mountain, by themselves. 2 And he was transfigured before them, and his face shone like the sun, and his clothes became dazzling white. 3 Suddenly there appeared to them Moses and Elijah, talking with him. 4 Then Peter said to Jesus, "Lord, it is good for us to be here; if you wish, I will make three dwellings here, one for you, one for Moses, and one for Elijah." 5 While he was still speaking, suddenly a bright cloud overshadowed them, and from the cloud a voice said, "This is my Son, the Beloved; with him I am well pleased; listen to him!" 6 When the disciples heard this, they fell to the ground and were overcome by fear. 7 But Jesus came and touched them, saying, "Get up and do not be afraid." 8 And when they looked up, they saw no one except Jesus himself alone.*

9 As they were coming down the mountain, Jesus ordered them, "Tell no one about the vision until after the Son of Man has been raised from the dead." 10 And the disciples asked him, "Why, then, do the scribes say that Elijah must come first?" 11 He replied, "Elijah is indeed coming and will restore all things; 12 but I tell you that Elijah has already come, and they did not recognize him, but they did to him whatever they pleased. So also the Son of Man is about to suffer at their hands." 13 Then the disciples understood that he was speaking to them about John the Baptist.

1-3   The time indication, "six days later," cannot be identified as referring to a previously specified point in time (16:13, or the unspecified "from that time on" of 16:21, 24). Rather, it has a symbolic sense; but precisely what sense? It cannot be a reference to the Feast of Tabernacles, beginning six days after the great Day of Atonement, when messianic expectations were especially keen. In conjunction with the reference to the lofty mountain (which does not mean the one identified today as Tabor) and with Moses, it is a harking back to the theophany granted to Moses, here fulfilled anew and in a more exalted form in the theophany to the disciples. The reference is to Exodus 24:16: "The glory of the LORD settled upon Mount Sinai, and the cloud covered it for six days." In that context Aaron, Nadab, Abihu, and the seventy elders are identified as Moses' companions (Exod. 24:9); after gazing on God, they still "ate and drank" (Exod. 24:11). This epiphany forms the conceptual background of the Christophany before the disciples, however modified, expressed in Christian terms, and surpassed in being transferred to Jesus. The natural, human Jesus appears in a blaze of light *(kābôd)*. Not only do his robes become a brilliant white but his face shines like the sun (cf., for God's face, Num. 6:25; Pss. 4:6; 17:15; 31:16; 67:1; and frequently; Matt. 18:10); his clothing becomes "[a blaze of] light" (cf. Ps. 104:2). "Transformation" has a role in Greek mythology as well *(metamorphōsis)*, but it is used here as an expression of transfiguration in the sense of dazzling glory (cf. Dan. 12:3; *Ethiopian Enoch* 62:16; *4 Ezra* 7:97; *Syrian Apocalypse of Baruch* 51:5, 10, etc.). Moses and Elijah "appear" (a reference to their rapture and return?), likewise transfigured, not as representatives of "the law and the prophets," but as rapt in heavenly glory (conversing with Jesus) and as witnesses to Jesus.

4-7   Peter's reaction brings to expression the blessed rapture of this experience of the proximity of God. The "dwellings" are reminiscent of the Feast of Tabernacles, which anticipates the atmosphere of the messianic eschaton (Zech. 14:16) but also of the "eternal homes" (Luke 16:9) or "heavenly dwelling places" (John 14:2), a familiar picture in Judaism (*Ethiopian Enoch* 39:7; 41:2;

Slavonic Enoch 61:2-3). The words of Peter (who is not rebuked) form a transition to the theophany accompanied by the "bright cloud" and the voice of God, which here (in a different way than in Jesus' baptism) ends with the admonition, "Listen to him" — an allusion to Deuteronomy 18:15, the announcement of the Moses-like prophet who fulfills Moses' revelation. God appears and endorses Jesus, who appears in transfigured form, as his "Beloved Son" (see Matt. 3:17), and points the disciples to the one who preaches the divine words "among [his] own people" (Deut. 18:18). The "pillar of cloud" that led (Exod. 13:21-22) and protected (Exod. 14:19-20) the people in their wandering in the wilderness, and that covered Mount Sinai (Exod. 24:15), radiating light ("bright" cloud) as does the transfigured Jesus (Matt. 17:2), creates an atmosphere of the presence of God. By "overshadowing" those present at the scene (not only the transfigured persons but the disciples as well), that is, covering them with its shadow, the cloud indicates God's salvific presence (cf. Luke 1:35), just as on Mount Sinai. With the emphatic, transitional "behold" (omitted in the New Revised Standard Version), its meaning becomes audible in the divine voice that specifies Jesus as the herald of divine revelation. In the wider context the disciples are being admonished to hearken to the prediction of the passion and at the same time encouraged, through the transfiguration and theophany, to accept that prediction. Now the disciples' reaction is to listen — to prostrate themselves — in holy fear. As surely as this fear ("they were overcome by fear") is the standard reaction to a divine appearance, the "hearing" and "falling to the ground" (only in Matthew) suggest obedience and worship (cf. 2:11; 4:9; 26:39). Trembling with fear before the majesty of the Transfigured One, the disciples now see Jesus approaching them in his usual form. He touches them — near them again in an earthly fashion — and calms their fear (cf. 14:27; 28:10).

8-9 The three disciples dare once more to lift their eyes to the natural Jesus, now restored to them (in Mark 9:8 they "look around"). The celestial visitor is gone; Moses and Elijah, too, have disappeared. As they descend the mountain, Jesus bids them tell no one of their "vision" until the Son of Man has been raised from the dead — a reference to the Christ-revelation that is comprehensible only now that the disciples have beheld the transfiguration, a reminder that the proclamation of Jesus' resurrection is bound up with the prediction of the passion (16:21). The narrative of the Christophany is sketched against the background of Easter. It is not to be regarded historically but as grounded in experiences of Jesus' majesty by disciples closely bound to him. It is a "Christ story," like Jesus' baptism or the Christophany on the lake.

10-13 Matthew retains (again in v. 14) the connection of the narrative with the descent from the mount (v. 9), but shapes the conversation concerning Elijah, occasioned by the latter's appearance, more explicitly and more compactly than Mark as a teaching device about the ancient prophet's return. For Matthew, Elijah, who was awaited as the forerunner of the Messiah according to Malachi 3:1, and the restorer of Israel according to Malachi 4:5-6, has clearly come in John the Baptist (Matt. 11:14). But for the primitive church this raised the problem of how the suffering and death of the Son of Man was to be brought into the picture. Jesus' response to the disciples calls their attention to the death of John (14:3-12), who, like Jesus, has fallen victim to human beings' malice and mercilessness. Thus his death brings him into closer proximity with the destiny of the Son of Man. With Mark we have something more like a riddle; with Matthew, the disciples now understand that Jesus is speaking of John the Baptist. To be sure, how the "restoration of all things" fits into this view (cf. Acts 1:6, 3:21; Matt. 19:28) remains without explanation.

Jesus Cures a Boy with a Demon (17:14-20)

14 *When they came to the crowd, a man came to him, knelt before him,* 15 *and said, "Lord, have mercy on my son, for he is an epileptic and he suffers terribly; he often falls into the fire and often into the water.* 16 *And I brought him to your disciples, but they could not cure him."* 17 *Jesus answered, "You faithless and perverse generation, how much longer must I be with you? How much longer must I put up with you? Bring him here to me."* 18 *And Jesus rebuked the demon, and it came out of him, and the boy was cured instantly.* 19 *Then the disciples came to Jesus privately and said, "Why could we not cast it out?"* 20 *He said to them, "Because of your little faith. For truly I tell you, if you have faith the size of a mustard seed, you will say to this mountain, 'Move from here to there,' and it will move; and nothing will be impossible for you."*

14-20 Following the route of the Markan presentation (the descent from the mountain), Matthew now sets forth the healing of a youth who is subject to seizures; but he rather notably abbreviates and alters the account. The abbreviation corresponds to his usual procedure (compare the healing stories in Mark 5 with Matt. 8:28-34; 9:18-26). In stylistic genre, Jesus' deeds are recounted in the broad narrative form of a short story with a moral, consisting of an account of Jesus' deeds, concentrating on the disciples' faulty faith ("little faith"), intended as a paradigm, and climaxing in Jesus' words. Thus the pericope fits better with the concern of the entire passage — full faith in the Lord, who attains to resurrection through suffering and the cross. It is subdivided into Jesus' healing of the youth with seizures (vv. 14-18) and Jesus' dialogue with the disciples, which thus appears, not as in Mark, as an appendage but precisely as the objective of the narrative.

14-18   The hapless father of the sick youth approaches Jesus "kneeling," and addresses him as "Lord," for Matthew surely as a sign, like "worship," of the reverence that is Jesus' due (see 2:11; 8:2; 9:18; 14:33; 15:25; 28:9, 17). The designation of the patient as an "epileptic" (only in Matthew; also 4:24) means, in the prevailing view, subject to seizures; cf. Galen 9.903: "The moon holds the epileptic's periods in its grasp." This diagnosis corresponds to the father's portrayal of the youth's affliction (v. 15b) and to the acute attack in Jesus' presence, described in Mark 9:20, which Matthew, however, omits. But Jesus' painful outcry concerning the "faithless [Matthew: 'and perverse'] generation" was important to Matthew, who adopts similar, even more powerful, words on other occasions (11:16; 12:39-45; 16:4), and here lays the groundwork for the theme of "little faith." The added questions, taken over from Mark, "How much longer must I be with you? How much longer must I put up with you?" remind the reader of Jesus' way to Jerusalem and his taking on himself his passion (16:21). Matthew has passed over Jesus' "dialogue on faith" with the father in Mark 9:22b-24, since the conversation with the disciples was more important to him. Only briefly (v. 18b) does he report the cure, which is understood as the expulsion of the demon of illness.

19-20   The actual teaching that the faith community is to draw from this story is that of overcoming "little faith," against which Matthew has often warned (6:30 and par.; Luke 12:28; in Matthew only in 8:26; 14:31; 16:8). The disciples are not, as they are in Mark 6:52, hard-hearted and without understanding; they simply have a weak, disheartened faith (Matt. 8:26), inclined to doubt (14:31; 28:17). Too little do they see Jesus' glory in his earthly works (cf. 16:9-10), indeed, not until after his resurrection (28:17). That is why it is here that Matthew speaks about faith, which, even if it is as small as a mustard seed (see 13:31), can move a mountain (v. 20). It is a paradoxical statement, one that shows "little faith" in its positive aspect. The logion is transmitted in a double tradition, in Q with a different image (the mulberry transplanted into the sea, Luke 17:6), in Mark 11:23-24 (= Matt. 21:21) in conjunction with the prayer that is sure to be heard. After all, in the prayer that vanquishes all doubt the believer calls on the God of might. This is likewise the implication of the response by Jesus in Mark 9:29. Matthew does not explicitly identify the prayer, but presumes it in the concluding clause (v. 20): ". . . and nothing will be impossible for you," an echo of Mark 9:23: "All things can be done for the one who believes." Charismatically stronger, a "faith that removes mountains" (1 Cor. 13:2) arises and develops in an unreserved confidence in God the Father. Later copyists have interpolated "and fasting," reflecting early Christian thought — based in Judaism itself — as also occurs in the spurious verse 21.

Second Prediction of Jesus' Passion and Resurrection: Instructions for the Community (17:22–18:35)

Jesus Again Foretells His Death and Resurrection (17:22-23)

> 22 *As they were gathering in Galilee, Jesus said to them, "The Son of Man is going to be betrayed into human hands,* 23 *and they will kill him, and on the third day he will be raised." And they were greatly distressed.*

22-23   The second proclamation of the passion (the first being in 16:21), positioned as in Mark, differs essentially from Mark only in the comments pertaining to framework. Matthew speaks not of a journey through Galilee but of a gathering in Galilee. By "they" he probably means the disciples just indicated (17:19) since all three predictions of the passion are addressed to the disciples. Only in 19:2 is a multitude of persons finally spoken of as following Jesus, doubtless because of the appended conversations. The declaration itself is more trenchant than the first in that it sharpens the contrast between "humans" and God, who once more is in the background of the expression that Jesus is to be "raised." Matthew does not speak of a lack of understanding on the part of the disciples, or of their fear of putting questions to Jesus. They understand very well, but are extremely saddened. Their protest (Peter, 16:22-23) is silenced. In what follows the community is once again addressed in the person of the disciples, as in 16:24-28 (cf. the discourse to the community, chap. 18).

Jesus and the Temple Tax (17:24-27)

> 24 *When they reached Capernaum, the collectors of the temple tax came to Peter and said, "Does your teacher not pay the temple tax?"* 25 *He said, "Yes, he does." And when he came home, Jesus spoke of it first, asking, "What do you think, Simon? From whom do kings of the earth take toll or tribute? From their children or from others?"* 26 *When Peter said, "From others," Jesus said to him, "Then the children are free.* 27 *However, so that we do not give offense to them, go to the sea and cast a hook; take the first fish that comes up; and when you open its mouth, you will find a coin; take that and give it to them for you and me."*

24-27   The additional pericope here inserted by Matthew can only be interpreted, as with 14:28-31, as an instruction to the community in the guise of a narrative. Like the scene on the lake, it features Peter, who for the Matthean community is the decisive intermediary of Jesus' words and intentions (see Intro., no. 6). The story of the temple tax is dependent on Jewish-Christian tradition, and indeed on a time when the community was still in contact with Judaism. For the Jewish-Christian part of the community, it was doubtless a question, until the destruction of the temple, whether Christians ought to continue to pay the temple tax. All Israelites over twenty years of age, except priests, were expected to pay this tax for the upkeep of the temple, one-half silver shekel (Exod. 30:11-16; Josephus, *Antiquities* 18.312) or, in Greek coinage, two drachmas, until, after the destruction of the temple, the tax was collected by the Romans for the Capitoline Jupiter (Josephus, *The Jewish War* 7.218). Peter's affirmative response to the tax collectors (Matt. 17:25) is consonant with his pliability on the occasion of the incident at Antioch (Gal. 2:12). But Jesus, anticipating him, instructs him (and the community) through a pedagogical dialogue on the correct attitude of God's "children." As the children of earthly kings are exempt from any obligation to make such contributions, so also God's children are free of any obligation to make payments for the maintenance of the temple, God's house (Matt. 17:26). If they do make such payments, let them do so not out of a sense of duty, but freely. Jesus endorses Peter's willingness to have the tax paid through the procurement of a stater (a coin worth two double drachmas) from the mouth of a fish that Peter will catch by angling — a miraculous narrative motif with parallels in the literature of the age. In this story it is the gift of a good God to his children (a distribution miracle). "Do not give offense" (v. 27a) corresponds to Peter's attitude as intermediary in the charged atmosphere of the primitive church. Matthew has included this narrative, peculiarly his own, in the "church" passage (17:22–18:35) to remind the community of the freedom given them as God's children, which, however, requires regard for particular circumstances.

The Great Community Discourse (chap. 18)

Here is the fourth in the series of the five great discourses marked off with a concluding formula (7:28; 11:1; 13:53; 19:1; 26:1). It takes up basic questions for the life of the community, and Matthew skillfully composes it from a variety of elements of tradition. He draws his main material from the outline of the discourse to the disciples assembled by Mark in Mark 9:33-50, which follows the second prediction of the passion and resurrection of the Son of Man. But he is not slavishly attached to it: he omits the scene with the intruding exorcist (Mark 9:38-41) and the logia of the salt (Mark 9:49-50), and expands the discourse with other material (Matt. 18:10-35). He adapts the parable transmitted in Luke 15:3-7 to the community situation (Matt. 18:12-14), offers a disciplinary rule out of Jewish-Christian tradition (vv. 15-17), and complements the parable with further logia (vv. 18-20). In the same conceptual framework follows Peter's question — how many times must one forgive one's sibling? — and Jesus' reply, reinforced with the parable of the merciless slave (vv. 21-35), which Matthew has composed from his own material. In this way the lesson to be learned is tailored to the needs of the community and concerned with the relationship of community members, both in principle and in concrete expression.

The division of the community discourse is disputed. Not a few exegetes hold only to the brief recognizable and interwoven textual units (compare v. 5 with v. 6; v. 10 as a transition from v. 9 to v. 12, continued in vv. 15-20). It is important to observe that the words "little" in vv. 1-14, and brothers and sisters in verses 15-34 are key expressions. However, verses 1-5 do not entirely fit (keyword, "child") into this schema. Matthew has adopted "children" and "little ones" from Mark 9:33-37, as well as related the "little ones" to endangered and straying community members (vv. 10-14); but from there on he has listed his instructions under being brothers and sisters, which was most important to him for his understanding of the community (see 5:22 and frequently, esp. 23:8)

True Greatness (18:1-5)

> 18:1 *At that time the disciples came to Jesus and asked, "Who is the greatest in the kingdom of heaven?" 2 He called a child, whom he put among them, 3 and said, "Truly I tell you, unless you change and become like children, you will never enter the kingdom of heaven. 4 Whoever becomes humble like this child is the greatest in the kingdom of heaven. 5 Whoever welcomes one such child in my name welcomes me.*

1 With the disciples' introductory inquiry, Matthew turns Mark's scene (Mark 9:33-34), the "dispute about rank," into a fundamental, all-but-doctrinal question, while he reserves the disciples' contention about greatness for the pericope concerning the sons of Zebedee (Matt. 20:20-28). The logion on being great and being a servant likewise appears in the latter passage (20:26-27), which Mark presents in a somewhat different form, in Jesus' response in the present passage (9:35). The question here is not who is the greatest among the disciples but who is the greatest in the Reign of heaven. What is meant by "Reign of heaven" — the coming Reign of God, which one can enter only with the necessary change (5:20; 7:21; 18:3; 19:23-24; 23:13-14), or the already present Reign of heaven, which has its estate in the church (cf. 13:24, 41)? For Matthew this would be a false question: the community is already, or ought to be, an anticipation, a realization in advance, of the coming Reign. As in 5:19, Matthew's concern is the conduct one must display in the community now in order to share one day in the Reign of God.

2-4 Matthew takes the scene with the child from Mark 9:36 but omits the loving embrace of the child, which is more consonant with the blessing of the children (Mark 10:16; cf. Matt. 19:15 without this verb). The proximity of the two scenes in Mark is also intentional on Matthew's part, since he transfers the logion on "becoming like children" from the blessing of the children (Mark 10:15) to the present passage (Matt. 18:3), and perhaps even couches it in a more primitive form. "Change and become like children" could, in the Aramaic, mean "*again* become as children" (J. Jeremias). Such an understanding would explain the further development of the original logion and its application to baptism in John 3:3, 5. Matthew 18:3, however, contains the thought of "conversion" as well, which is necessary for the spiritual attitude of being a child ("*like* children"). This becomes even more clear in the appended logion, shaped by Matthew, on "becoming humble" (v. 4), which presupposes personal effort: those who humble themselves will be exalted by God, doubtless a saying from Q (Luke 14:11; 18:14; see also Matt. 23:12). "This child" is referred to only by Matthew, in order to conform the logion to the scene of verse 3. We may scarcely attribute it to an attitude of humility on the part of "this" child. Being a child before God comports with being small before the always greater God as well as, however, a trustful looking to him, the Father. Being small in the community (Matt. 18:2, end) has to do with the importance of mutual service (Matt. 20:26; 23:11).

5 Mark's appended 9:37, concerning "welcoming such a child," may be asking for concern for the children in the community (cf. the blessing of children), especially for the orphaned and needy, and thus for works of charity (cf. 25:35-40). This is apparently how Mark has understood the close connection between Mark 9:36 and 9:37. But the ensuing "that one welcomes not me but the one who sent me . . ." is reminiscent of another logion, in which everyone who so much as hands a cup of water to one of "these little ones," that is, to a disciple sent by Jesus, will receive a reward (see Matt. 10:42; Mark 9:41). "Children" and "little ones" are synonymous in the primitive Christian tradition. Matthew 18:5 suggests, in context, the interpretation: those who receive such disciples in Jesus' name, who abase themselves and become as children (v. 4), are received by Jesus himself (cf. Matt. 25:40).

Temptations to Sin (18:6-9)

6 *"If any of you put a stumbling block before one of these little ones who believe in me, it would be better for you if a great millstone were fastened around your neck and you were drowned in the depth of the sea.* 7 *Woe to the world because of stumbling blocks! Occasions for stumbling are bound to come, but woe to the one by whom the stumbling block comes!*

8 *"If your hand or your foot causes you to stumble, cut it off and throw it away; it is better for you to enter life maimed or lame than to have two hands or two feet and to be thrown into the eternal fire. 9 And if your eye causes you to stumble, tear it out and throw it away; it is better for you to enter life with one eye than to have two eyes and to be thrown into the hell of fire."*

6-9 The logia on "putting a stumbling block" are added, as in Mark 9:42-47, under the key expression "these little ones." The first group (vv. 6-7) has a parallel in Q (Luke 17:1-2), and this is Matthew's source for the cry of woe concerning the scandals that must come, and concerning the one who causes them (v. 7). The second group (vv. 8-9) takes a different viewpoint, inasmuch as the scandals occasioning sin now arise from the human being as such (from that being's bodily members). The linkage in terms of keywords is "cause to stumble," and the concept of "stumbling," which in the first group of sayings bears on tempting someone to a lapse of faith and in the second refers to temptation to grave sin.

6-7 The Greek verb rendered by the German Ecumenical Translation as "tempt to evil" signifies grave consequences since such evildoers are threatened with loss of salvation, or exclusion from the Reign of God (see 13:41-42; cf. 7:23). Since "these little ones" is followed by "who believe in me," what is being referred to is a shaken faith. This is the gravest risk for the "little ones," simple disciples with a childlike faith, whom Jesus also has in mind when he says "immature" — those to whom the Father has revealed the works of Jesus (see 11:25). Jesus praises as blessed the one who takes no offense at him (11:6) — who refuses to be disconcerted by his appearance on the earthly scene. He predicts to the disciples that they themselves, in the night of his arrest and passion, will take offense at him (26:31). In this urgent time before the end of the age, Matthew takes account of the fact that many will "stumble" — falter in faith (24:10). And only such an extreme threat to salvation can explain the expression of the threat to the corrupter in such a drastic image — it would be better for such a person to be fastened to a millstone and drowned in the depths of the sea, a logion that shows Jesus' earnestness (26:24, to Judas) and the force of his language (17:20; 19:24; etc.). The "ass's millstone," literally, is the large, "upper" grinding stone of a mill, which consists of one stone on top of another.

The threat is reinforced by the reduplicated woe (v. 7). Woe to the world, in which scandals must come (a realistic view of the world!); but, despite the inevitability of scandals, nevertheless woe to the one who causes them. In view of the cries of woe against the scribes and Pharisees (23:13-30), Matthew could have in mind a seduction to a lapse in faith such as that occasioned by contemporary Judaism. But in this discourse to the community it is more likely that he has arrogant people in view, who drive simple believers away from the faith by their speech and conduct.

8-9 The double logion on the bodily members that seduce to sin (hand and eye; in Matthew, the foot is cited only incidentally), once more in a powerful crescendo, is meant just as urgently. Human beings can endanger their salvation through their own sins as well, leading them to eternal judgment (hellfire; see 3:10; 5:22; 13:42, 50). Matthew has already used the intentionally exaggerated saying concerning the cutting off or tearing out of bodily members in his warning against lust (see 5:29-30), in the opposite order (eye, then hand) and in a somewhat different form, better accommodated to sexual desires. Here the logion stands for all serious sins arising from human beings' corporeality — their desires and passions (thus often in Paul; cf. Gal. 5:16, 24; Rom. 13:14; etc.). Indeed, it is a warning against those grave sins that separate a person from God, including anger (see 5:22) and mercilessness (18:35).

Another interpretation of this pair of sayings understands the "members" to be cut off as members of the community, from whom the community ought to separate itself. In this case we would have an anticipation of the "disciplinary rule" (vv. 15-17); but this is unlikely since other material intervenes, the Pauline image of the community as the body of Christ occurs nowhere else in Matthew, and the wording fails to fit in well ("with one hand or one foot," "with one eye"). Matthew does not understand the unit of logia differently than does Mark.

The Parable of the Lost Sheep (18:10-14)

> 10 *"Take care that you do not despise one of these little ones; for, I tell you, in heaven their angels continually see the face of my Father in heaven. 12 What do you think? If a shepherd has a hundred sheep, and one of them has gone astray, does he not leave the ninety-nine on the mountains and go in search of the one that went astray? 13 And if he finds it, truly I tell you, he rejoices over it more than over the ninety-nine that never went astray. 14 So it is not the will of your Father in heaven that one of these little ones should be lost.*

10-14 Still under the heading of "the little ones" follow a logion found only in Matthew (v. 10) and the parable of the lost sheep from Q (Luke 15:3-7) — two pieces offered by Matthew in a conscious application to the community (again the plural "you"). In the community there is the danger of seduction (cf. 24:4-5, 11, 24), or going astray. In context, the reference is to community members who have wandered from the right path. How this has occurred, through corruption by others (vv. 6-7) or through the wanderer's own fault (vv. 8-9), is not specified. In view of vv. 15-17 one could think of sinners; but unlike the case in vv. 15-17, they are not reproached for their wandering. The purpose of the parable is to show the shepherdly care that goes into the search for all who have strayed and are in danger.

10 This saying, couched in Jewish conceptual idiom and whose origin cannot be identified, ties the logion unit of verses 6-9 with the parable of verses 11-14. The warning against "contempt" may be directed against corrupters, or already indicate care or concern for the wandering. The concept of guardian angels was prevalent in early Judaism (Raphael in the book of Tobit; Ps. 91:11-12; cf. Matt. 4:6); but here the angels concerned for the "little ones" ("their" angels) stand before the face of God. In Judaism this is the highest group ("angels of the face," 1QSb 4:25-26; 1QH 6:13), to which the guardian angels do not necessarily belong (cf., however, Tob. 12:15). As with Raphael, their service is immediately determined by God and effective before God — in context, as witnesses for the little ones and as accusers of those "despise" them. The primitive church continued to believe in individual guardian angels (Acts 12:15) and in the community's connection with God's angels (1 Cor. 11:10; Heb. 12:22; messages to be dispatched in Rev. 2:1–3:14). The interpretation of the "little ones" as referring to children rests on a narrowing of denotation (see v. 5). Through the angels, the face of God itself is turned toward Jesus' simple disciples.

11-14 A typically Matthean formula introduces the parable of the lost sheep, which, unlike the more primitive formulation in Luke 15:3-7, shifts the message of God's joy over the finding of a lost sinner to the admonition of a shepherdly concern for a wandering community member. In view of the purpose of the recital, the image of the shepherd's behavior, slightly varied by Matthew ("mountains" instead of "wilderness"), should not be faulted as "unrealistic" (leaving the ninety-nine sheep?). Everything in Matthew is concentrated on "searching" for the stray (v. 12); this is also the reason for the omission of the scene in which friends are assembled (Luke 15:6). Just as God seeks the wandering (Ps. 119:176; Ezek. 34:4-16), so it is the will of God (v. 14) that the community prevent the "being lost" not of one of its members but of this believer's salvation ("destruction"; see 7:13; 10:6, 28; 16:25). This task is incumbent on the entire community; there is no evidence of a special injunction to its leaders.

Reproving Another Who Sins (18:15-20)

> 15 *"If another member of the church sins against you, go and point out the fault when the two of you are alone. If the member listens to you, you have regained that one.* 16 *But if you are not listened to, take one or two others along with you, so that every word may be confirmed by the evidence of two or three witnesses.* 17 *If the member refuses to listen to them, tell it to the church; and if the offender refuses to listen even to the church, let such a one*

be to you as a Gentile and a tax collector. 18 *Truly I tell you, whatever you bind on earth will be bound in heaven, and whatever you loose on earth will be loosed in heaven.* 19 *Again, truly I tell you, if two of you agree on earth about anything you ask, it will be done for you by my Father in heaven.* 20 *For where two or three are gathered in my name, I am there among them."*

15-18 The second part of the community discourse (vv. 15-35), under the theme of membership in the community, is influenced by the Q tradition present in Luke 17:3-4 (just as Matt. 18:7 was influenced by Luke 17:1), in which the subject under consideration is correction of fellow members and repeated forgiveness. Since Matthew takes up both subjects, one following the other in Matt. 18:15 and 18:21-22, we must see his main concern in these, and not exaggerate the importance of the appeal to the community as set forth in vv. 17-18. But he is aware of a Jewish-Christian practice that, in the case of a recalcitrant refusal of conversion on the part of a community member, provides for that member's exclusion from the community (v. 17). Evidently this is Matthew's intent with the statement as to binding and loosing (v. 18). Subsequently, however (as early as vv. 19-20), he harks back to the positive aspects of community membership.

15-17 Correction of fellow members (instead of hatred and revenge) is required of the Israelites in Leviticus 19:17-18 as well. It is urged and cultivated in the Qumran community (1QS 5:24-26; CD 7:2; 9:8). For the Christian community, an additional motive is Jesus' urgent admonition to be reconciled and to forgive (see 5:24; 6:12; 7:1-5; 18:32-33). In Luke 17:3-4 the thought seems to be of the sin of one member against another, who should forgive him; in the Matthean disciplinary rule it is a matter rather of grave transgressions against the community: the mention of two or three witnesses and then of a presentation of the matter before the community supposes a case that seriously threatens community life. This kind of step-by-step procedure against a deviating member of the community is likewise in evidence in the Qumran texts. There the community rule reads: "No one shall bring a matter before the many unless there has previously been a reprimand before witnesses" (1QS 6:1). The rule of witnesses in Deuteronomy 19:15 ("two or three witnesses") was strictly observed in Judaism (cf. Matt. 26:60; Acts 6:13), and still echoes in primitive Christianity (John 8:17; Rev. 11:3). A similar disciplinary procedure was certainly practiced in the Jewish-Christian communities: a person sentenced to exclusion from the community is to be regarded as "a Gentile and a tax collector," a formulation (see Matt. 5:46-47) possible only in such a community. How the community *(ekklēsia)* here (unlike 16:18) made its decision, in full assembly (cf. "the many" in 1QS 6:1) or through a group of judges (CD 10:4-6), is not completely clear. But since Matthew does not cite "elders" (as in Acts 15:6, 22;

21:18), and in the primitive church the community as such shared in crucial decisions, doubtless a full community assembly is meant.

18 The fresh start, with "Truly I tell you" and the new style (conferral of authority) with the address in the second person plural, shows that this saying was appended to the disciplinary rule as a postscript, probably by Matthew, in order to establish the community's sovereignty and liberty in making such a decision. For an understanding of the content of the logion, see 16:19b). The tension, so frequently regarded as puzzling, between the plural form of the authority logion here and the singular in 16:19b, which emphatically assigns to Peter full authority of binding and loosing, cannot readily be resolved in terms of a division of duties: doctrinal and instructional authority for Peter and disciplinary power for the community. Nor will a conscious continuation, simply a further extension of function, be the solution: what has already been assigned to Peter is now transferred to the community. Instead, both sayings are rooted in the commission of the Risen One (28:19-20; John 20:23). They are directed to the entire community of disciples, which in the Easter scene is represented and commissioned in the "eleven disciples." In the church, as Vatican Council II recognized (*Lumen Gentium*, 17; *Ad Gentes*, 5), the mission conferred by Christ is continued, with all of the authority invested in Christ himself. For Matthew, and for his view of Peter, who exercises the function of a rock for the church, there is no contradiction between the assignment of the power of binding and loosing on one occasion to Peter and then to the community that is in concord with Peter. From their common origin, he applies the two versions of the logion according to context — at one time to Peter, at another to the community. How the community is formally constituted plays no special role for him; only in subsequent development did further-reaching questions arise as to the concrete exercise of the authority given by the Risen Lord, whether it was to be exercised by the community or by specific officers of the community. The authority of the apostles as preachers of the gospel called by the Lord himself (see 10:2), is of course unquestionable for Matthew.

19-20 The pair of individual sayings here appended as a new beginning (indicated by "Again . . . ," probably Matthew's own device; cf. 5:33; 13:45, 47; 22:1) do not fit verses 15-18 well conceptually: they no longer speak of gaining or excluding a sinful member or of the community's authority, but of the prayer of two community members in concord, which gets a hearing from the heavenly Father (v. 19).

The second saying grounds the first in the presence of Jesus when two or three are gathered in his name and thus introduces a new thought. Both logia, which need not have originally belonged together, indicate their Jewish-Christian origin but may have been formulated by Matthew.

19 The prayer of petition is a frequent concern of Matthew (6:8; 7:7-11;

21:22), although only here is it common prayer in mutual accord. "Anything" no longer applies to the case of the member who sins, although prayer on behalf of such a one is conceivable (cf. 1 John 5:16). This saying is connected with the logion on full authority (v. 18) by association with the words "on earth . . . in heaven," which is as valid a logion as the present one ("Truly I tell you . . ."). Does Matthew wish to suggest to the community that, rather than making use of its full authority, it implore God through the power of prayer? The saying concerning authority keeps both possibilities in view: to bind and to loose, and to loose means to permit or enable someone to enter the Reign of God (cf. the image of the keys of the Reign of heaven, 16:19a). But the prayer of petition is placed on a different level than that of the exercise of full authority. It summons the might of God, according to 17:20; 21:21-22, through an undoubting faith. Here it becomes effective through the agreement of those making the prayer. No longer is the community as a whole at issue; now it is a matter of only two community members — an encouraging saying when it comes to small group prayer.

20   This logion, which is the basis of the preceding ("For . . ."), is a Christian version of the Jewish expression: "As often as two sit together and busy themselves with the words of the Torah, there amidst them is the 'Shekinah' — 'the abiding' — an expression for the presence of God" (*'Abot* 3:2b). This testifies to a high appreciation for the study of the Torah, the investigation of the will of God, among the Jews. For Christians, the assembly for prayer, which deserves further attention (here somewhat extended, "two or three"), receives its dignity and consecration through the presence of Christ. The transfer of God's presence to the abiding of Christ among those gathered in his name is to be explained by Christians' fixing their gaze on the risen Lord, who has promised his disciples that he will be with them always, even to the end of the age (Matt. 28:20). "God with us" (Emmanuel) is the Messiah's name even as a child (1:23), and this "being-with-us" continues in the community. As God once accompanied the people in the wilderness, so now Christ is among those who gather in his name, that is, when they think of him, call upon him, and appeal to him. Prayer addressed to God (v. 19) becomes effective through Christ (cf. John 14:13-14; 15:7; 16:23-24).

On the Duty to Forgive and the Parable of the Unforgiving Servant (18:21-35)

21-23   Peter's inquiry of Jesus how often he must forgive a sinful brother marks a new division within the community discourse, inasmuch as it corresponds to the inquiry of the disciples in the exordium (v. 1; cf. "came to Jesus") and yet ties the succeeding passage to the foregoing (esp. v. 15) since it adopts the tradition contained in Luke 17:3-4. The question concerning behavior toward a sinful brother or sister is continued with the question of how often one must forgive. As Matthew extends the instruction in Luke 17:3 from his own tradition (Matt. 18:16-20), so he adds a tradition of his own to Jesus' response in v. 22, this time the parable of the unforgiving servant (vv. 23-35). That this parable did not originally belong to Jesus' response is shown by the fact that it makes no reference to the question of how often one must forgive, but simply illustrates the urgency of merciful forgiveness by reason of the mercy one has experienced from God oneself. But the Matthean presentation fittingly rounds out the instruction on responsibilities to fellow members.

Forgiveness (18:21-22)

21 *Then Peter came and said to him, "Lord, if another member of the church sins against me, how often should I forgive? As many as seven times?"* 22 *Jesus said to him, "Not seven times, but, I tell you, seventy-seven times."*

21-22 Peter has already been the disciples' spokesperson in Mark 8:29; 9:5; 10:28, and (not in Matthew) 11:21, and additionally in Matthew 15:15 and in the present passage. This corresponds to the Matthean image of Peter (cf. Matt. 10:2, "first"; 14:28-31; 17:24-27). The words addressed to Peter have the greatest importance for the community. Peter's "seven times," which he regards as a high number, dwindles in comparison with Jesus' answer: "seventy-seven times" (cf. Gen. 4:24; *Testament of Benjamin* 7:3-4), or seventy times seven, that is, again and again, limitlessly. Thus Matthew goes further than Jesus' instruction in Luke 17:4, which, however, is meant in exactly the same way.

The Parable of the Unforgiving Servant (18:23-35)

23 *"For this reason the kingdom of heaven may be compared to a king who wished to settle accounts with his slaves.* 24 *When he began the reckoning, one who owed him ten thousand talents was brought to him;* 25 *and, as he could not pay, his lord ordered him to be sold, together with his wife and children and all his possessions, and payment to be made.* 26 *So the slave fell on his knees before him, saying, 'Have patience with me, and I will pay you everything.'* 27 *And out of pity for him, the lord of that slave released him and forgave him the debt.* 28 *But that same slave, as he went out, came upon one of his fellow slaves who owed him a hundred denarii; and seizing him by the throat, he said, 'Pay what you owe.'* 29 *Then his fellow slave fell down and pleaded with him, 'Have patience with me, and I will pay you.'* 30 *But he re-*

fused; then he went and threw him into prison until he would pay the debt.
31 *When his fellow slaves saw what had happened, they were greatly distressed, and they went and reported to their lord all that had taken place.* 32 *Then his lord summoned him and said to him, 'You wicked slave! I forgave you all that debt because you pleaded with me.* 33 *Should you not have had mercy on your fellow slave, as I had mercy on you?'* 34 *And in anger his lord handed him over to be tortured until he would pay his entire debt.* 35 *So my heavenly Father will also do to every one of you, if you do not forgive your brother or sister from your heart."*

23-35   The parable, which tells a story (a parable in the strict sense) and opens with the Matthean introductory formula (see 13:24), portrays, in crass terms, in contrast to God's unexpected and immense mercy, the mercilessness of a person who, despite the mercy he has experienced, deals cruelly with a fellow human being. The consciously intended contrast is shown in the following elements: (1) The king cancels an enormous debt (10,000 talents are equal to 100 million denarii) on behalf of a high official ("slave"), while the slave brutally constrains payment of the comparatively small debt of one hundred denarii by his own debtor (a "fellow slave"). (2) Both debtors make their entreaty with the same words: "Have patience with me, and I will pay you everything," but with opposite results. (3) The lord (the king) has compassion on the official and sets him free (v. 27); but the slave seizes his debtor by the neck (v. 28) and throws him into prison (v. 30). The recital is not concerned solely with mercy shown or not shown. Its point is that, in view of the abounding mercy shown him, the indebted slave ought likewise to have been merciful to his fellow slave. We readily see the meaning of the story for Jesus' message: God has willed to forgive completely a person who cannot personally cancel sin and debt, but expects that person to be prepared for a like forgiveness of other human beings. The petition in the "Our Father" (6:12) presumes both, and Luke 6:36 expresses it as a requirement of Jesus.

There is no gainsaying the authenticity of the parable as that of Jesus. The specifications of the scene, which do not fit Palestine but rather a great realm of the time with its power structures (see below), constitute no evidence to the contrary since Jews were sufficiently aware of such contexts. The attempt to split off the last part (vv. 31-34) on grounds of literary criticism, as if it now called God's great goodness once more into question, ignores the concept of judgment that sounds forth in Jesus' preaching — granted, not the first concept, but nevertheless the other side of the coin of his message of grace, for those who refuse to be converted (see 10:15; 11:22-24; 12:41-42; 24:45-51). This does not exclude certain Matthean additions or alterations: besides the introductory formula (see above), especially the concluding verse 35, the application, entirely composed by Matthew (cf. 5:16; see also 6:14-15; 18:14); perhaps also "king" (v. 23); "greatly distressed" (v. 31; cf. 17:23; 26:22).

23 In Judaism "king" is a familiar symbol for God, also used by Matthew in the parable of 22:2-14. While the king is subsequently designated as "lord" (in contradistinction to the "slaves"), nevertheless the thought is of an Eastern potentate. The "slaves" are therefore high-ranking officers of state.

24 The large debt refers to the embezzlement or squandering of the amount of tax to be collected from this man. But 10,000 talents are far too much (nowhere was a tax this high), intentionally, in order to give some idea of the human being's debt before God.

25 The sale of all the merciless slave's possessions, including his spouse and children, could never cover the debt but is conceived as a punitive or coercive measure. In Jewish law, the sale of an Israelite as a slave was permitted only in a case of theft, that of his spouse never (Billerbeck, *Kommentar zum Neuen Testament*, 1:798).

27 Besides releasing the slave (from prison), the lord cancels the entire debt (in Greek, actually "the loan").

30 The "seizing by the throat" (v. 28) describes the debtor's arrest. In prison he was to work off the small sum owed, or have it paid by others (in the instance of a sentence of the guilty, cf. 5:25)

31 The denouncement by the "greatly distressed," or rather outraged, fellow slaves, other officials, is understandable. It fits the rest of the story, the punishment of the forgiven civil servant by the lord.

33 The words of the infuriated lord reveal the point of the story.

34 Naturally the refunding of the entire debt is illusory. Its expression indicates everlasting punishment. Tortures (by the "torture slaves") were customary in the East, and here emphasize the harshness of the punishment.

35 Matthew points to the "heart" (cf. 6:21; 11:29; 12:34; 15:8) since true forgiveness may not simply hang from the lips.

The parable is well understood in a framework of Jesus' preaching of the Reign of God as well: it shows God's mercy today, which frees a person forever, but only if one answers God's love with a similar love for one's fellow human beings. The scene is presided over by God (not by the Son of Man, as in 16:27; 25:31, 34) as sovereign King — in grace and in judgment.

Important Community Themes, along with the Third Prediction of Jesus' Suffering and Resurrection (19:1–20:34)

With Matthew 19:1-2 a new section begins, indicated by Jesus' departure from Galilee and his accompaniment by large crowds; but it still stands in intrinsic relationship with the great community discourse of chapter 18 inasmuch as important community themes now come to expression: divorce and celibacy (19:3-12), the position of children (19:13-15), wealth and poverty (19:16-30), and sovereignty and service (20:20-28). Thus Matthew follows the Markan outline. The third prediction of Jesus' suffering, now broadly explained in anticipation of the report of the passion, stands this time not at the beginning of the passage but, appropriately, before the pericope concerning the sons of Zebedee (20:17-19). After all, here would be the best place to present the description of Jesus' passion as addressed only to the Twelve — and in their name to the community — especially as it presents such a strong contrast to the disciples' ambitious striving for supremacy. Renunciation of any supremacy, and extreme readiness to serve, imaging Jesus (20:25-28): here is the climax of the entire community instruction. Matthew has inserted a special tradition available to him, the parable of the laborers in the vineyard, and this as an appendage to the passage on wealth and poverty (20:1-16). Matthew takes the healing of the blind men of Jericho (20:29-34) from Mark, as it is so pregnant with meaning for the community (seeing and following) and at the same time forms a transition to the journey to Jerusalem (21:1-9).

Teaching about Divorce (19:1-12)

19:1 *When Jesus had finished saying these things, he left Galilee and went to the region of Judea beyond the Jordan.* 2 *Large crowds followed him, and he cured them there.*

3 *Some Pharisees came to him, and to test him they asked, "Is it lawful for a man to divorce his wife for any cause?"* 4 *He answered, "Have you not read that the one who made them at the beginning 'made them male and female,'* 5 *and said, 'For this reason a man shall leave his father and mother and be joined to his wife, and the two shall become one flesh'? 6 So they are no longer two, but one flesh. Therefore what God has joined together, let no one separate."* 7 *They said to him, "Why then did Moses command us to give a certificate of dismissal and to divorce her?"* 8 *He said to them, "It was because you were so hard-hearted that Moses allowed you to divorce your wives, but from the beginning it was not so. 9 And I say to you, whoever divorces his wife, except for unchastity, and marries another commits adultery."*

10 *His disciples said to him, "If such is the case of a man with his wife, it is better not to marry."* 11 *But he said to them, "Not everyone can accept this teaching, but only those to whom it is given. 12 For there are eunuchs who have been so from birth, and there are eunuchs who have been made eunuchs by others, and there are eunuchs who have made themselves eunuchs for the sake of the kingdom of heaven. Let anyone accept this who can."*

1-2   The framework observed here is altered vis-à-vis Mark. After the formula concluding the community discourse (v. 1a), Matthew sets in relief the change of scene from Galilee to Judea, without distinguishing (v. 1b) this region from the area "beyond the Jordan," as Mark does ("and"). Thus Jesus is now in "Judea," on his way to Jerusalem (16:21; 20:17-18), and at the same time in an area located between Galilee, where the gospel was first preached, and Jerusalem, where the sharpest confrontations with Jesus' adversaries arise. Matthew is not concerned with a description of the route — Jesus' ascent to Jerusalem along the eastern route, by way of Perea. Rather, his specification is symbolic, as in 4:24. The referral to this place is shown in two ways (v. 2): great crowds followed Jesus (cf. 4:25), and he healed them, that is, he healed the many sick among the people (Mark: "he taught them"). In this region Jesus is still active as the savior of the people, while in Jerusalem no more cures are reported. Once more the community must know that it is being addressed — summoned to discipleship (cf. 19:21, 27-28; 20:34) and strengthened by Jesus' healing powers.

3-12   The pericope concerning marriage and divorce is adapted, vis-à-vis Mark 10:2-12, to the community situation through the following peculiarities: (1) The dispute with the Pharisees has instead become an instructional conversation, which also takes into consideration the Matthean clause concerning a sexual offense (see 5:32), and this in the concluding words (v. 9). (2) From the private instruction of the disciples "in the house" in Mark 10:10-12, Matthew is drawn into another conversation of the disciples with Jesus. Their objection to marriage (v. 10) leads to a lesson from Jesus on celibacy (vv. 11-12). Here Matthew is evidently relying on a special tradition.

3-9   The Pharisees' question, which presupposes a knowledge of Jesus' position on the matter, is broadened by the addition over against Mark of "for any cause." This is usually understood as a question as to whether one might adhere to the liberal interpretation of Rabbi Hillel (an "offensive matter" could simply be displeasure with one's wife) or must follow the stricter direction of Shammai (only moral transgressions are to be settled through divorce). But why should this be a trap for Jesus? The Greek version can also be understood as a heightening of the question in Mark 10:2 of whether one may dismiss a wife (at all): ". . . for any cause?" In that case, the persons asking the question expect the answer from Jesus: "For no cause." This response is presupposed when Jesus at once begins to instruct them with words from Scripture (otherwise than in Mark, who follows a different sequence). The appeal to Scripture, which takes the wind out of the sails of his treacherous questioners, is a combination of Genesis 1:27 and Genesis 2:24 (according to the Greek text). Jesus traces his quotation from Scripture back to the Creator, who has created man and woman and has pronounced the binding of man and woman into "one flesh" to be his express will. Thus God is the founder of monogamy, and the consequence is that the human being must not sunder what God has bound together (Matt. 19:6). In Judaism, on the occasion of entry into a marriage, God was seen as the founder of matrimony. Jesus stands on Jewish ground with this appeal to the will of the Creator. Married Qumran Essenes were forbidden to marry two women in their lifetime, likewise with an appeal to Genesis 1:27 (CD 4:21). The Qumran prohibition is directed against a different practice in Judaism (polygamy), but is also based on the "foundation of creation." While the combination of the Scripture quotations may stem only from Hellenistic Judaism or Jewish Christianity, the authenticity of Jesus' appeal to the nature of creation is nonetheless credible.

Only now, according to Matthew (v. 7), do the Pharisees present their objection to Jesus' prohibition of divorce, from Deuteronomy 24:1 (presentation of a bill of divorce).

The bill of divorce, a statute of Moses (for the protection of the wife), did suppose, they want to say, the permissibility of the dismissal of the wife ("Why then . . ."). Jesus answers: It was a *concession* on Moses' part, but one that does not nullify the will of God at creation (v. 8). "Because you are so hard-hearted" may, in the Matthean context, mean "because you are so stubborn" (as in the German Ecumenical Translation); but in terms of the Markan text (Moses "wrote this commandment for you," Mark 10:5) it can also mean: "in order that your hearts may become hard," in order that your hardness of heart may become evident. Jesus is not attacking Moses' statute here, but is harking back to "the beginning," in terms of what is valid according to God's will. This determination was not impossible for a Jewish understanding of the law (cf. Qumran). The concluding sentence (v. 9) confirms this in a formulation that essentially means almost the same as 5:32: Dismissal of a wife (except in the case of indecency) in order to enter into a new marriage is adultery, is sin. The formulation of this passage is influenced by Mark 10:11.

This pericope, sketched out as a dispute or lesson, remains questionable as a historical scene but is indubitable in its core, Jesus' prohibition of divorce, as the (older) logion tradition Matthew 5:32 par. Luke 16:18 confirms. Jesus was concerned for the primordial will of God, and the rooting of his prohibition in the order of creation is in keeping with his viewpoint.

10-12 The disciples' remark in verse 10 is a skillful transition, but it may also be transmitting an opinion held in the community (cf. 1 Cor. 7:8, 26-28, but with a different motive!). It sounds as if marriage were being disparaged; but this is not what Jesus has in mind. But there is indeed a case for which he validates renunciation of marriage, and it is presented in the "eunuch logion" (v. 12). Matthew probably had a special tradition at his disposal, which moved from natural or constrained celibacy to voluntary celibacy "for the sake of the kingdom of heaven." With "this teaching" (v. 11) what is meant are not the words about divorce (v. 9), let alone the words of the disciples (v. 10), but the subsequent logion concerning eunuchs, as is shown by the linking word "for." After the three-part saying, a sentence follows that probably already belonged to the tradition, and which corresponds to verse 11. If the first part reads, "Not everyone can accept this teaching, but only those to whom it is given [by God]" to do so, nevertheless the concluding sentence demands, "Let anyone accept this who can." This means not merely a mental "accepting" or appreciation but also a ready and willing "making room." This parenthesis establishes, for the logion being transmitted: voluntary celibacy is not appropriate for all; it is the gift of a grace from God (Paul: a charisma; 1 Cor. 7:7). Whoever thinks he possesses it, however, can and ought to make use of it. The eunuch-saying pictures first a natural, congenital or accidental, incapacity for marriage, then the widespread creation of eunuchs (castration for the purpose of creating harem attendants) especially in Eastern courts at the time, and sets these involuntary manifestations in contrast to voluntary renunciation of marriage. Self-mutilation is certainly not being recommended: "eunuchs" is a matter of metaphorical imagery. The harsh-sounding expression here could be owing to other Jews' sneering at Jesus, or at individual disciples who renounced marriage in following Jesus (cf. Luke 14:26; 18:29), as "eunuchs" (J. Blinzler, *The Trial of Jesus* [Westminster, Md., 1959], ad loc.); but this is not certain. In Judaism matrimony was not only highly esteemed but was regarded as an obligation, for the purpose of begetting children; according to Deuteronomy 23:1, castrated men were not to be received into the community. But there were also exceptions to the general rule of marriage: it is possible that the ancient prophets Elijah and Elisha were unmarried. The prophet Jeremiah was enjoined by God to take no wife and to have neither sons nor daughters, and this was to be a warning to the people rejected by God (Jer. 16:1-2). Celibacy is attested in the main branch of the Essenes at Qumran, as in John the Baptist. The motives of the Qumran monks are disputed; Jesus' own renunciation of marriage is for the purpose of total dedication to the proclamation of the Reign of God and his sacrifice for human beings, and this motive is also decisive for disciples who follow him in that renunciation. "For the sake of the kingdom of heaven" refers first of all to being free for the service of proclamation, but it can also, as in religious orders whose members make a vow of chastity, be understood (the "counsel" of perpetual virginity) as a living sign of the coming Reign of God, when the institution of matrimony will no longer exist (Matt. 22:30). Priestly celibacy is a church law, not a divine one, and supposes the charisma of celibacy: it is meaningful only when practiced with the motive named in the text at hand.

Jesus Blesses Little Children (19:13-15)

> 13 *Then little children were being brought to him in order that he might lay his hands on them and pray. The disciples spoke sternly to those who brought them;* 14 *but Jesus said, "Let the little children come to me, and do not stop them; for it is to such as these that the kingdom of heaven belongs."* 15 *And he laid his hands on them and went on his way.*

13-15   After the theme of marriage and celibacy, Matthew takes the blessing of the children from Mark. It is a brief recital from Jesus' life — to be understood, however, not as an idyllic episode, but as instruction for the community on how they are to behave toward children. Children here are not a paradigm for the disciples' attitude, as they are in 18:3-4: Matthew has struck out the logion on "becoming like children" and moved it ahead, to the community discourse (see 18:3). Children are a group in the community of whom special care must be taken. From his knowledge of Judaism, Matthew is aware of the custom of blessing: parents bless their children, and scribes their students (Billerbeck, *Kommentar zum Neuen Testament*, 1:807-8). He may be thinking of the custom (admittedly, only later attested in the Talmud) whereby parents had their children fast with them on the Day of Atonement and then took them to the scribes to have them blessed. Why the disciples "spoke sternly to" those who presented the children to Jesus is not stated; that Jesus became indignant that they did so (Mark 10:14) is passed over by Matthew. The disciples' conduct serves as a negative foil for Jesus' explanation: "Let the little children come to me." "Do not stop them" is Matthew's subsequent phraseology and forms a transition to the basis for these directives of Jesus: to "such" — namely, to weak, helpless children — belongs the Reign of Heaven (the same expression occurs in Matt. 5:3, 10). Thus children receive their place in the community, which is meant to be a threshold to the coming Reign of God (see 18:1). The opinion that the expression, "What is to prevent me from being baptized?" (Acts 8:36), means that the church is being urged to practice infant baptism is not adequately grounded. It suffices that it is being enjoined to a high esteem for children, their full membership in the community, and care for them. Indirectly, we have an acknowledgment of family life and an admonition to foster it in the communities.

The Rich Young Man (19:16-30)

> 16 *Then someone came to him and said, "Teacher, what good deed must I do to have eternal life?"* 17 *And he said to him, "Why do you ask me about what is good? There is only one who is good. If you wish to enter into life, keep the commandments."* 18 *He said to him, "Which ones?" And Jesus said,*

"You shall not murder; You shall not commit adultery; You shall not steal; You shall not bear false witness; 19 *Honor your father and mother; also, You shall love your neighbor as yourself."* 20 *The young man said to him, "I have kept all these; what do I still lack?"* 21 *Jesus said to him, "If you wish to be perfect, go, sell your possessions, and give the money to the poor, and you will have treasure in heaven; then come, follow me."* 22 *When the young man heard this word, he went away grieving, for he had many possessions.*

23 *Then Jesus said to his disciples, "Truly I tell you, it will be hard for a rich person to enter the kingdom of heaven.* 24 *Again I tell you, it is easier for a camel to go through the eye of a needle than for someone who is rich to enter the kingdom of God."* 25 *When the disciples heard this, they were greatly astounded and said, "Then who can be saved?"* 26 *But Jesus looked at them and said, "For mortals it is impossible, but for God all things are possible."*

27 *Then Peter said in reply, "Look, we have left everything and followed you. What then will we have?"* 28 *Jesus said to them, "Truly I tell you, at the renewal of all things, when the Son of Man is seated on the throne of his glory, you who have followed me will also sit on twelve thrones, judging the twelve tribes of Israel.* 29 *And everyone who has left houses or brothers or sisters or father or mother or children or fields, for my name's sake, will receive a hundredfold, and will inherit eternal life.* 30 *But many who are first will be last, and the last will be first."*

This composition offers a detailed treatment of the topic of wealth and poverty, which was of current importance for the life of the community. It splices together three texts, different in kind: a narrative from Jesus' life, being the encounter with the rich man who, on account of his possessions, evades the call to discipleship (a "biographical apophthegm," vv. 16-22); a discourse of Jesus with the disciples on riches as an obstacle to entry into the Realm of God (vv. 23-24), whose core is a saying from tradition on the difficulty of entering the Realm of heaven for a wealthy person (v. 24); finally, by way of contrast, Jesus' logia on the reward of poverty in his discipleship (vv. 27-30). In this conjunction of various traditions (expanded by Matthew with the saying concerning the sitting of the Twelve on twelve thrones, v. 28), the community is impressively, and in climactic style, called to voluntary poverty — an abiding lesson for dealing with ownership and wealth. We would do well to examine each passage individually.

16-20 Matthew gives the introduction briefly, in his style ("Then someone came to him"). He alters the man's question and Jesus' answer in striking fashion. Obviously he had trouble with Mark's "Why do you call me good?" (Mark 10:18). And so he transfers the question about the "good" into the person's inquiry itself (Matt. 19:16), and has Jesus answer, "Why do you ask me about what is good?" (v. 17). The subsequent little sentence, "There is only one who is good" namely, God, does not fit very well into the conversation, or, at most, fits in as a reflection on "being good." God, the One who is good, gives a person who inquires after the good the response: "Keep the commandments" (v. 17b). This sentence, which clearly refers to the Decalogue (vv. 18-19), had a lasting effect on the church (as a heading for its moral doctrine). Although, in the antitheses of the Sermon on the Mount, Matthew seeks to surpass the commandments (5:20-48), the tables of the law have an orienting function for him, as we have already seen (see 15:19); but this is not the last word to the rich young man (see v. 21).

The commandments of the Decalogue are itemized, corresponding to the man's desire to *do* good, in terms of the second table — the commandments dealing with actions toward one's fellow human beings. The order followed is the same as that of the Old Testament (the fifth through the ninth commandments), except that the duty to one's parents is kept for last. This is the only positive commandment, and has already received special emphasis in 15:3-6. Matthew appends the commandment of love of neighbor (Lev. 19:18), which for him is most intimately bound up with the commandment of love for God (Matt. 22:39-40) and which definitively tips the scales in the tribunal of the Son of Man (25:31-46). The inquirer, who is still young, as Matthew gathers from Mark 10:20 ("since my youth"), is not boasting, but he seeks to do even more, to go beyond the commandments (Matt. 19:20). He spontaneously asks what he still lacks, while in Mark it is Jesus who suggests this to him.

21-22 In Jesus' response, Matthew places an exclamation point for the reader: "If you wish to be *perfect.* . . ." The Sermon on the Mount contains the summons to be perfect as the Father in heaven is perfect (see 5:48) — the climax and objective of the antitheses. The "perfection" (only in Matthew) demanded of all Christ's disciples leaves the commandments of the Decalogue intact (cf. v. 17), but surpasses them in the manner of their observance, in a love that takes its measure from God's love and knows no limits. This call, embedded in Jesus' proclamation of God's Realm (see 5:20), assumes concrete forms in the following of Jesus — here as renunciation of earthly possessions. The motive, "treasure in heaven" (see 6:19-21), is reminiscent of the undivided service of God that excludes an enslaving dedication to "wealth" (6:24). In this way Jesus' response also indicates the "greatest and first commandment," love for God "with all your heart" (22:37-38), and validates it with an incentive. No excuse remains to the rich man in the presence of the will of God as Jesus proclaims it. For him it is not mere "counsel" but an obligating summons from Jesus. His refusal (v. 22) is a failure for which there is no excuse. There is no other way for readers to understand his "grief-filled" departure.

There can be no question of a two-tiered or two-degree morality, providing for "keeping the commandments" by all, and reserving "following the counsels" for the "perfect." At the same time, it must not be overlooked that the account here is of a concrete, individual case, intended as an admonitory paradigm for all of Jesus' disciples and yet attached in its particularity to this wealthy young man. Through the call, "Come, follow me" (v. 21), it becomes the story of a vocation, like other such stories (4:18-22; 9:9; cf. 8:18-22), although, of course, with a negative result. When a disciple is called, Jesus' will alone is normative. Not even the primitive church could conjecture why Jesus called these persons, and not others, to his more intimate discipleship. The later church therefore assumed a special call by Jesus to certain "followers," and from there developed its doctrine of the "evangelical counsels" (cf. also 19:12). Persons who recognize such a call with certainty are obliged to follow it; but there will often be doubt about a special vocation. "Perfection," as Thomas Aquinas teaches, must be pursued by all, in love; the "counsels" merely can and should enable one to do so.

23-26   The ensuing sayings in the text now present Jesus' reaction to the rich young man's refusal. In terms of the history of the tradition, the logia are not necessarily bound up with the situation. The first logion (v. 23), introduced by Matthew with "Truly," speaks only of the difficulty of a rich person's entering the Realm of God, without, however, unconditionally denying that entrance. But the second saying, unmistakably an original expression of Jesus, basically excludes the possibility of a wealthy person's gaining it, with its extremely powerful image (a camel going through the eye of a needle). Only in Matthew does this exaggerated declaration of Jesus occasion a tremendous shock on the part of the disciples and their question, "Then who can be saved?" (v. 25). In this question, and Jesus' answer, discussions in the primitive church are certainly being reflected, and their echo was long-lasting (cf. Clement of Alexandria's *What Rich Person Can Be Saved?*). Jesus' response, that for God all things are possible, takes up a concept running from the Old Testament to the New (Gen. 18:14; Job 42:2; Zech. 8:6; Luke 1:37) and rooted in faith in the ever greater God. This conviction also lends strength to limitlessly trustful prayer that calls on God's omnipotence. Under this aspect — from God's side — there is hope for redemption and salvation even for seemingly unredeemable persons.

However, the logion of the camel and the eye of the needle must not be watered down in its message of the threat to salvation occasioned by wealth. Attenuating interpretations of the character of the image — the "Needle's Eye" as a narrow gate in the Jerusalem wall, or "camel" as a mistranslation of *kamilos*, "nautical rope" — are unconvincing. The logion is an exaggerated (hyperbolic) one, calculated to describe something impossible through the crass opposition of a large animal and a tiny opening — intended to shock, like the "log in your own eye" (7:3-5). The threat against the wealthy in Jesus' preaching is not open to doubt; but even the primitive church had understood that, for such people as well, there can be good news if they listen to Jesus' words (cf., in this respect, Luke 19:1-10; 16:9).

27-30   As in the Markan textual arrangement, the question of the danger of wealth is followed by that of the reward of poverty for the disciples who, in following Jesus, have left all things. This time Peter is at hand as the mouthpiece of the circle of disciples in the Markan text itself. A new element is the insertion of an additional logion concerning sitting on twelve thrones and judging the twelve tribes of Israel (v. 28): it addresses the "twelve disciples," that special group listed by name as the "twelve apostles" in 10:2-4. However, the added promise of a "hundredfold reward" consisting of "everlasting life" is, as in Mark, addressed to everyone who has left home, family, and possessions for Jesus' sake (v. 29). To be sure, Matthew omits the reward "in this age," the replacement of one's original family with the earthly family of God (the community). The last saying (v. 30) is a floating logion, here chosen as the conclusion of the entire composition.

28   Special attention is called for by this strange, much disputed logion, which probably stems from Q (cf. Luke 22:30b) but is not clear in its origin and sense. Is it a special reward for the "twelve"? This is possible since it stands over against the following saying (v. 29), which is addressed to all. The eschatological perspective is unequivocal; but what does "at the renewal" mean? Of Greek-sounding origin, in Flavius Josephus the expression can denote the restoration of the Jewish people after the Captivity (*Antiquities* 11.66), or in Philo the revival of the world after the great Flood (*Life of Moses* 2.65); here, however — corresponding to the "age to come" in Mark 10:30 — it means the eschatological re-creation of the world (Rev. 21:5). This concept has a broad tradition in Judaism (Isa. 65:17; 66:22; *Jubilees* 1:29; *Ethiopian Enoch* 45:4-5; 72:1; *4 Ezra* 7:75; *Syrian Apocalypse of Baruch* 32:6; 44:12; etc.) as well as in Qumran, where 1QS 4:25 uses the cognate expression, "make new." However, sitting on twelve thrones and judging the twelve tribes of Israel draws attention to the judgment connected with the re-creation (cf. Dan. 7:9-10; *Ethiopian Enoch* 62:1-3; *4 Ezra* 7:113; etc.). What is new is not the judgment to be presided over by the Son of Man, but the participation of the "twelve" in it, and their "judging" ("reigning over" would be an understatement) the ancient twelve-tribe people. According to Paul, Christians will one day judge angels (1 Cor. 6:3); but judging Israel (the "new Israel," the church, is not meant) has no parallel and sounds polemical, as if it were a continuation of 8:11-12. Just as Jesus has chosen the "twelve" as representatives of the twelve-tribe people that he wished to usher into the Realm of God in its full complement, so here they are promised judgment over a people that has failed to accept this invitation — a logion inserted, doubtless, only in a Jewish-Christian view (cf. 10:23). Since neither with Luke (the Upper Room) nor with Matthew can we determine the original situation, this particular logion remains problematic. For Matthew, doubtless the emphasis lies with the regal thrones of judgment at the side of the Son of Man, the reward given to them by God (cf. 20:23).

29 The enumeration of what the disciples have abandoned is identical with that of Mark (Luke adds, "or wife"); the motive in Matthew is "for my name's sake," that is, for my sake, for the sake of my call (cf. 10:22, 42; 18:20). The "hundredfold" reward is precisely eternal life, sharing in the future Realm of God (compare 7:14 and 18:8-9 with 19:23-24). Matthew's omission of the distinction, introduced by Mark and more briefly by Luke, between an earthly, present reward and a future, heavenly one is surely intentional, based on his strict eschatological orientation when it comes to understanding the reward (cf. 5:12; 6:5-6, 14-18; 10:41-42).

30 This logion, concerning the first and the last and formulated in general terms, is found again (20:16), in reverse order, at the end of the parable of the laborers in the vineyard, and is placed by Luke in yet another place (Luke 13:30). It acquires its respective sense in each context: here it functions as the conclusion of the composition on wealth and poverty. In its view of the rich, regarded as the "first," and of Jesus' disciples, who count as "last," whom God evaluates precisely the other way around, it is a paradoxical logion like 18:4; 23:12. In the topsy-turvy values of the Realm of God, "being last" on earth has a positive ring (cf. Mark 9:35; 1 Cor. 4:9; 15:8-10).

The Laborers in the Vineyard (20:1-16)

20:1 *"For the kingdom of heaven is like a landowner who went out early in the morning to hire laborers for his vineyard. 2 After agreeing with the laborers for the usual daily wage, he sent them into his vineyard. 3 When he went out about nine o'clock, he saw others standing idle in the marketplace; 4 and he said to them, 'You also go into the vineyard, and I will pay you whatever is right.' So they went. 5 When he went out again about noon and about three o'clock, he did the same. 6 And about five o'clock he went out and found others standing around; and he said to them, 'Why are you standing here idle all day?' 7 They said to him, 'Because no one has hired us.' He said to them, 'You also go into the vineyard.' 8 When evening came, the owner of the vineyard said to his manager, 'Call the laborers and give them their pay, beginning with the last and then going to the first.' 9 When those hired about five o'clock came, each of them received the usual daily wage. 10 Now when the first came, they thought they would receive more; but each of them also received the usual daily wage. 11 And when they received it, they grumbled against the landowner, 12 saying, 'These last worked only one hour, and you have made them equal to us who have borne the burden of the day and the scorching heat.'* 13 *But he replied to one of them, 'Friend, I am doing you no wrong; did you not agree with me for the usual daily wage?* 14 *Take what belongs to you and go; I choose to give to this last the same as I give to you.* 15 *Am I not allowed to do what I choose with what belongs to me? Or are you envious because I am generous?'* 16 *So the last will be first, and the first will be last."*

1-16 Under the heading "last and first," and by association with the "reward," Matthew here inserts a parable (in the strict sense) from his own material, which, it is true, departs from 19:27-30 in content and in application. The "hundredfold" reward of the disciples, although entirely a gift of God's grace, is yet a recompense for renunciation of earthly goods; the present story, at bottom and despite the imagery, is one not of a "reward" but of God's unexpected bounty, as in the parable of the generous father in Luke 15:11-32. Accordingly, the title ought rather to read "The Parable of the Generous Householder" (R. Hoppe). The introduction (Matt. 20:1a), with its Matthean orientation to the proclamation of the Realm of Heaven (see 13:24-31, etc.), and the concluding verse have been introduced by Matthew. The parable (20:1b-15) tells of the lord of a manor who, at harvesttime, hires laborers for his vineyard at various hours of the day, and in the evening has them paid. Thus the narrative is divided into two integrated parts (vv. 1b-7, 8-15). The lesson comes to light in verses 14b-15: out of pure generosity the householder decides to give the laborers hired last the same wages he pays the others, who have borne the burden and heat of the day. That is how God proceeds, and Jesus' hearers ought to understand this and affirm it. Concluding with a question, the story directs one's gaze to Jesus, who, in his message and behavior, conveys to human beings an appreciation of the unexpected, incomprehensible goodness of God. What Jesus recounts here occurs in his appearance on the scene and in his deeds. Thereby the parable becomes an advertisement for the gospel and an encouragement to his audience to place themselves under God's reign of grace, currently dawning. The dealings in the parable first move against a background of the ordinary: the proprietor of the vineyard, who calls into his vineyard the laborers standing about (or sitting about) in the marketplace, agrees with those he calls earliest on one denarius, the customary daily wage (v. 2), and promises those taken on later a wage that is "right." The laborers hired last — an hour before the end of the working day — must not be regarded as averse to work, or their words seen as a lazy protest. The problem of unemployment existed in those days, too. The surprising thing, which does not correspond to the ordinary, happens only in the second part of the parable. That the last hired are the first to be paid is of course constrained by the narrative; otherwise the earlier workers would not learn of their lord's generosity. Their murmuring, to the effect that they are not paid more (vv. 9-12), is altogether understandable. After all, they are human beings. But the lord of the manor teaches one of them, in amicable fashion ("Friend"), that they suffer no injustice (v. 13); he *wishes,* however, to give these last, out of generosity, out of pure goodness, as much as the others. It is an unusual trait, just as unusual as that of the father in the parable of the "prodigal son" (Luke 15:20b-24).

The intent of the parable is not to draw hard-and-fast lines for the "just wage," humane regulations for labor relations, the consideration of a living wage, or the like, although the story may incidentally encourage us to reflection. It is solely oriented to the conduct of God, and is an advertisement calling people to understand God in terms of goodness and mercy. God's goodness ought also to lead to a different relationship with one's fellow human beings. At the time Jesus was probably aiming at the unreasonableness and stubbornness of certain groups among his people ("Are you envious because I am generous?"), but even beyond that he was probably seeking to win over everyone — even these persons — to his proclamation of God, as is illustrated even more clearly in the second part of the parable of the generous father. Matthew will have understood the parable in more sharply polemical terms, as one may suppose from the logion he appends of the last and the first (Matt. 20:16; cf. also 21:28-32). But we should go back to Jesus' original intent in uttering these words: in this parable he reveals his exalted view of God.

A Third Time Jesus Foretells His Death and Resurrection (20:17-19)

17 *While Jesus was going up to Jerusalem, he took the twelve disciples aside by themselves, and said to them on the way,* 18 *"See, we are going up to Jerusalem, and the Son of Man will be handed over to the chief priests and scribes, and they will condemn him to death;* 19 *then they will hand him over to the Gentiles to be mocked and flogged and crucified; and on the third day he will be raised."*

17-19   The third proclamation of the passion, arranged as in Mark, presents a summary of Jesus' suffering in anticipation of the presentation of the passion. The introduction, shorter than Mark's, concentrates on the twelve disciples, whose number is already specified here in view of the subsequent pericope (vv. 20-28). The contrast between Jesus' passion, which, along with physical pain, includes mental humiliation ("mocked"), and the ambition of the power-hungry disciples is impossible to overlook. A new element is the handing over of Jesus "to the Gentiles," who together with the high priests and scribes are responsible for Jesus' crucifixion (cf. 27:2, 20-26), here explicitly referred to. The primitive Christian kerygma of cross and resurrection is obvious.

The Request of the Mother of James and John (20:20-28)

> 20 Then the mother of the sons of Zebedee came to him with her sons, and kneeling before him, she asked a favor of him. 21 And he said to her, "What do you want?" She said to him, "Declare that these two sons of mine will sit, one at your right hand and one at your left, in your kingdom." 22 But Jesus answered, "You do not know what you are asking. Are you able to drink the cup that I am about to drink?" They said to him, "We are able." 23 He said to them, "You will indeed drink my cup, but to sit at my right hand and at my left, this is not mine to grant, but it is for those for whom it has been prepared by my Father."
>
> 24 When the ten heard it, they were angry with the two brothers. 25 But Jesus called them to him and said, "You know that the rulers of the Gentiles lord it over them, and their great ones are tyrants over them. 26 It will not be so among you; but whoever wishes to be great among you must be your servant, 27 and whoever wishes to be first among you must be your slave; 28 just as the Son of Man came not to be served but to serve, and to give his life a ransom for many."

20-28 This pericope is divided into Jesus' conversation with the sons of Zebedee and their mother (vv. 20-23) and instruction addressed to all of the disciples (vv. 24-28). Jesus' response to the pair in verse 23, of course, itself undercuts the disciples' power struggle; but only in the universal and fundamental law of service, which Jesus imposes on all disciples, does the obligation become incumbent on the later church and the climax of all previous instructions and admonitions for community life. The connection between the historical setting pictured for the request of the sons of Zebedee and the logion, occurring a number of times in the tradition, concerning being first or last was created later, like the bond between the account of the rich young man and the words on the danger of wealth (19:16-22 and 23-26). The link is skillfully constructed: the rest of the disciples become resentful of the arrogance of the sons of Zebedee (v. 24), and this forms the transition from the conversation to the instruction. Both passages contain important statements bearing on Jesus' way and mission (vv. 22-23, 28).

20-23 The intervention of the mother (usually identified with Salome; compare 27:56 with Mark 15:40) of the sons of Zebedee, James and John (10:2), is to be explained by the effort to spare the two distinguished disciples the imputation of ambition — an apologetic twist like that of Matthew 19:17. The request in verse 21 refers to places of honor at Jesus' side in his Realm (Mark: "in your glory"). As the Realm in Matthew is always the Realm of the Son of Man (13:41; 16:28), we must not imagine an earthly realm of Israel, although historically such an expectation can arise in the minds of the as-yet-unenlightened disciples (cf. Luke 19:11; 24:21; Acts 1:6). Matthew avoids the "coming kingdom of our ancestor David" (Mark 11:10) in the acclamations at Jesus' entry into Jerusalem (Matt. 21:9). Rather, Matthew has in view, in the spirit of 19:28, the disciples' joint reign with Jesus in the coming Realm of God: the regency in which James and John struggle for places of preference at Jesus' right and left. Jesus gives them two answers, which were surely connected even before Mark but which point in different directions. First they are told that joint reign with Jesus means antecedently accompanying him along his route of suffering and death; then their gaze is drawn to God's sole disposal (Matthew explains, "by my Father").

The "cup" that Jesus will drink is, according to a frequent, graphic Old Testament expression, the chalice of God's vertiginous wrath, which the peoples and all sinners must drink (Ps. 75:8; Isa. 51:17; Jer. 25:15; Ezek. 23:33; etc.), and therefore not simply a "bitter cup of suffering" but an image of God's wrathful judgment. If Jesus applies this image to himself (Matt. 26:39; John 18:11), the thought behind it may be that he takes God's judgment upon himself and is willing to bear the most extreme pain for human beings' sake. Thereby the disciples are reminded that, in order to reach preeminence with Jesus, they must follow him on the way of the cross (Matt. 10:38-39; 16:24-25). The image of "baptism" in Mark 10:38-39 (Luke 12:50), immersion in menacing, rushing water, to be understood in the same sense, is omitted by Matthew. Jesus' foreknowledge of his death does not necessarily include an interpretation of its purpose, which is first expressed in 20:28.

The overconfident, arrogant declaration by the sons of Zebedee that they can drink the cup of suffering and death (cf. Peter, 26:33-35) is followed by Jesus' prophecy in verse 23a, which was fulfilled in James's case early, according to Acts 12:2, although for his brother less surely, as only later and uncertain testimonials are available. The historical question of the death of the apostle John, which plays a role with respect to the composition of the Gospel of John — although it is no longer so acute since the beloved disciple could be someone other than the apostle — can scarcely have posed itself for Matthew. Matthew adopts the prophecy from tradition, but, like Mark, he passes at once to another lesson of Jesus, which rejects the demand for places of honor under a higher aspect: such decisions are the Father's alone, who has decided and "prepared" all things in advance (cf. 25:34). Rank in the Realm of God can be spoken of only figuratively and paradoxically (see 5:19; 11:11b; 18:1-4). Indeed, God's exclusive disposition over all future things is set in relief by Jesus (24:36; cf. 24:40-41; Luke 17:20).

26-27 In Jesus' response to the irate disciples, there is a certain note of contrast between "You know" and what he has told the sons of Zebedee: "You do not know what you are asking" (v. 22). Human knowledge is limited to earthly things. Jesus' words concerning the mighty rulers who abuse their power to oppress their peoples show his realistic assessment of what goes on in the world. Striving for power and abuse of power characterize human inclinations. In stark contrast, Jesus lays down a statute for the disciples: "It will not be so among you," that is, that is not the rule imposed upon you. Then follows the postive instruction, which becomes the fundamental law for the entire community of disciples: the one among you who would be great is to be your servant; the one among you who would be first is to be your slave. The tradition offers the same logion five times, here in its original form of a pair of lines, in a crescendo from "great" to "first" and from "servant" to "slave," with the emphatic repetition of "among you." No image more powerfully differing from the ways of society can be expressed, and it is to become a reality in the community of disciples, in society and in church.

28   The saying concerning the Son of Man who has come only to serve was appended early in the development of the tradition, in order to drive home Jesus' instruction as powerfully as possible. While, as with other logia, its "I came" betrays primitive Christian interpretation (see 5:17; 10:34-35; Luke 19:10), still it fits Jesus' basic attitude to a T — his dedication to human beings to the hilt (his "existence for"). In Luke 22:27, in the Upper Room, Jesus designates himself as the one who serves in their midst; in John 13:1-17, the same thought becomes clearer in the washing of the feet. In Jesus' last meeting with the disciples, the same meaning attaches to the logion of "ransom" for many, which in terms of content agrees with the saying, at the Eucharist of the chalice, "my blood of the covenant, which is poured out for many" (Matt. 26:28). It is the thought of the vicarious death of atonement prophesied for the Servant of God, who "bore the sin of many, and was numbered with the transgressors" (Isa. 53:12). The giving up of life in the case of the Servant is regarded as a "guilt offering" and here as a "ransom" — for many, that is, for the totality — in the primitive Christian understanding, for all — "for the forgiveness of sins" (Matt. 26:28; cf. John 1:29; 1 Peter 1:18-19; Tit. 2:14). The meaning of Jesus' voluntary sacrificial death cannot be seized in a "scapegoat" theory but only under the concept of loving surrender. Jesus receives God's redemptive will and love, in view of his rejection by human beings, into his own love, and delivers himself up for all, to the very death (cf. Rom. 8:32; Gal. 1:4; 2:20; Eph. 5:2, 25).

Jesus Heals Two Blind Men (20:29-34)

29 *As they were leaving Jericho, a large crowd followed him.* 30 *There were two blind men sitting by the roadside. When they heard that Jesus was passing by, they shouted, "Lord, have mercy on us, Son of David!"* 31 *The crowd*

sternly ordered them to be quiet; but they shouted even more loudly, "Have mercy on us, Lord, Son of David!" 32 *Jesus stood still and called them, saying, "What do you want me to do for you?"* 33 *They said to him, "Lord, let our eyes be opened."* 34 *Moved with compassion, Jesus touched their eyes. Immediately they regained their sight and followed him.*

29-34   The story of the healing, which Matthew takes from the Markan tradition, now forms a transition to Jesus' days in Jerusalem. The profession of the blind men, made to Jesus as the "Son of David," ties the story to the call of the crowd at the entry into Jerusalem (21:9) and to the children in the temple (21:15). But, reduced by Matthew to essential aspects — the two blind men with their profession, Jesus' majesty ("Lord") and mercy, his being followed by the beneficiaries of the healing — the narrative displays typical traits important for the concept of discipleship. Let us therefore leave it (with the German Ecumenical Translation) parallel with the passage on community themes. Striking alterations vis-à-vis Mark are two blind men versus one, identified by name in Mark (Bartimaeus); the triple address of Jesus as "Lord"; the omission of the portrayal in Mark 10:49-50; Jesus' compassion, and his touching of the eyes, in Matthew 20:34. Here we must also attend to similarities and differences in the story of the healing of the blind men recounted earlier (9:27-31).

29-31   Having no interest in the route followed by Jesus (see 19:1-2), Matthew begins with the situation: "As they were leaving Jericho" (otherwise in Luke 18:35). The presentation of two blind men instead of Mark's one is to be explained, as with the two demoniacs in Matthew 8:28 and the two blind men in 9:27, in terms of a peculiarity of Matthew (Intro., p. 4). Here the intent may be to reinforce the testimonial to Jesus by presenting two people (see 18:16). They are not characterized as beggars, as they are in Mark and Luke. As members of the crowd "following" Jesus, they already know him, but at the end they become actual "followers" (v. 34). Their faith in Jesus is expressed in the connection between "Lord" and "Son of David." The two terms together resemble Jesus' claim (cf. 22:41-45). "Son of David" in Matthew's Gospel has a positive ring: it denotes the Messiah descended from David, although in another sense than as awaited by the Jews (see 1:1; 12:23; 15:22; 21:9, 15). Not a few interpreters suppose that the acclamation, "Lord, have mercy on us," actually was influenced by the liturgical formula "Kyrie, eleison," whereas the case is doubtless the other way around. The blind men refuse to be disconcerted by the others' castigations, but call out even louder — they are confessors of Jesus who will not be intimidated. Typically of a Matthean presentation, Mark's already striking form of address, "Son of David," becomes still more meaningful: while according to 12:23 the question only comes up, in this case we hear a clear profession of Jesus as the "Son of David," which Matthew later reiterates (21:9, 15).

32-34   Jesus' "compassion" for the blind men corresponds to the mercy he shows the people as the messianic shepherd (9:36; 14:14; 15:32). The touching of the eyes is a gesture of healing (8:3, 15) that Matthew has already cited in an earlier account (9:29). In comparing the two healings of blind men that he presents, however, a further step is worth noticing: in 9:28-29 Jesus inquires about the blind men's faith and only then performs the cure; at Jericho the blind men profess their faith first and then implement it by following Jesus. In 9:30 Jesus forbids publicity about the event, while 20:34 stresses, with approval, that the healed ones followed him.

In this way the story acquires the character of an example: the one who, through Jesus, "regains his sight" is to follow him. "Seeing," for the primitive church, has a deeper sense. It becomes the sign of a believing recognition and comprehension, doubtless as early as the healing of the blind man in Mark 8:22-25, and clearly by the cure of the man born blind as reported in John 9. In the Matthean context, readers are being admonished to affirm Jesus' journey to Jerusalem (Matt. 16:21; 20:17) in faith, and to go that way following him.

THE DAYS IN JERUSALEM (CHAPS. 21–25)

With Jesus' arrival in Jerusalem the horizon darkens. His entry into the Holy City, which sheds a hopeful light on the mood of the people (21:1-11), is followed by the cleansing of the temple, which provokes the protest of the high priests and scribes (21:12-17). In the cursing of the unfruitful fig tree (21:18-22), Jesus sets forth a sign of the looming rejection of Israel, and his dispute with the leaders over the authority conferred on him (21:23-27) affords a surmise of the unbridgeable chasm between them. Polemically, the parables of the two sons and of the wicked tenants (21:28-45) are aimed at the same governing groups, intent on Jesus' elimination. The appended parable of the wedding banquet as well, drawn from a special tradition (22:1-14), makes this point, although Matthew broadens it to an address to the Christian community. The subsequent tradition complex, taken over from Mark, with four weighty questions (22:15-46), is ordered to this perspective more clearly (as a dispute) than it is in Mark. Thereupon Matthew presents an expanded discourse, drawn from the Sayings Source but specially shaped by him as an anti-Jewish polemic against the scribes and Pharisees (chap. 23). In counterpoint he offers the primitive church the great eschatological discourse (chaps. 24–25), which he offers as the last of Jesus' discourses to the community (cf. 26:1). Here he gathers and combines a great deal of traditional material from Mark 13 and Q, but fills it out with his own, namely, with the parable of the ten bridesmaids (Matt. 25:1-13) and with the portrayal of judgment on the world (25:31-46).

Matthew does not intend this carefully thought out arrangement of material to be a historical picture of the last days in Jerusalem, although they do shed light on the hostility of the leading groups as it comes to a head and issues in the decision to have Jesus put to death. But his presentation is also transparent, especially in the discourse of chapter 23, with respect to the relationship with Judaism as governed by Pharisees after A.D. 70. Matthew decidedly takes his distance from this Judaism that rejects the Christian faith and persecutes Christian emissaries. But at the same time he continues his instructions and admonitions for the Christian community, which is no less being tested (cf. 22:11-14; 23:8-12; 24:43-44, 45-51; chap. 25). This transparency for Christian life in the world, these lessons on the fruitbearing of the new people of God (21:43), on watchfulness (25:13), and on standing the test (25:21, 23), especially in works of love (25:31-46), retains its currency today, and deserves all the more attention.

The Entry into Jerusalem, the Cleansing of the Temple, and the Question of Authority (21:1-27)

Jesus' Triumphal Entry into Jerusalem (21:1-11)

> 21:1 *When they had come near Jerusalem and had reached Bethphage, at the Mount of Olives, Jesus sent two disciples,* 2 *saying to them, "Go into the village ahead of you, and immediately you will find a donkey tied, and a colt with her; untie them and bring them to me.* 3 *If anyone says anything to you, just say this, 'The Lord needs them.' And he will send them immediately."* 4 *This took place to fulfill what had been spoken through the prophet, saying,*
> 5 *"Tell the daughter of Zion,*
>   *Look, your king is coming to you,*
>   *humble, and mounted on a donkey,*
>   *and on a colt, the foal of a donkey."*
> 6 *The disciples went and did as Jesus had directed them;* 7 *they brought the donkey and the colt, and put their cloaks on them, and he sat on them.* 8 *A very large crowd spread their cloaks on the road, and others cut branches from the trees and spread them on the road.* 9 *The crowds that went ahead of him and that followed were shouting,*
>   *"Hosanna to the Son of David!*
>   *Blessed is the one who comes in the name of the Lord!*
>   *Hosanna in the highest heaven!"*
> 10 *When he entered Jerusalem, the whole city was in turmoil, asking,* *"Who is this?"* 11 *The crowds were saying, "This is the prophet Jesus from Nazareth in Galilee."*

1-11 Even in Mark, Jesus' entry into Jerusalem, which historically can have presented itself only as the arrival of a great pilgrimage from Galilee and its solemn liturgical entry into the temple, has become an account concentrated on the person of Jesus. The innocence of this event, in which, of course, Jesus stood at the center of interest within the festival throngs, is shown by the fact that his adversaries took no offense in it, nor made any indictment of it at his trial. Matthew has taken over this Markan presentation in its entirety, but has added some further accents: on Jesus' entry on the colt of a donkey, along with a fulfillment quotation (vv. 4-5); on the cry of the people, with the title "Son of David" for Jesus (v. 9), and on the observation that the entire city of Jerusalem was caught up in excitement (v. 10) and that the people said, "This is the prophet Jesus from Nazareth in Galilee" (v. 11).

1-6 The starting point for the solemn entry into Jerusalem is Bethphage, at the Mount of Olives. Bethany, additionally named in Mark and Luke, is omitted by Matthew, probably because it lay somewhat farther from Jerusalem and confused the order of place indications. The strange account of the discovery and release of the riding animals after Jesus' instruction comes from the same stratum of tradition as the later account of the room for the Passover meal (26:17-19). In both narratives Jesus demonstrates a miraculous knowledge of the future and a sovereign disposition, with which the people involved comply. Reflection by the primitive church on the event as it was transmitted and on the person of Jesus — still from Mark — influenced this presentation. The mounting of a donkey recalls the prophecy of Zechariah 9:9, according to which the messianic King comes not on a steed, with instruments of war, but in lowliness, on a donkey, the royal mount of early times (Gen. 49:11) — a prince of peace who plans no political action. This can be read out of Mark itself, but Matthew has clarified it with the quotation from Zechariah 9:9 — making two riding beasts of one, in terms of a literal understanding of the Greek text ("on a donkey, *and* on a colt, the foal of a donkey"). He then retains this picture for finding the beasts and Jesus' mounting them (Matt. 21:7). How this precisely occurred does not preoccupy him. But the citation of both beasts reinforces the exact fulfillment of the prophecy from Zechariah, which Jesus demonstrates as the messianic Prince of peace. It is the same image of the Messiah that, in another form, in 12:18-20, radiates from the song of the Servant of God in Isaiah 42:1-4. In introducing the quotation, Matthew adds: "Tell the daughter of Zion . . ." (Isa. 62:11) — Israel must now know and be aware of who Jesus is. If we look up the text of Isaiah 62:11 in the Septuagint, we find further overtones: "Behold, now your salvation comes; . . . all whom he has won go before him." In the image of Jesus' entry into Jerusalem, the people will be shown the fulfillment of their yearning for redemption.

7-9 The disciples lay clothing across the animals' backs, as was customary in the case of individuals of exalted rank. Numerous people spread clothing ahead of Jesus as he came, as is recounted at the enthronement of Jehu as king of Israel: "All took their cloaks and spread them for him on the bare steps" (2 Kings 9:13). At the two miles' distance from Jerusalem yet to be covered, the meaning here can only be symbolic, the honoring of the messianic King (cf. 1 Kings 1:38-40), which is reinforced by the "carpet" of branches and leaves cut from trees. The outcries (acclamations) evince the sense of this behavior. In Matthew Jesus is celebrated outright as the "Son of David" (see 20:30-31). The "Hosanna" (Heb. *hôshî῾â(n)nā*, "Save, we pray"), a cry of petition and salutation, was familiar to the people from Psalm 118:25. This psalm, a liturgy of thanksgiving, was originally a blessing pronounced by the priests on the pilgrims entering the temple (Ps. 118:26), but here it is shouted to Jesus by the crowd. *He* is the blessed one, the one who comes in the name of the Lord (cf. Matt. 11:3). Through its repetition, the Hosanna acquires a liturgical ring, as in Judaism itself, where it was chanted at the shaking of the festal flowers at the Festival of Tents. It was also adopted by the Christian liturgy (*Didache* 10:6). "In the highest" points to God and the court of heaven (cf. 18:10), where the cry of praise is heard and resounds.

10-11   These concluding sentences, found only in Matthew, characterize the entire action as a mighty assembly of the people for the messianic King, of David's line, and it throws all of Jerusalem into turmoil (cf. 2:3). The thought of the Sonship of David may stand behind the Jerusalemites' question (see 12:23). The Galilean pilgrims answer, "the prophet Jesus from Nazareth in Galilee," for Matthew a designation of the Christ/Messiah (see 2:23) but at the same time of the Messiah refused by the Jews. In spite of the people's attraction to this "prophet" (21:46), he is indignantly rejected by the high priests and scribes, as the appended scenes in the temple show (21:15-16).

Jesus Cleanses the Temple (21:12-17)

> 12 *Then Jesus entered the temple and drove out all who were selling and buying in the temple, and he overturned the tables of the money changers and the seats of those who sold doves.* 13 *He said to them, "It is written,*
>> *'My house shall be called a house of prayer';*
>> *but you are making it a den of robbers."*
>
> 14 *The blind and the lame came to him in the temple, and he cured them.* 15 *But when the chief priests and the scribes saw the amazing things that he did, and heard the children crying out in the temple, "Hosanna to the Son of David," they became angry* 16 *and said to him, "Do you hear what these are saying?" Jesus said to them, "Yes; have you never read,*

'Out of the mouths of infants and nursing babies
you have prepared praise for yourself'?"
17 *He left them, went out of the city to Bethany, and spent the night there.*

12-17   The narrative adopted by Matthew from Mark 11:15-19 acquires emphases through special traits. (1) For Matthew, it is in close relation to the entry into Jerusalem. According to Mark 11:11, Jesus leaves Jerusalem for Bethany with the Twelve on the evening of the day of the entry, while in Matthew this occurs only after the cleansing of the temple (Matt. 21:17). With Matthew, the entry into Jerusalem and the cleansing of the temple are one messianic act. (2) The cursing of the fig tree (21:18-19), which in Mark frames the occurrence in the temple, takes place in Matthew only afterward, so that it functions as an additional symbolic scene. It has its own weight. (3) In the scriptural quotation concerning the "house of prayer," Matthew omits "for the nations." In doing so, he preserves a Jewish orientation and sharpens the opposition to the high priests and scribes. (4) In the temple, blind and lame persons approach Jesus, who heals them, and children continue the cry raised at the entry, "Hosanna to the Son of David!" Alongside the criticism of the old temple worship, Jesus' promising messianic activity enters the picture, an activity through which a new salvation community, practicing authentic divine worship, is being formed — probably the Matthean interpretation of the event handed down in the tradition. At the same time the two scenes divide the passage.

12-13   Jesus' action is recounted almost verbatim in the words of Mark. The expulsion of the buyers and sellers takes place in the broad outer precinct (Court of the Gentiles), where the temple authorities permitted, indeed supported, the sale of sacrificial animals and currency exchange for the temple tax (see 17:24-27). In itself the procurement of sacrificial animals, namely, doves (the offering of the poor, Lev. 5:7; 14:22; cf. Luke 2:24, etc.), was necessary, just as was the exchange of the coins in common use for old Tyrian or Hebrew currency (one-half silver shekel for the temple tax). But the conducting of business in the sacred temple area itself, and probably, over and above this, the behavior of the higher-ranking priests, provoke Jesus' sharp criticism. What he does — the disciples are not mentioned — can only be a limited symbolic demonstration in holy zeal, a protest against the desecration of the sanctuary (cf. John 2:17), not with the intent to perform an act of violence, nor even with a political objective. Two scriptural quotations, placed on the lips of Jesus himself, reveal the sense: the "house of God," the temple (1 Sam. 1:7, 24; 1 Kings 6; 8:27-30), is to be a "house of prayer" (Isa. 56:7), but, in sharp contrast, "you are making it a den of robbers" (Jer. 7:11). Prophetic criticism of outward worship of God (Jer. 7:1-15) sounds forth in the words from Isaiah as well (understanding the future tense as a warning), just as in Matthew 15:8-9. The outlook on all peoples, which Mark 11:17 retains in the quotation, may be in Matthew's mind when, in the second scene (Matt. 21:14-16), he now thinks of a new people of God (cf. 8:11; 21:43; 28:19). But his concern here is the sharp confrontation with the high priests, who were in charge of the temple, and the scribes, who taught in the temple.

14-17 Jesus does something else in the temple (only in 21:23 do we hear of his "teaching" there): he heals the blind and the lame and he accomplishes "wondrous deeds," as is proper at the dawn of the era of salvation (see 11:5). His cures, which Matthew constantly emphasizes (see 4:23-24; 9:35; 14:14, 35-36; 15:30), are the proclamation of the gospel in deeds. They signify a new age and order. After all, according to 2 Samuel 5:8 the lame and the blind are excluded from the house of the Lord; we see the same thing more clearly in the Qumran community (cf. 1QSa 2:5-8). Jesus renders these handicapped people, who otherwise would continue to eke out their existence as beggars at the gates (Acts 3:2; cf. John 9:1-7), capable of participating in the worship and life of their community. He fulfills the promise that, as the physician of his people, he intends to heal all illnesses (Exod. 15:26). He is the "Son of David" professed by the children in their cry, like the blind men of Jericho (see Matt. 20:30-31). Matthew understands this, in terms of Psalm 8:2, as praise of God, "to silence the enemy and the avenger," as the same verse goes on to say. Thus Jesus resists the demand of the high priests and scribes (Matt. 21:15-16) that he forbid the children to continue their loud calling, allows them to remain, and leaves the temple.

The cleansing of the temple, beyond any doubt a historical event, is not fully clear, in its original sense, in Jesus' intent. Criticism of temple worship to the point of rejecting it? Prediction of the destruction of the temple? Proclamation of a new divine worship? Formation of a new salvation community (cf. the temple logion, Mark 14:58 and pars.)? The primitive church further interpreted it in terms of its own self-concept, especially as a sign of the dissolution of the old worship, bound up with the temple, and the initiation of the new way of access to God through Jesus' death on the cross (cf. Mark 15:38 par. Matt. 27:51), and in Matthew, besides, the transcendence of the former sacrificial practice through love and mercy (cf. Matt. 9:13; 12:7). For the church, with its new divine worship, which culminates in the Eucharist, the Matthean pericope, especially the second part (vv. 14-16), is a constant summons to reflection on the extent to which that church's worship actualizes Jesus' will to love and mercy.

Jesus Curses the Fig Tree (21:18-22)

> 18 *In the morning, when he returned to the city, he was hungry.* 19 *And seeing a fig tree by the side of the road, he went to it and found nothing at all*

*on it but leaves. Then he said to it, "May no fruit ever come from you again!"
And the fig tree withered at once.* 20 *When the disciples saw it, they were
amazed, saying, "How did the fig tree wither at once?"* 21 *Jesus answered
them, "Truly I tell you, if you have faith and do not doubt, not only will you
do what has been done to the fig tree, but even if you say to this mountain,
'Be lifted up and thrown into the sea,' it will be done.* 22 *Whatever you ask for
in prayer with faith, you will receive."*

18-22   This peculiar story, which should not be designated a "punishment
wonder" (the only one in the Gospels! — punishment of vegetation?), must be
seen rather as one of Jesus' "signs in action." In Mark the cursing of the fig tree
occurs on the way to the temple and its withered condition is discovered after
the cleansing of the temple, so that the pair of accounts frame the temple event.
In Mark, then, the story of the fig tree is certainly to be interpreted in the sense
that Jesus' action in the temple is a judgment upon Israel. Matthew, who joins
the two parts, retains this view, as the context of his Gospel suggests. He intensifies the miracle: the fig tree withers "at once" (vv. 19-20). Precisely this picture
forms for him the transition to Jesus' dialogue with the disciples, who "are
amazed" at it. Jesus' answer, taken over from Mark, goes in another direction
from that of his action signs: it is an admonishment to faith that does not doubt
and prayer sure of being heard. Matthew is making a transition: with the miracle of the mountain transported into the sea, the disciples can through their
prayer surpass even the miracle of the withered fig tree (v. 21). That is intended,
but perhaps the conversation with the disciples has for Matthew a function
similar to that of the scene with the sick and the blind after the cleansing of the
temple: the gloomy, menacing event is followed by a bright new outlook. In
terms of content, the cursing of the fig tree and the dialogue with the disciples
must be considered independently.

18-19   The fig tree became a symbol of Israel in the prophetic preaching
of the Old Testament itself (Hos. 9:10; Joel 1:7; Mic. 7:1), in the prophecy of di-
saster for the disobedient people (Jer. 8:13; 24:1-10; 29:17). Like the grapevine,
the fig tree, prized for its fruit, is a fitting image of God's love for Israel, as well
as of God's divine disappointment with the chosen people. In this sense the
parable of the sterile fig tree in Luke 13:6-9 is related, although it is not likely
that our story is concocted from it. Still more different, even further distant, is
the comparison with the fig tree in Mark 13:28-29 and parallels. The cursing of
the fig tree that stood along the way to Jerusalem indicates the rejection of Israel as the people of salvation because of its sterility. It is not open to interpretation as a punitive judgment on the temple or Jerusalem since the fig tree nowhere appears as their symbol. Matthew places stronger accents: *one* fig tree,
only leaves on it, no fruit *coming from* it. It is the same view found in 21:43:

"The kingdom of God will be taken from you and given to a people that produces the fruits of the kingdom." One must also bear in mind, however, the historically conditioned polemic against the Jewish people (cf. 27:25), which admits of no interpretation in terms of a judgment upon Israel's salvific destiny. Jesus' "signs in action" can also be understood in terms of the concept of threat, like his cries of woe in 11:20-24.

20-22 Despite their association with amazement, Matthew understands Jesus' words to the disciples as a warning to his community not to become hard, like unbelieving Israel, and fairly wither, but to bear fruit in faith and prayer. He has already presented the logion on the faith that moves mountains in 17:20. Here it differs slightly from the parallel in Mark: "only the size of a mustard seed" is missing, and "if you do not doubt" is added. Little faith (17:20) and doubt (cf. 14:31; 28:17) are both defects in the disciples' faith. Charismatically stronger faith requires the bulwark of the prayer that expects God to grant all petitions. Matthew's formulation is shorter than Mark's; however, he has already enjoined on the community of disciples trusting prayer to the heavenly Father in the Sermon on the Mount (see 7:7-11; further, 18:19). Matthew has omitted the admonition to forgive brothers and sisters, which Mark appends (Mark 11:25), since it has already resounded in the "Our Father" as well as been set in relief by Matthew in the immediate appendix to that prayer (6:14). As for Jewish unbelief, nothing is as important as an unshakable faith, bound to the prayer that through God's help and power can perform wonders.

The Authority of Jesus Questioned (21:23-27)

> 23 When he entered the temple, the chief priests and the elders of the people came to him as he was teaching, and said, "By what authority are you doing these things, and who gave you this authority?" 24 Jesus said to them, "I will also ask you one question; if you tell me the answer, then I will also tell you by what authority I do these things. 25 Did the baptism of John come from heaven, or was it of human origin?" And they argued with one another, "If we say, 'From heaven,' he will say to us, 'Why then did you not believe him?' 26 But if we say, 'Of human origin,' we are afraid of the crowd; for all regard John as a prophet." 27 So they answered Jesus, "We do not know." And he said to them, "Neither will I tell you by what authority I am doing these things."

23-27 In the course of the Matthean presentation, Jesus' entry into Jerusalem, the cleansing of the temple, and (the next day) the cursing of the fig tree are immediately followed by the question of authority. But at the same time polemical dialogues now begin to be held with the Jewish leaders. Is the question of authority still connected to the cleansing of the temple? To what does "these things" refer in the question put by the high priests and elders of the people? The reference to Jesus' "doing" betrays the cleansing of the temple as the occasion of the interrogation. Jesus' "teaching," which Matthew introduces instead of Mark's "going about," in the temple might indicate only the setting of the scene, or the "instructional dialogue" that Jesus conducts with his critics on the baptism administered by John the Baptist. But although the conversation is constructed in the style of a rabbinical disputation — question/counter-question/concluding sentence — it transcends the framework of such a disputation: the adversaries are exposed and overcome. For the Christian reader, Jesus' "full authority" is revealed in every respect, in his action and in his teaching (cf. 7:29; 8:9, 13; 9:6; 10:1; 28:18). In this way the question of authority becomes a fundamental emphasis.

23   In Matthew those who call Jesus to account are the "chief priests," as Jewish higher authorities, and the "elders of the people," as representatives of the people; these are then the ones who orchestrate Jesus' arrest and handing over to Pilate (26:3, 47; 27:1). The twin questions bear on the manner and the origin of Jesus' authority. If, like the scribes, Jesus lays claim to the power of teaching, law, and discipline (cf. the "binding and loosing," 16:19), it is of first importance for him to be able to say from whom he possesses it. And that could trigger judicial proceedings against him (as a "false prophet"). Jesus' counter-question, as to the authority of John the Baptist, implies the answer, "From God." But Jesus could not openly give such an answer to the Pharisees' question without occasioning his sure sentence to punishment at the hands of these interrogators (cf. 26:64-66).

24-26   Jesus' counterquestion, which shifts the interrogation to a dialogue on equal footing, takes as its point of reference the baptism of John, who, for Jesus and the primitive church, was, without prejudice to his secondary status to Jesus, a prophet sent from God (3:1-10; 11:7-19). John's baptism to repentance, in spite of the qualification it incurred through its reception by Jesus (3:13-17), is acknowledged. While Matthew specifies "many Pharisees and Sadducees" among the candidates for John's baptism (see 3:7), this does not prevent him from depriving these inquirers, representatives of the Jewish authorities, of any faith in the Baptist's mission (v. 25c), just as in 21:32. Any opportunity to proclaim their unbelief in this prophet is counterbalanced by their fear of the people (cf. 21:46; 26:5). The reflections engaged in by Jesus' adversaries, secretly among themselves or silently in their minds (cf. 3:9; 9:3; 16:7-8), are revealed by way of Christian tradition: they themselves, of course, do not verbalize them.

27   The humiliating response, "We do not know," which they had to blurt out in front of the people, entitles Jesus, in terms of verse 24, to leave their

own question unanswered. The layout and design of the dispute clearly show the slant of the narrative: Jesus' authority is endorsed, and his opponents' hypocrisy rendered blatant (cf. 23:28!), through their embarrassment. But viewed historically, Jesus' being called to account by the temple authorities on account of his behavior in the temple is credible.

Three Polemical Parables (21:28–22:14)

In place of the one parable of the wicked vinedressers of Mark 12:1-12, Matthew presents three parables, all making the same polemical point against the ruling groups in Jerusalem — for Matthew "the chief priests and the Pharisees" (21:45). He reinforces the transmitted parables in this respect by way of redactional additions: after the parable of the two sons, which is from his own material, in a chiding expression (21:32); after the parable of the vinedressers, in a saying dealing with the Reign of God, which will be taken from them (21:43); in the powerfully developed parable of the wedding banquet, especially in the outlook on the looming destruction of Jerusalem (22:7), which for him has already occurred. However, his perspective opens out as well on the call of sinners (21:31b-32), the formation of a new people of God (21:43), and the church composed of good persons and bad (22:10-14). All this reveals the evangelist's way of seeing things: in terms of "salvation history" (cf. Intro., pp. 7 and 10-11).

The Parable of the Two Sons (21:28-32)

> 28 "*What do you think? A man had two sons; he went to the first and said, 'Son, go and work in the vineyard today.' 29 He answered, 'I will not'; but later he changed his mind and went. 30 The father went to the second and said the same; and he answered, 'I go, sir'; but he did not go. 31 Which of the two did the will of his father?" They said, "The first." Jesus said to them, "Truly I tell you, the tax collectors and the prostitutes are going into the kingdom of God ahead of you. 32 For John came to you in the way of righteousness and you did not believe him, but the tax collectors and the prostitutes believed him; and even after you saw it, you did not change your minds and believe him.*"

28-32 The original text of the first parable begins, "A man had two sons" (the antecedent question is a Matthean introduction; see 18:12), and ends with Jesus' question as to who has done the father's will. Verses 31b-32 are an application to the two groups: on the one hand, the tax collectors and prostitutes, and, on the other, Jesus' adversaries, both addressees in the passage. The change of mind or heart of the two sons, expressed at the center of the parable, is presupposed rather than expressed in the case of the tax collectors and prostitutes but only demanded in the case of the adversaries. The content is reminiscent of the logion in Luke 7:29-30 and a tradition in the Sayings Source standing behind the Lukan material. In the light of stylistic indicators, Matthew himself may have tied these sayings together in the parable of the two sons, or at least adapted them. The connection with the question of John's baptism (21:25) also suggests this.

In terms of textual criticism, each of the two possibilities as to what the original order was between the son who said "Yes" and the son who said "No" has about the same weight. As the German Ecumenical Translation suggests, and against the text as edited by Nestle-Aland and not a few more recent interpreters, it is more probable that the first named is the one who consents but then does not obey, and that the second is the one who refuses but changes his mind (reverses, changes, his decision) and fulfills his father's will: both sons illustrate the audience's attitude to Jesus' proclamation, and the purpose of the parable is to give an opportunity for conversion and doing the will of God. That purpose is better attained if the son who ultimately obeys comes at the end. Matthew could have changed the order on the basis of his polemical tendency. But even his order is understandable: just as in the other two parables, he is thinking in terms of salvation history. Then the "first" son corresponds to the wedding guests first invited (22:3, 8), while the other matches those invited later, who follow God's call. In terms of content the difference between the two orders is not very significant: either way, the accent falls on doing the divine will.

28-31a The narrative material on the "two sons" is also found in the parable of the "prodigal son" (Luke 15:11-32); but it is cited so differently there that no connection is possible from the standpoint of tradition history. There we have joy at the finding of a lost son, here praise for an obedient son; there our eyes are on God, whose compassion is so inconceivably great, here they are on human beings and their conduct in the presence of God's call. A parable taken from real life is in line with Jesus' style; nor, indeed, is this his only parable depicting labor in a vineyard (see 20:1-15; 21:33; Luke 13:6; 14:28-30). The first son still lives at home, and his "Yes" corresponds to his duty of obedience vis-à-vis the father, while his disobedience is a culpable matter. Just the other way around, the second son's initial refusal is offset by his reversal, his conversion. The response to Jesus' question (cf., similarly, Luke 7:43, subsequent to the parable of the two debtors), which is clear to his audience, may have been added in the original context itself.

31b-32 The tax collectors and prostitutes are not characterized as earlier resisters of the will of God: only their faith in the Baptist's proclamation is brought out. Faith means trusting, obedient acceptance of the word of God, and it here includes submission to John's baptism and "fruit worthy of repentance" (3:8). Prostitutes are singled out here, alongside tax collectors, as notorious "sinners" (9:10-11; 11:19). In an entry logion (see 5:20), they are assured of a portion in the Realm of God, while others who in unbelief and disobedience have closed themselves off from the message of John the Baptist are denied entry. The "precedence" of the tax collectors and prostitutes is to be understood not chronologically, as if those addressed would indeed still be received into the Realm of God, but in an excluding, indicting sense (cf. 5:19). Those who fail to fulfill God's will in their actions must face the condemning words of the Son of Man (7:21; 13:41-42; 25:45). The expression, "kingdom of *God*," instead of the Matthean "kingdom of heaven," permits a connection with the antecedent logion (cf. 12:28; 19:24; 21:43). The turn of phrase, "John came to you in the way of righteousness," is certainly Matthew's own (see 3:15; 5:6, 20, and frequently), is emphatically reminiscent of the Old Testament (Job 24:13 in the Greek; Prov. 8:20; 12:28; 16:31; and frequently), and means that the Baptist himself practiced right behavior before God, preached it to others, and required it from all. Jesus had acknowledged this righteousness (cf. Matt. 11:7-11) and submitted to it (3:15); thus, behind John's route, Jesus' own route becomes visible. One who rejects the Baptist only opposes Jesus' message all the more. The logion of verse 31b is also a mirror for the conscience of all subsequent believers in Christ.

The Parable of the Wicked Tenants (21:33-46)

33 *"Listen to another parable. There was a landowner who planted a vineyard, put a fence around it, dug a wine press in it, and built a watchtower. Then he leased it to tenants and went to another country.* 34 *When the harvest time had come, he sent his slaves to the tenants to collect his produce.* 35 *But the tenants seized his slaves and beat one, killed another, and stoned another.* 36 *Again he sent other slaves, more than the first; and they treated them in the same way.* 37 *Finally he sent his son to them, saying, 'They will respect my son.'* 38 *But when the tenants saw the son, they said to themselves, 'This is the heir; come, let us kill him and get his inheritance.'* 39 *So they seized him, threw him out of the vineyard, and killed him.* 40 *Now when the owner of the vineyard comes, what will he do to those tenants?"* 41 *They said to him, "He will put those wretches to a miserable death, and lease the vineyard to other tenants who will give him the produce at the harvest time."*

42 *Jesus said to them, "Have you never read in the scriptures:*
'The stone that the builders rejected

has become the cornerstone;
this was the Lord's doing,
and it is amazing in our eyes'?
43 *Therefore I tell you, the kingdom of God will be taken away from you and given to a people that produces the fruits of the kingdom.* 44 *The one who falls on this stone will be broken to pieces; and it will crush anyone on whom it falls."*

45 *When the chief priests and the Pharisees heard his parables, they realized that he was speaking about them.* 46 *They wanted to arrest him, but they feared the crowds, because they regarded him as a prophet.*

33-46   This parable, taken from Mark 12:1-12, is composed even more transparently for the history of Israel, and Jesus' destiny, in Matthew than in Mark, as we also see from the conclusion in verses 45-46. The original parable, whose form may come somewhat into view in the *Gospel of Thomas* 65 (twice a slave is sent, then the son), was further interpreted by Mark himself (esp. in 12:5). Matthew goes beyond this and develops a view in line with salvation history that traces Israel's behavior over against its prophets and the destiny of God's last emissary, the "Son." Among the striking characteristics introduced by Matthew are: (1) the proprietor of the vineyard requires "his produce" (v. 34), and not merely "his share of the produce," as in Mark 12:2. The importance of fruits to be produced is shown again in the addition that the owner will lease the vineyard to other vinedressers, "who will give him produce at harvest time" (v. 41), and completely in verse 43: the Reign of God will be given to a people that "does" its fruits, that is, produces them through their actions. (2) Instead of slaves being sent one after the other, groups of slaves are dispatched twice, obviously an allusion to the prophets (as suggested in Mark 12:5 itself). The second group is more extensive; perhaps the later prophets are meant. (3) The son is not first killed and then cast out of the vineyard (Mark 12:8), but driven out of the vineyard and subsequently killed (Matt. 21:39), a representation of the destiny of Jesus, who was crucified outside the holy city (cf. Heb. 13:12). From the post-Easter perspective (cf. the quotation in Matt. 21:42), the parable (like the following one of the wedding banquet) becomes a sketch of the history of salvation and reprobation as believers in Christ conceptualized it.

Then has the parable itself not perhaps been formed and developed only out of the matrix of the primitive church? This is the opinion of critical exegetes who hold the still recognizable original story to be unrealistic, and impossible on the lips of Jesus. According to scholars of the Palestinian context of the times, however, we can construct a simple, credible story that Jesus could indeed have narrated: a large landholder leases his landed property — here a vineyard — stipulates in the contract that he receive a certain proportion of the proceeds, and goes on a journey. The delivery of this proportion is to be effected by one or more emissaries. The poor farmers are enraged with the wealthy proprietor, probably an absentee landlord, and therefore abuse the emissary or emissaries. Finally, they reflect whether they should kill the son: if the sole heir dies, the vineyard becomes ownerless property, which, according to Jewish legal principles, can be appropriated by anyone, simply by taking possession of it. The son, then, in the framework of the account, would be a realistic personage, and not designed as a christological figure. True, we are taken aback by the naive unconcern with which, after the experiences with the slaves, the proprietor nevertheless sends his son. But the man could have expected to succeed in asserting his rights more readily through his son. The latter's murder, which shows the despicable character of the wicked vinedressers, is a frightful felony. Jesus introduces other transgressions of the law into his parables as well, as with the weeds among the wheat (see 13:24-30), the treasure in the field (see 13:44), and the impatient judge (Luke 18:2-5). Other authors refer to a Hellenistic Jewish-Christian theology they allege to surface in the presentation; but the Palestinian coloring of the original narrative permits us to ascribe it to Jesus, and only the interpretative expansions and the conclusion (Matt. 21:42-46) to the community transmitting it. The original parable threatened judgment against Israel and its leaders, as with the cursing of the fig tree.

33-41   Taking up the various details, the beginning may simply have read: a man had a vineyard and entrusted it to farmers. The portrayal of his care in laying it out originates in the vineyard song of Isaiah 5:1-7, whose second verse is quoted, in heavy dependence on the Greek text. This ingredient is certainly a contribution of the Greek-speaking community; the vineyard as a symbol of Israel was familiar to Jesus' audience. Matthew calls the owner, literally, "master of the house" (Mark merely says "man"), a symbolic word for God or Christ elsewhere as well (10:25; 13:27; 20:1, 11). Examples of the abuse and killing of prophets are found in the Old Testament (1 Kings 19:14; 2 Chron. 24:20-22; Jer. 26:20-24; 37:15-16; 38:6), as in later legends (*Martyrdom of Isaiah* 2:16; 5:1-14). This view of the hard lot of prophets and the righteous (cf. also Acts 7:52; Heb. 11:36-38) is adopted by Matthew in 23:34-35 by way of accusation. The exclusively Matthean "stoning" is also used in 23:37. A crescendo of misdeeds with each successive dispatch of emissaries is not found; instead, Matthew at once directs the reader's gaze to the son. While he does not characterize him as the "only, beloved" son, it is clear that he identifies him with Jesus. The concluding question, what the master of the vineyard will do with these vinedressers, is answered in Matthew by the audience, whom we ought to think of as ordinary persons (cf. v. 46) rather than as the leaders. "To bring the evil to ruin in an evil way" was an expression current in classical Greek itself, and in Matthew betokens the menace of imminent judgment.

42-46 A new beginning follows, with a christological continuation originating with the primitive church. The quotation concerning the stone that the builders rejected, made by God the cornerstone (hardly the keystone), is taken literally from Psalm 118:22-23 in the Greek, an important christological testimonial for the primitive church (Acts 4:11; 1 Peter 2:7; cf. Eph. 2:20). Jesus, executed on the cross by human beings, attains a unique significance by being raised by God. Upon him is founded the new community of salvation (the church), to which even the erstwhile heathen belong (cf. 1 Peter 2:9-10). He alone is the source of redemption and salvation for all human beings (Acts 4:12). After the murder of the son in the parable, the primitive church wished to introduce the concept of Jesus' resurrection. Jesus' way does not end in a catastrophe, but is rendered consummately meaningful by God — an astonishing, wondrous event. Other "stone" passages (the chosen, precious cornerstone, Isa. 28:16; the stone that for the contemptuous becomes the stone of scandal and fall, Isa. 8:14-15) were seen as connected with this one, as 1 Peter 2:6-8 shows. For Matthew, whose thinking is in the context of the church, the most important thing is the formation of a new people of God. In the logion of verse 43, which reveals his overarching concern, the key concepts are the "kingdom of God," the "people" — here not the ancient people of God *(laos)* but the new people *(ethnos)*, one that includes the Gentile peoples (Matt. 12:18-21; 28:19) — and the "fruits" that this new people is to produce. In the Matthean view, Jesus' cross and resurrection accomplish the transition from the ancient people of God to the new. Israel is not denied the Reign of God for its time; but now, after the crucifixion of its Messiah, that Reign is taken from it and — after the raising of the crucified one — given to another people. At the same time we are aware of the pervasive Matthean concern that this new people yield the corresponding moral fruits (7:21-23; 13:41-43; 25:31-46; 28:20).

Verse 44 adds another "stone" logion, one that echoes Daniel 2:34-35, 44 — the vision of the stone that breaks away from the mountain and smashes the statue of the realms of the world. However, the first part transcends the image from Daniel and is doubtless reminiscent of Isaiah 8:14-15. If verse 44, which surfaces in Luke 20:18 as well, was introduced by Matthew himself, its position here can be elucidated as follows. It interprets in terms of the new people of God of verse 43 the judgment to be rendered upon those who despise the "stone" laid by God, and thereby forms an appropriate transition to the concluding observations of verse 45.

The Parable of the Wedding Banquet (22:1-14)

22:1 *Once more Jesus spoke to them in parables, saying:* 2 *"The kingdom of heaven may be compared to a king who gave a wedding banquet for his son.*

3 *He sent his slaves to call those who had been invited to the wedding banquet, but they would not come.* 4 *Again he sent other slaves, saying, 'Tell those who have been invited: Look, I have prepared my dinner, my oxen and my fat calves have been slaughtered, and everything is ready; come to the wedding banquet.'* 5 *But they made light of it and went away, one to his farm, another to his business,* 6 *while the rest seized his slaves, mistreated them, and killed them.* 7 *The king was enraged. He sent his troops, destroyed those murderers, and burned their city.* 8 *Then he said to his slaves, 'The wedding is ready, but those invited were not worthy.* 9 *Go therefore into the main streets, and invite everyone you find to the wedding banquet.'* 10 *Those slaves went out into the streets and gathered all whom they found, both good and bad; so the wedding hall was filled with guests.*

11 *"But when the king came in to see the guests, he noticed a man there who was not wearing a wedding robe,* 12 *and he said to him, 'Friend, how did you get in here without a wedding robe?' And he was speechless.* 13 *Then the king said to the attendants, 'Bind him hand and foot, and throw him into the outer darkness, where there will be weeping and gnashing of teeth.'* 14 *For many are called, but few are chosen."*

1-14   This much discussed parable, explained in many different ways in the history of interpretation, was developed by Matthew from a much simpler narrative. Luke 14:16-24 and the *Gospel of Thomas* 64 offer the story of a man who issues invitations to a banquet, but who is "left in the lurch" and snubbed, and then invites other persons. However, in each of these versions of the parable, various expansions and special tendencies are also recognizable. In terms of tradition history, we are dealing with the same material; a literary relationship between Luke and Matthew must have rested on a common basis in the Sayings Source, which each of the two evangelists would then have worked out in his own fashion. The original narrative on Jesus' lips may have been a polemical parable against the leading classes in contemporary Judaism, who close themselves off from God's call heard in Jesus' gospel, and are put to shame by the poor, the despised, and sinners (cf. 21:28-32). Matthew has put together a broad showcase of salvation history here, as he likewise has in the parable of the wicked vinedressers, the "model" for which can be seen to be repeated in the present parable of the royal wedding banquet. The actual parable of the first invited, with their lame excuses, and then the second, the guests who accept the invitation, goes to verse 10. The interpolation, "bad and good," leads at once to the second part, which is shaped with the new community in process of formation, the church, in mind. Whether verses 11-13 present an originally independent parable of a "man not wearing a wedding garment" or what we have is a Matthean redactional formation is disputed to our day. Since such a parable is not easily integrated into the rest of the Jesus tradition, the latter possibility is more likely, although with the reservation that Matthew was perhaps inspired by familiar material (cf. the rabbinic parable of the king's banquet in Billerbeck, *Kommentar zum Neuen Testament,* 1:878). The aphorism of verse 14 is Matthew's conclusion, added as a warning to the Christian community, as in 19:30; 20:16.

On the imagery of verses 2-8: Matthew has made the dinner banquet a wedding feast, hosted by a king — in Judaism a frequent symbol for God — for his son. The personage of the son has been suggested by the parable of the vinedressers (21:37-39), but he plays no role in the further course of events: it suffices to indicate his wedding, his glory, and his magnificence. Besides, God (the king) is the only actor. However, in other passages Christ is identified with or described as the bridegroom who conducts his bride (the church) to the wedding (Matt. 25:1-10; 2 Cor. 11:2; Rev. 19:6-9). Still, this primitive Christian imagery has been coined in advance in the Old Testament through the symbolism of God's "marriage" with Israel (Hos. 2:16; 3:1; Isa. 54:5-8; 62:4-5; Ezek. 16:7-8). In the view of the primitive church, God brings salvation history to its fulfillment by having Jesus Christ, his Son, triumph at the end in salvation and judgment. A celebratory meal is also a picture of the awaited final salvation, the future Realm of God (see Matt. 8:11; 26:29). All of these motifs blend here in a presentation that is topical and yet focuses on the glorious end of salvation history. Israel's history is drawn in, through the destruction of Jerusalem (v. 7); yet the eschatological wedding, from which the unworthy are excluded (v. 8), constitutes the actual viewpoint.

1 Taking up the details, Jesus "answers" the hostile intentions of the high priests and Pharisees (21:45-46), as the Greek text reads (as in 11:25, without an antecedent question), once more with a parable.

2 The exordium places this parable among the eschatological parables of the "kingdom of heaven" and is Matthean in content and tone (as are 13:24; 18:23; 25:1).

3-4 The double dispatch of slaves corresponds to the parable of the wicked tenants (21:34-36) and, as there, has the Old Testament in view. In addition, perhaps, with the second dispatch, it actually portrays Christian heralds of the faith. In the parable of the great banquet in Luke 14:16-17, a slave is also sent twice, probably in accordance with the Eastern custom of a second invitation, to follow the first, at the hour of the banquet.

5-6 The excuses of those first invited are more restricted in Matthew: only the purchase of a field, or "business." (In the *Gospel of Thomas* 64, "business" is broadened and viewed as entanglement in the world.) Instead of the third example (the wedding), Matthew presents, once more in connection with the parable of the tenants, the abuse and murder of the slaves who had been sent. The king's punitive expedition against the murderers, with the razing of the city, is completely out of keeping with the course of the narrative. Everything is ready for the wedding, the fatted calf has been slaughtered — how can there be time for a military mission? Furthermore, all of those declining to attend the wedding are in one city, "their" city. There can be no missing Matthew's allusion to Jerusalem and its destruction in A.D. 70. Granted, what is explicitly stated depicts the characteristics of an event in any war, but here it is applied to a determinate case.

8-10   The guests who replace those first invited are led from the "exits of the streets," that is, from the outskirts of the city. Here is an indication that Matthew is thinking of non-Jews (the Gentiles), as with the second group, the substitutes, in Luke 14:23. In the first group of substitutes, Luke lists "the poor, the crippled, the blind, and the lame" (Luke 14:21; cf. 14:13). That may have been the actual intent of the original parable — to counterpoise the leaders with those they looked down upon; but Matthew is thinking now of the church as made up of Jews and Gentiles. All are called to it, and God achieves the goal of his salvation plan, to host the banquet of the divine Reign. With the present church in view, however, Matthew speaks of the "bad and good": the church is still a *corpus mixtum*, and the separation of the two occurs only at the end of the age (Matt. 13:36-43).

11-14   Matthew illustrates the expulsion of the wicked members of the church as the story continues. It is surprising and unsettling that the guests assembled on such short notice are supposed to have wedding robes (clean, laundered clothing). The hypothesis that they receive this from the king as they enter the wedding hall is not a solution since then everyone would have had one; and the custom is not actually established. Matthew does not bother about the new situation. The picture is that of the church, which has suffered the entry of unworthy persons among its members. It is probably not a matter of the baptismal garment, many members not having kept it; the expelled man obviously brings his soiled garment along with him. Experiences of the missionary church surely form part of the background; but the missionary situation is not immediately recognizable. With the eviction of the unworthy guest, Matthew is holding up a mirror and warning of pretense before the eyes of his community. This expulsion into the outer darkness, with howling and gnashing of teeth, is not Matthew's only use of the image for exclusion from the Reign of God and the punishment involved (Matt. 8:12; 13:42, 50; 24:51; 25:30). Another warning to the community is constituted by the general statement of verse 14, which does not logically fit verses 11-13: the wedding hall is full, and the "chosen" cannot be few. But it is an appeal to the hearer and reader: see to it that you do not lose your vocation! Just as in 7:13-14 "many" and "few" are not meant numerically. Divine choice and human probation are not mutually exclusive and are not to be played off against each other as the gift of grace and human effort.

Four Significant Questions (Disputations) (22:15-46)

Matthew has taken over the next passage, with four important questions for the Christian community, from Mark with little change. Mark divides the questions according to the functions of each: the Pharisees (imperial tax), the Sadducees (resurrection of the dead), a scribe (the greatest commandment), and Jesus himself (the son of David). Some interpreters contend that we are dealing with a rabbinic schema with four types of questions: a question of law *(halakah)*, a deriding question, a question of conduct, and, finally, a haggadic question (the apparent contradiction between two scripture passages). However, a rabbinic construction is improbable. Instead, what we have are themes of intimate concern to the Christian, more specifically the Jewish-Christian, community for its living in the world according to Jesus' guiding principles and its faith in Christ. At the same time Jesus' superiority to his challengers is indicated, so that they dared ask him no more questions (Mark 12:34, after the third question; Matt. 22:46, after the fourth). The consideration of these questions in connection with Jesus' last days in Jerusalem is easily understandable and says nothing about the original situation. As for the structure of the conversations, the primitive church was clear as to Jesus' intent and could certainly rely on credible traditions coming down from Jesus' days. Likewise, one must attend to the formation of these texts in four units and to their contribution to the application of Jesus' guidelines in their own times. Their openness to later times remains helpful and orientating for the church of today as well.

Through the observations embedded in his framework (the introduction and conclusion of the conversations), Matthew reveals the current nature of his interests. He upbraids the Pharisees and their legal scholars (cf. 22:34-35) most emphatically, just as he does subsequently in the great anti-Pharisaic discourse of chapter 23. As to the question of the tax, the Pharisees make a formal resolution and send "their disciples," accompanied by the Herodians, to Jesus. Matthew does not take the occasion of the theme broached by these inquirers to change the Sadducees' inquiry, but has the Pharisees, assembled for this express purpose (22:34), emphatically pose once more the question of the greatest commandment of the law. Again, Jesus poses the question concerning the son of David to the assembled Pharisees (22:41). It is no wonder, then, that the first three exchanges (including that concerning the greatest commandment) are characterized as struggles or disputes, introduced by a cunning, ill-willed question (22:18), one calculated to "tempt" Jesus, to trick him into showing his hand (the Sadducees' question). Only Jesus' question concerning the son of David reduces his adversaries to silence (22:45-46). Matthew is stepping back further from the historical situation and constructing a polemic against the Pharisees, even though in the question of the resurrection of the dead Jesus does stand with them against the Sadducees. Jesus' original intent is not represented by Matthew's current polemics.

The Question about Paying Taxes (22:15-22)

15 *Then the Pharisees went and plotted to entrap him in what he said.* 16 *So they sent their disciples to him, along with the Herodians, saying, "Teacher, we know that you are sincere, and teach the way of God in accordance with truth, and show deference to no one; for you do not regard people with partiality.* 17 *Tell us, then, what you think. Is it lawful to pay taxes to the emperor, or not?"*

18 *But Jesus, aware of their malice, said, "Why are you putting me to the test, you hypocrites?* 19 *Show me the coin used for the tax." And they brought him a denarius.* 20 *Then he said to them, "Whose head is this, and whose title?"* 21 *They answered, "The emperor's." Then he said to them, "Give therefore to the emperor the things that are the emperor's, and to God the things that are God's."* 22 *When they heard this, they were amazed; and they left him and went away.*

15-17 The entire group of Pharisees (after A.D. 70 the prevailing group in Judaism) comes together, according to Matthew, and passes a resolution to attempt to lead Jesus to speak in such a way as to fall into a trap. In the situation portrayed, however, they send only their "disciples," a word used only here in Matthew (not in 9:14, as in Mark 2:18), together with the "Herodians," who, as partisans of Herod and collaborators of the Romans, would have reported a politically dangerous answer on Jesus' part. Otherwise Matthew avoids mentioning the Herodians (cf. Matt. 12:14 with Mark 3:6). One is struck by the emissaries' lengthy expressions of flattery, providing an effective atmosphere for a crisp and clear answer by Jesus. Matthew presents only the positive assertions: Jesus is truthful, and teaches "in accordance with truth," without falsification, the "way of God" — that is, all that God tells human beings in the law (*halakah*, instruction for the way) for their life conduct (cf. Psalms 1, 119, etc.). Jesus promptly substantiates the negative statements ("You do not regard people") by unmasking his interlocutors' malice and hypocrisy (Matt. 22:18). Without the questioners' intending it, the material content of their insidious flattery accords with Jesus' actual attitude.

The question concerning the imperial tax, the "poll tax," or tax on each individual, which everyone who lived in the Roman Empire had to contribute in the amount of one denarius (about a day's wages; cf. 20:2), touched raw nerves. Its introduction in Judea in A.D. 6, under the procurator Coponius, met with vehement opposition from the Zealots (the uprising led by one Judas), who were willing to acknowledge only God as king over Israel. Their resistance, however, was considered rebellion against Rome. If Jesus rejected the poll tax, he could be brought to trial; if he came out in favor of it, he would become not only unpopular with the people but suspect of not taking the sovereignty of God in real earnest. The forked-tongue inquirers evidently sought to impel Jesus to reject the poll tax since they knew that he proclaimed God's sovereignty.

18-22 Having scolded the "hypocrites" (a favorite word of Matthew, occurring thirty times), Jesus answers with both gestures and words. He requires them to produce the coin of tribute since he is not carrying it, and the questioners do so: they have and use such coins. In the general conception of antiquity, the right of coinage, and the economic order it facilitates, accords with a recognition of government. Jesus' question as to the image and inscription on the coin also belongs to his action. The coin of Emperor Tiberius featured, on the obverse, the bust of the emperor with a crown of bay leaves and the inscription, "Tiberius Caesar Divi Augusti Filius Augustus" ("Tiberius Caesar Augustus, Son of the Divine Augustus"), emphasizing his divine dignity. Thus, the inquirers bow to pagan hegemony, which sparkled with divinity. The Pharisees did accept Roman hegemony, though unwillingly, doubtless with the thought that God uses even pagan rulers as tools of the divine world order (Nebuchadnezzar, Jer. 27:5-8; 28:14; Cyrus, Isa. 41:2-4; 44:28; 45:1), though with the reservation that God deposes kings and establishes them (Dan. 2:21), and will one day hale them before his judgment seat (*Ethiopian Enoch* 89–90). Accordingly, Jesus' celebrated expression, "Give to Caesar" what belongs to him (not "restore" or "reimburse" what belongs to him), goes beyond what the emissaries are asking: "and give to God the things that are God's." Here is the whole emphasis, and Jesus adds it deliberately. With this, he exalts God's claim above that of the emperor: God can demand more than can the state — he demands one's whole being (Matt. 6:24), and first and foremost (10:28). God's prerogative sets the bounds for the state: this is the proviso with which Jesus acknowledges the legitimate demands of the state. It is a basic instruction, although in the concrete, varying circumstances of reality it always requires new decisions (contrast Rom. 13:1-7 with Revelation 13).

The scene is significant for Jesus' "political" position. The Zealots, with their thoughts of a violent overthrow of the Roman government, have no ally in him. Rather, his position is the Pharisaic one. His word of orientation reveals his actual intent: to enable God's sovereignty to break through. But it admits of a variety of applications, as the history of its effect has always shown. Jesus has escaped the trap set for him — the tempters are compelled to withdraw — but the primitive church saw in his reply more than an evasion. It was an orientation for that church's own behavior, even vis-à-vis the Jewish authorities (Acts 4:19; 5:29).

The Question about the Resurrection (22:23-33)

> 23 *The same day some Sadducees came to him, saying there is no resurrection; and they asked him a question, saying,* 24 *"Teacher, Moses said, 'If a man dies childless, his brother shall marry the widow, and raise up children for his brother.' 25 Now there were seven brothers among us; the first married, and died childless, leaving the widow to his brother. 26 The second did the same, so also the third, down to the seventh. 27 Last of all, the woman herself died. 28 In the resurrection, then, whose wife of the seven will she be? For all of them had married her."*
>
> 29 *Jesus answered them, "You are wrong, because you know neither the scriptures nor the power of God. 30 For in the resurrection they neither marry nor are given in marriage, but are like angels in heaven. 31 And as for the resurrection of the dead, have you not read what was said to you by God, 32 'I am the God of Abraham, the God of Isaac, and the God of Jacob'? He is God not of the dead, but of the living." 33 And when the crowd heard it, they were astounded at his teaching.*

23-33 Matthew has taken the Sadducees' pericope almost literally, slightly condensed, from Mark. The introductory phrase, "The same day," may be an indication of how Jesus is harassed by the various leading groups in rapid succession. (For the conjunction of the Pharisees and the Sadducees cf. 3:7; 16:1, 6, 11-12.) For Matthew they form a unit, allied against Jesus, and Jesus warns against their doctrine (see 16:11-12). Then follows the "case history" of the seven brothers who enter into the Levirate matrimony (vv. 24-28). Jesus' answer in verses 29-32 sets two things in relief: his interlocutors' ignorance of Scripture and the power of God (v. 29), which Jesus establishes in reverse order. God's power is shown in the different mode of existence in the resurrection of the dead (v. 30); the proof from Scripture is set forth in terms of Exodus 3:6 (intentionally from the Pentateuch, which the Sadducees, too, regarded as binding). The two items converge in a deeper understanding of God. There is no adequate basis for holding the scriptural argument as a later interpolation by the Hellenistic Jewish-Christian community; from a narrative viewpoint the pericope is to be regarded as a unit. Matthew's own concluding observation (v. 33) is meant to convey the strong impression on the people of the teaching of Jesus, who speaks with sovereignty, with divine authority, as with the observation after the Sermon on the Mount (7:28-29). In context, the people clearly stand with Jesus (cf. 21:46; 23:1).

The resurrection of the dead was important to the primitive church (cf. 1 Corinthians 15; Acts 17:32; etc.), which was most profoundly convinced of it on the basis of the resurrection of Jesus. But in our pericope there is no reference to Jesus' resurrection (as there is in the prophecies of the passion in 16:21, 17:23, and 20:19). The frequently proposed post-Easter origin of the pericope from discussions between Christians and Jews ignores this fact. To what extent Jesus' response to the Pharisees can actually be ascribed to him depends on how strongly a belief in the resurrection prevailed in the Judaism of the time and on whether there are other traces of Jesus' sharing the belief. The present formation of the story, its artistic construction, on the part of the community handing it down need not be disputed.

24-28 The case history of the seven brothers is intended to show that a belief in the resurrection, which the Sadducees, unlike the Pharisees, rejected (cf. Acts 23:7-8; Josephus, *Antiquities* 18.16), is untenable. Fictitious narratives like this one served for purposes of disputation. Although it is a matter of a "mocking question," it is intended not to make belief in the resurrection actually laughable but simply to reduce it *ad absurdum*. Marriage to a brother-in-law — Levirate marriage (Deut. 25:5-10) — was introduced in Israel to regulate the inheritance of real estate — to ensure the legacy of buildings and land. But even in early Judaism, with a view to Leviticus 18:16; 20:21, it was suppressed, and by Jesus' time it was probably no longer in force. The Sadducees are using it simply as a "case," such as those used in moral instruction, and of course it presupposes the continuation of earthly relationships after the resurrection. True, conceptualizations of the resurrection of the dead (first attested in Dan. 12:2-3, and frequently since the time of the Maccabees) were considerably different, but generally speaking the world to come was thought of as analogous to the present one — only as a more blessed condition — including marital bliss and a wealth of children. The Sadducees' question was therefore not unjustified.

29-32 Jesus' answer is categorical: "You are wrong" (formulated in Mark as a question). The foundation, in verse 29, is the power of God, who, with the resurrection of the dead, creates a new world in which there is no longer any marriage, either for men ("they neither marry") or for women ("nor are they given in marriage"). The positive facet, "they are like angels in heaven," adopts the Jewish view that God has given the angels no wives, "for the spiritual beings of heaven have their dwelling in heaven" (*Ethiopian Enoch* 15:7). According to the *Syrian Baruch* 51:10, the resurrected righteous of the world to come live on high and are like the angels and stars. Judaism itself, then, grasps the otherness, the new manner of existence, of the resurrected, their exaltation into the transcendence of God. To read into this material a "sexlessness," as not infrequently occurred in the history of its Christian application, so that the sexual was devalued across the board, even for the earthly realm, is absurd. Jesus lays his whole emphasis on the power of God, who deals in a way different from anything human beings can conceive or imagine (see Matt. 19:26). Thereby he reveals the deepest foundation for a hope in the resurrection (cf. 2 Macc. 7:6, 9, 14, 23).

Jesus' scriptural argument is based on the same faith in that almighty, faithful God who is the God of life. In the revelation of God in the burning bush, the revelation to Moses, God is presented as the constant, faithful one, who has spoken words of encouragement to the ancestors and who will always keep his covenant. In spite of verse 32b, it is unlikely that the argumentation is to the effect that Abraham, Isaac, and Jecob are still alive and will live on until the resurrection: their life with God does not yet say anything directly about the future bodily resurrection. The argumentation begins rather with God, who will fulfill the divine promises of full life and salvation in the resurrection of the dead. Among the many biblical passages in which the Pharisees in rabbinism read, according to their methods of interpretation, evidence for the resurrection of the dead, Exodus 3:6 does not occur. What we have is a unique reference to a key text in the Pentateuch, which betrays profound reflection on the God of the Fathers. The three forefathers are likewise cited in the logion; see 8:11 on the participation of Gentiles in the eschatological banquet in the Reign of God. This material, like many judgment logia, may presuppose the resurrection of the patriarchs since resurrection and judgment were seen in intimate conjunction. From such indications in other logia of Jesus we may conclude that Jesus shared the belief, widespread among the people, in the resurrection, even though it comes to explicit expression only in our pericope.

A hope in the resurrection is of great importance for the concept of God, as it is for that of human beings. God summons human beings to full participation in the divine life, and this includes, in the holistic biblical view, human corporeality. But since the world to come is different from the present one, it is also a different corporeality — a transmuted or transfigured one, as Paul has so clearly seen. For Paul, bodiliness will be formed in the likeness of the risen Christ (cf. Rom. 8:23, 29; 1 Cor. 15:35-55; 2 Cor. 5:2-5; Phil. 3:21).

The Greatest Commandment (22:34-40)

34 *When the Pharisees heard that he had silenced the Sadducees, they gathered together,* 35 *and one of them, a lawyer, asked him a question to test him.* 36 *"Teacher, which commandment in the law is the greatest?"* 37 *He said to him, "'You shall love the Lord your God with all your heart, and with all your soul, and with all your mind.'* 38 *This is the greatest and first commandment.* 39 *And a second is like it: 'You shall love your neighbor as yourself.'* 40 *On these two commandments hang all the law and the prophets."*

34-40 This pericope is essentially altered vis-à-vis Mark 12:28-34. It is no pedagogical exchange with a good-willed student of the Scriptures to whom Jesus says, in conclusion, "You are not far from the kingdom of God," but a test

(Matt. 22:35), to which Jesus, however, responds with the same superior prowess that he shows concerning the resurrection of the dead. In Mark, Jesus posits the commandment of love of God and that of love of neighbor as the "first" and "second" in succession; in Matthew, love of neighbor is "like" the "greatest and first commandment" (vv. 38-39). However, this is only a more precise way of saying what Mark actually means. The Matthean response takes into consideration the Jewish rabbinic view. As the concluding sentence shows (v. 40), for Matthew the entire law and prophets depend on (literally, depend "in") these two commandments. Matthew's context is that of the conversation with Judaism after A.D. 70.

In terms of tradition history, it is disputed whether Matthew uses, besides Mark, another version that we would find in a different context in Luke 10:25-28 and that could originate in the Sayings Source. Here the legal expert poses the same question as does the rich young man in Luke 18:18 (Lukan redaction?) and gives the answer himself, while in Mark and Matthew the response is reserved for Jesus. Some linguistic points of contact with Luke are striking: the expression for "lawyer" (Gk. *nomikos*), which we have in Matthew only here; "asked him a question to test him" (absent in Mark); the same kind of expression with the modifiers of the formula for love of God, namely, "in," and not, as with Mark, "from" (your whole heart, etc.). Should Luke be using an actual variant tradition known also to Matthew, Jesus' answer would seem to be deprived of its historical authenticity. At all events, not a few scholars think that the condensation of the many commandments into the first and second commandments of love stems only from the Hellenistic Jewish-Christian community since this view appears in Hellenistic Judaism (cf. *Testament of Issachar* 5:2; 7:6; *Testament of Daniel* 5:3; Philo, *On the Special Laws* 2.63). However, the twofold commandment itself rests on the intention of Jesus, recognized by the later community, to bind the love of God and the love of neighbor most intimately together. Love of God, as in Judaism, occupies the highest place but must be evinced and effectuated in love of neighbor. This is the basic characteristic of Jesus' proclamation (cf. Matt. 5:44-48; 18:23-35; 25:31-46; Luke 10:30-37; etc.) and is utterly basic and essential to his moral doctrine. And the intimate connection between love of God and love of neighbor describes its actual inner requirements.

34 Singling out the various details, the Pharisees again enter the scene, following the Sadducees, almost as in a criminal interrogation, with the interrogators "taking turns." For Matthew they are the dominant groups (cf. also v. 41).

35-36 The question of the "greatest" commandment in the law refers neither to more or less easily observable commandments nor to more or less significant ones (cf. the "smallest commandments," 5:19), but to a commandment embracing all the others and in this sense the "most important." This question of the fullness of the commandments was the subject of lively discussion in Judaism (later 613 commandments were numbered: 365 prohibitions and 248 positive injunctions; cf. Billerbeck, *Kommentar zum Neuen Testament,* 1:900-901) and led to different responses, such as, with Hillel, the Golden Rule, with Rabbi Akiba the love of neighbor. The "test" to which Jesus is subjected is not the same as the "case" presented in 22:15, but is intended to examine his knowledge of and fidelity to the Torah.

37-38 The commandment of love of God in Deuteronomy 6:5 (without the introductory "Hear, O Israel," Deut. 6:4) is cited in a form that deviates from Mark and Luke, who present four modifying phrases. With Matthew there are three modifiers, as in the Hebrew text; but instead of "with all your strength" he has us read "with all your mind" *(dianoia),* a Greek word that is placed alongside "strength" in Mark and Luke as well. The turns of phrase that the Jews interpreted separately ("soul" = life, "strength" = ability or possessions) are obviously being used synonymously, reinforcing the concept of comprehensive love.

39 The commandment of love of neighbor, likewise much appreciated by the Jews, is found in Leviticus 19:18 and thus in a different place. Nowhere in Judaism are Deuteronomy 6:5 and Leviticus 19:18 cited in tandem. The Christian understanding, which goes back to Jesus, is unambiguous: the two commandments are of equal importance. Love for God is the vehicle and motive force of everything else, but it must prove itself in love of neighbor and extend even to love of enemies, in character and in deed (cf. 1 John 3:17-18; 4:19-21).

40 As if hanging on a hook, the entire law and prophets "hang" on the two commandments — a manner of expression attested in Judaism. These constitute the epitome of everything given by God by way of injunctions and commands in the divine revelation ("the law and the prophets," Matt. 5:17; 7:12). The same phrase is used in 7:12 as a compendium of the requirements of the Sermon on the Mount and called the Golden Rule, which is a practical yardstick for the practice of love of neighbor. Indirectly, Matthew is referring to the understanding of the divine law in Jesus' presentation as developed in the Sermon on the Mount.

The Question about David's Son (22:41-46)

> 41 *Now while the Pharisees were gathered together, Jesus asked them this question:* 42 *"What do you think of the Messiah? Whose son is he?" They said to him, "The son of David."* 43 *He said to them, "How is it then that David by the Spirit calls him Lord, saying,*
> 44 *'The Lord said to my Lord,*

"Sit at my right hand,
> *until I put your enemies under your feet"'?*

45 *If David thus calls him Lord, how can he be his son?"* 46 *No one was able to give him an answer, nor from that day did anyone dare to ask him any more questions.*

41-46 Having fended off his adversaries' cunning questions, Jesus counterattacks at once, and demonstrates his superiority in a manner such that no one now dares pose him a question. Inasmuch as Matthew moves this observation to the end of the four dialogues (appearing in Mark 12:34b earlier, immediately after the third question, the one concerning the greatest commandment), he lays stronger emphasis on Jesus' majesty, since in the question of David's son we hear the community's attribution to the Messiah of "Lordship." For Matthew the Pharisees are the actual addressees of this last question, which is placed on the lips of Jesus. As in verse 34, the Pharisees are "gathered" — a council assembled before Jesus. Again we discern the evangelist's current situation: the religious dialogues between Christians and Jews after the year 70.

Another Matthean alteration is worthy of note: in Matthew Jesus explicitly asks (v. 42) whose son the Messiah is. In Matthew and Luke, only the fact that David calls his son "Lord," is set forth, as an apparent contradiction; Matthew is opening the conversation for the positive question, which calls for more emphatic attention. For Matthew the answer is beyond all doubt: David's son is the Son of God (see 14:33; 16:16; 26:63; 27:43, 54). Even more clearly than Mark, Matthew draws the curtain back before the Christian response.

This is of importance for a historical assessment of the pericope. There is no doubt that the question of the Messiah engaged the attention of the Judaism of the time, and that the prevailing view, widespread among the people, was to the effect that the Messiah would come of the seed of David and be the deliverer and righteous king. Here we have reliable testimony from the *Psalms of Solomon,* dating from the first century B.C., probably issuing from circles connected with the Pharisees (cf. *Psalms of Solomon* 17:21-43; 18:7-9). David's son rules over the Realm of God, of which "the Lord himself is king" (*Psalms of Solomon* 17:34). The expectation of this king of salvation is based on the prophecy of Nathan imparted to King David (2 Sam. 7:14-16; cf. Ps. 2:5-9). But the concept of the son of David as an earthly ruler is not shared by Jesus or by primitive Christianity (see Matt. 20:30-31; 21:9-15). Jesus' Davidic ancestry stands (1:1-17, 20), but his Messiahship is fulfilled in another way, in virtue of his enthronement at the right hand of God. Only with the resurrection has God elevated the Crucified One "to both Lord and Messiah" (Acts 2:36); for the primitive church he has thereby become Lord (Gk. *Kyrios*) and, as such, the one who brings salvation. With divine authority he exercises a Lordship of heavenly origin, which is different from that awaited by Israel. The same understanding is attested in the old formula that antedates Paul: Jesus Christ, "descended from David according to the flesh and declared to be the Son of God with power according to the spirit of holiness by resurrection from the dead" (Rom. 1:3-4).

A prominent role in this primitive Christian understanding belongs to Psalm 110:1 (in the Greek), a text cited here almost literally, according to the Greek Bible (Acts 2:34; 1 Cor. 15:25; Eph. 1:20; Col. 3:1; Heb. 1:3, 13; etc.). Psalm 110 was not interpreted in terms of the Messiah in early Judaism (cf. Billerbeck, *Kommentar zum Neuen Testament,* 4/1:452-65), although whether this was in reaction to the Christian appeal to it (thus Billerbeck) remains questionable. The entire train of thought here is based on a messianic understanding of the passage. David is considered the author of the Psalms and inspired by the Holy Spirit, and it is presupposed that the psalm concerns the Messiah, the son of David. When the Psalm says, "The LORD [= God] says to my lord" (the son of David), this is unusual and a seeming contradiction, which of course is resolved here in favor of the Christian conceptualization specified above.

Considering this view of the son of David, possible only after Easter, this will have to be the background of the dialogue. As with Peter's messianic confession (see Matt. 16:16), the full primitive Christian confession of Jesus as the Messiah and the Son of God, the "Lord," is presupposed. Granted, the son of David is not expressly called "Son of God"; but the question in verse 42 tends in that direction. Likewise open to the Christian interpretation is the question of the high priest in 26:63, which leads to the heart of the confrontation between Jewish and Christian belief. Adding Jesus' response to that of the high priest (see 26:64), we may say: Jesus has veiled his claim and expressed it indirectly; the post-Easter community has clarified it and put it into words. With the conversation concerning the son of David that it has molded, even Jesus' reticence concerning himself is preserved, although the sense of the question for the primitive church is completely in the open.

Discourse against the Scribes and Pharisees (chap. 23)

After the exchange with the ruling circles in Jerusalem, which has finally led to the silencing of the adversaries, Matthew also wishes to have a grand settlement of accounts with Pharisaic Judaism since the antipathy has become acute in his time. In the course of his presentation, this is the last discourse that Jesus hurls at his opponents in Jerusalem; afterward he speaks with them no more until he stands before the High Council (26:64). Unlike the five great addresses (see Intro., pp. 2-3), this sermon of punishment and threat is not marked with a special concluding formula. It is a special discourse, molded by Matthew, which bears no such proclamatory character as do the Sermon on the Mount, the speech to the disciples, the parabolic discourse, and the community instruction. The last of the five great addresses for the community, namely, the eschatological discourse, follows in chapters 24–25. From there Matthew goes on to recount the history of Jesus' passion and resurrection.

The discourse in chapter 23, where it is emphasized that Jesus addresses "the crowds and his disciples" (23:1), bears the special signature of the evangelist. True, he applies material from the sources he has been consulting, Mark and the Sayings Source — more precisely, the brief address of Mark 12:38-40 (cf. Luke 20:45-47) and the lengthier woe discourse against the Pharisees and scribes originating in Q and presented in Luke 11:42-52. As with the discourse of the dispatch of the disciples (Matt. 10:5-15), Matthew has assembled and developed this two-strand tradition in free style — complementing Luke's six cries of woe with a seventh, introducing new material (such as the various oath formulas, Matt. 23:16-22), and, at the end, appending a Q logion concerning Jerusalem (23:37-39 par. Luke 13:34-35). The free style does not always permit recognition of what Matthew has taken over from Jewish-Christian (oral) tradition (cf. vv. 2-3) and what he has introduced through his own redaction (cf. v. 5). He has clearly inserted one passage himself, with an eye to his community, namely, verses 8-12, a word of warning that is most revealing for his understanding of the community (a community of brothers and sisters!), a warning that sets aside for the moment the Christian/Jewish polemics and directly addresses the Christian community ("But you . . ."). In the development of the discourse, it stands as the conclusion of the first part, before the seven cries of woe.

We can distinguish three passages: vv. 1-12, against arrogant teachers and their behavior; vv. 13-33, the seven cries of woe; vv. 34-39, persecution of Christian messengers of faith and the judgment of God. The variety of material that Matthew uses, if we regard it carefully, entails something of a heterogeneity. Ought the Christian community depart altogether from the practice of Judaism, or should it merely continue it in another direction? The sharp polemics here, not actually detached from Jewish thought (oath formulas, tithing), partially reveals an attitude that fails to correspond to Jesus' words and behavior as otherwise attested.

Jesus Denounces Scribes and Pharisees (23:1-33)

23:1 *Then Jesus said to the crowds and to his disciples, 2 "The scribes and the Pharisees sit on Moses' seat; 3 therefore, do whatever they teach you and follow it; but do not do as they do, for they do not practice what they teach. 4 They tie up heavy burdens, hard to bear, and lay them on the shoulders of*

226

others; but they themselves are unwilling to lift a finger to move them. 5 *They do all their deeds to be seen by others; for they make their phylacteries broad and their fringes long.* 6 *They love to have the place of honor at banquets and the best seats in the synagogues,* 7 *and to be greeted with respect in the marketplaces, and to have people call them rabbi.* 8 *But you are not to be called rabbi, for you have one teacher, and you are all students.* 9 *And call no one your father on earth, for you have one Father — the one in heaven.* 10 *Nor are you to be called instructors, for you have one instructor, the Messiah.* 11 *The greatest among you will be your servant.* 12 *All who exalt themselves will be humbled, and all who humble themselves will be exalted.*

13 *"But woe to you, scribes and Pharisees, hypocrites! For you lock people out of the kingdom of heaven. For you do not go in yourselves, and when others are going in, you stop them.* 15 *Woe to you, scribes and Pharisees, hypocrites! For you cross sea and land to make a single convert, and you make the new convert twice as much a child of hell as yourselves.*

16 *"Woe to you, blind guides, who say, 'Whoever swears by the sanctuary is bound by nothing, but whoever swears by the gold of the sanctuary is bound by the oath.'* 17 *You blind fools! For which is greater, the gold or the sanctuary that has made the gold sacred?* 18 *And you say, 'Whoever swears by the altar is bound by nothing, but whoever swears by the gift that is on the altar is bound by the oath.'* 19 *How blind you are! For which is greater, the gift or the altar that makes the gift sacred?* 20 *So whoever swears by the altar, swears by it and by everything on it;* 21 *and whoever swears by the sanctuary, swears by it and by the one who dwells in it;* 22 *and whoever swears by heaven, swears by the throne of God and by the one who is seated upon it.*

23 *"Woe to you, scribes and Pharisees, hypocrites! For you tithe mint, dill, and cummin, and have neglected the weightier matters of the law: justice and mercy and faith. It is these you ought to have practiced without neglecting the others.* 24 *You blind guides! You strain out a gnat but swallow a camel!*

25 *"Woe to you, scribes and Pharisees, hypocrites! For you clean the outside of the cup and of the plate, but inside they are full of greed and self-indulgence.* 26 *You blind Pharisee! First clean the inside of the cup, so that the outside also may become clean.*

27 *"Woe to you, scribes and Pharisees, hypocrites! For you are like white-washed tombs, which on the outside look beautiful, but inside they are full of the bones of the dead and of all kinds of filth.* 28 *So you also on the outside look righteous to others, but inside you are full of hypocrisy and lawlessness.*

29 *"Woe to you, scribes and Pharisees, hypocrites! For you build the tombs of the prophets and decorate the graves of the righteous,* 30 *and you say, 'If we had lived in the days of our ancestors, we would not have taken part with*

them in shedding the blood of the prophets.' 31 *Thus you testify against your-selves that you are descendants of those who murdered the prophets.* 32 *Fill up, then, the measure of your ancestors.* 33 *You snakes, you brood of vipers! How can you escape being sentenced to hell?"*

1-7 23:1-7 constitutes an extremely sharp polemic, which does not really do justice to the conduct of the Pharisees and scribes, not even for the time of the alienation between Judaism and Christianity. Considering only the critical portrayal of the Pharisee in the parable of the Pharisee and the tax collector, one fails to notice that the Pharisee does observe the precepts of the law — fasting and tithing — and thus that his actions correspond to his words (not as in Matt. 23:3c-4). The parable reproaches the Pharisee's contempt for the sinful tax collector, who trusts in God's mercy as Jesus proclaims it; thus the parable makes a case for the gospel of grace. Jesus has hardly contested the earnest concern for legal righteousness observed in Pharisaic milieus but does criticize an outward "practice" of the law that leads its subject to smugness and arrogance (cf. 6:1-18; 15:8-9). In view of this, verses 5-7 represent Jesus' actual attitude. The scribes, who must be distinguished from the simple members of the Pharisaic "brotherhood" (*ḥăbērîm*, "comrades"), studied the Torah, interpreted it, and concluded various injunctions from it, which they imposed on others. That they themselves failed to hold to them is as little demonstrable as that the burdens were heavy ones (v. 4a), burdens that persons must have felt as heavy. But for the Christian community, Jesus' words were normative and orienting, an "easy yoke and a light burden" (11:30).

From this standpoint, it may be surprising that verse 3 reads, "Do whatever they teach you and follow it." Previously we read that the scribes sat on the chair of Moses — scarcely in the sense that they did so illegitimately; rather, they laid claim to Moses' teaching authority ("chair," since a teacher taught seated; cf. the Chair of Peter in Rome), and that was certainly recognized by Jewish Christians. Here is the same position vis-à-vis the Jewish law that we have in 5:17-19, except that then the "fulfillment" of the law according to Jesus' interpretation follows. The critical words concerning the "tradition of the elders" in 15:2-9 are left out of consideration. Thus there is no denying a tension with other logia, especially 16:12, the warning against the "teaching" of the Pharisees and Sadducees. True, in 23:3 the expression "teaching" is avoided in the Greek version.

Verse 5 excoriates a striving to maintain fidelity to the law for appearance' sake. By "phylacteries" (the Greek word; actually "amulets") is meant the *tefellin*, capsules containing texts from the Torah, worn on the hand or forehead to recall God's commandments (cf. Exod. 13:16; Deut. 6:8; 11:18; see Billerbeck, *Kommentar zum Neuen Testament*, 4:250-76). The tassels (*ṣîṣit*) on the gar-

ments were sewn on the robes, also to remind the wearer of the commandments of God (cf. Billerbeck, 4:277-92). The Pharisees under attack here saw to
it that these signs were especially large and noticeable. In verse 6, their striving
for places of honor and the best seats is raked over the coals. For Matthew, all of
this is out of sheer smugness, "to be seen by others" (cf. 6:2, 5, 16). The Pharisees seek honor from human beings instead of from God, as we read in the similar polemics in John 5:44. It is a bitter criticism, which corresponds to the spirit
of Jesus, but which is not to be limited to the Jewish scribes, as Matthew himself
immediately reveals.

8-12 The word of admonition to the audience, with which Matthew
has the later community in view, demonstrates that there were teachers in the
Matthean community to whom Matthew here metes out a powerful lesson.
Verses 8-10 have been classified in terms of form criticism under "rule for the
community," which of course is remarkable in the version at hand. Verse 10
sounds like a repetition of verse 8 in a more graceful version since here — the
only time in the New Testament — appears a Greek expression (*kathēgētēs*) by
which Christ, too, is designated. In terms of content, verse 10 says nothing different than verse 8, namely, that one alone is "your teacher," Christ, since verse
10 denotes Jesus from a post-Easter perspective. The original admonition will
have comprised only verses 8-9; verse 10 was added in a Hellenistic environment. The form of address, "rabbi," in verse 8, is striking. Jesus himself is frequently addressed as "Rabbi" in the Gospels (literally, "My Lord," and so
[teaching] "Master") and even more frequently as "Lord," although he was not
a trained scribe (cf. John 7:15). Did Christian preachers and teachers soon
come to be addressed as "rabbi" in the community? Or is it a matter of converted Pharisees, who sought to establish a "rabbinate" in the Christian community like that in Judaism? Reliable indications are lacking. The title "father,"
rejected in verse 9, cannot be definitely established in the case of Jewish
scribes, but it can be regarded as probable on the basis of the title used of
prophets (2 Kings 2:12; 6:21; 13:14) and the reverence for the "fathers" in Judaism (forefathers, Sirach 44; Mishnah tractate *'Abodah Zarah*). For primitive
Christianity it was perhaps suggested by the "spiritual" fatherhood of the
preachers and founders of the community. The difficult original text occasions
diverse interpretations; but to understand, under "father," one's physical father, whom Christians were not to address owing to their bond with God, the
heavenly Father, is far-fetched. Rather, here too teachers are meant, who, as
older men, tried and true, received this honorific name. In any case, it is not
the designation of an office: a connection with the "presbyters" or elders in
other communities (Acts 11:30; 15:6 and frequently; 1 Tim. 5:1-2, 19; Titus
1:5; 1 Peter 5:1, 5) is not to be assumed. If these classes of title holders hark
back to an early (Jewish-Christian) time, verse 10 bears rather on community

teachers in Hellenistic communities, in which they exercised an important function (cf. Acts 11:26; 13:1). These verses hold up before everyone's eyes that there is only one true teacher, Christ.

If Matthew has adopted this sort of (mature) community rule, it is because it is very important to him that his community mature into a community of brothers and sisters, in which all members stand on the same level before Christ, their Lord and Master: "You are all siblings." "Brother" and "sister" were the prevailing terms of address among Christians, a designation that for Matthew expresses the life of the community and imposes the obligation of sibling behavior (Matt. 5:23-24; 7:3-5; 12:50; 18:15-17, 21-22). The ideal prevailed in all primitive Christian communities, but for Matthew it became the fundamental understanding of a community of Jesus Christ. The Christian scribes (see 13:52) and teachers ought to insert themselves into the community of brothers and sisters. While no "structure of offices" is observable, neither is any hostility to the notion of offices to be read into the text. As time went on, in different circumstances, it was possible to have a three-tiered level of offices, which was still understood as sacred service (high esteem of the "deacons"), as the *Letters of Ignatius* attest for Antioch.

11-12   The leading men in the community of the time — as of all later times — are shown the correct direction with the basic rule, "The greatest among you will be your servant," which originates with Jesus himself (see 20:26-27). Matthew founds it on another saying of Jesus, which Luke presents in two other places (Luke 14:11; 18:14). Matthew echoes it as early as 18:4, and it continues to be in vogue in the primitive church (James 4:10; 1 Peter 5:6). Finally, the belief prevails throughout the Bible that God humiliates the proud but exalts the lowly (1 Sam. 2:7-8; Prov. 3:34 in the Greek; Luke 1:52; etc.). Here the concept is applied to the self-humbling and service of brothers and sisters, which God will one day reward with a share in his and Christ's Lordship (cf. 19:28; Luke 22:29-30; Rev. 3:21).

13-33   In the prophetic, apocalyptic style of the "woe," raised as a lament or menace (Isa. 1:4; 5:8-23; 10:5; Jer. 23:1; Ezek. 24:6; Hos. 7:13; etc.), and encountered in a variety of uses and contexts (*Ethiopian Enoch* 94–100), Matthew holds up to the eyes of the "scribes and Pharisees" a mirror of their "hypocrisy." What is meant by "hypocrisy" is not a concealment of their true character, or playacting and fraud, as in Matthew 22:18, but the contradiction between their actions and true morality (6:2, 5, 16; 7:5; 15:7). "Hypocrite" has become invective. The six expressions of woe in Luke 11:42-52, three each for the Pharisees and scribes, in Matthew become three expressions of woe against the scribes and Pharisees together, with the scribes especially in his sights. The cry of woe introduced by later manuscripts in verse 14 and taken from Mark 12:40, against the consumption of the goods of widows, is spurious on grounds of textual criticism. But Matthew presents two special woe sayings not contained in Luke — in verse 15 against those who make converts or proselytes, and in verses 16-22 against the practice of taking oaths; the cry of woe expressed in Luke 11:46 has not been taken over by Matthew in this series, and is already taken into consideration in verse 4, without a "woe." Thus a Matthean composition has arisen, using a variety of materials and mirroring Jewish practice (while partially distorting it) of the law. Here it will suffice to make some remarks concerning the various woe sayings.

13 In Luke verse 13 stands at the end of the series, as the most important of the woe expressions, although in a secondary form ("key to recognition"). Matthew uses it to open his scathing, condemnatory indictment. The image of the key (see 16:19a) denotes authority and here stands in connection with a logion concerning admittance into the Realm of God (see 5:20). The terrible thing is that the scribes use their authority to lock people out. They do not enter themselves (cf. 21:31), and they prevent others from doing so. Matthew is thinking of the hostile defense measures taken by Judaism against the Christian mission (cf. v. 34): the leading Pharisees hinder conversion to the Christian church and thereby bar Jews from a share in the Reign of God.

15 An eagerness to win proselytes is also attested by Paul (Rom. 2:19-20), before the year 70. There was strong Jewish mission propaganda as early as the first pre-Christian century; see the book of *Joseph and Aseneth*. Full Jewish proselytes (with circumcision) were harder than the merely "God-fearing" (cf. Acts 13:43; 16:14; 17:4) to win over to the Christian faith. The woe in verse 13 blames the Pharisees for excluding such a person from the Realm of God, indeed for making him a "child of hell" (opposite of "children of the kingdom," 13:38; cf. 8:12), twice as bad as themselves, doubtless owing to seduction.

16-22 The expression of woe fashioned by Matthew (see above) uses the address "blind guides," an accusation already raised against the Pharisees in 15:14 (originally a logion from Q; cf. Luke 6:39). Paul, too, applies the image (Rom 2:19). The Pharisees' "blindness," applied to the purity logion of 15:11, is illustrated here by their oversubtle handling of oath formulas. Rabbis indeed used such distinctions (cf. Billerbeck, *Kommentar zum Neuen Testament*, 1:931-32), although it cannot be shown that it was to the extent indicated here. It is striking that swearing by God is approved, and thus the Jewish custom is rejected only in its abuse, while according to 5:33-37 Jesus forbids swearing altogether. The Jewish-Christian attitude is discernible here as in verse 3a, but Jesus' intention is absent.

23-24 An example of the Pharisees' distorted zeal for the law is also offered by the extensive tithing, that is, the contribution of the tenth or "tithe" of the harvest to the priests and Levites (Num. 18:11-13; Deut. 14:22-23). We find this woe in Luke 11:42 as well, but in somewhat different words. The expressly required contributions of grain, wine, and oil were extended by the Pharisees to include garden produce ("mint, dill, and cummin"). It is not this for which they are reproached here, but for their omission of the "heavier matters of the law." What is meant are the moral duties (cf. chap. 15!), "justice" (literally, "being right"), "mercy," and "fidelity." All three expressions are found in the Bible, and similarly grouped there (Mic. 6:8; cf. Zech. 7:9). *Pistis* here does not mean faith, as elsewhere in Matthew, but fidelity, as often in the Old Testament (Prov. 3:3; 14:22; Wis. 3:14; Sir. 1:27; 15:15; etc.). The Jewish-Christian attitude is shown in the appended declaration, "These you ought to have practiced without neglecting the others [the prescriptions of the tithe]." The rejection of the ceremonial laws has not yet taken place, as it will in the second century *(Letter of Barnabas)*. Verse 24, a drastic image, probably proverbial, is absent from Luke and once again introduced with "blind guides."

25-26 The fifth woe, not occurring in Luke 11:39 as a woe, extends the theme of "inner" and "outer." It refers to the painfully careful outer cleansing of table vessels. The point was to make sure that bowls and mugs consecrated by the table blessing did not run over, and to rinse them on the outside. Otherwise they were reckoned as unclean. The "interior" of the vessels is said to be "full of greed and self-indulgence," that is, metaphorically transferred to the depravity that the Pharisees have heaped up in themselves. This characteristic application is certainly occasioned by the purity logion of 15:11. The "blind Pharisees" should first overcome the measureless acquisitiveness in their interior; then what they do externally will come clean as well.

27-28 The next woe saying is added under the same contrast of outer and inner, with a new image of "whitewashed tombs." We have evidence of the custom of whitening tombs with lime in the springtime, in order to identify them as places where one could become unclean through contact with the bones of the dead. Again Matthew applies the picture metaphorically to the Pharisees, who look elegant on the outside but teem on the inside with all kinds of impurity. Verse 28 is a typical Matthean clarification: they are seemingly "righteous," but in reality full of "hypocrisy" and "lawlessness," all favorite Matthean words.

29-33 The outline of the woe concerning the tombs leads to a new accusation in the last expression of woe: outwardly, hypocritically, the Pharisees build tombs for the "prophets" and decorate the graves of the "righteous" (the same pair as in 13:17), and in this way seek to keep their distance from the murders of the prophets that occurred in the days of their forebears (cf. 21:35-41; 22:6). But inasmuch as they erect monuments to the deceased prophets, they proclaim their bond with their fathers, continue their work, and share their mortal guilt. Maintenance of "sepulchres of the saints" was highly regarded in Judaism, and in certain cemeteries is still to be seen in our day. In verses 32-33 (now absent in Luke) the woe saying is elevated to a threat of judgment. With bitter irony, the scribes and Pharisees are invited to fill up the measure (of guilt) of their forebears. Then they are addressed as "snakes, brood of vipers" (see 3:7) and threatened with the same judgment as in the preaching of John the Baptist (3:7). Verses 32-33 are added by Matthew to prepare for the threat of judgment hurled against the persecutors and murderers of the messengers of the Christian faith (vv. 34-36).

The entire discourse of the woes is well thought out — composed with associative transitions and with clear, gradual intensification. It is a dismal picture, understandable from the viewpoint of confrontation with contemporary Judaism but failing to do justice to the religious efforts of the Pharisaic scribes. The religious conversation between Christians and Jews conducted by Justin, as early as mid-second century, is in a different spirit. In his dialogue with the Jew Trypho, he writes: "We hate you [plural] not; rather we pray that, if you are not converted, you all find mercy with the compassionate, merciful Father" (108:3).

Judgment for Persecutors (23:34-36)

> 34 *Therefore I send you prophets, sages, and scribes, some of whom you will kill and crucify, and some you will flog in your synagogues and pursue from town to town,* 35 *so that upon you may come all the righteous blood shed on earth, from the blood of righteous Abel to the blood of Zechariah son of Barachiah, whom you murdered between the sanctuary and the altar.* 36 *Truly I tell you, all this will come upon this generation."*

34-39 The last passage in this discourse is divided into words about the judgment to befall the persecutors and murderers of the emissaries of God in this very generation (vv. 34-36) and the lament over Jerusalem (vv. 37-39). Thus we have two distinct passages. While verses 34-36 constitute the immediate continuation of the woe sayings (so also in Luke 11:49-51), the lament over Jerusalem stems from another context. In Luke it appears in 13:34-35, from the outlook of Jesus' destiny of death in Jerusalem. Where this moving lament, which Luke and Matthew present in almost the same words, stood in the Sayings Source is uncertain. But since this particular passage bears on the murder of the prophets, it suited Matthew as a continuation of verses 34-36. For him the threatened judgment occurs as punishment for the persecution and slaying of Christian missionaries, and he has in mind the fall of Jerusalem in the year 70, with the destruction of the temple. This is shown by the fact that Matthew places the prediction of the razing of the temple immediately afterward (24:1-2). Still, 23:37-39 has a different tone from that of the harsh indictment of verses 34-36.

It is a wistful lament over a blinded city, which murders the messengers of God and resists Jesus' loving invitation.

34-36 In Luke "wisdom" speaks of the killing of the prophets. In the Sayings Source, the wisdom of God is an active force (see 11:19 par. Luke 7:35), and in Matthew 11:28-30 wisdom address is applied to Jesus himself. Thus, here Matthew has Jesus himself pronounce the words of wisdom: *he* sends "prophets, sages, and scribes" to the Jews. Here only Christian heralds of the faith can be meant: "prophets" as in 10:41; "the sages" (an echo of wisdom discourse?) — here, otherwise than in 11:25, in a positive sense; "scribes" as in 13:52. The lot of these Christian emissaries is to be slain, like the Old Testament prophets. Examples abound: Stephen, James the brother of John (Acts 12:2), later James the brother of the Lord (Josephus, *Antiquities* 20.200), Peter (cf. John 21:18-19), Paul, and Antipas (cf. Rev. 2:13). Although these martyrdoms are not laid to the account of the Pharisees, the persecution (in the A.D. 80s) seems to have become more acute under their influence (cf. John 16:2). Matthew adds, from his area of experience, floggings in the synagogues (see 10:17; Paul, 2 Cor. 11:24) and pursuits from city to city (Matt. 10:23). Thus the Pharisees heap up the guilt of their ancestors who murdered the prophets (vv. 31-32), and call down upon themselves the punishment for the entire torrent of blood from righteous Abel, whose blood "cried out" to God (Gen. 4:10), to the last prophet to be murdered — a thought that is still indebted to ancient Israelite views (cf. Exod. 34:7; Deut 5:9; differently Jer. 31:29-30; Ezekiel 18). "Zechariah" is the son of the priest Jehoiada, who was stoned to death in the temple court (2 Chron. 24:20-22), the last death of an innocent person in the Old Testament. His father is mistakenly called Barachiah; Berechiah was the father of the canonical prophet Zechariah (Zech. 1:1). Still another Zechariah, a leading Jerusalemite murdered by the Zealots in the Jewish War (Josephus, *Jewish War* 4.334-43), is not in mind in this passage about prophets. On Jesus' lips "this generation" means Jesus' contemporaries (12:39, 41-42, 45); Matthew uses the expression to include the Jews living afterward, upon whom the judgment of God, in Matthew's view, fell in the Jewish War (cf. 27:25). The cries of woe attain their confirmation through that punishment (in Matthew with "Truly").

The Lament over Jerusalem (23:37-39)

> 37 "*Jerusalem, Jerusalem, the city that kills the prophets and stones those who are sent to it! How often have I desired to gather your children together as a hen gathers her brood under her wings, and you were not willing!* 38 *See, your house is left to you, desolate.* 39 *For I tell you, you will not see me again until you say, 'Blessed is the one who comes in the name of the Lord.'*"

37-39 The lament over Jerusalem, stemming from Q, which presupposes a frequent sojourn of Jesus in the Holy City and which is credibly placed on Jesus' lips, was handed down early and certainly mirrors the emotion of Jewish-Christian missionaries who, with all of their failures, had maintained a great love for Jerusalem. The picture of the hen who gathers her chicks under her wings, an image of protection and loving solicitude, recalls that of Isaiah: "Like birds hovering overhead, so the LORD of hosts will protect Jerusalem; he will protect and deliver it, he will spare and rescue it" (Isa. 31:5; cf. Deut. 32:10-11; Pss. 36:7; 57:1; 61:4; and frequently). But the call of Jesus, God's last emissary, to the Holy City has been refused by the leading Jews; therefore God will withdraw his presence from them (cf. Jer. 12:7). Their "house" will become desolate, abandoned. This can mean the land of Israel, Yahweh's inheritance (Jer. 12:7), the city of Jerusalem (*Ethiopian Enoch* 89:50), or the temple (Jer. 26:6; *Syrian Apocalypse of Baruch* 8:2). Matthew is thinking of the destruction of the temple (Matt. 24:1-2) and Jerusalem (cf. 22:7; 24:15-16). If the Jews no longer wish to see Jesus (Matthew: "from now on"; cf. 26:29, 64) until they call out to him in the name of the Lord who comes, what the evangelist has in mind is the time span between Jesus' death and parousia. The original call to the pilgrims (Ps. 118:26), already applied to the entry of the Messiah, the Son of David, into Jerusalem in Matthew 21:9, is now applied to the King of the parousia. Will there then be forced homage to the Judge (cf. 26:64)? Or are we now in the presence of the glimmer of hope, in this logion of blessing, for the conversion of Israel? Opinions are divided to this very day. Otherwise, precisely in Matthew there is no trace of a conversion of the ancient people of God (unlike the case of Paul, Rom. 11:25-27). Still, the encoded word may originally have conveyed this hope.

The Great Eschatological Discourse (chaps. 24–25)

The polemics against outsiders are followed by a lengthy discourse pointedly addressed to the disciples (24:1), intended for the faith community and looking to the future. Through its outlook on the parousia and the end of the world (24:3, 29-31), and the traditions taken over concerning the time before the end (24:4-28), it is an "eschatological discourse," but in such a way that the community is addressed in its current situation. All three Synoptics present such an "eschatological discourse" of Jesus (see also Mark 13; Luke 21); in addition, Luke transmits an address with a similar tendency from the Sayings Source (Luke 17:20-37). Matthew has then redeveloped these discourses into a single, extensive composition, in the first part (Matt. 24:4-36) primarily in line with Mark (except for the passage set forth that follows Matt. 10:17-21), and as he went on, according to elements from the Sayings Source, supplemented with his particular material (the parable of the bridesmaids, 25:1-13; the last judgment, 25:31-46). Matthew's tendency in writing this composition can be explained from the divisions and headings that he has selected in this commentary. Following the chronologically antecedent presentation up to the parousia (from "the beginning of the birthpangs" [24:8] to the "great suffering" [24:21] to the coming of the Son of Man [24:30-31]), the question of *when* is discussed (24:32-42, partially following Mark, partially following Luke 17). Then the community is summoned to watchfulness, readiness, and preparedness through parables (24:43–25:13). Finally, they are reminded more emphatically of their responsibility for their conduct in the world (entrusted talents, 25:14-30; works of love in the portrayal of the judgment, 25:31-46). Even previously, in his portrayal of the end, however, Matthew is concerned to show the community their duty. After the first passage (the beginning of woes) he uses "then" *(tote)* to introduce the admonition to be steadfast to the end (24:9-14); and after the second passage, on the great suffering, likewise beginning with "then," he warns against seducers (24:23-28). The imminent expectation of the end is underplayed although not given up, and the instruction to the community in the world is worked out all the more emphatically. The world judgment opens up a universal horizon ("all nations"), resumed in the final scene of the Gospel (28:16-20) and culminating in the promise, "I am with you always, to the end of the age."

The Destruction of the Temple Foretold (24:1-2)

24:1 *As Jesus came out of the temple and was going away, his disciples came to point out to him the buildings of the temple.* 2 *Then he asked them, "You see all these, do you not? Truly I tell you, not one stone will be left here upon another; all will be thrown down."*

1-2   Jesus' departure from the temple may be an echo of the pericope on the widow's offering (Mark 12:41-44), made in the temple, which Matthew omits. But Matthew may also be taking his cue from the prophecy of 23:38. In that he presents the anti-Pharisaic discourse of chapter 23 in the temple precincts, his leaving the temple takes on a symbolic sense as well: Jesus turns away from the ritual religion of Judaism and toward his new community. As we know, "the disciples" (in Matthew it is "one of the disciples") represent the later church. The reference to the beautiful temple installations (cf. Josephus, *Antiquities* 15.391-402; *Jewish War* 5.190-227) that Herod took so long to build (cf. John 2:20) leads to Jesus' prediction that not a stone will be left upon another. Such a prophecy on Jesus' part, after similar threatening words by prophets (Mic. 3:12; Jer. 26:4-6), after Jesus' criticism of temple worship (Matt. 21:12-13), and after the admittedly opaque words about the temple that play a role in his trial (Mark 14:58 and pars.; cf. Acts 6:13-14), is altogether credible. The actual destruction of the temple followed in the year 70 (Josephus, *Jewish War* 6.249-66).

Signs of the End of the Age (24:3-8)

> 3 *When he was sitting on the Mount of Olives, the disciples came to him privately, saying, "Tell us, when will this be, and what will be the sign of your coming and of the end of the age?"*
>
> 4 *Jesus answered them, "Beware that no one leads you astray. 5 For many will come in my name, saying, 'I am the Messiah!' and they will lead many astray. 6 And you will hear of wars and rumors of wars; see that you are not alarmed; for this must take place, but the end is not yet. 7 For nation will rise against nation, and kingdom against kingdom, and there will be famines and earthquakes in various places: 8 all this is but the beginning of the birth-pangs."*

3 Although Matthew divorces the disciples' question on the Mount of Olives more distinctly from the foregoing scene than does Mark (without Mark's "opposite the temple"), nevertheless it is connected with it. "Tell us, when this will be" can here, as in Mark, refer only to the destruction of the temple. The disciples approach Jesus, as before (v. 1) — the same disciples (in Mark there are four disciples, singled out) — but now ask "privately." This calls attention to the fact that the following address is intended only for the community. Matthew clearly states the object of the entire discourse: the parousia (Greek for the arrival, or appearance, of a ruler), his special expression for the coming of the Son of Man (24:27, 37, 39), which Paul as well applies to the coming of the "Lord" (1 Thess. 2:19; 3:13; and frequently), and the "consummation of the age" — that is, the end of the world (Matt. 13:39-40, 49; 28:20), which coincides with the parousia. What he means by the "sign" is uncertain; he may be thinking of the "sign of the Son of Man" (see 24:30), cited only by him. No close connection between the destruction of the temple and the parousia is evident.

4-14 The portrayals and admonitions that follow, until the prediction of the parousia (vv. 30-31), are striking in many respects: certain typical expressions like "the end" (vv. 6, 13), "the beginning of the birthpangs" (v. 8), and the "great suffering" (vv. 21, 29), unrealistic portrayals that are difficult to understand (vv. 15, 22, 29), and a timetable dependent on the will of God ("This must take place," v. 6). All of this stems from apocalyptic thought, arising with the book of Daniel and developing in other apocalypses. The present world, ruled by the evil one, is coming to an end; the moment and its signs are the object of inquiry (*4 Ezra* 6:7; 9:1-6). This sort of thought saturates primitive Christianity; but the reminder is ever present that Jesus has resisted apocalyptic "curiosity" (cf. Luke 13:23-24; 17:20-21), and, despite his expectation of the imminent coming of the Reign of God, has not announced a specific moment (see vv. 36-42). A great deal of Matthew 24 must be regarded as constituting contemporary references; with the sources and traditions that he uses, Matthew remains bound to the apocalyptic worldview, which for us has disappeared — apart from our hope, without our being able to imagine it, that God will one day bring the phenomenon of the world to an end, to a fulfillment accomplished in the coming of the glorified Christ. To attempt to read apocalyptic "signs" into the text, that is, data of future history enabling a calculation of the moment of the end, is to fall victim to an outmoded way of thinking or to a new fanaticism.

Matthew essentially follows Mark 13 in his presentation of the passage up to the parousia, but he also places accents of his own, which lead one to suppose that he no longer sees his community in the same situation as Mark saw his. Mark seeks to deal with an explosive situation: an imminent expectation of the parousia precipitated by the destruction of the temple in A.D. 70. In our passage, Matthew 24:4-14, the following alterations are worthy of note: an emphatic reference to the future (v. 6); a generalized "all this" (v. 8); the addition "by all nations" (v. 9); and especially, the appending of verses 1-12 and verse 14. Overall, we recognize a postponement of the expectation of the parousia and a horizon broadened to include the entire world.

4-8 The warning against seducers, repeated and intensified in the next passage (on the great suffering, vv. 23-26), is intended as an antidote to false declarations that the Christ of the parousia has already returned. Persons will step forth in the name of Jesus and maintain that they are the Messiah, as Matthew ("I am the Messiah"), unlike Mark, makes clear. This look into the future is meant to banish the fear with which such false pretenders will exert their pressure ("See that you are not alarmed"). After all, " 'this must take place" — a citation from Daniel 2:28 in the Greek, Daniel's interpretation of Nebuchadnezzar's dream, in which he unveils the plan of God for the "end of days." The predicted frightening events, in verse 7 wars between great nations, starvation, and earthquakes, are conventional images of terror (cf. the "Four Horsemen of the Apocalypse," Rev. 6:1-8; cf. also Rev. 6:12; 11:13; etc.). They are understood precisely not as signs of the end but only as the "beginning of the birthpangs." The expression is of not infrequent occurrence in apocalyptic discourse. As early as the "apocalypse of Isaiah" we read: "Like a woman with child, who writhes and cries out in her pangs, . . . so were we because of you, O LORD" (Isa. 26:17). And we find this image used often after this (*Ethiopian Enoch* 62:4; 1QH 3:7-12) — in rabbinism as the "pangs of the Messiah" (Billerbeck, *Kommentar zum Neuen Testament,* 1:950). Here the expression is used in a Christian view of history and means that the Christ of the parousia is still afar off.

Persecutions Foretold (24:9-14)

> 9 *"Then they will hand you over to be tortured and will put you to death, and you will be hated by all nations because of my name.* 10 *Then many will fall away, and they will betray one another and hate one another.* 11 *And many false prophets will arise and lead many astray.* 12 *And because of the increase of lawlessness, the love of many will grow cold.* 13 *But the one who endures to the end will be saved.* 14 *And this good news of the kingdom will be proclaimed throughout the world, as a testimony to all the nations; and then the end will come."*

9-14 An application to the community follows: Christians, too, will be hard pressed, especially preachers and missionaries. This is why Matthew has taken over the announcement of Mark 13:9-12 earlier, in the discourse for the dispatch of the disciples (see 10:17-21), retaining only the declarations that apply to all members of the community: they will be killed, and they will be hated by all peoples (universally!) because of Jesus' name. The Gospel of John speaks in a similar fashion, citing the hatred of the world (John 15:18-21). But for Matthew it is even more shocking that many in the community itself will be seduced, will fall away from the faith ("take offense"; cf. Matt. 13:21; 18:6), will deliver one another over to tribunals, and will hate each other. The community orientation becomes even more clear in verses 11-12: by "false prophets" Matthew obviously means the dangerous false prophets of 7:15, who confuse the community; and the multiplication of "lawlessness" recalls the "evildoers" of 7:23 and 13:41. The result is a cooling of love throughout the community — a shattering experience, discernible here and constituting an ever threatening danger for the church. Nevertheless, these are no grounds for despondency but an impulse to constancy and perseverance. The expression "endures to the end," occurring earlier in 10:22b, admonishes constancy even should it mean martyrdom (24:9b). An encouraging and consoling meaning also invests the prospect of the proclamation of the gospel throughout the world (24:14), which Matthew has taken from Mark 13:10. The witness to all peoples (as earlier in 10:18) indicates a missionary perspective (cf. 28:19). Despite internal difficulties, the Matthean church developed a strong missionary sense. In this certainty it can see the end, as does Luke (cf. Luke 21:24), to be still at a rather great distance in time.

The Desolating Sacrilege (24:15-28)

> 15 *"So when you see the desolating sacrilege standing in the holy place, as was spoken of by the prophet Daniel (let the reader understand),* 16 *then those in Judea must flee to the mountains;* 17 *the one on the housetop must*

not go down to take what is in the house; 18 *the one in the field must not turn back to get a coat.* 19 *Woe to those who are pregnant and to those who are nursing infants in those days!* 20 *Pray that your flight may not be in winter or on a sabbath.* 21 *For at that time there will be great suffering, such as has not been from the beginning of the world until now, no, and never will be.* 22 *And if those days had not been cut short, no one would be saved; but for the sake of the elect those days will be cut short.* 23 *Then if anyone says to you, 'Look! Here is the Messiah!' or 'There he is!' — do not believe it.* 24 *For false messiahs and false prophets will appear and produce great signs and omens, to lead astray, if possible, even the elect.* 25 *Take note, I have told you beforehand.* 26 *So, if they say to you, 'Look! He is in the wilderness,' do not go out. If they say, 'Look! He is in the inner rooms,' do not believe it.* 27 *For as the lightning comes from the east and flashes as far as the west, so will be the coming of the Son of Man.* 28 *Wherever the corpse is, there the vultures will gather."*

15-28　This passage, most difficult for our understanding, deals, in the progress of the presentation, with the "great suffering" to occur before the parousia (cf. v. 29). Apart from a few rather small changes, Matthew has adopted this passage up to verse 25 from Mark 13:14-23. The passage presents considerable problems even in the Gospel of Mark. What is meant by the "desolating sacrilege" (from Dan. 9:27; 11:31; 12:11)? What is the sense of the admonition to flight to the mountains, to be taken in such urgent haste? What does it mean that a great suffering will occur such as has never been nor will ever be again, and that those days will be shortened by God in order to rescue the elect? An important key to understanding the passage is found in the parenthetical remark, "Let the reader understand," which Matthew (v. 15) takes over from Mark 13:14. Today it is assumed that what we have is a portrayal from a writing (a pamphlet) that circulated among Palestinian Christians (whatever its origin) during the Jewish War, summoning them to flight to the mountains at the terrifying prospect of the capture of Jerusalem and the desecration of the temple. It was an apocalyptic composition focusing on the book of Daniel, and hence doubtless understood by many Christians in the sense that, with the destruction of Jerusalem, the parousia of Christ was at hand. These Christians then interpreted the Jewish catastrophe as a sign of the impending end, and it seems that Mark sought to quell this burning imminent expectation (cf. Mark 13:33-36). But this situation was scarcely still at hand for Matthew when he looked back on the destruction of Jerusalem (Matt. 22:7) and no longer had to deal with an insistent imminent expectation in his community (cf. 24:48; 25:5). What, then, is this text saying as it now looks back on a decade or more without the parousia? Is Matthew simply retaining this material from Jewish-Christian circles as he has in 10:23 and 16:28, or does he understand the portrayal in a new sense, so that it remains current for a later time as well? In the latter case, verses 15-25 must no longer be interpreted in terms of contemporary events but eschatologically, and therefore in terms of events to occur in the further course of history, especially with the approach of the end. But, then, what is Matthew thinking of as the "desolating sacrilege standing in the holy place" (v. 15)? Is this all simply borrowed eschatological imagery and speech? The answer is scarcely clear. In any case, Matthew agrees with the notion of an intense darkening of world history, with heavy burdens and temptations for Christians. They can hold fast through all of this only in the hope of the coming of the Son of Man. Matthew's view and admonition resemble the later ones in the book of Revelation.

Comparing verses 15-28 with verses 4-14, we can once more distinguish a portrayal of future events (vv. 15-22) and an admonition to the community, again marked off with "then" in verse 23. Matthew has supplemented the admonitory verses with verses 26-28, a passage stemming from the Sayings Source (cf. Luke 17:23-24, 37). The text reinforces the warning against seducers and prepares for the portrayal of the parousia in verses 29-31.

15-22 The "desolating sacrilege," explicitly identified by Matthew as an expression of Daniel in that apocalyptic book (Dan. 9:27; 11:31; 12:11), is a coded reference to the idolatrous altar, or the image of a pagan god that Antiochus IV had installed upon the altar of burnt offerings in the temple in Jerusalem in 167 B.C. (1 Macc. 1:54-55, 59; 2 Macc. 6:2). This prophecy is transferred to Matthew with the "desolating sacrilege," which Mark 13:14 interprets as being a person but which is no longer viewed as such in Matthew 24:15. Who or what is meant by the desolating sacrilege has always been disputed. The antichrist (a long influential interpretation)? An occurrence in the Jewish War? Or the desecration of the temple at the storming of Jerusalem? Since the warning to flee in verses 16-20 is inseparable from the observation regarding the desolating sacrilege, the reference in the original writing is certainly to a concrete event, but one that we can no longer identify. With his emphatic reference to Daniel, Matthew may have wanted to leave the interpretation open. The portrayal of the flight presupposes a Palestinian situation. One is struck by the addition, in verse 20, of "not on a sabbath." Since the time of the Maccabees, the strict sabbath commandment was no longer observed when there was danger of death (1 Macc. 2:32-41). Doubtless the observance of a "sabbath's journey" (880 meters) is in mind here (cf. Acts 1:12), a prescription by which Jewish-Christians continued to feel bound.

Seemingly attached to time and place, the portrayal acquires another dimension in the following verses (vv. 21-22). Suffering greater than there has been since the beginning of the world, or ever shall be, transcends the scale of the concrete historical. It is once more a prophecy of the future focusing on

Daniel, a quotation from Daniel 12:1, complemented by the indication that such suffering "will never again be." This moves the prophecy into the eschatological perspective, as an announcement of the last great torment and cosmic shock before the appearance of the Son of Man (v. 29). The days shortened by God also constitutes an apocalyptic concept (*Ethiopian Enoch* 80:2; *Syrian Apocalypse of Baruch* 20:1; *4 Ezra* 4:26). Such declarations ordinarily have a threatening sense; here the shortening of the days for the sake of the "elect" (also an apocalyptic expression) becomes a motif of consolation.

As we consider this eschatological horizon, we may regard this urging to and portrayal of flight as a graphic picture of Matthew's understanding of the heightened misery that will occur before the end; and if Matthew conceives of the parousia not as an event of the immediate future, then the prophecy becomes a discourse for the later church: all believers must reckon with the end, but without being led astray concerning God's salvific will.

23-28 In the address to the audience or readers that Matthew once more sounds here, first comes a warning, as in verse 5, against seducers who will come forward with the claim to be a Messiah or a prophet. A new element is that these, too, will work great signs and wonders, an echo of Deuteronomy 13:1-4. Matthew knows such wonder-workers, who boast to be such, from his own community (7:22-23). But one must lend them no credence; Jesus has foretold it. Then Matthew appends words from the Sayings Source having the same general sense. More clearly than in Luke 17:23, such seducers are said to entice people into the wilderness to meet the Messiah. According to Jewish thought, the Messiah-Prophet may reveal himself in the place sanctified by the wandering in the wilderness, as is well illustrated by an actual seducer of this kind, one Theudas, whom Josephus reports to have been followed by a great throng to the Jordan, where he sought to facilitate an easy crossing, as Joshua had long before (Josephus, *Antiquities* 20.97-98; cf. Acts 5:36). According to another view, the Messiah would at first remain concealed (cf. John 7:34), and doubtless "He is in the inner rooms" refers to this view. By contrast, the saying concerning the lightning assures one that the parousia of the Son of Man will be unmistakable for all human beings. The comparison with lightning here is intended to express, not suddenness, but the visibility of the parousia throughout the world. The proverbial expression concerning the carcass and the vultures, in Luke 17:37 probably referring to the judgment, is here not yet, as it is in Luke 17:34-35, related to the division of human beings at the judgment (cf. Matt. 24:40-41; 25:32-33), and means that the Christ of the parousia can no more be overlooked than the vultures that gather over a carcass. However, the comparison is only to the event, not to Christ or human beings. With this anticipatory look toward the parousia Matthew makes a transition to the next passage, on the event of the parousia.

The Coming of the Son of Man (24:29-31)

> 29 *"Immediately after the suffering of those days*
> *the sun will be darkened,*
> *and the moon will not give its light;*
> *the stars will fall from heaven,*
> *and the powers of heaven will be shaken.*
> 30 *Then the sign of the Son of Man will appear in heaven, and then all the tribes of the earth will mourn, and they will see 'the Son of Man coming on the clouds of heaven' with power and great glory.* 31 *And he will send out his angels with a loud trumpet call, and they will gather his elect from the four winds, from one end of heaven to the other."*

29-31 Now the event constituting the object of the disciples' question (v. 3) and the entire presentation up to this point are presented in apocalyptical language. The connection with Mark 13:24-27 is evident, and yet characteristic differences are recognizable: the sign of the Son of Man in the sky, the cries of woe of the peoples (v. 30), and smaller deviations, among them the trumpet in verse 31. Two emphases are remarkable in Matthew: the obviousness and cosmic shock of the event and the concept of the judgment. On the other hand, Matthew shows no hesitation in expressing the "imminence" of the parousia (v. 29), while Mark, owing to the false expectation of that imminence, portrays a delay in 13:24 ("in those days"). True, Matthew scarcely wishes to fan the flames of expectation but seeks at most to indicate the surprising element in the eschatological event (cf. Matt. 24:37-41). The presentation itself remains entirely within the purview of apocalyptic imagery.

29 The unusual natural phenomena — the darkening of the sun and moon (return to chaos and darkness) and the falling of the stars (regarded as ruling over the universal order; cf. Gen. 1:14-18), along with the quaking of the powers of heaven — are part of the scenery of the eschatological drama and must not be taken to mean the catastrophic destruction of the world. In terms of natural science, these images teach no lesson. They stem, as their actual wording shows, from Isaiah 13:10 (judgment upon Babel) and Isaiah 34:4 (judgment upon Edom), images now portraying God's judgment on the "day of the Lord." In apocalypticism, then, the imagery is indeed of an actual dissolution of the natural order (cf. *Ethiopian Enoch* 80:4-6; *4 Ezra* 5:4-5; *Sibylline Oracles* 3.796-803, etc.). The portrayal given here, too, is akin to this thought. The "shaking of the powers of heaven" may mean a trembling of the angelic powers that until now have ruled the world (cf. Eph. 6:12), or it may be a comprehensive expression for the previously mentioned falling of the stars (in Isa. 34:4 in the Greek the expression is encountered in one group of manuscripts).

243

On the whole, this portrayal is an indication of the judgment of God over the whole earth, a judgment plummeting from the sky (cf. also Heb. 12:26).

30 Matthew emphasizes the judgment more strongly than does Mark, through the quotation from Zechariah 12:10(12): "All the tribes of the earth will mourn," a text also reflected elsewhere in primitive Christianity (John 19:37; Rev. 1:7). Matthew omits, "They look on the one whom they have pierced," thereby avoiding a reference to the Crucified One and retaining only the cry of woe of the peoples. But what does he mean by the "sign of the Son of Man"? An old interpretation refers it to the cross (doubtless as early as *Didache* 16:6); but then why does Matthew pass over the words about the one pierced in the citation from Zechariah? Others think of a burst of light from heaven (cf. the words about lightning in v. 27, which, however, is merely a comparison). Probably the "sign" is the Son of Man himself, an explanatory genitive. An allusion to Isaiah 11:10, 12 (the shoot from the root of Jesse as a sign to the peoples) is questionable because in Isaiah the sign is salvific while in Matthew it is menacing. "The sign" could be an answer to the disciples' question in verse 3: there is no other sign of the parousia than the Son of Man himself. But this is not certain. The sequence indicated by "then . . . and then" probably means: at the first appearance all peoples raise their cries and lamentations. Then they see him coming on the clouds of the sky with great power and glory — the primitive Christian interpretation of Daniel 7:13(14) (cf. 26:64; Rev. 1:7, 13; 14:14). Whoever the one like a son of man meant in the prophetic passage, for the primitive church he was the Christ coming with power, none other than the earthly Jesus (Matt. 8:20; 9:6; 11:19; and frequently) — now, however, with divine power, also ascribed to the one like a son of man in Daniel 7:14. Only the Christ of the parousia comes *from the sky,* "on the clouds of heaven," as on a divine vehicle. His enthronement at God's side is presupposed (cf. 26:64). His function as judge is stressed by Matthew (see 16:27; 25:31-32).

31 But the Son of Man comes not only in judgment; he comes also for the gathering of the elect. He sends forth his angels, who are his heavenly retinue and messengers — for Matthew representing the divine exaltation of the Son of Man. "His" angels, Matthew calls them (also 13:41; 16:27), since the angels generally play a special role for Matthew as God's fighting force (26:53) and executors of divine judgment (13:39; 25:31). The great trumpet (in Hebrew the *shofar,* or ram's horn) is named as the instrument of an eschatological sign in 1 Thessalonians 4:16 and 1 Corinthians 15:52 as well, just as in *4 Ezra* 6:23 the Son of Man becomes not only visible but audible through the sound of the trumpet. The eschatological event, perceptible throughout the world, culminates in the assembling of the elect "from the four winds" (cf. Zech. 2:6). In Isaiah 27:13 the blowing of the "great trumpet" had this function. "From one end of heaven to the other," that is, from one horizon to the other, underscores the universal gathering of all the scattered "elect." In Israel, the prophecy was meant for its members scattered among the Gentiles (Deut. 30:3-4 and frequently); against a Christian background, those who are intended are the children of God scattered throughout the world (John 11:52). It is the vision of the union of the church with its Lord (Rev. 19:9; 21:2, 9-10).

The passage may neither be divested of its eschatological garb (be "demythologized") nor, on the other hand, regarded as providing any pattern of concrete data for the end time. But faith gains a perspective of hope — it is able to realize a goal: at the end of world history, in spite of all the darkness and growing shock, the fulfillment of the salvific event is to be awaited, a fulfillment indicated in the earthly Jesus' message of the Realm of God and in the resurrection of the Crucified One, his sojourn in the transcendent world of God — a fulfillment that will follow precisely in this Jesus Christ, through the power of God.

The Lesson of the Fig Tree and the Necessity for Watchfulness (24:32-42)

32 *"From the fig tree learn its lesson: as soon as its branch becomes tender and puts forth its leaves, you know that summer is near.* 33 *So also, when you see all these things, you know that he is near, at the very gates.* 34 *Truly I tell you, this generation will not pass away until all these things have taken place.* 35 *Heaven and earth will pass away, but my words will not pass away.*

36 *"But about that day and hour no one knows, neither the angels of heaven, nor the Son, but only the Father.* 37 *For as the days of Noah were, so will be the coming of the Son of Man.* 38 *For as in those days before the flood they were eating and drinking, marrying and giving in marriage, until the day Noah entered the ark,* 39 *and they knew nothing until the flood came and swept them all away, so too will be the coming of the Son of Man.* 40 *Then two will be in the field; one will be taken and one will be left.* 41 *Two women will be grinding meal together; one will be taken and one will be left.* 42 *Keep awake therefore, for you do not know on what day your Lord is coming."*

32-42 The question of the moment of the parousia, which was a concern of the primitive church again and again (see 2 Peter), is also taken up by Matthew. He follows the text of Mark 13:28-32 almost literally, thereby adopting the characteristic tension and dialectic that arise in this passage through the juxtaposition of references to an impending event ("is at the very gates," Matt. 24:33; "this generation," 24:34), and knowledge that belongs to the Father alone (24:36). Matthew omits the conclusion of the discourse (Mark 13:33-37) and instead appends words from the apocalypse of Q (Luke 17:26-27, 31-35) that shed light on the critical situation of the dawn of the parousia and its suddenness. For Matthew these words will continue to stand in the context of the question of the moment of the end. He presents admonitions to watchfulness and readiness, which recall Mark 13:33-37, only afterward, with other material. But how do things stand, for Matthew, with the question of the end?

32-33   On Jesus' lips, the parable of the fig tree may originally have portrayed the Reign of God as proclaimed in the signs of his activity, like the weather signs of Luke 12:54-56 (cf. Matt. 16:2b-3). As the fig tree announces the coming of summer by sprouting twigs and leaves, so Jesus' salvific deeds proclaim the awaited Realm of God. In Mark 13:29 "these things" can refer only to the previously portrayed eschatological occurrences. Matthew writes "all these things," denoting the entire eschatological event. For Matthew the "woes," the "great suffering," and the coming of the Son of Man are a single set of events, whose extension in time is scarcely intended to indicate anything specific. All of this indicates only that the end is in store for the community. Whether the implied subject of "at the very gates" is the parousia (cf. Matt. 24:3), "the end of the age" (24:3), or the Son of Man (cf. v. 30) is unclear. In Luke 21:31 it is the "kingdom of God."

34-36   "This generation," in Jesus' statements, is the contemporary generation, and for Matthew is certainly the persons living in his time (cf. 23:36). Since he twice designates "this generation" as "evil and adulterous" (absent in Mark) because it demands a "sign" (see 12:39; 16:4), the question has arisen whether this is perhaps meant qualitatively: this wicked type of person that will not die out until the very parousia. In context, however, this is improbable. In the chronological sense, the sentence is akin to 16:28, in terms of tradition history possibly deriving from it. In this case Matthew would be adopting an early Jewish-Christian tradition that included an imminent expectation, without his having to share that expectation. The powerful assurance of verse 35 is similar for Matthew to 5:18 as well, concerning the validity of the law to the very end of the world. His addition of "until all these things have taken place" reveals his eschatological thinking: everything, the observance of the law as well as world events, must be fulfilled according to the will of God, or the words of Jesus. All things run their course toward the "accomplishment of the time of the world," and this course includes the mission to the Gentiles (24:14; 28:19-20); thus for Matthew surely no intense imminent expectation underlies verses 34-35. This is confirmed by verse 36: the knowledge of the day and the hour (more closely bound together than in Mark) of the parousia is reserved for the Father. It can be unsettling that not even the Son knows this point in time: Does the Son not stand in an intimate relationship with the Father (cf. 11:27)? Many interpreters think that the "nor the Son" is not an original reading in Matthew and has been introduced, on the basis of Mark 13:32 (Luke omits the entire verse), only by later copyists. But it is equally plausible that Matthew casually names the Son (cf. the statements concerning the Father in 20:23; 25:34), and that this reference was only later suppressed in the much read Gospel of Matthew on dogmatic grounds. The reading "nor the Son" is far better attested in terms of the manuscript tradition. For many interpreters, the unusual reference to the Son is an indication that we have an authentic logion of Jesus since the primitive church would scarcely have dared to make such a reference. For others, the unmodified "Son" indicates a wording composed by the primitive church. In any case, it is a testimony to the consciousness of primitive Christianity that the "last things" are hidden from human intelligence and knowledge, and this is certainly Jesus' attitude as well.

From the "little apocalypse" of Luke 17:22-37, from which Matthew has already quoted in 24:27-28, he now adds logia concerning the parousia as something that overtakes persons unexpectedly. The verses confirm the quality of the end as unknowable and the situation of crisis that will suddenly descend upon people, but are also intended as a transition (cf. Matt. 24:42) to the admonitions that are then developed in further parables. The comparison with the generation of the Flood (Luke 17:26-30, adding the inhabitants of Sodom) portrays the casual attitude with which people go about their daily business, but who in their unconcern and unwillingness to learn are suddenly overtaken by catastrophe. The twin image of the pair of men working together in a field (a different image in Luke) and the pair of women grinding grain at a mill together is intended to portray redemption and judgment. "Taken" (with the Son of Man) stands first in each comparison and represents the redemption of the elect, while "left" (in the devastating catastrophe) stands for the victims of the judgment. This is no arbitrary act on the part of God; rather, it presupposes either standing up to or failing the trial: judgment occurs according to works (see Matt. 16:27; 22:11-13; 25:46). Thus Matthew appends the admonition to watchfulness. That the Son of Man comes at an unexpected hour is also a basic presupposition in the following parables (24:44-50; 25:6).

> 43 *"But understand this: if the owner of the house had known in what part of the night the thief was coming, he would have stayed awake and would not have let his house be broken into.* 44 *Therefore you also must be ready, for the Son of Man is coming at an unexpected hour."*

43-44 The little parable stemming from the Sayings Source (cf. Luke 12:39-40) is one of the "crisis parables" and fits in well for Matthew after 24:37-42. Originally it was not the Christ of the parousia that was its focus of attention, but the critical situation, in which one must be watchful and ready. The thief, then, is not an image of the Son of Man. The primitive church has taken Jesus' parable and subjected it to further meditation. According to 1 Thessalonians 5:2, the "day of the Lord" comes like a thief in the night. In Revelation 3:3; 16:15

it is Christ himself. But in every instance, watchfulness and readiness are urged as the Christian attitude.

The Faithful or the Unfaithful Slave (24:45-51)

45 *"Who then is the faithful and wise slave, whom his master has put in charge of his household, to give the other slaves their allowance of food at the proper time? 46 Blessed is that slave whom his master will find at work when he arrives. 47 Truly I tell you, he will put that one in charge of all his posses-sions. 48 But if that wicked slave says to himself, 'My master is delayed,' 49 and he begins to beat his fellow slaves, and eats and drinks with drunk-ards, 50 the master of that slave will come on a day when he does not expect him and at an hour that he does not know. 51 He will cut him in pieces and put him with the hypocrites, where there will be weeping and gnashing of teeth."*

45-51 Like Luke, Matthew attaches to the parable of the watchful master of the house the one of the slave supervisor, who is entrusted with the oversight of the household. Matthew has made little alteration in the text, which he has taken from the Sayings Source (cf. Luke 12:42-46). He characterizes the ne-glectful slave as "wicked," casts him among the "hypocrites" (v. 51a), and de-picts his agony in the place of punishment as "weeping and gnashing of teeth," a favorite Matthean metaphor (see 8:12; 13:42-50; 22:13; 25:30). The parable does not deal with two different slaves but only one, who has been given re-sponsibility for the other servants and handmaids. Depending on whether he fulfills his duty to see to their bodily needs or coarsely neglects it, he will receive reward or punishment from his lord when the latter returns. On Jesus' lips, the parable may have been an admonitory address against the leaders of Israel, who ought to have concerned themselves with the people entrusted to them. In the Matthean context, as earlier in Q, it is applied to Christ (the "Lord"), awaited by the community, and thus carried over to the new, post-Easter situation. Luke, as we may learn from the introduction he has composed (Luke 12:41), obviously has the leaders of the community in mind (cf. Luke 22:26-27), while Matthew means all Christians in their responsibility for one another, since he scarcely knows of such community leaders. The parable of the bridesmaids, too (Matt. 25:1-12), is addressed to everyone.

No valid basis exists for ascribing the parable a priori to the community. What suggests this — that the lord postpones his return — is apposite to the development of the narrative: it motivates the wicked dealings of the slave su-pervisor (v. 48). Of course, verse 50 places a stronger accent on the community element: the lord comes at a day and hour when the slave least expects him (cf.

24:36, 44; 25:13). But in line with other crisis parables (cf. 24:38-41, 43-44), this, too, belongs plausibly to Jesus' preaching. The reader is struck by the harsh punishment meted out to the slave who beats his fellow servants (Luke, "men and women") and celebrates banquets with his companions. The lord will "cut him in pieces," literally, a way of execution cited elsewhere as well (*Greek Apocalypse of Baruch* 16:3; cf. Sus. 55-59 and extrabiblical literature). But then how can the man be "put with the hypocrites" (Luke 12:46: the "unfaithful" or untrue)? Here it is God's everlasting judgment that comes to the fore (cf. 1QS 2:17: May God "set his lot among the eternally cursed"). Granted, Joachim Jeremias' suggested solution (*Die Gleichnisse Jesu* [Göttingen, 6th ed., 1962], p. 54, n. 2), that we presume a misunderstood text, "He will mete him out blows and deal with him as useless," fits in well with the account as it is narrated but remains questionable: the misunderstanding would have to have infiltrated before Q (orally?). The text transmitted in Q goes from image to fact — punishment in God's final judgment — and Matthew underscores this fact by adding verse 51b. For Matthew this judgment also threatens Christians who have failed the test (Matt. 22:11-13; 25:41, 46).

The Parable of the Ten Bridesmaids (25:1-13)

> 25:1 *"Then the kingdom of heaven will be like this. Ten bridesmaids took their lamps and went to meet the bridegroom. 2 Five of them were foolish, and five were wise. 3 When the foolish took their lamps, they took no oil with them; 4 but the wise took flasks of oil with their lamps. 5 As the bridegroom was delayed, all of them became drowsy and slept. 6 But at midnight there was a shout, 'Look! Here is the bridegroom! Come out to meet him.' 7 Then all those bridesmaids got up and trimmed their lamps. 8 The foolish said to the wise, 'Give us some of your oil, for our lamps are going out.' 9 But the wise replied, 'No! there will not be enough for you and for us; you had better go to the dealers and buy some for yourselves.' 10 And while they went to buy it, the bridegroom came, and those who were ready went with him into the wedding banquet; and the door was shut. 11 Later the other bridesmaids came also, saying, 'Lord, lord, open to us.' 12 But he replied, 'Truly I tell you, I do not know you.' 13 Keep awake therefore, for you know neither the day nor the hour."*

1-13 Matthew appends a parable from his own tradition bearing on the same aspect of readiness and watchfulness (24:44, 50; 25:13). He thereby presents two rather large problems: (1) Is the narrative cohesive, and can it be regarded as representing an actual wedding custom? (2) Can the account have originated with Jesus himself, or is it a post-Easter composition by the community, drawn up in terms of the parousia and shot through with allegorical characteristics? It is scarcely Matthew's own creation. The introduction corresponds (right to the use of the future tense) to three Matthean parables: that of the weeds among the wheat (13:24), that of the pitiless slave (18:23), and that of the wedding banquet (22:2). The Matthean admonition, "Keep awake therefore," does not fit the narrative, in which all of the bridesmaids fall asleep. Unusual characteristics are also to be found in the three other parables: whatever their origin, Matthew has scarcely fashioned them on his own.

1-5 The situation recounted is not altogether clear. In the Jewish wedding, the "leading home," the introduction of the bride to the house of the groom, was the decisive act. Apart from an interpolation (clearly secondary) in verse 1 in one group of manuscripts, there is no mention of the bride at all. Where is she — still with her parents in their house (the most obvious hypothesis), or already in the groom's house, where the groom will follow her when he has concluded the negotiations that have delayed the wedding (cf. Jeremias, *Die Gleichnisse Jesu*, pp. 172-73). The bridesmaids, who wait at a meeting place, are to encounter the bridegroom and accompany him with lamps (probably wind lanterns) in solemn procession to the bride. Owing to the groom's delay, they all grow weary and fall asleep.

6-9 The second scene takes place at midnight. The beginning of a wedding banquet at midnight is unusual, although (owing to the groom's negotiations with the bride's relatives) not impossible. The scene at midnight would then be well understandable. Even the urgent prompting of the "wise" maidens to the others, that they go to the dealers and get themselves some oil, need not be out of keeping with the story since in the case of such a wedding celebration merchants were certainly still to be reached.

10-12 The third scene portrays the bridegroom's procession into the wedding hall together with the wise maidens, and the rejection of the foolish maidens who have come too late. Can the harsh rebuff of the latter, too, be understood in the framework of the narrative? Even if the bridesmaids are the wedding household's own servants, this would be difficult. Further, this passage echoes other texts that bear on the eschatological event: the call of "Lord, Lord" of those condemned in the judgment (7:22), the vain knocking on the locked door (Luke 13:25), and the formula of rejection, "I do not know you" (Matt. 7:23; cf. Luke 13:27). Thus the image of the judgment is woven into the narrative.

Assessment

(a) The material for a wedding parable is ready to hand, for the Old Testament (Yahweh's marriage to Israel; cf. esp. Hos. 2:19-20; Isa. 62:5) as well as for the Jesus tradition (see Matt. 9:15; 22:2). However, in Judaism the bridegroom is not a metaphor for the Messiah and Jesus will not have seen himself as such, although the primitive church will have (cf. Matt. 9:15; further, John 3:29; 2 Cor. 11:2; Rev. 19:7; 21:2, 9). This speaks for an origin in the community, although here the community will be represented by the bridesmaids, not by the bride. (b) An origin in the Christian Easter celebration, which was extended to midnight and in which, at this time, the parousia was expected (F. A. Strobel, *Die Stunde der Wahrheit* [Tübingen, 1980]), remains questionable. To cite this *Sitz im Leben* for the narrative of the ten bridesmaids would be purely a product of the imagination. Besides, a midnight parousia of Christ is discounted elsewhere (Mark 13:35; cf. Luke 12:38). (c) The detail that the lord or bridegroom (25:5) delays his arrival fits the narrative since this detail is plausible in the order of events. The delay must not constitute the starting point from which the story is constructed, for example, by primitive Christian prophets proclaiming such a delay. (d) The formation of the parable remains a complex problem. Possibly there were starting points for it in authentic logia of Jesus. The parable of the lord who returns home in the night (Luke 12:36-37) seems related to it, as that one in turn has points of contact with the parable of the lord returning from a journey (Mark 13:34-35; Matt. 24:50 par. Luke 12:46). Evidently the primitive church has applied such elements of imagery in various ways, even joining them with new eloquent images. The story of the ten bridesmaids is not a crisis parable (the image of the wedding is out of keeping), but an admonitory summons to constant readiness, which for Matthew is connected to the warning to watch (cf. Matt. 24:44 with 25:13). The moment of the parousia remains uncertain.

The Parable of the Talents (25:14-30)

14 *"For it is as if a man, going on a journey, summoned his slaves and entrusted his property to them;* 15 *to one he gave five talents, to another two, to another one, to each according to his ability. Then he went away.* 16 *The one who had received the five talents went off at once and traded with them, and made five more talents.* 17 *In the same way, the one who had the two talents made two more talents.* 18 *But the one who had received the one talent went off and dug a hole in the ground and hid his master's money.* 19 *After a long time the master of those slaves came and settled accounts with them.* 20 *Then the one who had received the five talents came forward, bringing five more talents, saying, 'Master, you handed over to me five talents; see, I have made five more talents.'* 21 *His master said to him, 'Well done, good and trustworthy slave; you have been trustworthy in a few things, I will put you in charge of many things; enter into the joy of your master.'* 22 *And the one with the two talents also came forward, saying, 'Master, you handed over to me two tal-*

ents; see, I have made two more talents.' 23 His master said to him, 'Well done, good and trustworthy slave; you have been trustworthy in a few things, I will put you in charge of many things; enter into the joy of your master.' 24 Then the one who had received the one talent also came forward, saying, 'Master, I knew that you were a harsh man, reaping where you did not sow, and gathering where you did not scatter seed; 25 so I was afraid, and I went and hid your talent in the ground. Here you have what is yours.' 26 But his master replied, 'You wicked and lazy slave! You knew, did you, that I reap where I did not sow, and gather where I did not scatter? 27 Then you ought to have invested my money with the bankers, and on my return I would have received what was my own with interest. 28 So take the talent from him, and give it to the one with the ten talents. 29 For to all those who have, more will be given, and they will have an abundance; but from those who have nothing, even what they have will be taken away. 30 As for this worthless slave, throw him into the outer darkness, where there will be weeping and gnashing of teeth.'"

14-30 In the course of the Matthean presentation, this parable, like the three preceding, is intended to inculcate in the community the correct attitude toward the span of time between the departure and return of the Lord. But while the other parables summon to watchfulness and readiness, the point here is life in the world — the observance of the will of God in deed. The parable of the entrusted money is appropriate for Matthew in terms of his preoccupation with the fulfillment of the righteousness required by the Reign of God (5:20; 7:21; 13:41-43, 49; 21:43; 23:3), and forms a good transition to the portrayal of the last judgment, at which works of love are the decisive element. The eschatological perspective is established by the man's return "after a long time" and his settling of accounts with his slaves. Here there is nothing about "delaying" (24:48; 25:5), but Matthew seems to be thinking of a rather long interim.

In view of the parable's clear and unambiguous applicability to the community, it is difficult to imagine what might have been the origin of its tradition and its meaning on the lips of Jesus, if the parable goes back to him. Unlike the parable of the bridesmaids, this one is a variant reading of Luke 19:12-27; and despite significant deviations, we may argue for a tradition in the Sayings Source. We can scarcely reconstruct anymore how the parable ran there, of course, since both evangelists have altered it considerably depending on their intentions — Luke, in view of the delay of the parousia (cf. Luke 19:11), through the insertion of a story of a pretender to the throne; Matthew through other interventions, such as that of the huge difference in the entrusted money (talents instead of minas), and through the transcendence of earthly relationships in his portrayal of reward and punishment. On Jesus' lips, the parable may have been directed against the frequently attacked Jewish leaders (cf. the parable of the slave supervisor, Matt. 24:45-51), in view of the emphasis on the failure of the useless slave. But it may also have been intended to summon all hearers of Jesus' message to yield fruit corresponding to God's gift of grace (the entrusted money).

The redoubled version of the parable, which we cannot here investigate more closely, once more reveals the freedom with which the primitive church and the evangelists dealt with the Jesus tradition, especially through a post-Easter transformation of that tradition. The returning lord is Christ at his parousia. Just as in the parable of the bridesmaids, certain metaphors and motifs are adopted: the man who journeys afar (cf. Mark 13:34), the assignment of the task (compare the doorkeeper, Mark 13:34, with Luke 12:36), the settling of accounts (cf. Matt. 18:23; Luke 16:2), reward and punishment, a banquet of celebration, and the darkness of hell. What has belonged to the "story line," the events portrayed in the original parable narrative, now gains a much deeper meaning, a metaphorical sense.

The construction of the parable is simple and comprises basically only two scenes: in verses 14-18 a man about to undertake a lengthy journey entrusts his household slaves with money, and the slaves handle it differently; in verses 19-30 he returns, calls them to account, and metes out reward and punishment. The first scene is the necessary preparation for and setting of the stage for the second scene, which is worked out in greater detail. Verses 14-18 are to be regarded as a unit since they depend on the behavior of the slaves throughout (cf. the connective "at once," v. 16). The second scene develops the actual point: the entrusted talents must be "invested." One can distinguish the rewarding of the good servants from the punishment of the useless one; but the layout in terms of the hallowed "three"consecrated triad reveals the combination in its unity.

14-18 The crisp appending of these verses to the foregoing ("For it is as if . . .") is perhaps a sign that Matthew knew this parable, like the previous one of the bridesmaids (25:1), as a parable of the Realm of God (cf. also Luke 19:11). The "property" entrusted to the slaves bears only on the entrusted money. Originally the amount was certainly in minas. A mina had the value of one hundred drachmas; a talent, however, was a great amount, worth several thousand dollars (see 18:24). Matthew has substituted the large sum because he was thinking of God's great gift (as previously in 18:24-27) — here not of God's boundless forgiveness but of the treasure of the Reign of God (cf. 13:44, 45-46). The unequal distribution of the money according to the capacity of each slave is more credible in the story than the equal conferral of one mina to each slave, as we have it in Luke, as is the number of the slaves — three here instead of Luke's ten. That the servants are to deal with the money is presupposed (in Luke the nobleman expressly says so). The first slave, the one with five talents, goes at once and works with it, and the second does the same. The third buries the money, which in those days was considered the best security. Thus the scene is set for act two.

19-30   The two good, reliable servants are requited in Matthew with the same reward (not so in Luke). This is deliberate on Matthew's part — an important aspect of God's goodness (cf. 20:1-15). The entry "into the joy of your master" can be seen, in terms of earthly relationships, as partaking at the lord's table (banquet of celebration), a rewarding with the lord's common fare. Of course, Matthew is already thinking of the metaphorical heavenly, eschatological banquet (cf. 8:11; 22:1-10; 25:10). The disproportion between the "few things" and the "many things" will be Christians' promise of God's superabundant reward of grace (cf. 19:29).

The excuses offered by the slave who has buried his talent are cover-ups for his sloth, and he will be taken by his "harsh" lord at his own word and sentenced. The dialogue belongs to the logic of the narrative, and does not authorize a harsh picture of God. The story is setting forth not an inexorably demanding God but the sloth and guilt of the slave. The order that the lazy servant is to be deprived of his talent and have it given to the one who has received ten talents is peculiar. In the framework of the account, this can be thought of as a humiliation. The appended verse 29 is found in 13:12 as well, and there is adopted from Mark 4:25. Whether it was originally in our parable, in spite of the parallel in Luke 19:26, is questionable. It may also be experiential material of a wisdom sort, shifted to a new perspective and added here in light of the order just given in the story. It shows the overflowing goodness of God (cf. Luke 6:38; Mark 4:24), here God's superabundant reward and the impoverishment befalling guilty human beings — a logion susceptible of various applications. The punishment of the useless servant in verse 30 is described by Matthew as comparable to that of the man without a wedding garment (22:13), both with metaphors of eternal divine judgment — a warning for his Christian readers.

The Judgment of the Nations (25:31-46)

> 31 *"When the Son of Man comes in his glory, and all the angels with him, then he will sit on the throne of his glory. 32 All the nations will be gathered before him, and he will separate people one from another as a shepherd separates the sheep from the goats, 33 and he will put the sheep at his right hand and the goats at the left. 34 Then the king will say to those at his right hand, 'Come, you that are blessed by my Father, inherit the kingdom prepared for you from the foundation of the world; 35 for I was hungry and you gave me food, I was thirsty and you gave me something to drink, I was a stranger and*

you welcomed me, 36 I was naked and you gave me clothing, I was sick and you took care of me, I was in prison and you visited me.' 37 Then the righteous will answer him, 'Lord, when was it that we saw you hungry and gave you food, or thirsty and gave you something to drink? 38 And when was it that we saw you a stranger and welcomed you, or naked and gave you clothing? 39 And when was it that we saw you sick or in prison and visited you?' 40 And the king will answer them, 'Truly I tell you, just as you did it to one of the least of these who are members of my family, you did it to me.' 41 Then he will say to those at his left hand, 'You that are accursed, depart from me into the eternal fire prepared for the devil and his angels; 42 for I was hungry and you gave me no food, I was thirsty and you gave me nothing to drink, 43 I was a stranger and you did not welcome me, naked and you did not give me clothing, sick and in prison and you did not visit me.' 44 Then they also will answer, 'Lord, when was it that we saw you hungry or thirsty or a stranger or naked or sick or in prison, and did not take care of you?' 45 Then he will answer them, 'Truly I tell you, just as you did not do it to one of the least of these, you did not do it to me.' 46 And these will go away into eternal punishment, but the righteous into eternal life."

31-46 Matthew knows how to build up a story to its dramatic climax, as in 16:13-20 and at the end in 28:16-20. So also in the eschatological discourse, after the first peak, the parousia (24:29-31), the second follows: the last judgment, the judgment upon the world. That this is a deliberate composition is shown by the adoption of the image of the parousia: the Son of Man in his glory, with the angels accompanying him. "All nations," too, are cited once more (cf. 24:30). But the scene of the last judgment now receives its own stamp: it is a juridical process, with a judge's bench and an indictment, a setting apart of the guilty from the righteous, and finally the execution of a sentence (v. 46). It is not a parable but a revelatory discourse with a graphic portrayal, a painting with shining colors and moving themes.

The construction of this eschatological scene is artistic and carefully thought through. The scene is set in verses 31-33. In verses 34-45 the central event of the judgment is proclaimed. The pronouncement upon the righteous in verses 34-40 and the pronouncement upon the guilty in verses 41-45 run perfectly parallel, except that the enumeration of the works of love is stylistically abbreviated in the second passage. Third, and last, the execution of the judgment is announced, in which the condemned are dealt with first, and afterward the righteous (a summary of the preceding presentation). The broadly constructed main part also reveals a carefully considered twin structure: pronunciation of the sentence (vv. 34, 41), grounds for the sentence (vv. 35-36, 42-43), request for a clarification or objection on the part of the defendants (vv.

37-39, 44), and explanation of the sentence or overruling of the objection (vv. 40, 45). The whole is a rhetorical work of art, developing the decisive point with the most extreme sharpness: the criterion of judgment is constituted by works of love on behalf of the "least," namely, those in trouble and need (v. 45).

The much discussed portrayal of the judgment mainly presents the following problems: (a) Where does this uniquely Matthean presentation come from? (b) Is there a plurality of traditions or redactions here, especially in view of the switch from "Son of Man" (v. 31) to "king" (vv. 34, 40)? (c) Who are the "least" (members of God's family) to whom, according to the pronouncement of judgment, the works of love were to be shown? (d) How is one to assess the relationship between the Son of Man and the "least" (members of God's family) in terms of his "you did it to me" or "you did not do it to me"? The last two questions, especially, call for a clear choice among the various answers given. Deeds of love to primitive Christian missionaries in their troubled situation? Deeds of love toward those suffering need at the hands of non-Christians, so that it is these latter who are put on trial? Deeds of love toward all in need, which the Son of Man demands of Christians and non-Christians? Lately, two opposite views have crystalized (each with a variety of modifications): one more narrow, centering on certain groups, and one universal, embracing all peoples and every individual. Let us follow the text in such a way as to be able to take a stand on this question.

31-33   "When the Son of Man comes" harks back to the prediction of the parousia in 24:30. "In *his* glory, . . . on the throne of *his* glory" places the Son of Man in the center of the scene as the focus of attention. With him come "all the angels," who are also cited in 24:31 ("*his* angels"). Matthew's special viewpoint comes still more sharply to the fore in that the Son of Man now sits "on the throne of his glory"; only Matthew expresses himself in this way (cf. 19:28). In Revelation 4 God is the one on the throne; in Revelation 5:6 the Lamb stands between the throne and the four living beings, and judgment is reserved to God (Rev. 20:11-15). This is also the prevailing Jewish view: only in the imagery of *Enoch* is the "Elect" or the "Son of Man" seated on the throne of his glory (*Ethiopian Enoch* 45:3; 51:3; 55:4; 61:8; 62:2-3, 5; 69:27, 29). However, there the hosts of angels are not mentioned, nor the assemblage of all peoples. This is a motif of the Old Testament and apocalyptic portrayals of the "day of the Lord" (Isa. 66:18; Joel 3:1-2, 11; Zech. 14:2-3, 12; *Ethiopian Enoch* 62:3; etc.). For Matthew, "all nations" gains more importance (cf. Matt. 24:9, 14) through the commission of the Resurrected One to go and teach them (28:19). The scenario of verses 31-32a is obviously designed (redacted) by Matthew.

The division of good and evil, righteous and sinners, likewise belongs to current expectations, although the Judgment is usually described as a punitive judgment upon sinners (cf. *Jubilees* 5:10-15; *Ethiopian Enoch* 1:7-9; *Testament of Levi* 5:4; *Testament of Benjamin* 10:8-9; *4 Esdras* 7:33-38; *Syrian Apocalypse of Baruch* 54:21-22). Granted, the image of the division of the (white) sheep from the (black or dark brown) goats does not occur elsewhere, but it does correspond to Palestinian life: during the day all of the animals graze together, but in the evening they are separated because goats need a warmer place. What we have is symbolic speech: on the right hand is the positive or good side; white is the color of purity.

34-45 Surprisingly, we now hear of a "king" — usually a symbol of God (cf. 5:35; 18:23; 22:2) but here clearly referring to the Son of Man. Is this an indication that another tradition is being adopted here, one that originally had God as the Judge? But the subsequent portrayal, especially in verses 40 and 45, can refer only to Jesus, the Judge who comes. The identification of Son of Man and king is to be explained from the Christian designation of Jesus as a king — here in his glory (cf. 21:5; 27:37, 42; John 18:37; Rev. 17:14; 19:16). The royal Son of Man executes the decree of God, who from the very creation of the world has contemplated its end, and decreed the portion of the good in his Realm (v. 34) and the punishment of the wicked in the place of damnation (v. 41). God's blessing and curse are set forth to the Israelites in Deuteronomy 11:26-28, and in chapter 28 are more nearly detailed (cf. Josh. 8:34), depending on whether they abide by, or transgress, his law. In the judgment by the Son of Man this comes out in the open, and indeed for all peoples. The linguistic composition betrays Matthew's signature: we read of those blessed "by my Father," of the "inheritance" of the Realm of God (Matt. 5:5; 19:29), of the Father's "determination" of people's lot (20:23). The accursed will be cast into the "eternal fire" (cf. 13:42, 50; 18:8-9) that is prepared for "the devil and his angels." The word "devil" (Gk. *diabolos*) is selected, besides, in the story of the temptation (4:1-11) and in 13:39, along with the older expression, "Satan." Matthew does not otherwise mention the devil's angels; cf., however, Revelation 12:7-9.

A sentence is pronounced in accordance with each individual's deeds (see 16:27) — more specifically, in accordance with the works of love that those standing before the judgment seat have done or have omitted. If this is now not a "judgment upon the peoples" but an individual judgment, we need not be surprised. In the assembly of all peoples, after all, each individual is judged. Even in Jewish texts, the individual judgment of sinners stands (cf. *Psalms of Solomon* 2:34-38; 15:11-15; 1QS 2:1-18; 3:25–4:15) alongside the older expectation of punitive judgment upon peoples and realms. The enumeration of six works of "material help" (but they are not only "material"!) is not intended to be exhaustive but merely illustrative. Nor is it anything new and original: there are abundant examples in Egypt (in the "Book of the Dead") and in Judaism, although with variations, and suited to a given context (Isa. 58:4-8; *Testament of Joseph* 1; *Slavonic Enoch* 9; 42:8-9; *Midrash on Psalm 118,* para. 12). In Tobit

1:16-20; 2:3-8, the work of love of burying the dead is added. In our text, these deeds of love gain their special standing through their relationship to Jesus Christ. What the merciful have done for one of the "least of the members of my family," they have done to him. "My family" may not be stricken on the basis of tradition criticism, for example, because it is missing in Matthew 25:45. For the words of the Judge, it is essential that the righteous have encountered him in their good works on behalf of the "least," and the latter include those who have closed themselves off from the call of mercy. That the Son of Man and king is none other than the earthly Jesus and that the Jesus who worked on earth has practiced and demanded such mercy are presupposed. For Matthew, mercy, love in action, is a priority (cf. 5:7; 9:13; 12:7; 23:23); and for primitive Christianity, as the fulfillment of the commandment of love, it is the most powerful effect of Jesus' preaching (cf. Luke 10:37; John 13:34-35; Rom. 12:13-21; Gal. 5:14).

But in what sense does the eschatological Judge identify himself with the least ones? Not in the sense of a mystical identification, as if he were hidden in the robes of the needy and oppressed; nor in the sense of a simple human solidarity. Rather, the Son of Man can speak in this way because he once lived among men and women, lived and required such mercy, and now steps forward as the one who lives with God and as the eschatological judge demands an accounting. Judaism has said that *God* credits it to the account of his children who have given to the poor to eat as if they had given to him to eat (*Midrash on Tannaim* 15:9, in J. Jeremias, *Die Gleichnisse Jesu*, p. 205). Now God has been replaced by the Son of Man, and he says the like of himself, only more clearly and more powerfully: the least ones are his brothers and sisters. The idea of brothers and sisters, originally applied to the members of the community (Matt. 5:22-24 and frequently; 23:9), can, against the horizon of world judgment, be expanded to include all women and men. To understand only Christians or Christian missionaries as among the "least," on the ground of places in which "little ones" refers to disciples of Jesus, Christian missionaries, or insignificant members of the community (see 10:42; 18:6, 10, 14), is to overlook the fact that "in the name of a disciple" (10:42) is absent here. In the judgment upon "all the nations," the horizon of the time of mission is past: all the people of the world at the end of time are in view. Similarly questionable is the other restricting view, to the effect that here the Gentiles are being addressed and a pathway is being opened to them by which, with the practice of love in the sense of Jesus, they may yet stand the test in the court of the Son of Man (J. Jeremias, *Gleichnisse*, ad loc.). Granted, "all the nations" includes the Gentiles, who are yet to be evangelized (28:19). But in the mind of the evangelist, it also includes the members of the church at the scene of judgment. Frequently enough, these are threatened with the judgment of the Son of Man if they fail him (7:22-23; 13:41-42; 22:11-

13; 25:12). Each will be requited by the Son of Man as his or her deeds deserve (16:27): this exclusively Matthean expression is fulfilled in the judgment portrayal of the eschatological discourse. Christians and non-Christians alike are dealt with in the Judge's pronouncement of sentence. Their astonishment, expressed in their question as to when they have served, or not served, the Judge, is explained by the unexpected establishment of the grounds of the judgment. Christians will have thought that they knew the Son of Man; Gentiles will not have considered such credit for their deeds of love. But for everyone there is only this one criterion: an urgent cry of warning to believers in Christ, hope for those who do not (yet) know the Son of Man.

46 The brief proclamation of the execution of judgment foresees only eternal punishment for those who have spurned the commandment of merciful love of neighbor, and eternal life for the righteous. Consolingly, the merciful are named last.

Where does this text come from? The part contributed by the evangelist (vv. 31-32a; certain turns of phrase in the middle part; v. 46) has already become clear. The main portrayal, however, is adopted from a tradition that, in view of the christological outlook in verses 40 and 45, must come from Christian circles, probably from Hellenistic Jewish Christianity. The core concepts go back to Jesus, but they are shifted into a post-Easter context. The primitive church has developed the thought of Jesus' demand of love and has presented it in this impressive manner. The portrait of the judgment cannot be interpreted as a real, concrete event; but the words of the Son of Man and Judge retain their trenchancy.

JESUS' PASSION AND RESURRECTION (26:1–28:20)

In its external course the Matthean history of the passion follows Mark's presentation very exactly. Matthew skips over only a little of what Mark sets forth: details in the preparation for the Passover meal (Mark 14:13-14), a young man's following Jesus at his arrest (Mark 14:51-52), Pilate's wonderment at Jesus' quick death (Mark 15:44), the musing of the women as they walk to the tomb (Mark 16:3-4; but see below). On the other hand, he has introduced much new material: Judas's question, at the prediction of the betrayal, whether the traitor is himself, and Jesus' affirmative response (Matt. 26:25); Jesus' declaration at his arrest that he could summon twelve legions of angels (26:52-54); Judas's end (27:3-10) after Jesus was handed over to Pilate; the intervention of Pilate's wife (27:19) in the Roman trial; Pilate's verdict of innocence and the acceptance of guilt by "the people as a whole" (27:24-25); further striking occurrences after Jesus' death (27:51b-53); and the posting of guards at the tomb (27:62-66).

Matthew gives a great deal of attention to Jesus' resurrection, which in Mark is announced only to the women, at their visit to the tomb, by an angel (16:1-8). Thus he considerably reshapes the Markan scene: he tells of an appearance of Jesus to the women (28:9-10), of the bribing of the guards at the tomb (28:11-15), and, finally, of an appearance of the Risen One to the disciples in the striking concluding scene of his Gospel (28:16-20). This expansion of the Easter stories sheds light on the alterations and tendencies in the story of the passion: the glory of the Risen One shines forth in the passion itself. Jesus' passion and resurrection are inseparable for Matthew.

As to the origin of the additional material introduced by Matthew, we must make a distinction. It surely comes in part from oral tradition in Jewish-Christian circles (Judas's end, the wife of Pilate, the guards at the tomb) and in part from the evangelist's own intention in the way he shapes his Gospel (26:52-54; 27:24-25, 51b-53; 28:2-4). The appearances of the Risen One have a broader tradition in the primitive church. Matthew has taken over what is most important to him — strikingly, not Jesus' appearance to Peter (but cf. 16:17-19); on the other hand, the appearance to the disciples, to which Paul testifies in 1 Corinthians 15:5, and which Luke and John present each in his own way, is carefully thought through theologically in Matthew and is of the highest importance for the image of the church.

As for Matthew's special tendencies, we may cite the following. (1) Theologically, he continues to seek to show the fulfillment of Old Testament writings in the concrete events of the passion, even more strongly than in what he has already presented in his Gospel (Matt. 26:15, 54, 56; 27:9-10, 43). The last fulfillment citation is found in 27:9-10. (2) Christologically, he seeks to bring to light the traits of the suffering and risen Son of Man combined in the person of Jesus (cf. the predictions of the passion, 16:21; 17:22; 20:18-19), Jesus' status as Messiah and Son of God (26:63-64; 27:22, 40-43, 54), and the complete authority of the Risen One (28:18). (3) Ecclesiologically, the enactment of the new covenant through Jesus' blood (26:28) and the continued presence of the Risen One in his community (28:20) are important. The church spreads outward, becoming the church of all nations (28:19), but continues to need direction, Jesus' doctrine and instruction. The traitor Judas steps into the spotlight as a deterring example. The women play a salient role as intermediaries of the Easter message. The disciples, despite all earlier failure, are the recipients of full power and mission through the Risen One. (4) Historically, the line followed until now continues: the Jewish leaders are indicted, but the entire ancient people of God are included in the declaration of guilt and punishment (27:25). The perspective is that following the catastrophe of the year 70, one of waxing hostility between the church and the synagogue. It sets forth the positive thrusts of Matthean theology, namely, Matthew's understanding of the church in terms of the history of the time.

From the Conspiracy of the High Council
to the Hour in Gethsemane (26:1-46)

The Plot to Kill Jesus (26:1-5)

26:1 *When Jesus had finished saying all these things, he said to his disciples,* 2 *"You know that after two days the Passover is coming, and the Son of Man will be handed over to be crucified."*

3 *Then the chief priests and the elders of the people gathered in the palace of the high priest, who was called Caiaphas,* 4 *and they conspired to arrest Jesus by stealth and kill him.* 5 *But they said, "Not during the festival, or there may be a riot among the people."*

1-2 The customary concluding observation after Jesus' five great addresses (see Intro., pp. 2-3) emphasizes that Jesus has finished *all* of his discourses. It refers not simply to the long eschatological discourse of chapters 24–25 but to Jesus' speeches in the world and to the disciples altogether. Jesus professes before the High Council that he is the one sitting at God's right hand and proclaims the coming Son of Man (26:64), but otherwise he is mute (cf. 27:12-14). From now on, his words are replaced by fulfillment in suffering, as he has predicted. The entire history of the passion is recounted to a faith community that is already familiar with it.

3-5 In his report of the death sentence pronounced by the High Council, Matthew names, along with the high priests, not the scribes, as in Mark 14:1, but the elders of the people (cf. 21:23; 26:47) — doubtless because they are regarded as representatives of the Jewish people, who cannot escape responsibility for Jesus' condemnation (27:25). The leaders have long since sought to arrest Jesus, but fear the popular crowds (21:46). They now think of a ruse — an arrest in secret, and for this purpose Judas's offer comes just at the right time (vv. 14-16). The other consideration, "not during the festival" (or in the festival crowd) is justified, as popular uprisings often took place on Jewish feasts (Josephus, *Jewish War* 1.88).

The Anointing at Bethany (26:6-13)

6 *Now while Jesus was at Bethany in the house of Simon the leper,* 7 *a woman came to him with an alabaster jar of very costly ointment, and she poured it on his head as he sat at the table.* 8 *But when the disciples saw it, they were angry and said, "Why this waste?* 9 *For this ointment could have been sold for a large sum, and the money given to the poor."* 10 *But Jesus, aware of this, said to them, "Why do you trouble the woman? She has per-*

formed a good service for me. 11 *For you always have the poor with you, but you will not always have me.* 12 *By pouring this ointment on my body she has prepared me for burial.* 13 *Truly I tell you, wherever this good news is proclaimed in the whole world, what she has done will be told in remembrance of her."*

6-13 Matthew has somewhat smoothed out the story he has adopted from Mark, but he has left it unaltered at its core. It is specified as to place and situation through the citation of Bethany and the banquet at the house of "Simon the leper," although not precisely as to time (only in John 12:1: "six days before the Passover"). But the story belongs in the last days before Jesus' passion since Jesus' reference to his burial (v. 12) is inseparable from the narrative. Bethany lay on the eastern slope of the Mount of Olives, outside the confines of Jerusalem (unlike Bethphage, 21:1), and seems to have been Jesus' home in those days, where he also found relative protection from the assault of the Jewish authorities (cf. 21:17). The presentation is inserted into Jewish thinking: highly regarded as almsgiving to the poor was, it is transcended by personal deeds of love: the unnamed woman (named only in John 12:3, "Mary," the sister of Martha) prepares an especially highly regarded work of love, anointing for burial. But the point of the story is reached only with the observation that she does this work of love for Jesus. It is presupposed that Jesus knows of the death looming before him (cf. 26:29, 36-39). A particular trait of the Matthean presentation is that it is not "some" (of those present) who become excited and speak "to one another," but "the disciples" (v. 8), and that Jesus recognizes it and answers *them* (v. 10). In John 12:4-6, Judas then comes in for special blame and is suspected of theft. In Matthew, Jesus' instruction is addressed to the community. The community should recognize Jesus' glory: the woman has done him a good deed, in an unconscious and yet prophetic outlook on his death. The closing words, exactly the same as in Mark, have even greater weight for Matthew: the observation on the proclamation of the gospel throughout the world rings out frequently (Matt. 10:18; 12:21; 13:38; 24:14; 28:19). If in this way the deed of the nameless woman will be told "in remembrance of her," this is an acknowledgment of the women who carried that proclamation with them and reinforced it through their faith, like the women at the tomb (28:7-8, 9-10).

7 Singling out some of the details, for a woman to enter a banquet hall where men were feasting was scandalous for observers of the law (cf. Luke 7:36-50, a story with another accent but with striking points of contact with the anointing in Bethany). The history of the tradition is difficult to bring to light. In addition, Matthew refrains from naming the kind of oil or stating its worth ("very costly"). Such alabaster jars in various forms were numerous.

11 "You always have the poor with you" recalls Deuteronomy 15:11, which says that "there will never cease to be some in need on the earth." There the conclusion is drawn that one has an obligation to help one's needy, poor neighbor. Contempt for the poor is forbidden throughout Jesus' preaching; here the words stand only in the special perspective of the woman's deed of love. "You will not always have me" recalls Matthew 9:15b.

12 This verse looks ahead to Jesus' burial, which took place without an anointing. But the story is not based on that.

13 In the Old Testament, "in remembrance" often calls to present memory God's salvific deeds; but here, "in remembrance of her" means that the woman will be remembered, not in the sense that God will remember her, but in that the church will constantly recall her in the proclamation of the gospel and will tell of her, as the adoption of the pericope into the Gospels establishes. Historic deeds belong immortally to the message of Jesus Christ.

Judas Agrees to Betray Jesus (26:14-16)

14 *Then one of the twelve, who was called Judas Iscariot, went to the chief priests* 15 *and said, "What will you give me if I betray him to you?" They paid him thirty pieces of silver.* 16 *And from that moment he began to look for an opportunity to betray him.*

14-16 Judas Iscariot's visit to the chief priests presents a sharp contrast to the loving deed of the woman in Bethany. Here is a person who, though a member of the inside circle of the disciples (10:4), is willing to deliver Jesus to his enemies, and this for money. By contrast with Mark 14:10-11, where the chief priests promise to give him money, in Matthew Judas asks what he will be given. While in Mark the real motive remains concealed, that of greed is now unambiguously decisive. The real motive that has driven Judas to his shameful deed can no longer be historically established. The legend of Judas has richly proliferated from the beginning, and has led to various interpretations. With Matthew the story goes on from our pericope to Judas's second visit to the chief priests, which leads to his suicide (27:3-5). The two passages are connected by the bribe, which in verse 15, in an indirect quotation from Zechariah 11:12, is said to be thirty pieces of silver. In Zechariah this is seen as a small sum, which must have insulted God. In Matthew God's plan shows through: the Greek verb that is usually rendered "betray" can also mean "deliver up," with the connotation that the Son of Man will be given over into the hands of men (17:22; cf. 20:19; 26:2, 24, 45). According to Luke 22:3 and John 13:27, Satan entered into Judas. God's adversary seeks to thwart the divine plans; yet he is only constrained to fulfill them more profoundly.

From a historical viewpoint Jesus' last supper presents certain difficult problems, especially the question whether it was a Passover meal. According to the Johannine chronology, it could not have been since Jesus is placed before the Roman judge before the Jews have eaten the Passover meal (John 18:28), and his death obviously followed at the hour when the Passover lambs were slaughtered in the temple (cf. John 19:31, 36). The question of which chronology should be followed is disputed even today. According to our passage, in which Matthew follows Mark's presentation while considerably abbreviating it, the disciples are to prepare the paschal meal. At the supper itself, strikingly, there is no mention of eating the paschal lamb, although the actions portrayed — reclining at the table in the evening (Matt. 26:20), dipping into the dish (26:23), the institution of the Eucharist during the meal (26:26), and the hymn (26:30) — are consonant with the course of a Passover celebration. The preparation for the Passover meal is portrayed in a fashion similar to that of Jesus' entry into Jerusalem (21:1-3), with majestic mastery and foreknowledge on Jesus' part. The part of the story dealing with the man carrying water in Mark 14:13-14 is, to be sure, omitted by Matthew. Both preparation scenes (for the entry into Jerusalem and for the supper) place strong accents on Jesus as the "Lord" (21:3) or "Teacher" (26:18). In both instances Matthew stresses that the disciples did what Jesus had assigned them to do (21:6; 26:19).

To what extent this credible presentation records historical details is difficult to say. Many scholars now picture a situation in which Jesus held a Passover celebration with his disciples in the fashion of the Essenes, at a different time than the other Jews, after the slaughter of the Passover lambs in a special area of the temple precinct. They hold that the information concerning the water carrier and the supper chamber (on Mount Zion, where the Essenes had standing accommodations) refers to this. Other scholars assume that Jesus' last supper was not a Jewish Passover meal but took place with the Passover meal in mind (cf. Luke 22:15-16), and that the above references to the Feast of Passover are derived from the "Christian Passover" (the feast of Easter), a new, "reinstituted," Passover feast. Christ was "sacrificed as our paschal lamb" (1 Cor. 5:7). This idea seems more likely to me.

The Passover with the Disciples (26:17-25)

17 *On the first day of Unleavened Bread the disciples came to Jesus, saying, "Where do you want us to make the preparations for you to eat the Passover?"* 18 *He said, "Go into the city to a certain man, and say to him, 'The Teacher says, My time is near; I will keep the Passover at your house with my disciples.'"* 19 *So the disciples did as Jesus had directed them, and they prepared the Passover meal.*

20 *When it was evening, he took his place with the twelve;* 21 *and while*

they were eating, he said, "Truly I tell you, one of you will betray me." 22 And they became greatly distressed and began to say to him one after another, "Surely not I, Lord?" 23 He answered, "The one who has dipped his hand into the bowl with me will betray me. 24 The Son of Man goes as it is written of him, but woe to that one by whom the Son of Man is betrayed! It would have been better for that one not to have been born." 25 Judas, who betrayed him, said, "Surely not I, Rabbi?" He replied, "You have said so."

17   The Festival of Unleavened Bread (seven days) was at that time connected with the Feast of Passover and was celebrated along with it as a double festival. Here the day of Passover is meant. In the evening the household celebration for the family, or some other group of some twelve to fifteen persons, began. Jesus could have celebrated such a Passover *Habura* with his disciples.

18   Part of the preparation consisted of setting up a room and readying everything necessary for the Passover meal. Jesus, as the father of the household or the presiding person, is set in relief ("my"), and he alone is mentioned. For the Christian community, Jesus is now in the foreground owing to the institution of the Eucharist. The "large room" of Mark 14:15 is not mentioned by Matthew; however, he does quote Jesus, meaningfully, as saying, "My time is near," an allusion to the impending passion (cf. 26:45).

20-25   Although the reader has already been instructed in verses 14-16 concerning the "delivery" of Jesus by Judas, now the prediction of the betrayal is impressively portrayed during the meal. The christological tendency of this passage on the betrayal has already been powerfully developed in Mark 14:17-21. Jesus knows of the "betrayer"; but this "delivery" into the hands of human beings is ordained by God, foretold in Scripture, and established in the route to be followed by the "Son of Man": he "passes on" what stands written of him. The shocking thing is that a fellow diner commits this scornful deed, and the shock of the disciples present comes to expression in their troubled question, "Surely not I, Lord?" The shock of the primitive church echoes in Jesus' cry of woe over the one who will deliver up the Son of Man.

Matthew has taken over this meal scene from Mark almost verbatim, but he has added a meaningful appendix: Judas's question whether it is he, and Jesus' affirmative reply (v. 25). We recognize an enhanced interest in the person of the betrayer. Judas addresses Jesus, as at the arrest (Matt. 26:49), with "Rabbi," and Jesus' answer, "You have said so," catches the disloyal disciple with his, Jesus', knowledge of the deed. We learn nothing further: whether those present observed it (in John 13:25-26 Jesus reveals it to the "one whom he loved"), or whether Judas then left the room (John 13:30). Even in Matthew, and, later, more explicitly, in John, reflections on the part of the primitive church are betrayed. An exact reconstruction of the events at the meal is no longer possible, nor is it sought in the presentation. This is true as well for the later raised and variously answered question of the "Judas communion": the primitive church was not yet interested in this. According to Matthew, the "disciples" (Matt. 26:26), who are not distinguished from the earlier cited "twelve disciples," were present at the institution of the Eucharist. Again, Judas must have withdrawn before Jesus' arrest. However, there is no consideration of this. Each of these pericopes stands on its own in its power of testimony for the community.

It may seem curious that Matthew omits the allusion to Psalm 41:9 in Mark 14:18. But on the other hand he emphasizes, by Jesus' indication of the common dipping into the bowl (v. 23), "[This] one will betray me" (or "deliver me up"). The woe upon that person (cf. 18:7) does not necessarily predict eternal damnation, any more than does the continuation, that it were better for him had he never been born, an expression one often meets in Jewish literature (*Ethiopian Enoch;* rabbinic literature; cf. Billerbeck, *Kommentar zum Neuen Testament,* 1:989). But it is a terrible threat, which for Matthew is confirmed in Judas's awful end (27:5) and suggests what God's judgment might well be.

The Institution of the Lord's Supper (26:26-29)

> 26 *While they were eating, Jesus took a loaf of bread, and after blessing it he broke it, gave it to the disciples, and said, "Take, eat; this is my body."* 27 *Then he took a cup, and after giving thanks he gave it to them, saying, "Drink from it, all of you;* 28 *for this is my blood of the covenant, which is poured out for many for the forgiveness of sins.* 29 *I tell you, I will never again drink of this fruit of the vine until that day when I drink it new with you in my Father's kingdom."*

26-29 The high point of Jesus' last supper with his disciples is the institution of the Eucharist. Here the new Christian Passover feast, which probably comes into view in the preparation itself (vv. 17-19; see above), finds its basis and at the same time its reversed image. The historical basis, Jesus' unique behavior, which these verses report, is as little doubtful historically as its effect on the later celebration in the communities and the concrete formulation of Jesus' words. Since the primitive church practiced the "breaking of the bread" or "Lord's supper" from the beginning, and no other grounds for this characteristic celebration can be alleged but Jesus' actions at the last supper, the reports of its institution cannot be drawn from later customs of worship ("etiological worship legend"). But the diverging reports in Paul (1 Cor. 11:23-25), Luke 22:19-20, and Matthew and Mark compel one to accept a joint formation of reports through the vehicles of tradition, that is, the communities. Essentially, two shapes of the tradition are recognizable: the Pauline-Lukan and the Markan-Matthean. Which is older or "more original," or what single original form can perhaps be reconstructed from them, cannot be dealt with here. We shall follow Matthew's transmission and understanding, which is closely related to Mark's.

26 The new beginning (in parallel with v. 21), "while they were eating," shows that we are dealing with an independent unit of tradition. Not everything that happened during the meal is recounted, but only what was meaningful for the community. The special character of what Jesus now does is recognizable from the gestures that Matthew, like Mark, identifies: he takes bread, says a blessing over it, breaks the bread, and gives it to the disciples. In principle, the blessing of the bread by the father of the house signals the beginning of the meal; here Jesus takes a piece of bread during the meal. In "taking" the bread, Jesus shows that he intends to do something out of the ordinary. Jews never omitted praise of God, the creator and giver of everything good. We do not learn the wording of this blessing of the meal by Jesus; the later communities formulated it in their own particular ways, as we see, for example, in the "Teaching of the Twelve Apostles" (*Didache* 9:1-4). The breaking of the bread is explained first of all by the shape of loaves of bread in that time — flat and brittle — but here must be seen in relation to "giving" and the connecting word "took." Jesus breaks the bread and distributes it to the disciples. It is a gesture that establishes community (and not a symbolic act that indicates the "breaking" of Jesus' body). But Jesus does not give the sign that all should now eat by eating the bread himself, as was the case at the Jewish meal, but only hands the bread to the disciples. Matthew goes further than Mark in explaining this, in that he adds, "Take, eat." Jesus himself does not eat of the bread, which has a special meaning: "This is my body." In terms of the Greek verb form, the "breaking" of the bread and the speaking of these words are the primary statement; this explains the early designation of the Eucharist as the "breaking of the bread." The sense is clear: through this bread distributed by Jesus, which is his body, those at the table receive a share in him (cf. 1 Cor. 10:16): "body" stands for the entire person, as does the blood, if in a special way. The double expression "body" and "blood" includes the body, too, under the concept of devotion to death, as is expressly stated in the Pauline-Lukan tradition form: "my body, which is given for you." The words that are at the heart of the meaning here, "This is my body," are pronounced in view of Jesus' death, which will be for the disciples and "for many," as Jesus says over the cup, and reveals what he wished to do as the extreme consequence of his being-for-others. The bread that he hands the disciples to eat is sign and reality in one: the sign of the event of the cross and actual participation in fellowship with Jesus and with one another.

27-28 The handing of the cup to the disciples is narrated immediately after that of the bread (in Paul, in 1 Cor. 11:25, it occurs only "after supper"). Instead of "blessing," as over the bread, now Jesus "gave thanks." Both of these — "eulogy" and "eucharist" — originally meant the same thing — praise and thanks; the second expression, nevertheless, later gave its name to the entire Christian celebration (*Didache* 9:1). In Matthew the thanksgiving over the cup is formulated in a way parallel to the action with the bread: "Drink from this, all of you" corresponds to the imperative, "Eat." Mark says, "All of them drank from it." The Matthean form is an accommodation to the community's liturgy. Both formulations testify that it was a community cup. At the Jewish Passover meal, each participant probably had his own drinking cup. Jesus' farewell legacy emphasizes the community, which, in view of his imminent death, Jesus founds with his disciples at this meal.

The thanksgiving ("Eucharist") over the cup gives the sacred action still another special meaning: Jesus' blood is the "blood of the covenant, which is poured out for many." The expression "blood of the covenant" looks back on the enactment of the covenant on Sinai, at which Moses erected an altar, presented burnt offerings, and sprinkled the people with the blood of the victims, saying: "See the blood of the covenant that the LORD has made with you" (Exod. 24:4-8). The concept of the covenant is now transferred to Jesus' bloody death, in which God's covenants with his chosen people are fulfilled in a new and definitive way. This concept, that God, through the blood of the Son of God, forms a new chosen people (Acts 20:28) and in Jesus founds a "better covenant" (Heb. 7:22; 8:6; and frequently), which is likewise sealed in blood (cf. Heb. 9:22, 26; 10:14; 12:24), is developed in the primitive church, namely, in the Letter to the Hebrews. For the newness of this covenant, by which God gives a new heart and forgives all guilt, appeal was also made to the prophecy of Jeremiah 31:31-34 (Heb. 8:8-12; 10:16-17), as we recognize in the Pauline-Lukan formulation, "the new covenant in my blood." Both versions of the Eucharist of the cup agree in the concept of the covenant. The Old Covenant of Sinai is definitively fulfilled in Jesus' blood, and the eschatological promise of the "New Covenant" becomes a reality through Jesus' blood. At the same time, with the turn of phrase "for many" (Luke: "for you"), the concept of the vicarious sufferer and worker of expiation, the Suffering Servant of Isaiah 53, is brought in — the one who "shall make many righteous, and . . . bear their iniquities" (Isa. 53:11) and who "poured out himself to death" for them (Isa. 53:12). The "many" are not meant restrictively (in contrast with "all") but denote the totality of those for whom this One is a substitute. Originally Israel was meant, but now, in the primitive Christian understanding, it is the whole of humanity (cf. 2 Cor. 5:14-15, 19; Gal. 3:13-14; 1 Tim. 2:5-6). Matthew appends, ". . . for the forgiveness of sins," an addition that explains the essence of the New Covenant as the effect of Jesus' expiatory death (cf. Col. 1:14; Eph. 1:7). The words of the Eucharist of the cup are enriched with primitive Christian theology, but they are meant only to bring Jesus' intention all the more clearly to consciousness.

29 From the present event Jesus looks ahead to the meal of the community in the coming Realm of God. The words that imply Jesus' knowledge of his imminent death are important for his self-understanding. Although he proclaimed the coming Realm as in the near future (4:17; 10:7), he is not mistaken in his message since the majority of the people refused to show faith in him, the authorities persecuted him, and he saw the approach of his destiny of death. In this hour of farewell, Jesus assures the disciples that he — Matthew adds, "until that day" — will no more drink of the fruit of the vine (not a "vow of abstinence" but prophetic certitude), and yet that he will drink it "new" in the Realm of his Father. Matthew adds, "with you." "New" refers to the "otherness" of the world to come (cf. Matt. 22:29-30; 2 Peter 3:13; Rev. 21:1, 5): the present meal community finds its fulfillment in a new way. A meal, already understood in a deeper sense in the Eucharist, is once more lifted metaphorically to the status of an image of the fulfilled community in the Realm of God (see Matt. 8:11; cf. 22:2-10; 25:10, 21, 23). This eschatological outlook, in Luke 22:18 actually at the beginning of the farewell meal, is fittingly placed in connection with the institution of the Eucharist, and was important to the primitive church for its Lord's Supper (1 Cor. 11:26; cf. the "Our Lord, come" of 1 Cor. 16:22; Rev. 22:20).

Peter's Denial Foretold (26:30-35)

> 30 When they had sung the hymn, they went out to the Mount of Olives.
> 31 Then Jesus said to them, "You will all become deserters because of me this night; for it is written,
> 'I will strike the shepherd,
>   and the sheep of the flock will be scattered.'
> 32 But after I am raised up, I will go ahead of you to Galilee." 33 Peter said to him, "Though all become deserters because of you, I will never desert you." 34 Jesus said to him, "Truly I tell you, this very night, before the cock crows, you will deny me three times." 35 Peter said to him, "Even though I must die with you, I will not deny you." And so said all the disciples.

30-35 This brief pericope, with negligible deviations from Mark 14:26-31, can be divided into the setting of the situation (v. 30), the prediction of the scattering of the disciples (vv. 31-32), the prophecy of Peter's denial of Jesus (vv. 33-34), and Peter's protest to the contrary, like that of the other disciples (v. 35). But everything is bound together internally, and develops out of Jesus' words that the disciples will all take offense, that is, will be shaken in their faith and desert him (cf. 11:6; 13:57; 18:6; 24:10). Matthew complements this with "because of me this night." These are harsh words, and provoke Peter's contradiction. In his very grandiosity ("Though all become deserters, I will never") he falls. Even after Jesus' prediction of his denial, he contradicts him again. The dismaying words about the defection of the disciples in verses 31-32 are reinforced in two ways: through the quotation from Zechariah 13:7, concerning the shepherd who is struck down and whose sheep are scattered, and then through Jesus' prediction that he will go ahead of them to Galilee. The sense of the prediction is that there the disciples will gather once more. The view of the primitive church in the recollection of the disciples' behavior comes through. Verse 32 is an anticipation of the words of the angel in Mark 16:7 (parallel to Matt. 28:7), except that nothing is yet said about "seeing Jesus." The scattering of the disciples and Peter's denial are harsh facts, which the primitive church sought to grasp but which are to be understood in the Easter view — in God's salvific plan and in Jesus' foreknowledge. Jesus' predictions are fulfilled exactly: at the arrest the disciples flee (Matt. 26:56), and during Jesus' hearing before the High Council Peter denies him thrice, before the cock crows (26:69-75).

Jesus Prays in Gethsemane (26:36-46)

36 *Then Jesus went with them to a place called Gethsemane; and he said to his disciples, "Sit here while I go over there and pray."* 37 *He took with him Peter and the two sons of Zebedee, and began to be grieved and agitated.* 38 *Then he said to them, "I am deeply grieved, even to death; remain here, and stay awake with me."* 39 *And going a little farther, he threw himself on the ground and prayed, "My Father, if it is possible, let this cup pass from me; yet not what I want but what you want."* 40 *Then he came to the disciples and found them sleeping; and he said to Peter, "So, could you not stay awake with me one hour?* 41 *Stay awake and pray that you may not come into the time of trial; the spirit indeed is willing, but the flesh is weak."* 42 *Again he went away for the second time and prayed, "My Father, if this cannot pass unless I drink it, your will be done."* 43 *Again he came and found them sleeping, for their eyes were heavy.* 44 *So leaving them again, he went away and prayed for the third time, saying the same words.* 45 *Then he came to the disciples and said to them, "Are you still sleeping and taking your rest? See, the hour is at hand, and the Son of Man is betrayed into the hands of sinners.* 46 *Get up, let us be going. See, my betrayer is at hand."*

36-46 The hour of Jesus' death agony in Gethsemane, already portrayed by Mark in three moments of prayer, doubtless similarly shaped before Mark, is adopted by Matthew with certain stylistic deviations; only Luke 22:40-46 offers another version. In comparison with Mark, Matthew strikingly emphasizes Jesus' longing for community with the disciples even more strongly. Jesus goes "with them" to Gethsemane (v. 36); he calls on them to "sit here," and he rebukes them: "Could you not stay awake *with me* one hour?" (v. 40). This makes the admonition to the community even more forceful than it already is through the words taken over from Mark concerning watching and praying (v. 41).

Jesus' prayer to the Father is developed by Matthew in two stages: first, Jesus prays that the cup of death, if it be possible, may pass him by (v. 39); then he prays that, if it is not possible, the will of the Father may be done (v. 42, only in Matthew). This shows even more intensely Jesus' surrender and devotion to the will of God. In verse 39, in agreement with Mark, we have read: "Yet not what I want, but what you want"; in verse 42 the prayer reads: "Your will be done," an echo of the Matthean petition in the "Our Father" (6:10) that is worthy of note.

We also hear an echo of the "Our Father" in the encouragement to watch and pray: ". . . that you not come into the time of trial" (v. 41). There are trials that surpass the strength of a person (the "flesh"), even when the "spirit" is willing. Today we have found the antithesis between "flesh" and "spirit" (cf. as early as Isa. 31:3) illustrated in the Qumran texts: the weak "flesh," inclined to evil and sin (1QS 11:9; 1QH 4:29; etc.), takes the place of the person in a situation of struggle in this world; but from God comes "strength for the struggle against all wickedness of the flesh" (1QM 4:3). The spirit of the person, too, can waver (1QS 7:18, 23) unless God strengthens it (cf. 1QS 4:2-6). Watching and praying, a constant staying awake for prayer, is often enjoined on Christians (Luke 21:36; Eph. 6:18; Col. 4:2; 1 Pet. 4:7; cf. with 5:8).

Jesus' struggle in prayer in Gethsemane deeply concerned the primitive church (cf. also John 12:27-28; Heb. 5:7-8). The varying formation shows that Jesus' mortal agony, handed down historically, was intended to be presented with regard to the person of the "Son of Man" (cf. Matt. 26:45) in such a way that his persevering prayer to the Father should become instructive and exemplary for the community in its need and temptation (v. 41). Therefore the three separate moments of prayer cannot be taken literally, nor are Jesus' directly formulated words to be scrutinized: How can the distant or sleeping disciples hear? The disciples knew Jesus' pattern of prayer, with the special address of God as "My Father" (in Mark with the addition of the Aramaic "Abba," which Matthew omits), and they knew that Jesus had borne up under this hour of prayer in Gethsemane and went to meet the traitor with composure. The designation of place — an area of ground with the name (olive) "oil press" — is doubtless a reliable tradition.

From the Arrest of Jesus to His Delivery to Pilate (26:47–27:10)

The Betrayal and Arrest of Jesus (26:47-56)

> 47 *While he was still speaking, Judas, one of the twelve, arrived; with him was a large crowd with swords and clubs, from the chief priests and the elders of the people.* 48 *Now the betrayer had given them a sign, saying, "The one I will kiss is the man; arrest him."* 49 *At once he came up to Jesus and said, "Greetings, Rabbi!" and kissed him.* 50 *Jesus said to him, "Friend, do what you are here to do." Then they came and laid hands on Jesus and arrested him.* 51 *Suddenly, one of those with Jesus put his hand on his sword, drew it, and struck the slave of the high priest, cutting off his ear.* 52 *Then Jesus said to him, "Put your sword back into its place; for all who take the sword will perish by the sword.* 53 *Do you think that I cannot appeal to my Father, and he will at once send me more than twelve legions of angels?* 54 *But how then would the scriptures be fulfilled, which say it must happen in this way?"* 55 *At that hour Jesus said to the crowds, "Have you come out with swords and clubs to arrest me as though I were a bandit? Day after day I sat in the temple teaching, and you did not arrest me.* 56 *But all this has taken place, so that the scriptures of the prophets may be fulfilled." Then all the disciples deserted him and fled.*

47-56 The actual scene of the arrest, appended directly to the foregoing portrayal, is unchanged in Matthew vis-à-vis Mark, but is provided with accents, through *Jesus' words*, that show Matthew's attitude and intentions. In Mark Jesus speaks only to the crowd that has assembled in the place of his arrest; in Matthew Jesus responds to Judas as well (v. 50), and to the disciple who smites the servant of the high priest with a sword (v. 52). The lengthy insertion formulated by Matthew in verses 52-54 especially reveals the thoughts that Matthew seeks to transmit to his readers in this dark hour. Along with the admonition to nonviolence, Matthew emphasizes that the Scriptures must be fulfilled, and the Scriptures testify, "This must take place" (24:6). Throughout, the Matthean picture presents Jesus in his majesty and at the same time in his obedience to God, in his pain at human beings' conduct and at the same time in his knowledge of the "must" of salvation history. Jesus, who knowingly goes his way to his passion, presents a contrast with the disciples, who, in a spirit of desperation — the one who wields the sword sheds light on their mentality — show their lack of understanding and in the end all flee. The episode of the young man (Mark 14:51-52) is omitted by Matthew, doubtless because the evangelist does not wish to qualify his position that all of the disciples abandoned Jesus.

The pericope is divided as follows: (1) the arrival of the troop to arrest Jesus, the encounter with Judas, and Jesus' being taken into custody (vv. 47-50); (2) the drawing of the sword by one of those accompanying Jesus, and Jesus' reaction (vv. 51-54); and (3) Jesus' words to the crowd and the flight of the disciples (vv. 55-56). The description of the situation is not in a literal genre but conceived by the evangelist: Jesus is already arrested in verse 50, and then he speaks to various addressees, for which those arresting him would scarcely have allowed time.

47-50   The "large crowd" may mean for Matthew those accompanying the arresting troop, which is armed with swords and clubs (the clubs of the temple police were feared instruments) and is sent by the "chief priests and the elders of the people" (cf. 26:3). Attention is immediately focused on the betrayer. With the prearranged sign, a kiss of friendship, he greets the "Rabbi" (cf. 26:25). Jesus addresses him painfully as "friend," which may be intended to recall the community at the supper. The remainder of the sentence, rather disputed, is probably rendered correctly in the New Revised Standard Version. At once Jesus is taken into custody.

51-54   The one who draws the sword is a bystander in Mark, one of Jesus' companions in Matthew, and in John, Peter, where the one who is struck is named Malchus, the high priest's slave. For Matthew the interlude is an opportunity to bring to expression the renunciation of resistance and violence, for which he cites Jesus' words. "Do you think?" is typical Matthean phraseology (cf. 17:25; 18:12; 21:28; 22:17, 42; 26:66), just as is "My Father." Jesus' reprimand of the swordsman reinforces the instruction of the Sermon on the Mount concerning the renunciation of resistance (see 5:39-41). Jesus grounds his rebuke with words of a wisdom ring (cf. Sir. 3:26-28), but having a deeper foundation in the concept of God (cf. Gen. 9:5-6). In the *Targum to Isaiah* 50:11, we read: "All of you who kindle a fire, who grasp a sword, go, fall into the fire that you have kindled, and upon the sword that you have grasped. From my Memra (from God) you have this: You will return to your annihilation." Thus, primitive Christianity leaves vengeance to God (Rom. 12:19), and the persecuted submit to the decree of God if they must be executed by the sword (Rev. 13:10). Jesus' example at his arrest, which Matthew brings out even more powerfully with the statement concerning the twelve legions of angels, became a guideline and consolation to the communities in situations of persecution. But moral resistance to injustice was not forgotten. The reference to the fulfillment of the Scriptures is not to be taken here as referring to specific passages in Scripture but adopts the "must" of the divine decree and applies it to the passion of Jesus (16:21) and the suffering of the eschatological moment (see 24:6). It is the basic stance of primitive Christianity (cf. Luke 17:25; 22:37; 24:26, 44; 1 Cor. 15:3).

55-56   Jesus' teaching activity in the temple is mentioned by Matthew only in 21:23, but for the last days in Jerusalem is presupposed, up to 24:1 (cf. 22:16, 33). The rebuke to the crowd consists in this, that Jesus had daily sat among them as a teacher and they had not had him arrested, but in this hour of darkness they came out against him as against a robber. The night "hour," with which the passion of the Son of Man has begun, was understood by the primitive church in a deeper, symbolic sense (cf. 26:45; Luke 22:53; John 13:1, 30; 17:1). In this dark hour, too, all the disciples fled.

Jesus before the High Priest (26:57-68)

57 *Those who had arrested Jesus took him to Caiaphas the high priest, in whose house the scribes and the elders had gathered.* 58 *But Peter was following him at a distance, as far as the courtyard of the high priest; and going inside, he sat with the guards in order to see how this would end.* 59 *Now the chief priests and the whole council were looking for false testimony against Jesus so that they might put him to death,* 60 *but they found none, though many false witnesses came forward. At last two came forward* 61 *and said, "This fellow said, 'I am able to destroy the temple of God and to build it in three days.'"* 62 *The high priest stood up and said, "Have you no answer? What is it that they testify against you?"* 63 *But Jesus was silent. Then the high priest said to him, "I put you under oath before the living God, tell us if you are the Messiah, the Son of God."* 64 *Jesus said to him, "You have said so. But I tell you,*

> *From now on you will see the Son of Man*
> *seated at the right hand of Power*
> *and coming on the clouds of heaven."*

65 *Then the high priest tore his clothes and said, "He has blasphemed! Why do we still need witnesses? You have now heard his blasphemy.* 66 *What is your verdict?" They answered, "He deserves death."* 67 *Then they spat in his face and struck him; and some slapped him,* 68 *saying, "Prophesy to us, you Messiah! Who is it that struck you?"*

57-68 From a historical viewpoint, the judicial proceeding against Jesus, held at night before the High Council, raises a number of questions. Was it a regular process before the highest Jewish court, which concluded with the death sentence? Could such a process concerning a capital transgression be held at night, and, to boot, in a single sitting, a procedure that according to the (later) law of the Mishnah was not permitted (cf. *Sanhedrin* 4:1h)? How are we to picture the precise course of the procedure: the terms of the indictment, the interrogation of witnesses by the high priest? How are we to construe the adjuration of the high priest (v. 63)? Can Jesus' response be regarded as a literal record of his words? And so on. It is clear that our presentation, in essence existing even before Mark, stems from Christian circles and does not fail to betray their interest in Jesus' person and conduct before the Jewish court. But, by contrast with widespread earlier skepticism whether any historical data can be extracted from it at all, more and more studies are appearing that ascribe it considerable, indeed high historical credibility. True, many problems remain unsolved, including those springing from a comparison with Luke and John. Since we cannot broach these questions here, we will follow the Markan/Matthean report, try to work through the faith composition to the historical basis, but also attempt to recognize the tendencies prevailing in the primitive church that resulted in just this composition. A sure assessment, however, is scarcely possible.

Matthew follows Mark 14:53-65 except for rather minor deviations. The following alterations are worthy of note. (1) More precisely, verse 59 reads that the high priests and the entire High Council sought *false* testimony against Jesus. (2) The statement concerning the temple is weakened in verse 61: "I *am able* to destroy the temple of God. . ."; and the additions in Mark 14:58, "this temple that is made with hands" and "another, not made with hands," are omitted. (3) In verses 62-63, the high priest does not go "among" those assembled, as in Mark, but puts Jesus "under oath before the living God." (4) In Jesus' profession in verse 64, "from now on" is inserted. (5) The mocking of Jesus in verse 67 is portrayed somewhat differently. Throughout, we observe a tendency to sharpen the contrasts and to bring out Jesus' testimonial concerning himself.

The pericope can be divided into the introduction (vv. 57-58), with the mention of Peter in order to connect and contrast the subsequent story of the denial with the process against Jesus; the interrogation of witnesses (vv. 59-62); the solemn question of the high priest and Jesus' response (vv. 63-64); the indictment for blasphemy and the verdict that Jesus is guilty of a capital offense (vv. 65-66); and the mocking scene (vv. 67-68).

57-58 The residence of the high priest is traditionally shown in the upper city (today Zion). The High Council, which functioned as the highest judicial body, consisted of the high priest and seventy-one other members. Nowhere in Jewish literature, however, do we find that it met in the house of the high priest. Josephus (*Jewish War* 5.142-44) believes that its meeting hall was at the southern side of the first or oldest wall. Today not a few scholars assume that a distinction is to be made between a hearing before Caiaphas (or Annas and Caiaphas; see, e.g., John 18:13, 24) and a session held not before morning before the entire court (cf. Luke 22:66). Mark would therefore have skipped over this, as we may also conjecture from his unclear indication of the sentence of the Sanhedrin *in the morning* (Mark 15:1 par. Matt. 27:1). The supposition that only a first hearing before the high priest was held at his residence, and this by night, and then, in the morning, the session of the High Council in the court building followed, is highly probable. Matthew has taken over this hurried presentation of the hearing in the palace of Caiaphas and the judicial process with its climax, Jesus' interrogation by the high priest. However, he seems to have weakened it: he omits Mark's "all" (Mark 14:53). Peter's denial occurred precisely in the court of the palace of the high priest and, in order to synchronize the procedure against Jesus with it, and especially to contrast Jesus' self-profession with Peter's denial, the later judicial procedure could be moved forward.

59-62 In a Jewish process — unlike a Roman one, with the interrogation of the defendant (cf. 27:11-14) — the most important thing was the questioning of witnesses, and this was done very conscientiously (cf. the story of Susanna in chap. 13 of the Greek version of Daniel). Thus it was with the Jewish process against Jesus. Since the witnesses did not agree, however, it led to no indictment and sentence. That the members of the Council sought "false testimony" against Jesus is to be ascribed to Matthew's polemics. Indeed, the statements of "many false witnesses" did not "agree," as Mark says (Mark 14:56). We learn nothing more precise — only one accusation, brought, according to Matthew 26:60, by two witnesses (the required number according to Deut. 17:6; 19:15), is reported: words of Jesus concerning the temple that they claimed to have heard. An assault on the temple, the prediction of its destruction, would certainly have been grounds for sentencing for the high priest's circle, and they could have counted on the support of the Romans. Here the story of Jesus the son of Ananias is instructive. A prophet of woe, from A.D. 62 on he called out his warnings over Jerusalem and the temple to deaf ears (Josephus, *Jewish War* 6.300-309). But neither did the testimony of these witnesses agree, as Mark indicates and Matthew tacitly assumes. Indeed, this is no wonder since even the Christians who transmitted these words concerning the temple disagreed with one another in handing them down. In addition to being found in the present passage, these words come up among the taunts at the foot of the cross (Mark 15:29 par. Matt. 27:40), at the cleansing of the temple in John 2:19, and at the indictment of Stephen in Acts 6:14 — an indication that they are a solid part of the tradition. But they cannot be fixed either chronologically or in their wording. At most we might think of a connection with the cleansing of the temple. The prophecy of the destruction of the temple is intimated in Matthew 23:38 as well, and is pronounced openly before the disciples in 24:2; but nothing is said there about a rebuilding in three days. In the primitive church the statement doubtless circulated as a riddle *(māshāl)* and was variously interpreted. Matthew forgoes Mark's interpretative additions but weakens Jesus' alleged expression to "I *am able* to destroy . . ." in order to deprive the accusation of any force. Matthew's interest is in Jesus' power, as in 26:53. The question of the high priest, who is the judge, is an attempt to bring Jesus to break his silence. But Jesus gives him no answer —

a prudent move, which places the high priest in an awkward situation. Many interpreters think that it is an allusion to Isaiah 53:7.

Jesus' silence leads the high priest to an unusual step but not an implausible one, given the sensation that Jesus has caused. He poses to him the question whether he is the Messiah — in Matthew with a solemn adjuration that Jesus cannot sidestep. It is the "hour of truth" (A. Strobel, *Die Stunde der Wahrheit*). The only question is whether the addition "Son of God" (in Mark, "Son of the Blessed One") is probable on the lips of the high priest, or whether it represents a Christian interpretation. "Son of God," it is true, is unusual with the Jews as a designation of the Messiah, but it is not impossible (cf. 2 Sam. 7:14; Ps. 2:7; 4QFlor 1:11-12; 4Q 243). If the high priest could elicit from Jesus a profession that he was the awaited Messiah, he presumably would ask further how he could prove this. When he did not succeed in doing so, as the high priest obviously presumed he could not, he could be indicted as an "impostor" and sentenced. The accusation that Jesus was an "impostor" crops up repeatedly on Jewish lips, as in Matthew 27:63-64 (this "impostor"), in John 7:12 (cf. 7:47), and in later anti-Christian polemics (cf. Justin, *Dialogues* 69:7; 10:1; also in the Talmud). But Jesus' answer spares the high priest further investigation. Jesus confesses himself as the Messiah: the Matthean "You have said so" scarcely means anything different from the Markan "I am" (cf. Matt. 26:25), perhaps with a certain reserve (cf. 27:11). Jesus adds a declaration that clarifies his claim and is threatening for the Sanhedin that sits over him as a court: he designates himself as the "Son of Man," whom his judges (plural) will see "seated on the right hand of Power [= God] and coming on the clouds of heaven." In contradistinction to the Jewish understanding of the Messiah — the earthly ruler of David's line — Jesus must emphasize his salvific claim in all its specificity. But did Jesus say precisely these words? In the form at hand they are a combination of two passages in Scripture that play an important role in primitive Christian Christology: Psalm 110:1 (see Matt. 22:44) and Daniel 7:13 (see Matt. 24:30). Accordingly, we must regard these words as of primitive Christian composition. But it is to be assumed that Jesus brought to expression his impending justification by God, his exaltation to the presence of God (cf. Luke 22:69), and probably also the office of judge assigned to him (as "Son of Man"), and all of this as now hanging threateningly, which Matthew (like Luke) stresses with his "from now on." In view of his expected death sentence, Jesus places his judges under the judgment of God, a judgment soon to descend upon them and entrusted to himself (cf. Matt. 23:39). In this dramatic confrontation the high priest has all that he could wish: he believes that Jesus is not the Messiah but a seducer of the people, and now Jesus has laid explicit claim to his Messiahship. Now the high priest can act in all conviction; but his judgment as to Jesus' claim stands diametrically opposed to that of the early church, and the latter is just as firm as his own. This opposition governs the conflict between church and synagogue to our very day.

65-66 With Jesus' self-profession, the situation of the trial has changed. The high priest finds blasphemy in Jesus' words. The Messiah's sitting at the right hand of God and exercising judicial judgment in the name of God was, it is true, not an implausible concept for Judaism (cf. *Ethiopian Enoch* 46:1-6; 48:2; 49:2; 62:2-5; 69:27), but it could occur only by divine legitimation, which Jesus, in the high priest's understanding, does not possess. Thus this claim must be regarded as an assault on God's authority and interference with exclusive divine rights. Legally that was blasphemy, although later the requirements for such an assessment were made more strict. As a sign of it the high priest tears his clothes, as was prescribed, and calls those present to witness that the blasphemy has been committed, as they themselves have just heard. The verdict is unanimous: Jesus has committed a capital offense. The penalty for blasphemy was stoning to death; but it is not clear whether a formal verdict had been handed down at this point, so that this penalty would have to be paid. It is enough to observe that Jesus has been pronounced guilty of a capital offense by the High Council.

67-68 The mockery of Jesus is cruel. In Luke it takes place at the hands of Jesus' guards even before the convening of the High Council (Luke 22:63-65). In Mark the culprits are "some," necessarily meaning, in the sequence of the passage, members of the High Council. The derision presupposes the popular opinion that Jesus is a prophet (Mark 6:15; 8:28 par. Matt. 14:5; 21:11, 46); Matthew, however, has Jesus addressed additionally as "Messiah," obviously with verses 63-64 of this chapter in mind. For Matthew it is an unheard-of scene of derision at the hands of members of the High Council. Historically, however, this is implausible. Judaism's administration of justice was carefully ordered, and a like *faux pas* on the part of the supreme judge is scarcely imaginable. The scene will have been played out when Jesus is in the custody of his guards, perhaps even before the session of the High Council, as Luke presents it.

Peter's Denial of Jesus (26:69-75)

> 69 Now Peter was sitting outside in the courtyard. A servant-girl came to him and said, "You also were with Jesus the Galilean." 70 But he denied it before all of them, saying, "I do not know what you are talking about." 71 When he went out to the porch, another servant-girl saw him, and she said to the bystanders, "This man was with Jesus of Nazareth." 72 Again he denied it with an oath, "I do not know the man." 73 After a little while the bystanders came up and said to Peter, "Certainly you are also one of them, for your accent betrays you." 74 Then he began to curse, and he swore an oath, "I do not

know the man!" At that moment the cock crowed. 75 Then Peter remembered
what Jesus had said: "Before the cock crows, you will deny me three times."
And he went out and wept bitterly.

69-75 Peter's denial, whose historicity it would be unjustified to seek to contest, is recounted by all the evangelists, in somewhat different ways, with the strongest deviations in John 18:15-18, 25-27. The story is not fabricated since the primitive church could hardly have had any positive interest in it. In all four accounts the denial is a triple one, as Jesus has said it would be (Matt. 26:34). The narrative deviations with respect to the persons who accuse Peter, the places of the accusations, the words spoken, whether the denial is complete before the first cock's crow or the second, and so on, belong to the conventional freedom of narrative at the time and place of our Gospels.

Matthew follows Mark 14:66-72 rather exactly, but introduces a dramatic ascent to a climax. First Peter denies to all that he has been Jesus' follower (Matt. 26:70), then he does so with an oath (v. 72), and finally his denial is accompanied by cursing and an oath (v. 74). Here Matthew is thinking of Jesus' prohibition against swearing (5:33-37). As deep as is his fall — unfaithful to Jesus, denial of fellowship with him, a false statement sworn to with an oath — so great is his repentance: at the cock's crow, recalling Jesus' words, he recognizes his sin, goes out, and "weeps bitterly," as verse 75 reads, in agreement with Luke 22:62.

Matthew sets the scene as follows. Peter enters the courtyard of the high priest and approaches the fire because of the cold, and there a maid accuses him. Then he returns to the darker entrance hall, and another maid (in Mark the same one) recognizes him. As he lies once more, those standing about approach him and throw out to him his Galilean dialect. In this threatening situation Peter is even more emphatic than before: he engages in cursing and swearing. Only with the cock's crow does he leave the building. Considering the high authority that Peter held for Matthew and his community (cf. Intro., p. 8), this revelation of his human weakness (cf., however, as early as 14:30-31) is astounding. Peter is not mentioned again in Matthew's Gospel. What we have is an urgent warning to the community not to trust in one's own strength, to be mindful of the danger of temptation (26:41), but also to seek forgiveness through repentance and conversion, since forgiveness is guaranteed through Jesus' blood (26:28).

Jesus Brought before Pilate (27:1-2)

27:1 When morning came, all the chief priests and the elders of the people
conferred together against Jesus in order to bring about his death. 2 They
bound him, led him away, and handed him over to Pilate the governor.

27:1-2 Jesus' handing over to Pilate, the Roman procurator, leads to the Roman proceeding against Jesus. The "jurisdiction of blood," the execution of death sentences, was reserved to the Roman governor (cf. John 18:31), although this is often disputed. In the morning session, at which the Jewish judicial procedure against Jesus probably took place (cf. 26:57-58), "all" the members of the Council — as we now read, otherwise than in 26:57 — passed the resolution to "hand over" (here a judicial expression) Jesus to Pilate. It is not likely that they sought only the execution of a sentence handed down by themselves; rather, they sought a Roman trial with the indictment of rebellion, whose penalty was necessarily crucifixion, as is established in 27:11-14, 26, and 37.

The Suicide of Judas (27:3-10)

3 *When Judas, his betrayer, saw that Jesus was condemned, he repented and brought back the thirty pieces of silver to the chief priests and the elders.* 4 *He said, "I have sinned by betraying innocent blood." But they said, "What is that to us? See to it yourself."* 5 *Throwing down the pieces of silver in the temple, he departed; and he went and hanged himself.* 6 *But the chief priests, taking the pieces of silver, said, "It is not lawful to put them into the treasury, since they are blood money."* 7 *After conferring together, they used them to buy the potter's field as a place to bury foreigners.* 8 *For this reason that field has been called the Field of Blood to this day.* 9 *Then was fulfilled what had been spoken through the prophet Jeremiah, "And they took the thirty pieces of silver, the price of the one on whom a price had been set, on whom some of the people of Israel had set a price,* 10 *and they gave them for the potter's field, as the Lord commanded me."*

3-10 This presentation of Judas's end and the reaction of the high priests constitutes a first more extended insertion by Matthew into the Markan history of the passion. Here Matthew will have relied on oral narratives in Jewish-Christian circles. The fulfillment quotation (vv. 9-10), connected with the payment for the betrayal, may be Matthew's own insertion, or Matthew may have taken it from Christian scribes. In Acts 1:18-20 Judas's death and the purchase of the "Field of Blood" (by Judas himself!) are presented considerably differently; in addition, another reference to Scripture is added (Ps. 69:25). Accordingly, our pericope, which has nothing directly to do with Jesus' passion, does not have the same "historical reliability" as does the rest of the passion story. The betrayer's unhappy death recalls other stories of the terrible end of villainous persons (Antiochus IV Epiphanes, according to 2 Macc. 9:5-12; Herod the Great in Josephus, *Antiquities* 17.169; Herod Agrippa in Acts 12:21-23); this is also true for the short observation in Matthew 27:5. The "Field of Blood" is a locality in Jerusalem probably to be found in an area where the three valleys of the Kidron, the Tyropoeon, and the Hinnom converged and where potters lived. The place is not "thought up" on the basis of the remarkable combination of citations in verses 9 and 10; rather, the latter presupposes the place with its designation, "Potter's Field." How it came to be known as the "Field of Blood" is unsure; but "to this day" suggests a later time; the Aramaic account in Acts 1:19, however, suggests Jews who knew the names of places. Throughout, popular transmissions, the fulfillment of Old Testament prophecies, and details of Jerusalem topography are bound together in a narrative of its own kind.

When Matthew cites Judas' "repentance" at this point, soon after Peter's denial of Jesus (Matt. 26:69-75), Jesus' two disciples are being presented in their contrasting reactions to their denials: the one "weeps bitterly," the other hangs himself in despair. The figure of Judas is intended to shock and deter; but the most important thing is his confession, "I have sinned by betraying innocent blood." Jesus is shown to be innocent through Judas's end; Jesus' blood comes upon those who have spilled it (cf. 23:35; 27:24-25).

The fulfillment quotation (the last one in Matthew's Gospel) is a characteristic combination of Zechariah 11:13, "I took the thirty shekels of silver and threw them into the treasury of the house of the LORD," and allusions to potters or pottery in Jeremiah 18:2-3; 19:11, or the purchase of a plot of ground in Jeremiah 32:6-15. The citation from Zechariah 11:13 is pivotal: the "treasurer" named there, who smelts the pieces of silver, has suggested the "potter," the place of judgment (Jer. 19:4, 6, 11), and the purchase of the field. The entire Scripture quotation is ascribed (summarily?) to Jeremiah. Probably the Christian interpreter has sought places in Scripture that would ground the tradition of the "Potter's Field," which was later named "Field of Blood" and which lay along the valley of the Hinnom, a difficult "Scripture fulfillment" (cf., similarly, Matt. 2:23), which is supposed to reveal scriptural grounds for happenings after the fact. It is at most a piece of evidence for the zeal of primitive Christian "scribes" in searching for instances of fulfillment of Scripture.

The Hearing before Pilate, the Mocking of Jesus, and His Crucifixion, Death, and Burial (27:11-66)

The procedure against Jesus initiated by the chief priests and elders before the Roman governor (not merely a petition for endorsement of their sentence) is presented without a preponderance of juridical elements, and accordingly cannot be traced in its precise development. The greatest interest is in Pilate's attempt to set Jesus free on the grounds of "Passover amnesty." Thus the contrast between the rebel Barabbas and Jesus, "who is called the Messiah," is meant to show Christian readers Jesus' innocence and majesty but also the chief priests' incitement of the people, which finally leads to Jesus' sentencing and execution as a political rebel. Matthew also introduces the intervention of Pilate's wife on Jesus' behalf (27:19), to which Pilate's declaration of Jesus' innocence corresponds (27:24). The anti-Jewish tendency of Matthew's writing is considerably reinforced by the scene in verses 24-25. The Roman procurator, whose disposition appears weakly and compliant, as in Mark, is not relieved of his responsibility; but the greater blame for the unjust verdict is shifted to the Jews with their pressure on Pilate. For a historical assessment, the question of the "Passover amnesty" and the attitude of the Roman judge is important; but the Christian presentation affords scant understanding of the person and attitude of Pilate. The passage is divided into the following scenes: (1) the indictment and hearing (vv. 11-14); (2) the attempt to release Jesus on grounds of the Passover amnesty (vv. 21, 26; cf. v. 15); (3) Barabbas and Jesus (vv. 15-23); and (4) the sentencing of Jesus (vv. 24-26).

Pilate Questions Jesus (27:11-14)

> 11 *Now Jesus stood before the governor; and the governor asked him, "Are you the King of the Jews?" Jesus said, "You say so."* 12 *But when he was accused by the chief priests and elders, he did not answer.* 13 *Then Pilate said to him, "Do you not hear how many accusations they make against you?"* 14 *But he gave him no answer, not even to a single charge, so that the governor was greatly amazed.*

11-14 After being handed over to Pilate (27:2), Jesus now "stands" before the Roman judge. According to Roman judicial procedure, a formal (written) indictment was necessary. Here that indictment is based on Pilate's question whether Jesus is "King of the Jews." According to Roman procedure, the initial duty of the judge was primarily to examine, through an interchange with the defendant, whether or not the latter was a political rebel, who, on grounds of *crimen maiestatis,* that is, incitement to uprising against the Roman state, was to be sentenced to death. For non-Romans, this sentence, especially in the provinces, was ordinarily carried out by crucifixion. Thus the procedure against Jesus by his Jewish accusers is shifted to the political level — with a certain consistency, to be sure, since the High Council regarded Jesus as "an impostor," who endangered the Jewish theocratic body politic, recognized as such by the Romans. Under the messianic designation "King of the Jews," from the viewpoint of a Roman Pilate could scarcely visualize anyone but a political rebel. Nevertheless, the chief priests must have been conscious of the emptiness of such an accusation. Jesus' response, "You say so," which in this case Mark also gives (Mark 15:2; cf. "I am," Mark 14:62), may connote a certain distancing here. Speaking for himself, Jesus will not admit full agreement with the accusation because of the political overtones (cf. John 18:33-38). When Jesus then refuses to answer the many accusations (listed in Luke 23:2), he is understood as being extremely insolent in the face of Roman authority. Matthew underscores this silence (vv. 12, 14), and may be thinking of the silence of the suffering righteous person (Pss. 38:13-15; 39:9-10) or of the atoning Servant of God (Isa. 53:7).

Barabbas or Jesus (27:15-23)

> 15 Now at the festival the governor was accustomed to release a prisoner for the crowd, anyone whom they wanted. 16 At that time they had a notorious prisoner, called Jesus Barabbas. 17 So after they had gathered, Pilate said to them, "Whom do you want me to release for you, Jesus Barabbas or Jesus who is called the Messiah?" 18 For he realized that it was out of jealousy that they had handed him over. 19 While he was sitting on the judgment seat, his wife sent word to him, "Have nothing to do with that innocent man, for today I have suffered a great deal because of a dream about him." 20 Now the chief priests and the elders persuaded the crowds to ask for Barabbas and to have Jesus killed. 21 The governor again said to them, "Which of the two do you want me to release for you?" And they said, "Barabbas." 22 Pilate said to them, "Then what should I do with Jesus who is called the Messiah?" All of them said, "Let him be crucified!" 23 Then he asked, "Why, what evil has he done?" But they shouted all the more, "Let him be crucified!"

15-18 In one group of manuscripts, Barabbas's name is given as "Jesus Barabbas": "called Jesus Barabbas" (v. 16); "'Whom do you want me to release for you, Jesus Barabbas or Jesus called the Messiah?'" (v. 17). Although the majority of manuscripts do not set forth this reading, it is taken into the text in verse 16, in brackets, by Nestle and Aland (*Novum Testamentum Graece*, ad loc.), since internal probability argues for Barabbas's having the name of Jesus as well, and for its having been dropped out of reverence for Jesus the Messiah.

The "notorious" Barabbas is designated in Mark 15:7 as a member of a group of insurgents who had committed a murder in the course of an uprising. He was probably their leader; the two men crucified with Jesus (Matt. 27:38) may have been members of the same group: the Greek word for "robber" is also used by Flavius Josephus to denote such a freedom fighter. Matthew does without a more exact characterization of Barabbas: he is more interested in the contraposition of this (Jesus) Barabbas with Jesus the Messiah. For Christians, it was a profound insult that this worker of violence was preferred to their peace-loving Messiah (cf. 12:18-21; 20:30-31; 21:1-10). The amnesty granted by Pilate to a prisoner — according to legal custom, inasmuch as he released him at Passover time — was long contested as a historical fact, but was shown to be possible in the writings of Josephus (*Antiquities* 20.208-9, 215) and in a place in the Mishnah (*Pesaḥim* 8:6a). The point was to obtain the release of imprisoned Jews in order that they might be able to take part in the Passover meal. Festival amnesties were also customary elsewhere in the ancient world, and the Romans offered amnesty procedures at the time of Augustus *(Pax Romana)*. Pilate doubtless hoped that Jesus was more popular than Barabbas. He holds Jesus' indictment to be unfounded: it is "out of jealousy," as we read in verse 18. Perhaps it is rather "jealousy" in the original sense that is meant, a zeal for their religious convictions, a zeal for the law as they understood it; or "jealousy" may express their discontent with Jesus' great popularity.

19 Pilate's wife's reference to a nightmare that she has had corresponds to the general belief in antiquity, including Judaism (cf., e.g., Nebuchadnezzar's dream in Daniel 4), in the preternatural meaning of dreams. Matthew has adopted the account of her intervention from popular material. For him the episode reinforces the evidence for the innocence of Jesus, who is designated as the "righteous" one, a Matthean expression (see Matt. 1:19; 13:17, 43; and frequently), although it also occurs in Luke 2:25; 23:47, 50.

20-23 Pilate's question to the people may have rested on a Roman legal practice of granting freedom, under certain circumstances, to a prisoner upon the petition of the people. Such a case is attested for Egypt on a papyrus from A.D. 85. Thus it may well be that Pilate's invitation to allow the people to decide by acclamation, or even at an assembly of the whole people called by the governor (cf. Luke 23:13), may have preceded the action of the chief priests and elders. The latter, it is true, cast their vote among the people for Barabbas, and since it is the question of a crowd in Jerusalem, which, even aside from the above, had less attachment to the "Galilean," the vote for Barabbas becomes understandable. The Jerusalemites surely looked more to the leading persons of the city. The extent to which the cries directed against Jesus, "Let him be crucified!" correctly record the situation is difficult to say. However, the chief priests may have convinced the throng that Jesus was a false prophet, who must be blotted out from Israel. Pilate sees that he is compelled by the people's vote to go on with Jesus' trial. His attempt to get rid of the inconvenient prisoner is shattered.

Pilate Hands Jesus Over to Be Crucified (27:24-26)

24 *So when Pilate saw that he could do nothing, but rather that a riot was beginning, he took some water and washed his hands before the crowd, say-*

ing, "I am innocent of this man's blood; see to it yourselves." 25 Then the people as a whole answered, "His blood be on us and on our children!" 26 So he released Barabbas for them; and after flogging Jesus, he handed him over to be crucified.

24-26 The scene of the pronouncement of sentence, which in Mark 15:15 is presupposed, in Matthew is framed graphically and dramatically. Pilate allows himself to be pressured by the uproar of the people, theatrically washes his hands — which we know to be a symbolic gesture among Greeks and Jews — and shifts the guilt to the assembled crowd. The character and conduct of the Roman procurator are viewed differently by different scholars. Along with the harsh conduct of the Roman, who saw no easy task facing him in Judea, greed and political maneuvering are attested. Upon entering his office, he had had imperial coins sent to Jerusalem, the Jews violently demonstrated against this, and he had given in (Josephus, *Jewish War* 2.169-74). At a similar tumult, when Pilate had sought to withdraw money from the temple treasury for the construction of an aqueduct, he acted with cunning and violence (Josephus, *Jewish War* 2.175-77). At Jesus' sentencing he probably acted out of political expedience (cf. John 19:12-16). According to Matthew, the people took the blame on themselves (27:25). "His blood be on us and on our children!" is a biblical expression (cf. Jer. 26:15; Acts 5:28; 18:6), and here harks back to Matthew 23:35, a prediction reinforced and recalled by the outcry of the people. A false interpretation of this passage later had disastrous effects on the relationship between the church and the Jews. An everlasting curse on the Jewish people, indeed the pronouncement of Ahasuerus the unrepentant Jew, must be decidedly rejected. On the other hand, the transfer of blame in Matthew's sense cannot be restricted to the assembled throng since the "people as a whole" in the Greek *(laos)* means Israel. But it is a Matthean interpretation, corresponding to his view that the Reign of God will be taken from those who have constituted the salvific people up to this point (see Matt. 21:43). Matthew is probably thinking of the punitive judgment over Jerusalem and the temple (22:7; 23:38). But this perspective, adopted in terms of the history of the time, must not be played up to the point of a basic declaration, as if the people of Israel were rejected. Seen historically, the responsibility for Jesus' sentence lies with the chief priests of the time, who, according to their conviction, believed that they must so behave, as well as with Pilate, who was willing to capitulate to their demand (cf. the Lukan view in Acts 4:27-28). Pilate has Jesus scourged (a penalty in itself? — cf. Luke 23:16, 22; John 19:1), an act the Romans used as a prelude to crucifixion. Then he hands Jesus over to the execution squad to carry out the sentence.

The Soldiers Mock Jesus (27:27-31a)

27 *Then the soldiers of the governor took Jesus into the governor's head-quarters, and they gathered the whole cohort around him.* 28 *They stripped him and put a scarlet robe on him,* 29 *and after twisting some thorns into a crown, they put it on his head. They put a reed in his right hand and knelt before him and mocked him, saying, "Hail, King of the Jews!"* 30 *They spat on him, and took the reed and struck him on the head.* 31 *After mocking him, they stripped him of the robe and put his own clothes on him.*

27-31a Jesus' mocking at the hands of Roman soldiers in the court of the praetorium, which was probably not at the ancient site of the Fortress Antonia (where pilgrims today begin the Way of the Cross) but in the former palace of Herod in the western area of the city, took place according to Mark and Matthew (otherwise in John 19:1-3) between Jesus' sentence and his way to crucifixion and is a credible tradition. The coarse mocking on the part of the soldiers presupposes Jesus' condemnation as "King of the Jews." Matthew recounts the scene even more graphically than does Mark: the Roman soldiers not only wrap a scarlet military cloak around him and place a crown woven of thorns on his head, but they thrust a reed into his right hand, with which they then strike him on the head. Matthew avoids the expression "knelt down" in his account of the cynical homage paid to Jesus by "bending the knee" since the Greek word for the former *(proskynein)* generally connotes "adoration" (see 2:11; 4:9-10; 14:33; 28:9, 17).

The Crucifixion of Jesus (27:31b-44)

Then they led him away to crucify him.

32 *As they went out, they came upon a man from Cyrene named Simon; they compelled this man to carry his cross.*

33 *And when they came to a place called Golgotha (which means Place of a Skull),* 34 *they offered him wine to drink, mixed with gall; but when he tasted it, he would not drink it.* 35 *And when they had crucified him, they divided his clothes among themselves by casting lots;* 36 *then they sat down there and kept watch over him.* 37 *Over his head they put the charge against him, which read, "This is Jesus, the King of the Jews."*

38 *Then two bandits were crucified with him, one on his right and one on his left.* 39 *Those who passed by derided him, shaking their heads* 40 *and saying, "You who would destroy the temple and build it in three days, save yourself! If you are the Son of God, come down from the cross."* 41 *In the same way the chief priests also, along with the scribes and elders, were mocking him,*

saying, 42 *"He saved others; he cannot save himself. He is the King of Israel;*
let him come down from the cross now, and we will believe in him. 43 *He*
trusts in God; let God deliver him now, if he wants to; for he said, 'I am
God's Son.'" 44 *The bandits who were crucified with him also taunted him in*
the same way.

31b-44 The old presentation, which Matthew adopts from Mark, forgoes a
portrayal of the physical torments connected with crucifixion and shifts the
painful events into the light of scriptural words concerning the suffering of the
Righteous One, especially according to Psalms 22 and 69. But Jesus' passion is
not developed in terms of these passages, since concrete details of his death
walk are connected with it: Simon of Cyrene's bearing the cross, the inscription
at the head of the cross, the crucifixion between two other men, and the allusion to the statement concerning the demolition and reconstruction of the
temple.

The mockery and insults that Jesus has to endure on the cross are portrayed in detail. They are the work of three groups: the passersby (Matt. 27:39-
40), the chief priests and scribes (vv. 41-43), and those crucified with him
(v. 44). The jeering words, which mock Jesus' powerlessness (v. 40) and even his
salvific activity (v. 42), reveal the emotional neediness of the crucified Messiah,
which immediately (v. 46) provokes Jesus' outcry.

In comparison with Mark, Matthew pays even more attention to scriptural echoes. The wine mixed with myrrh, which according to Mark 15:23 is offered to Jesus before the crucifixion and which was to function as a narcotic, in
Matthew 27:34 becomes "wine mixed with gall." This is an allusion to Psalm
69:21 in the Septuagint, where "gall" and "vinegar" are meant in a pejorative
sense (cf. likewise Matt. 27:48). In Matthew Jesus tastes it, and so takes something of the bitter drink (cf. 20:22; 26:39, 42). Matthew takes the casting of lots
over Jesus' clothing (v. 35; cf. Ps. 22:18) and the jeering shaking of their heads
by the passersby (v. 39; cf. Ps. 22:7) from Mark; but in verse 43 he presents a
new reference to Scripture: "He trusts in God; let God deliver him now, if he
wants to." The double mention of "Son of God" (Matt. 27:40, 43) is worthy of
note. This jeering is especially shocking for Matthew, who, with the church,
professes Jesus to be the Son of God in the full sense (see 14:33; 16:16). Other
changes are of lesser importance. The time indication in Mark 15:25, "It was
the third hour," is omitted by Matthew, who thereby avoids Mark's three-hour
division. Throughout Matthew makes use of the old (pre-Markan) history of
the passion, which understands Jesus' suffering as a test of the unjustly persecuted Righteous One. As early as Wisdom 2:18, the latter is called the "son of
God" or the "child of God" (Wis. 3:1). The concept of the atoning Servant of
God is not in question here.

The Death of Jesus (27:45-56)

> 45 *From noon on, darkness came over the whole land until three in the afternoon.* 46 *And about three o'clock Jesus cried with a loud voice, "Eli, Eli, lema sabachthani?" that is, "My God, my God, why have you forsaken me?"* 47 *When some of the bystanders heard it, they said, "This man is calling for Elijah."* 48 *At once one of them ran and got a sponge, filled it with sour wine, put it on a stick, and gave it to him to drink.* 49 *But the others said, "Wait, let us see whether Elijah will come to save him."* 50 *Then Jesus cried again with a loud voice and breathed his last.* 51 *At that moment the curtain of the temple was torn in two, from top to bottom. The earth shook, and the rocks were split.* 52 *The tombs also were opened, and many bodies of the saints who had fallen asleep were raised.* 53 *After his resurrection they came out of the tombs and entered the holy city and appeared to many.* 54 *Now when the centurion and those with him, who were keeping watch over Jesus, saw the earthquake and what took place, they were terrified and said, "Truly this man was God's Son!"*
>
> 55 *Many women were also there, looking on from a distance; they had followed Jesus from Galilee and had provided for him.* 56 *Among them were Mary Magdalene, and Mary the mother of James and Joseph, and the mother of the sons of Zebedee.*

45-56 The events before and after Jesus' death on the cross, which are impressively presented even in the old report, are still more extensively portrayed by Matthew in view of his inclination to dramatic portrayal — namely, in the cosmic occurrences after Jesus' death (vv. 51b-53). They have a symbolic sense, which Matthew sets forth using the stylistic elements of his time. In Jesus' very death the great turning point is reached: from mockery by human beings to justification by God, from Jesus' seeming helplessness, indeed abandonment by God, to the powerful revelation of his nearness to God, from death to life.

Matthew's construction is well balanced and proportioned. He recounts three events before Jesus' death: the darkness from the sixth to the ninth hour (v. 45); Jesus' cry of abandonment by God at the ninth hour (v. 46); the misunderstanding on the part of those standing about and the drinking of the vinegar. Then he recounts three occurrences after Jesus' death, namely, the rending of the veil of the temple, the earthquake, and the splitting of the rocks (v. 51); the raising of bodies of the saints who had fallen asleep in death and their appearance in the Holy City (vv. 52-53); and the confession of the Gentile centurion and his companions (v. 54). Thus Jesus' death (v. 50) stands in the middle of the presentation. The appended section (vv. 55-56) concerning the women who were present at these events is important to Matthew in terms of the primitive church's tradition but is somewhat tacked on here. It posits a connection with Jesus' burial (cf. 27:61) and the visit of the women to the tomb (28:1).

45-49 *Events before Jesus' death:* The darkness over all the land (v. 45) is not a natural eclipse of the sun: that is impossible at full moon, the time of Passover, as the ancients themselves (Origen and others) knew. The possibility of a darkening of the sun by a sandstorm has often been cited ("sirocco nights"). The event is probably intended to express symbolically the sympathy of creation, as in Amos 8:9, or God's wrath (cf. Isa. 13:10; Joel 2:1-2, 10, 31; 3:15; etc.). Jesus' loud, prayerful outcry (v. 46) is taken from Psalm 22:1 and in the old report is offered first in Aramaic, then in Greek (Mark 15:34), like other sayings of Jesus (Mark 7:34; 14:36). Matthew is not likely to be referring to the Hebrew since "Eli" also appears in Aramaic texts. His change of the address to God into "Eli, Eli" is to be explained by a concern to account for the misunderstanding of those who heard the cry: "This man is calling Elijah." Jesus' call, in the midst of his most profound need, is to be understood not as the despair of death (to the point of a "death of God theology"), but in the framework of the passion psalm, Psalm 22, in which the one who prays attains a new trust (cf. Ps. 22:4-5). On top of that, for Matthew it is not Jesus' last word, which is the cry "with a loud voice" with which he "breathed his last" (v. 50). Whether the drinking of the sour wine is intended to quench Jesus' terrible, tormenting thirst or to prolong his life and thus his suffering is difficult to say; probably the latter. The "sour wine" may be vinegar diluted with water as a refreshing drink (posca); but the expression recalls Psalm 69:21, where it has a pejorative sense (cf. Matt. 27:34). The scene as transmitted was subject to various interpretations (cf. Luke 23:36; John 19:28-30a).

Shortly after the drinking of the sour wine, Jesus must have died, and with a loud cry, which is unusual for someone crucified. Medical considerations as to the cause of the quick death and the possibility of such a cry (traumatic shock? tetanus cramps?) were of no concern to the primitive church. The cry refers (once more) to the first cry of prayer to God in verse 46, and in Matthew can be understood as a cry to the Father. In Mark 15:39 it moves the Gentile centurion to the profession that Jesus was "God's Son!"; in Luke 23:46 it is a trustful prayer in terms of Psalm 31:5; and in John 19:30 it is a cry of victory, proclaiming that his work is completed. The Matthean alteration, "he breathed" (literally, "he released") his spirit, instead of the simpler "he expired," may indicate Jesus' conscious, willing death (cf. John 19:30: "he gave up his spirit").

51-54 *Events after Jesus' death:* The occurrences after Jesus' death are even more pregnant with symbolism than those preceding it. With Mark, Matthew cites first the rending of the veil of the temple "from top to bottom, in two," a symbolic sign whose meaning, however, is not stated and is disputed among exegetes. Is it the inner curtain that is meant, between the Holy Place and the Holy of Holies (cf. Heb. 6:19; 9:3; 10:20), or the outer veil, visible to all, in front of the temple? Is it a sign of doom — the end of the old worship, presaging the destruction of the temple — and/or an indication of the new worship, the opening of the sanctuary to the Gentiles (cf. Mark 11:17)? For Matthew, it could have a cosmic meaning in view of the other events after Jesus' death. (Both veils, according to Philo, *Life of Moses* 2.87-88, with their four colors, corresponding to the four elements, represent the created universe — as also in Josephus, *Jewish War* 5.210-11.)

The earthquake that split the rocks and opened the tombs is the prelude to the awakening of many "bodies of the saints" who had fallen asleep. On Easter morning, too, as an angel comes down and rolls the stone from Jesus' tomb, a "great earthquake" occurs (Matt. 28:2). The strange awakening of dead persons of Old Testament salvation history, recounted only by Matthew, and their appearance in the Holy City (Jerusalem), stand, for Matthew, in the perspective of Jesus' resurrection, as well as function as a sign of the resurrection. Thus the text is to be understood only as a theological concept portrayed as an event. Extraordinary events at the deaths of famous persons, including earthquakes, are narrated elsewhere in antiquity as well (at the death of Caesar: Virgil, *Georgics* 1.475), along with appearances of the dead (Dio Cassius, *Roman History* 51, 17.5). Matthew was no doubt influenced by such Hellenistic notions; but for him they are directed toward Jesus' resurrection, which thus is announced in Jesus' very death. In the ancient church the text was repeatedly interpreted as Jesus' descent to the realm of the dead *(descensus ad inferos)* and the redemption of all of the righteous of the Old Testament (but in Matthew they are only "many bodies"), and the "Holy City" was understood as the heavenly world (but for Matthew it is Jerusalem; cf. Matt. 4:5). The portrayal of the situation is no longer bound to this point in time, that of Jesus' demise, since the awakened go to the Holy City only "after his [Jesus'] resurrection." But this may have been an early gloss, introduced into the text to safeguard the primacy of Jesus' resurrection (cf. 1 Cor. 15:23). The word used here for "resurrection" *(egersis)* is unusual and is used only once in the New Testament. The entire passage belongs to a stylistic genre peculiar to Matthew and is not to be analyzed historically (cf. Matthew 1, 2). Matthew imagines that the centurion and his men saw the earthquake and these happenings, and, seized with great fear, acknowledged Jesus as the Son of God. This, too, fits into the framework of such a narrative style.

55-56 The women who watch the event "from a distance" and who have followed Jesus from Galilee, where they had "provided for" him, are part of a reliable historical tradition (cf. Luke 8:2-3). This is vouched for by their names, which are multiplied in Luke 8:3, while not given separately in Mark and Matthew. Except for Mary Magdalene, who plays a salient role (cf. Matt. 27:61; 28:1; John 19:25; 20:11-18), precise identification is not easy. In the second place, a "Mary the mother of James and Joseph" is named (somewhat differently in Mark), called "the other Mary" by Matthew (27:61; 28:1). Third, there is "the mother of the sons of Zebedee" (cf. 20:20-21), who is held to be the Salome mentioned in Mark 15:40. The loyalty of the women, in contrast to the treachery of the disciples, who have fled at Jesus' arrest, is rightly recorded to their credit in the primitive church (cf. also 26:6-13).

The Burial of Jesus (27:57-61)

> 57 *When it was evening, there came a rich man from Arimathea, named Joseph, who was also a disciple of Jesus.* 58 *He went to Pilate and asked for the body of Jesus; then Pilate ordered it to be given to him.* 59 *So Joseph took the body and wrapped it in a clean linen cloth* 60 *and laid it in his own new tomb, which he had hewn in the rock. He then rolled a great stone to the door of the tomb and went away.* 61 *Mary Magdalene and the other Mary were there, sitting opposite the tomb.*

57-61 Jesus' burial in a rock tomb, which Joseph of Arimathea has made possible with his visit to Pilate to request that he be entrusted with Jesus' body, is credibly transmitted in Mark 15:42-47 in the old report. Matthew and Luke do not appreciably deviate from it. John 19:38-42 likewise records the fact as such, but it recounts the event of the burial somewhat differently and in detail; he knows that the tomb lay in a garden. Matthew is entirely dependent on Mark, but he condenses his report and introduces certain special emphases. Joseph of Arimathea is not referred to as a "respected member of the council," but as a wealthy man who has become a disciple of Jesus — a Matthean expression (Matt. 13:52; 28:19). That it was a courageous act to go to Pilate (Mark says, "he went boldly") is not emphasized in Matthew, nor does he give us Pilate's interrogation of the centurion. On the other hand, he concentrates on a description of the tomb: it is a *new* one, which Joseph has had hewn out in the rock *for himself.* A rock tomb like this one, which this disciple of Jesus places at the disposition of the executed Master, who otherwise would have been thrown into a common grave, shows the highest respect for Jesus. And so Joseph of Arimathea joins the woman who has poured out the costly ointment on Jesus' body before the passion (26:13) and whose deed is likewise included in the proclamation of the gospel. At the same time, this tomb becomes an honored place for Christendom. Both women, who sit "across from the tomb" (certainly also as witnesses), may represent the honor paid to this spot. The "tomb of Christ" shown today, in whose proximity other cemeteries lay (outside the second wall), is a credible location.

The Guard at the Tomb (27:62-66)

62 *The next day, that is, after the day of Preparation, the chief priests and the Pharisees gathered before Pilate* 63 *and said, "Sir, we remember what that impostor said while he was still alive, 'After three days I will rise again.' 64 Therefore command the tomb to be made secure until the third day; otherwise his disciples may go and steal him away, and tell the people, 'He has been raised from the dead,' and the last deception would be worse than the first." 65 Pilate said to them, "You have a guard of soldiers; go, make it as secure as you can." 66 So they went with the guard and made the tomb secure by sealing the stone.*

62-66 This story, recounted only by Matthew, which finds its continuation in 28:11-15, is understandable only from the viewpoint of its end: the rumor that Jesus' disciples came in the night and stole his body (28:13) is "still told among the Jews to this day" (28:15). The story of the guards at the tomb was current in Christian circles for apologetic reasons as well as to protect against the Jewish suspicion. The theft hypothesis, so gleefully embraced at the time of the Enlightenment (H. S. Reimarus), outlived Matthew's day as well, as we know from Justin, *Dialogue* 108 (from about the middle of the second century). In the apocryphal *Gospel of Peter,* dating probably from the same time, the story of the grave watch is embroidered even more extensively (*Gospel of Peter* 28–33). From a historical viewpoint, it is untenable. How could the chief priests know of a prediction by Jesus of his resurrection after three days? Why would Pilate have been persuaded to make Roman soldiers available to guard the tomb when the Jews could have done it themselves? The story of the bribing of the soldiers so that they would testify that the disciples came and stole the body while they themselves slept (Matt. 28:13) is implausible. The apologetic standpoint makes it understandable that such a legend should be accepted, one that has also influenced the following report concerning the women's visit to the tomb (28:2-4). Jesus' resurrection was solidly accepted in the primitive church as an event wrought by God (1 Cor. 15:4); did it need such a defense? The story, which irritates us today, can at most be justified in terms of stylistic usage of the time.

The "next day, that is, after the day of Preparation" (cf. Mark 15:42), is the Sabbath, which Matthew is probably unwilling to name directly because of the Sabbath rest. The designation of Jesus as an "impostor" (in Greek, *planos*) is important since this corresponds to his indictment as a "false prophet" or "impostor" (see above, the hearing before the High Council). The contraposition of the "last deception" (v. 64) to the "first" directs our gaze to the time after Easter (cf. the future tense in Greek). The "first" deception was Jesus' earthly work, while the "last" comes from the disciples with the proclamation that "he has been raised from the dead" (the same formula as in 28:7; cf. John 2:22; Rom. 6:4). The "last deception" is even worse since it involves more circles of people and has now turned many Jews to the Christian faith.

The Resurrection and
the Appearances of Jesus (28:1-20)

The Resurrection (28:1-10)

> 28:1 *After the sabbath, as the first day of the week was dawning, Mary Magdalene and the other Mary went to see the tomb.* 2 *And suddenly there was a great earthquake; for an angel of the Lord, descending from heaven, came and rolled back the stone and sat on it.* 3 *His appearance was like lightning, and his clothing white as snow.* 4 *For fear of him the guards shook and became like dead men.* 5 *But the angel said to the women, "Do not be afraid; I know that you are looking for Jesus who was crucified.* 6 *He is not here; for he has been raised, as he said. Come, see the place where he lay.* 7 *Then go quickly and tell his disciples, 'He has been raised from the dead, and indeed he is going ahead of you to Galilee; there you will see him.' This is my message for you."*
>
> 8 *So they left the tomb quickly with fear and great joy, and ran to tell his disciples.* 9 *Suddenly Jesus met them and said, "Greetings!" And they came to him, took hold of his feet, and worshiped him.* 10 *Then Jesus said to them, "Do not be afraid; go and tell my brothers to go to Galilee; there they will see me."*

1-8   In literary terms Matthew follows the Markan report, but in verses 2-4 he has presented a dramatically fashioned scene, also necessary because of the introduction of the guards at the tomb. The angel has already been described as a "young man" in white garments in Mark 16:5, but he now becomes a powerful, fear-inspiring messenger of God who rolls the stone away while the guards sink to the ground as if dead. By no means is Jesus' resurrection itself being described, nor the moment in time established, but the open grave described by Mark is probably being explained. Thus the concern of the women vanishes as to who will roll back the great stone for them (Mark 16:3). The Lord's angel, descended from heaven, is still there, and immediately proclaims to them the Easter message. Matthew does not explicitly say that they enter the tomb; but if the angel then says to them, "See the place where he lay" (Matt. 28:6), the women's entering the tomb seems to be presumed, since this will have been the intended purpose of their visit (v. 1). The casual presentation shows that Matthew is concerned not with an exact portrayal of the situation but with the message that the Crucified One has risen; Matthew adds, "as he said" (v. 6). In Matthew the proclamation that Jesus will go before the disciples into Galilee and the encouragement to tell the disciples of this "quickly" are pronounced emphatically by the angel: "This is *my* message for you" (v. 7). The angelic commission is indeed carried out "quickly" by both women (v. 8). Matthew deliberately alters the final sentence in Mark 16:8: the women are not seized with fright and shock, but are filled "with fear and great joy." Nor are they silent about what they have experienced, but hasten away and proclaim it to Jesus' disciples. The reshaping of the Markan report by Matthew is instructive for the Easter narratives of the primitive church. It inquires less into the exact circumstances and goes more into the overwhelming event that the Crucified One was raised by the power of God (Easter kerygma). Casually, it makes this event more visible and understandable for people of the time — indeed, it brings in new elements but in such a way as to preserve the mystery of Jesus' resurrection. There can be no doubt about the women's visit to the tomb on Easter Sunday; all the rest, however, escapes more exact historical examination. The limit of such a presentation is finally reached in the apocryphal *Gospel of Peter*, in which two men with blinding brilliance descend from heaven and the soldiers that observe this see three men leaving the tomb; the one who follows the two others is followed by a cross, and his head outshines the heavens in its splendor (chaps. 35–40).

Our passage is divided into the introduction — the two women's visit to the tomb (28:1) — the appearance of the angel, along with the earthquake and the "quaking" of the guards (vv. 2-4), the message of the angel to the women (vv. 5-7), and the women's execution of the angelic commission (v. 8).

1 The time indication is not to be understood as referring to evening (Vulgate: "Vespere autem sabbati"). The Greek expression is to be translated, with the New Revised Standard Version, as "after the sabbath." Then a more precise indication is given: at dawn on the first day of the week. Matthew cites only two women, both named Mary, as at the burial (27:61); Mark adds Salome. Nor do the women come to anoint Jesus' body; rather, they wish to visit the tomb.

2-4 The appearance of the angel is introduced with a great earthquake, as with the revelation of God on Mount Sinai (Exod. 19:18) and before Elijah on Mount Horeb (1 Kings 19:11). The motif is also found in Hellenistic theophany portrayals. The shining garment, white as snow, and the angel's appearance like a bolt of lightning are heavenly brightness as it also gleams over the earth in Jesus' transfiguration (Matt. 17:2). Lightning, which is also cited for Christ's parousia (24:27), here indicates the overwhelming force of the appearance, which makes the sentinels "quake" (the same expression as for the earthquake). The soldiers become "like dead men," hence incapable of acting. Thus Matthew neutralizes the guards he has introduced.

5-8 Now the angel addresses the women, in the standard style for the scene of a revelation, with the encouragement not to fear (cf. 1:20; 14:27; 17:7; 28:10). The Easter proclamation reads as in Mark, except that the women (and through them the community) are also reminded of Jesus' prediction (16:21; 17:23; 20:19; 26:32). They are to tell the disciples that the Risen One will go before them to Galilee and that they will see him there: this for Matthew is fulfilled in the appearance on the mountain in Galilee (28:16-20). The idea of the parousia (often erroneously ascribed to Mark) is out of the question for Matthew (cf. 28:20). If he does not mention Peter in the commission to the disciples, this is probably because no portrayal of the Risen One's appearance to this chief of the disciples (cf. John 21:15-19) was known, or at least was not of concern to him because of the final scene with all the disciples. Where and how the women met the disciples — they are to be thought of as still in Jerusalem (cf. Luke 24:22-23, 33) — is not reported: Matthew is content with their execution of the angelic commission.

9-10 For the Matthean presentation, Jesus' meeting with the women while they hastened to the disciples is meaningful. It could seem superfluous after the angel's commission and the women's obedience. But the women hasten "with fear and great joy," and through the meeting with Jesus their fear is overcome and their joy increased. The Greek address, "Greetings!" has a joyous echo (cf. 5:12; 18:13). If Jesus now calls the disciples "my brothers" ("siblings"), this may indicate that he forgives the cowardly disciples and promises them his intimate presence. Now they have the courage to follow his instruction and go to Galilee to "see" him there.

Has this encounter, narrated by Matthew alone among the Synoptics, been created by our evangelist to prepare for the final scene (28:16-20)? True, the language is recognizably Matthean, through many linguistic peculiarities: "And behold" (omitted in the NRSV), "there," "then" (= next), "worshiping" (= adore), and "brothers" (siblings). But Matthew may be making use of a tradition that he formulates in his own way. John 20:14-17 relates the encounter of the Risen One with Mary Magdalene, who becomes the emissary to the disciples, more in detail. One need not assume that the Johannine presentation was further developed only out of the short verses of Matthew since John suggests his own thread of tradition. Thus the tradition of an appearance of Jesus to the women, or to Mary Magdalene, is discernible that is valuable and important to Christians of today, especially to women. Historically, to be sure, it cannot be researched, as with the rest of the Easter stories.

"Taking hold" of Jesus' feet, cited before the "worshiping," probably indicates that the women sought to be convinced of Jesus' corporeality. True, they may have fallen down before him; but the Matthean "worshiping" denotes homage, indeed adoration (see 2:11), as is the case with the appearance of Jesus before the disciples (28:17).

The Report of the Guard (28:11-15)

11 *While they were going, some of the guard went into the city and told the chief priests everything that had happened.* 12 *After the priests had assembled with the elders, they devised a plan to give a large sum of money to the soldiers,* 13 *telling them, "You must say, 'His disciples came by night and stole him away while we were asleep.'* 14 *If this comes to the governor's ears, we will satisfy him and keep you out of trouble."* 15 *So they took the money and did as they were directed. And this story is still told among the Jews to this day.*

11-15   The account of the soldiers at the tomb had to be given at the end, after 27:62-66 and 28:2-4, and this is the only available place. Matthew inserts the reaction of the chief priests — their bribing of the guards — into the course of events. While the women hasten to the disciples, the guards go to the city and report what has occurred. From their actions arises an effective contrast between the believing acceptance of the Easter message by the women and its deliberate suppression by the Jewish authorities. The "chief priests and elders" are again, as in 27:3, 12, 20, cited only by Matthew, and then in Acts 4:23; 23:14; cf. 25:15, perhaps an indication of later formulas.

The event portrayed, the bribing of the guards, is conceivable in itself (cf. Matt. 26:15), but it is to be ruled out here (see above on 27:62-66). The apologetic intention to deprive the allegation of a theft of its plausibility does not allow the suggesting of further considerations regarding the hard-necked bad will and incredulity of the Jews.

The Commissioning of the Disciples (28:16-20)

16 *Now the eleven disciples went to Galilee, to the mountain to which Jesus had directed them.* 17 *When they saw him, they worshiped him; but some doubted.* 18 *And Jesus came and said to them, "All authority in heaven and on earth has been given to me.* 19 *Go therefore and make disciples of all nations, baptizing them in the name of the Father and of the Son and of the Holy Spirit,* 20 *and teaching them to obey everything that I have commanded you. And remember, I am with you always, to the end of the age.*

16-20   The concluding scene, bound to the preceding material by its introduction (v. 16), marked only in verse 17 as an "appearance" of the Risen One ("they saw him"), is a masterpiece of Matthean composition and the climax of the Matthean conception of salvation history (or of historical theology). The discourse of the risen Lord to his eleven disciples assembled on the "mountain in Galilee" and representing the entire later church is divided into the assertion of all authority (v. 18b), the commission to go forth (vv. 19a-20a), and the affirmation of his everlasting presence (v. 20b). Attempts have been made to explain this triple form according to various patterns: on the model of the baptismal liturgy; on that of the enthronement schema (exaltation, presentation, and enthronement — cf. Phil. 2:9-11; 1 Tim. 3:16); and in terms of the Old Testament form of God's address (revelation, instruction, and promise — but never bound together in this way in the Old Testament!). These attempts at an interpretation are not satisfactory. In terms of form and genre criticism, the text follows the same pattern as the decree of Cyrus in 2 Chronicles 36:23. Indeed, it is a royal discourse by a ruler, charged with exaltation and condescension alike. The focus is not on the parousia, at which the Son of Man will come in the glory of his Father (Matt. 16:27), with great power and glory (24:30), but on the present time of the world, the time of the church. In order that Jesus' work be continued in them, the Risen One sends forth the disciples to make disciples of all people. At the same time he gives them the promise that he is "with them" until the end of this age. These last words (v. 20b) are not simply a consoling and encouraging addition to the commission to go forth but an integral part of the entire revelatory address. It becomes a penetrating summary of what Jesus Christ, "God with us" ("Emmanuel," 1:23), is for his church. The words of commission, which also contain the command of baptism and the imposition of a duty to observe Jesus' instructions, together with the promise to be with the disciples "always," leave little to be desired in a compendious ecclesiological statement. Understood as a unit, the address of the Risen One gives the church its full self-understanding and thus becomes a "manifesto": a declaration of the meaning of the church. The great declaration concerning the church at the end of the first part of Matthew's Gospel (16:18-19) finds its continuation here. Jesus' intention, expressed in chapter 16, to build the church finds its sequel here — his promise there is here confirmed by the full power of the Risen One, and the promise given there finds its confirmation in the One who, despite his farewell, is constantly with his own on earth.

16 The "eleven" disciples — the number that Matthew now cites, differs from that in the formula of faith presented in 1 Corinthians 15:5 ("he appeared to the twelve") because of the elimination of the betrayer (cf. also Luke 24:9, 33; Acts 1:26; 2:14) — go to Galilee as instructed in verses 7 and 10. With this instruction the Gospel returns to its origin (see Matt. 4:15-16) and at the same time broadens out to all people. The "mountain" (mentioned for the first time) to which Jesus has summoned his disciples is not a specific place with a name but a symbolic expression for Jesus' activity, which has been performed in close

association with God and now has been endorsed by God. Likewise symbolic are the "mountains" of the Sermon on the Mount (5:1), the cures (15:29), and the transfiguration (17:1). Here, at the high point of his "course," Jesus is endorsed by God and identified as having all authority.

17   The encounter with Jesus, the Risen One, is expressed only with a participle ("when they saw him"), and does not convey anything else about the disciples' impressions or experience. The "seeing" is a primitive Christian expression elsewhere as well, and denotes what we usually call "appearances" (John 20:18, 25; 1 Cor. 9:1). The Risen One has made himself "visible to," or, better, available to the experience of, certain persons (cf. *ōphthē*, 1 Cor. 15:5). But the kind of experience of the people in question, which in the more lengthy Easter stories is described with great variety, does not imply a particular "seeing" (visions). The completely new experience of the presence of the Risen One transcends human power of expression. But the reaction of the disciples is characteristic: they prostrate themselves and worship (as also in Luke 24:52). Given the same self-revelation, it may seem surprising that "some doubted"; but this is a motif often found in Easter accounts (Mark 16:14; Luke 24:38; John 20:24-27), and it was important to Matthew on pastoral grounds (see Matt. 14:31).

18   The proclamation of Jesus' complete authority echoes Daniel 7:14, where it is said of the Son of Man, "To him was given dominion and glory and kingship." The prophecy from Daniel, applied in other places as well to the parousia of the Son of Man (24:30; 26:64), here refers to the transfer of all authority to the Risen One, which has now been accomplished (cf. the "from now on" of 26:64). The future parousia of the Son of Man is not in question here. But for Matthew the "Son of Man" is also the Jesus who has already come, who has been active on earth (8:20; 9:6; 11:19; 13:37; 16:13), and who goes his way to suffering and death and is raised by God (17:9). True, the title "Son of Man" does not occur, nor is this to be wondered at in this self-presentation of the Risen One. His authority is at the same time that of the "Son," to whom "all authority will be given over" by the Father (see 11:27). It is an all-embracing authority, here established with a special view to the world of people.

19-20a   The establishment of the universal focus is through the commission to the disciples to go to "all nations." The Gentile nations are meant first of all (24:9, 14; 25:32). Now the mission of the earthly Jesus to Israel is broadened, in the commission given by the Risen One, to include the entire world (24:14). The Jews are not positively excluded; it is only that Matthew does not have a mission to the Jews in mind. The goal of evangelization is to make all people disciples of Christ. This is a typically Matthean expression (13:52; 27:57) — used once by Luke as well (Acts 14:21). What Matthew understands by being disciples of Christ is evident from his entire Gospel, especially the Sermon on the Mount (see 5:1), the discourse to the disciples in chapter 10, and the discourse to the community (see 18:1); but here it is made explicit with respect to the church as well. "Make disciples" is the main clause, and the two dependent participles specify the means through which this occurs. Now, in the time of the church, the means are baptism and the obligation to obey Jesus' commands and instructions. That Matthew writes entirely against the background of his time and from the praxis of his church is demonstrated by his use of the tripartite, trinitarian baptismal formula. According to the testimony of the *Didache*, this formula had obviously become the usage of the Syrian church: baptism was administered in "living" (flowing) water, or else through a triple pouring of water on the head, "in the name of the Father and of the Son and of the Holy Spirit" (*Didache* 7:1-3). The oldest baptismal formula was the one "in the name" of Jesus Christ (cf. Acts 2:38; 8:16; 19:5; 1 Cor. 1:13; Gal. 3:27), but it was not in competition with the trinitarian formula (cf. *Didache* 9:5). From the outset the Holy Spirit is connected with baptism by water as his medium and effect (cf. John 3:5; 1 Cor. 6:11; 12:13; Gal. 3:26-27 with Gal. 4:6; Titus 3:5-6). The trinitarian formula establishes the origin of the Gospel of Matthew from the Syrian world (see Intro., p. 5). But also important to Matthew is the keeping of all that Jesus has commanded the disciples, that is, what he has laid down in the compendium that is the Sermon on the Mount. That has been Jesus' "teaching," a teaching in fullness of authority (see 7:28-29): this obligatory teaching is to be handed on by the disciples to all who, through their proclamation, through faith and baptism, now become new disciples of Christ.

20b Jesus' concluding words, his promise to be with the disciples, presuppose the long history of Yahweh's covenant with Israel and the transition to the "Church of Christ" (H. Frankemölle, *Jahwebund und Kirche Christi* [Münster, 1983]). In Jesus, who is called "God with us" as early as the "Pre-Gospel" (1:23), God's being-with and being-for the chosen people are fulfilled. The salvation history begun with the call of Abraham (cf. Matt. 1:1), with all of its peaks and valleys, flows to the promised shoot of David, taking a new turn through the Spirit-wrought birth of Jesus from the Virgin Mary (1:16, 20). This Messiah, of David's progeny, is to redeem his people from their sins (1:21), and this occurs through his blood, poured out for many (see 26:28). But the newly constituted people of God, emerging from Israel, which receives the Gentile people, the church of Jesus Christ, now goes its way into the future under the guidance and with the accompaniment of the Risen One. It bears in itself the promise that it will never be overcome by the powers of destruction (16:18). When even two or three are gathered in Jesus' name, he is there among them (18:20). From him the church on earth has the authority to bind and loose (16:19; 18:18). Those sent forth by him participate in his authority; in fact, he is with them and among them as only the Risen One can be. Thus this promise of accompaniment is the climax of all the divine promises to the church: with Christ, its Lord, it can stride into the future with full assurance, as long as this world lasts. At the end of its journey is the coming of the Son of Man in power and glory, to create the world anew (19:28).

Index of Subjects

Index of Scripture and Other Ancient Literature

7:18-19	22	**4QpPs**		11–13	78
9:8	176	37	47	16:3	78
10:4-6	176			16:6	244
		11QTemple			
1QH		57:17-19	58	*Gospel of Peter*	
3:7-12	238			28–33	292
4:29	271			35–40	294
6:13	175				
6:24-26	159	**RABBINIC**		*Gospel of Thomas*	
7:9	159	**LITERATURE**		64	213, 214
14:3	47			65	210
18:14-15	47	**Midrash**			
		Psalm 118, para. 12	257	**Hermas**	
1QM		Tannaim 15:9	258	*Mandates*	
4:3	271			6	77
14:7	47	**Mishnah**			
		ʾAbot		**Ignatius**	
1QS		3:2b	178	*To the Philadelphians*	
1:9-10	62	3:13	148	3:2	78
2:1-18	257				
2:17	249	*Sanhedrin*		**Justin**	
3:25–4:15	257	10:1-3	116	*Dialogue with Trypho*	
4:2-6	271			10:1	277
5:24-26	176	*Pesahim*		69:7	277
6:1	176	8:6a	284	108	292
7:18	271			108:3	233
7:23	271	*Sanhedrin*		140	32
8:5-9	159	4:1h	274		
8:13-14	30				
9:6	159	*Targum to Isaiah*			
9:19-20	30	50:11	273	**CLASSICAL AND**	
10:17-18	62			**HELLENISTIC**	
11:8	159			**LITERATURE**	
11:9	271				
		EARLY CHRISTIAN		**Dio Cassius**	
1Qsa		**WRITINGS**		*Roman History*	
2:5-8	203			17.5	290
		Barnabas		51	290
1QSb		19–20	77		
4:25-26	175			**Galen**	
		Didache		9.903	168
4Q		1–5	77		
243	277	7:1-3	299	**Josephus**	
		8:1	69	*Antiquities*	
4QFlor		9:1	268	2.205-9	25
1:11-12	277	9:1-4	267	11.66	190
		9:5	75, 299	15.391-402	236
4QTest		10:6	201	17.169	280
9:13	22